WORLD WHISKY

EDITOR-IN-CHIEF

CHARLES MACLEAN

WRITTEN BY

**DAVE BROOM, TOM BRUCE-GARDYNE,
IAN BUXTON, CHARLES MACLEAN, PETER MULRYAN,
HANS OFFRINGA, GAVIN D. SMITH**

REVISED BY

GAVIN D. SMITH

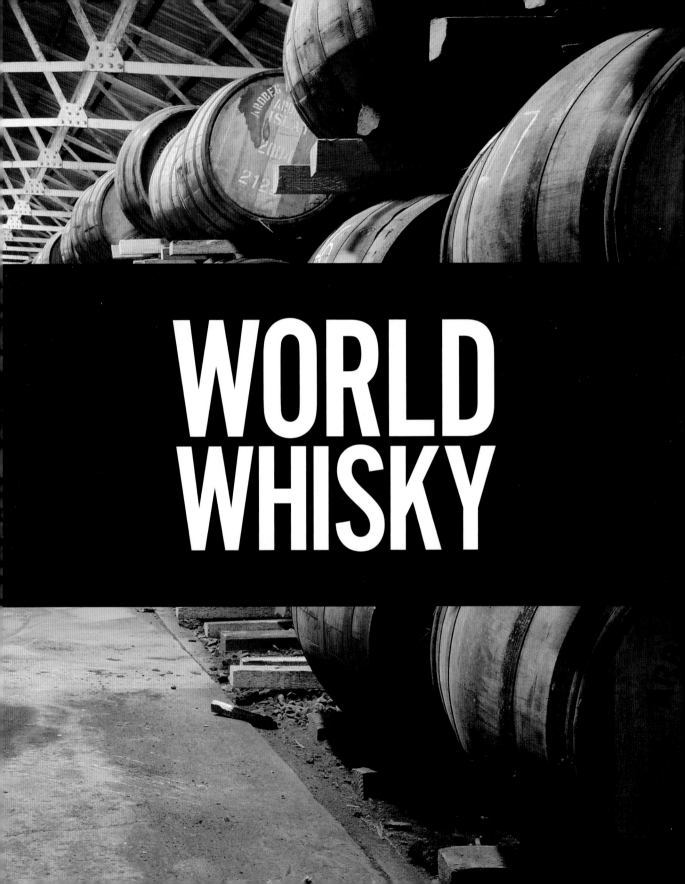

WORLD
WHISKY

DK UK
EDITOR Toby Mann
SENIOR DESIGNER Kathryn Wilding
JACKET DESIGNER Vanessa Hamilton
SENIOR PRE-PRODUCTION PRODUCER Robert Dunn
SENIOR PRODUCER Che Creasey
CREATIVE TECHNICAL SUPPORT Sonia Charbonnier
MANAGING EDITOR Angela Wilkes
MANAGING ART EDITOR Marianne Markham
ART DIRECTOR Maxine Pedliham
PUBLISHING DIRECTOR Mary-Clare Jerram
SPECIAL SALES CREATIVE PROJECT MANAGER
Alison Donovan

This revised edition published in 2016
First published in Great Britain in 2009 by
Dorling Kindersley Limited,
80 Strand, London, WC2R 0RL

Copyright © 2009, 2016, 2017
Dorling Kindersley Limited
A Penguin Random House Company
10 9 8 7 6 5 4 3 2 1
006-262225-Oct/2017

A CIP catalogue record for this book
is available from the British Library
ISBN 978-0-2413-3563-5

Printed and bound in China.

A WORLD OF IDEAS:
SEE ALL THERE IS TO KNOW

www.dk.com

CONTENTS

INTRODUCTION

Global interest in and enthusiasm for whisky has never been greater. In recent years, many new distilleries have opened in Australia, Europe, Taiwan, and Japan, as well as in Scotland. Most of these are small concerns, designed to meet local demand, but some are major production sites. Several leading malt distilleries have recently expanded capacity, and in Europe a handful of liqueur distillers are now producing whisky as well.

What has prompted this expansion and confident investment? Two factors: first, the interest in single malts, which continues to grow in every market, and, second, the anticipated demand from emerging markets in China, India, Russia, and Brazil.

The burgeoning interest in single malts is proved not only by the year-on-year rise in sales, but also the phenomenal enthusiasm for whisky festivals around the world – from Finland to New Zealand, San Francisco to Moscow. Once a taste for whisky is developed, particularly malt whisky, the passion for information about this beguiling subject is inexhaustible.

It is important to remember that the whisky made today cannot be sold as "whisky" until it has matured for at least two years in the US and at least three years in Scotland – and is often aged for far longer periods. The distiller must, therefore, peer into the future, gauge the likely demand in 5, 10, 15, or 20 years, in various markets, and gear production accordingly.

From time to time they get it wrong, and, to a large extent, the availability today of some very fine old whiskies, both single malts and blended, is a reflection of overproduction in the early 1980s. The point remains, though, that the excellence of the spirit will always be recognized. Fashions in drinks may come and go, but, for the discriminating consumer, whisky goes on forever!

The book you are holding offers a superb catalogue of the aforementioned whiskies that are available around the world today. Not only does it cover the output of major and lesser-known whisky distilleries, but it also includes a wide selection of blended whiskies. The main section of the book – Whiskies Worth the Wait – is broken down into countries. It catalogues in A–Z format first the key whisky-making nations of Scotland, Ireland, the USA, Canada, and Japan, followed by whiskies from other parts of Europe, South Asia, Australasia, and Africa. Secreted within this listing of world whiskies are features on the production processes and the varied types of whisky made, examinations of particular distilleries to divulge the secrets of their whisky-making, and tours that will guide you to the whisky regions of Scotland, Ireland, the USA, and Japan. For no experience adds more to the enjoyment of whisky than visiting a working distillery, to savour the aromas, appreciate the skill, dedication, and time that goes into making this profound spirit, and, of course, to sample a dram right at its source.

Charles MacLean

MAKING WHISKY

Whisky is both a simple product and an endlessly ponderable drink. It is made from just grain, water, and yeast, and yet the spectrum of aromas and tastes that emerge from a mature whisky can be wondrous and beguiling. How can such basic ingredients produce such an array of flavours? The answer lies in all the small variations in the whisky-making process: the grain(s) used, how the barley is malted, the shape of the stills, the angle of the lyne arms, the length of maturation, and types of casks used. But to understand those nuances, first you need to be familiar with the basics – the principal stages of whisky-making.

The first step is choosing the grain. Barley is the most commonly used grain in whisky-making. It is the sole grain in Scotch malt, and a percentage of malted barley is used in almost all whisky. Corn, wheat, and rye are the other grains used in whisky-making. Corn is the principal grain for making bourbon and Tennessee whiskey, and rye grain is, of course, the key ingredient in rye whiskey. The term "grain whisky" refers to whisky made principally from grains other than barley for primary use in making blended whisky. The main grains used for making grain whisky are either corn or wheat. For more on whisky types, *see pp. 12–13.*

1 MALTING

Barley goes through a malting process to activate enzymes and maximize its starch content, which is later converted to sugar and then alcohol. If peat is burned while drying the grains, the whisky will have a smoky flavour. Some distilleries have their own floor maltings *(above)*, but most use independent maltsters. *(See also pp. 38–39)*

2 MASHING

At the distillery, the malt is milled to produce a coarse flour called grist. The grist is then mixed with hot water in a mash tun *(above)* to extract soluble sugars. The sugar-laden water, known as wort, is piped off for use. Other unmalted grain can be combined with the grist in the mash tun for making non-malt whiskies.

3 FERMENTING

The wort is mixed with yeast and heated in a washback *(above)*. The yeast feeds off the sugars in the wort, so producing alcohol and carbon dioxide. This process, known as fermentation, lasts between 48 and 74 hours, and results in what is effectively a strong and rather tart beer, called wash.

4 DISTILLING

The next stage is for the wash to be distilled. Whether using a column still for continuous distillation or a pot still for batch distillation, the purpose is the same: to extract alcohol spirit from the wash. The essential process is simple: the wash is boiled and, as alcohol boils at a lower temperature than water, the alcohol is driven off the wash as vapour; this vapour is then condensed into liquid. With pot still distillation, the spirit is condensed either in a shell-and-tube condenser *(as above)* or an old-fashioned worm tub *(see p.167)*, which produces a heavier, oilier style of spirit. Most whisky is distilled twice – the first time in a wash still (known as a "beer still" in the US), the second time in a spirit (or "low wines") still. But Irish whiskey is traditionally triple-distilled to create an even purer spirit.

5 THE CUT

A spirit safe *(above)* is used at distilleries using pot still distillation to enable the distillers to assess the spirit. The first and last parts of the "run" during the second distillation are not pure enough for use. Known as the "foreshots" and the "feints", respectively, they will go back for redistillation along with the "low wines" from the first distillation. The desired and useable part of the distillation, however, is the middle section, and this is known as the "middle cut", or just "the cut". This useable spirit, which is called "new make", is drinkable and exhibits some of the characteristics that will be in the final whisky. However, it will not have achieved any depth of flavour or colour yet, and cannot legally be called whisky.

6 FILLING INTO CASKS

The new make will have its strength slightly reduced to about 63 or 64% ABV – the optimum strength to begin maturation. The spirit is then piped from a holding tank into oak casks *(above)*. In the US, the spirit is filled into new, charred barrels; in Scotland, it is filled into used casks.

7 MATURATION

The process that turns raw, clear, new make into the richly hued, complex-tasting drink we know as whisky is maturation. The length of time for maturation varies, depending on climatic conditions, the size and type of the casks used, and legal requirements – at least three years for Scotch. *(See also pp.66–67 and 72–73)*

8 BLENDING

The majority of whisky sold is blended whisky – a mix of malt whisky and grain whisky. As many as 40 or more whiskies may be combined in a blend, and the art of the blender *(above)* is to marry flavours so that they balance and unify. Blends tend to be tailored to specific tastes and markets. *(See also p.78)*

9 BOTTLING

The bottling of whisky is often carried out at automated plants *(above)*, but sometimes the bottling and labelling is done by hand. Most whisky is reduced with water to a bottling strength of 40 or 43% ABV, but cask strength bottlings are released at the strength they came out of the cask (in the region of 53–65% ABV).

WHISKY TYPES

There are several distinct types of whisky, and the variations depend upon the type and proportion of grains used and the methods employed in making the whisky. Barley, corn, wheat, and rye are the principal grains, while the variations in methods that lead to different classifications of whisky include the way of distilling (batch or continuous distillation) and the process and period of maturation. American whiskies are mostly aged in new oak, while Scotch and Irish whiskies employ re-used casks.

MALT Made solely from malted barley in copper pot stills, this is the "original" whisky of the Scottish Highlands. It has also been made in Japan since the 1920s, and is now made in Canada, parts of Asia, and (in small amounts) in almost every European country. "Single malt" is the product of an individual distillery. In Scotland, it must be matured for a minimum of three years. (See p.28)

GRAIN Distilled in a continuous still, grain whisky is typically made from wheat or corn (maize), along with unmalted and malted barley. Though mostly used for blending, some is bottled as grain whisky. (See p.163)

BLENDS A mix of malt whisky and grain whisky, blends typically have a proportion of 40 per cent malt to 60 per cent grain. More malt is used in deluxe blends, less in standard blends. They account for 92% of all Scotch. (See p.78)

BLENDED MALT Whereas single malt is the product of just one distillery, a blended malt is a mix of malt whiskies from more than one. *(See p.172)*

PURE POT STILL WHISKEY Made from a mix of malted and unmalted barley, pure pot still whiskey is unique to Ireland. *(See p.190)*

TENNESSEE WHISKEY Made much in the same way as bourbon, with a mashbill of at least 51 per cent corn, Tennessee whiskey has the distinction of undergoing filtration through a deep bed of sugar-maple charcoal. This is known as the Lincoln County Process. *(See p.228)*

BOURBON For a whiskey to be deemed bourbon, it must contain at least 51 per cent corn in the mashbill, the remainder being made up of barley, wheat, or rye. It has to be matured in new, charred white-oak casks for a minimum of two years. *(See p.221)*

RYE Although relatively uncommon today, rye is the original American whiskey. It must contain at least 51 per cent rye and be matured in new, charred white oak for at least two years. Canada produces a lot of rye whisky, though the process and classification is different to that of US rye. *(See pp.260 and 268)*

ALL ABOUT...
APPRECIATING WHISKY

Whisky is one of the world's most versatile drinks, and may be enjoyed in a variety of ways. But when it comes to appreciating fully its flavours and complexity, only a little water should be added. Flavour is a combination of aroma and taste, and to properly appreciate whisky, you must have a glass that will present the aroma to its best advantage (see pp.156–157). The addition of a dash of still water (how much depends on the individual whisky and personal preferences) disturbs the molecules in the liquid and tends to increase the aroma; by contrast, ice closes it down. Here are some pointers on the best way to appreciate whisky and some of the key flavours associated with the drink.

TASTING

When tasting whisky, use a clean glass for each drink, have a small jug of water to use when diluting the spirit slightly, and drink more water between each tasting to cleanse the palate. It's a good idea to keep notes as you go (see p.334).

1. Appearance Consider the whisky's colour (see p.73). Swirl the spirit in the glass and look at the "legs" that trickle down the inside. If they are slow-running and thick, it indicates good body, while skinny, fast-running legs suggest a thinner texture to the whisky.

2. Aroma Swirl the liquid and sniff it. Note first the physical effects (if any) – prickle, sharpness, warming, cooling. Then try to put words to the smells. Add a drop of water and repeat.

3. Taste By all means taste the whisky straight, but its character can best be appreciated once a little water has been added. Note the texture or "mouthfeel" – smooth, oily, waxy, drying, acerbic, and so on. Then consider the balance of the four primary tastes: sweetness, acidity, dryness, saltiness. Does the overall taste remind you of anything? Finally, how long is the finish, and does it leave a pleasant aftertaste?

4. Development After 10 minutes or so, sniff and taste the whisky again to see if it has changed.

A glass that narrows towards the rim is ideal for appreciating whisky, as it concentrates the all-important aromas.

FLAVOURS

Whisky should smell and taste of whisky, but when we are appreciating it to the full, we go beyond this simple description to isolate and identify what the smells and tastes remind us of. Here are some of the key flavour groups:

CEREAL

As you might expect, this flavour comes from the grain. You can taste it in whiskies such as Knockando *(p.124)*, Tullibardine *(p.176)*, and McDowell's *(p.322)*.
• biscuits • breakfast cereals • porridge • bran • new leather • malt extract • corn mash (maize mash)

FRUITY

The fresh, fruity flavours develop in the spirit itself while being fermented and distilled. Dried and cooked fruit flavours come from the wood in which the whisky is matured. Glenmorangie *(p.100)*, Yoichi *(p.294)*, and Yamazaki *(p.297)* are examples of whiskies that offer different fruity flavours.
• fresh fruit (apples, pears, peaches) • citric fruits (oranges, lemons, tangerines) • tropical fruits (pineapples, lychees, bananas) • dried fruits (raisins, candied peel, figs, prunes, fruitcake) • stewed fruits • boiled sweets • solvent (nail-varnish remover)

FLORAL

Scottish Lowland malts are the archetypal floral whiskies. The flavour is well suited to aperitif-style whiskies, such as the younger offerings from Auchentoshan *(p.30)* and Glenkinchie *(p.97)*.
• florist's shop • scented flowers (rose, lavender, heather) • grass (clippings, dried grass, flower stems) • artificial perfume (air fresheners, Parma Violet sweets)

SMOKY

Peated malt gives us the smokiest flavoured whiskies, as exemplified by Islay malts such as Lagavulin *(p.126)* but also Talisker *(p.164)* and Longrow *(p.135)*.
• smoked meat, fish, cheese • charred sticks • bonfires, burning leaves • peat smoke • tobacco • soot, coal • tar • creosote

MEDICINAL

The medicinal tang is not a taste for everyone, but those who like it tend to really like it and head for the malts of Islay. Taste it in any Laphroaig *(p.128)*, in Benriach's Curiositas *(p.42)*, and in Ardbeg's 10-year-old *(p.24)*.
• bandages, plasters • hospitals • mouthwash • coal tar soap • iodine (sea salt) • antiseptic (Germolene, TCP)

WOODY

The influence of the cask is two-fold. The first flavour influence is in woody notes, as can be found in Balvenie *(p.36)* and Glenrothes *(p.104)*.
• new wood (sap, pine, bark, fresh oak) • scented wood (sandalwood, cedar, cigar boxes) • pencil shavings • sawdust

WOOD EXTRACTIVE

The second influence of the cask comes in the form of vanillins and tannins within the wood. Vanillins are particularly strong in American oak, and all bourbons feature these notes. European oak is richer in tannins, giving spicier and winey influences.

Tamdhu *(p.168)* displays the former; Glenfiddich Solera *(p.88)* the latter.
• vanilla (vanilla pods and essence, ice cream, custard, cake mix, pastry) • coconut (dessicated coconut, gorse bushes, sun-tan oil) • caramel (toffee, fudge, candyfloss) • honey • spicy (nutmeg, clove, cinnamon, ginger) • winey (sherry, prune juice, port, rum)

OILY

The heavier spirits tend to have an oily character, which you'll find in Dalmore *(p.70)* and Jura *(p.120)*. It also characterises pure pot still Irish whiskey, like Redbreast *(p.212)*, which use unmalted as well as malted barley.
• butter, fat • cream • crème brûlée • lubricating oil • grease (roasting tins) • unscented soap • cheese • leather polish, furniture polish

SULPHURY

Subtle sulphury notes can be found in great whiskies, such as Aberlour a'bunadh *(p.21)* and Macallan *(p.136)*.
• rubber • struck matches • Marmite • yeast • cooked vegetables

Some of the most clearly discernable flavours in whisky – from sweet vanillins to fragrant spices such as cinnamon, cloves, and nutmeg – derive from the cask in which the spirit was matured.

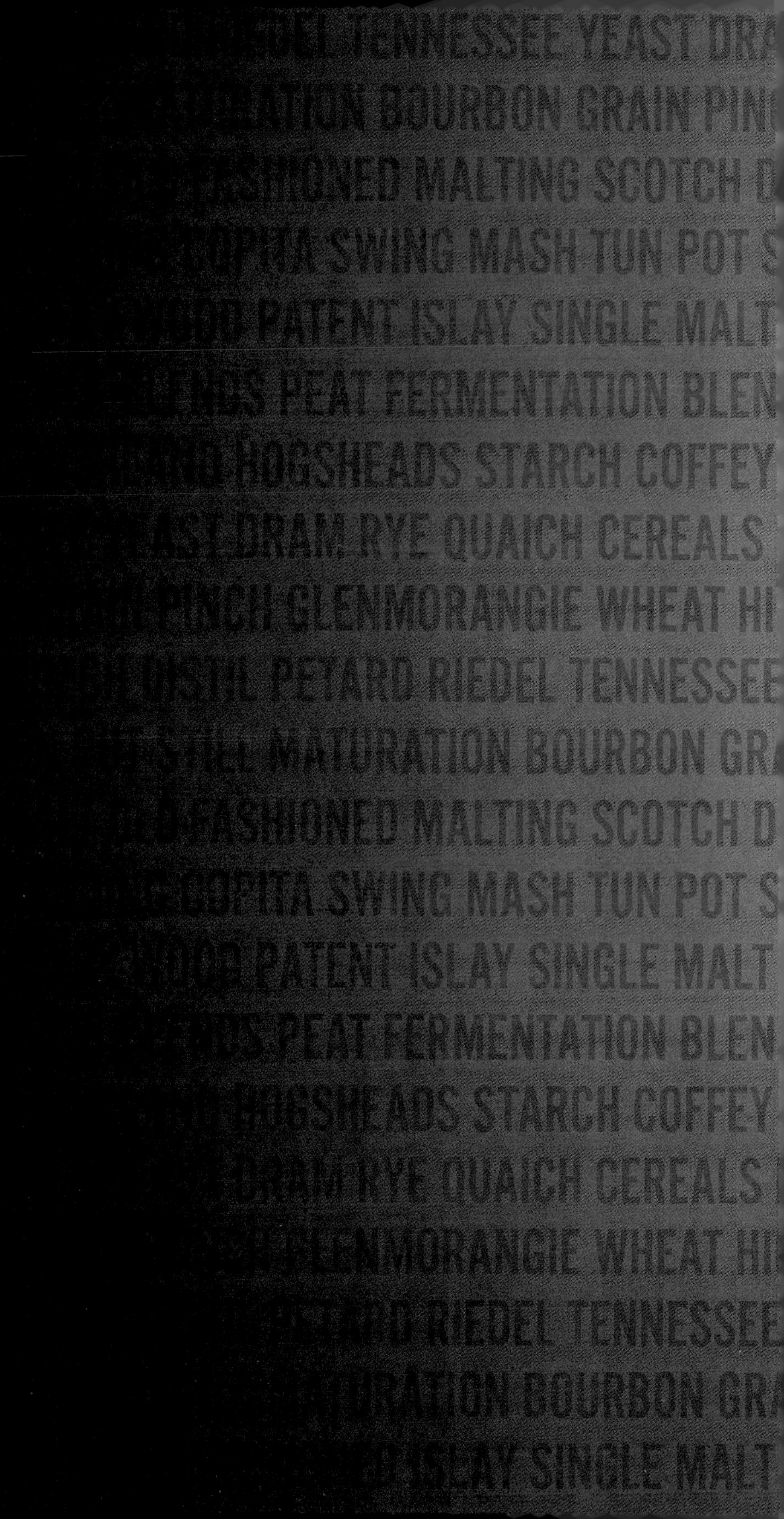

TENNESSEE YEAST DRA

ATION BOURBON GRAIN PIN

FASHIONED MALTING SCOTCH D

COPITA SWING MASH TUN POT S

OD PATENT ISLAY SINGLE MALT

DS PEAT FERMENTATION BLEN

HOGSHEADS STARCH COFFEY

AST DRAM RYE QUAICH CEREALS

PINCH GLENMORANGIE WHEAT HI

DISTIL PETARD RIEDEL TENNESSEE

STILL MATURATION BOURBON GRA

FASHIONED MALTING SCOTCH D

COPITA SWING MASH TUN POT S

OD PATENT ISLAY SINGLE MALT

DS PEAT FERMENTATION BLEN

HOGSHEADS STARCH COFFEY

DRAM RYE QUAICH CEREALS

GLENMORANGIE WHEAT HI

RD RIEDEL TENNESSEE

URATION BOURBON GRA

ISLAY SINGLE MALT

WHISKIES WORTH THE WAIT

KEY
NATIONS

SCOTLAND • IRELAND • USA
CANADA • JAPAN

Scapa · Highland Park

JOHN O'GROATS

Wolfburn

Old Pulteney

Clynelish

Abhainn
Dearg

Harris

ULLAPOOL

Balblair · Glenmorangie

Invergordon · Teaninich

Dalmore · Benromach

Glen Ord · Royal
Brackla

INVERNESS

CENTRAL
SPEYSIDE

Inchgower
Aultmore
Knockdhu
Strathisla
Strathmill
Glentauchers

Glendronach
Glen Garioch

Ardmore

ABERDEEN

Talisker

SKYE

Balmenach

Tomatin

Speyside

Dalwhinnie

Royal
Lochnagar

Ben Nevis

FORT WILLIAM

Fettercairn

Ardnamurchan

Tobermory

MULL

HIGHLANDS

Blair Athol · Glencadam

Edradour · Arbikie

Aberfeldy

Oban

DUNDEE

Glenturret

Tullibardine

PERTH

Strathearn

Eden Mill

Daftmill · Kingsbarns

Deanston

Jura

Loch Lomond

Glengoyne

Auchentoshan

Glasgow · Strathclyde

GLASGOW

EDINBURGH · Glenkinchie

Arran

LOWLANDS

Glen Scotia

CAMPBELTOWN

Springbank

Glengyle

Ailsa Bay

Girvan

DUMFRIES

Annandale

STRANRAER

Bladnoch

miles
0   50

0   50
kilometres

ISLAY

Bunnahabhain

Caol Ila

PORT
ASKAIG

Kilchoman

Bruichladdich · Bowmore

PORT ELLEN

Ardbeg
Lagavulin
Laphroaig

miles
0   5

0   5
kilometres

CENTRAL SPEYSIDE

Roseisle
LOSSIEMOUTH

Glenburgie
Glen
Moray
Miltonduff
Glenlossie
Glen Grant
Glenrothes
Dalmunach
Macallan
Cardhu
Tamdhu
Aberlour
Knockando
Dailuaine
Glenallachie
Benrinnes
Glenfarclas
Cragganmore
Tormore

Linkwood
Benriach
Longmorn
Glen Elgin
Auchroisk
Speyburn
Glen Spey
Craigellachie
Balvenie
Kininvie
Glenfiddich
Glendullan
Ballindalloch
Mortlach
Dufftown
Allt-a-Bhainne

Glen
Keith

Glenlivet

Tomintoul
Braeval

miles
0   5

0   5
kilometres

This map shows the location of active distilleries in Scotland, which in most cases have the same names as the Scottish whisky brands. It does not include the names of blended whiskies or independent bottlings that cannot be pinpointed geographically. The Speyside region has about 50 distilleries – the world's greatest concentration of whisky distilleries. Another major whisky region of Scotland is called simply the Highlands, which encompasses a huge area stretching roughly from Loch Lomond up to the north coast of mainland Scotland. Further south is the Lowlands region, which has a sprinkling of distilleries. Whiskies from the Islands region are sometimes called the maritime malts. The island of Islay to the west forms its own whisky region, with a clutch of distilleries that make good use of the island's peat. To the southeast of Islay, Campbeltown had a big whisky industry in the 19th century, though only three distilleries survive today.

BRUICHLADDICH – ISLAY

GLENKINCHIE – LOWLANDS

FETTERCAIRN – HIGHLANDS

TALISKER – ISLANDS

GLENLIVET – SPEYSIDE

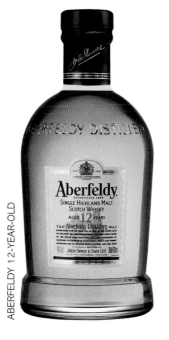

ABERFELDY 12-YEAR-OLD

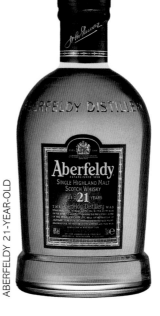

ABERFELDY 21-YEAR-OLD

ABERLOUR 12-YEAR-OLD DOUBLE CASK MATURED

100 PIPERS

Owner: Chivas Brothers

Created in 1965 by Seagram, and named after an old Scots song, 100 Pipers was originally a contender in the "value" sector of the Scotch whisky market, where it was an immediate success. The blend contains Allt-a-Bhainne and Braeval, and probably some Glenlivet and Longmorn as well. Seagrams developed the brand very effectively and it has continued to prosper under the new owners, Chivas Brothers (themselves owned by Pernod Ricard). It is one of the best-selling whiskies in Thailand, a dynamic market for Scotch, and is growing rapidly in many countries, especially Spain, Venezuela, Australia, and India.

100 PIPERS

BLEND 40% ABV
Pale in colour. A light and very mixable whisky, with a smooth yet subtly smoky taste.

ABERFELDY

Aberfeldy, Perthshire
www.aberfeldy.com

Plenty of malt distilleries claim to be the spiritual home of a particular blend, and celebrate the fact with a plaque on the wall or a large sign by the entrance. In its life-long bond with Dewar's White Label, Aberfeldy takes this a whole lot further: an impressive, fully interactive visitor's centre was opened in 2000 and the distillery effectively became the Dewar's World of Whisky.

Although visitors get to see the nuts and bolts of malt whisky distilling, the main emphasis is on the art of blending and the role of Tommy Dewar (1864–1930), arguably the greatest whisky baron of them all.

The distillery was built by John Dewar & Sons in 1898 with the express purpose of supplying malts for the company's blends. The site was chosen for its good, consistent

source of water and for the railway link to Perth, where the company was based. It was also a tribute to the original John Dewar, who was born in a bothy nearby and, according to legend, had walked from here to Perth in 1828.

Having spent most of the 20th century as part of DCL (now Diageo), Aberfeldy was bought by Bacardi as part of a billion-pound deal involving five malt distilleries and the gin brand Bombay Sapphire.

ABERFELDY 12-YEAR-OLD

SINGLE MALT: HIGHLANDS 40% ABV
The standard expression has a clean, apple-scented nose with a medium-bodied fruity character in the mouth.

ABERFELDY 21-YEAR-OLD

SINGLE MALT: HIGHLANDS 40% ABV
Launched in 2005, the 21-year-old has greater depth and richness than the 12-year-old, with a sweet, heathery nose and a slight spicy catch on the finish.

ABERLOUR

Aberlour, Banffshire
www.aberlour.com

Although Aberlour is not so well-known in its homeland, it is extremely popular in France, and it can claim to be one of the top ten best-selling malts in the world. As part of the old Campbell Distillers, it has been owned by the French group Pernod Ricard since 1975. Its malt is used in a great number of blends, particularly in Clan Campbell, but up to half the production is bottled as a single malt in a wide range of age statements and finishes.

The village of Aberlour lies a short distance from the Spey, and had only recently been founded when James Gordon and Peter Weir established a distillery on the main street in 1826. It survived for 50 years, but was then gutted by a fire. As a result, a new Aberlour Distillery was built in 1879, a couple of miles

ABERLOUR A'BUNADH

ABERLOUR 10-YEAR-OLD

upstream, by James Fleming, who already owned Dailuaine *(see p.69).* What you see today is a classic late-Victorian distillery, designed by Charles Doig after another bad fire in 1898.

ABERLOUR 12-YEAR-OLD DOUBLE CASK MATURED

SINGLE MALT: SPEYSIDE 40% ABV
Soft nose of cloves, nutmeg, and banana. The spicy pear and dark berry palate leads to a slightly bitter oak finish, with sherry and a wisp of smoke.

ABERLOUR A'BUNADH

SINGLE MALT: SPEYSIDE 60% ABV
A'bunadh (a-boon-ahh), "the origin" in Gaelic, is a cask strength, non-chill filtered malt matured in Oloroso casks. It has a sumptuous character of fruitcake and spice.

ABERLOUR 10-YEAR-OLD

SINGLE MALT: SPEYSIDE 40% ABV
Matured mainly in ex-bourbon casks, this has a caramel sweetness from the wood and a gentle nutty, spicy flavour.

ALLT-A-BHAINNE

Glenrinnes, Dufftown, Banffshire
Owner: Pernod Ricard

The building of Allt-a-Bhainne in 1975 is a testament to the post-war success of Chivas Regal. Having taken the US, Seagram's flagship Scotch was busy conquering Asia and Latin America. As sales boomed, so did demand for the malts needed for the blend. This primary blend-supplying role for the distillery has never changed, nor is it likely to under its present owner, Pernod Ricard, which is on a mission to make its Chivas Regal the world's number one 12-year-old blend. To date, there have been very few independent bottlings of the malt.

DEERSTALKER 18-YEAR-OLD

SINGLE MALT: SPEYSIDE 46%ABV
The nose is initially slightly astringent, with malt and brittle toffee. Light-bodied, with pears and ripe apples on the palate, leading to a medium-length finish.

ANCNOC VINTAGE 2000

ANCNOC 12-YEAR-OLD

ANCNOC 18-YEAR-OLD

ANCNOC

Knockdhu Distillery, Knock,
Huntly, Aberdeenshire
www.ancnoc.com

Named after the nearby "Black Hill", the springs of which supply its water, anCnoc is the core expression of Knockdhu Distillery.

With its solitary pair of stills and a capacity of just 900,000 litres (200,000 gallons) of spirit a year, Knockdhu Distillery is no giant. Yet, from this tiny acorn, planted in 1893, grew the mighty oak that is now Diageo. It was the first – and for years the only – distillery built by the Distillers Company (DCL), who preferred to grow by acquisition. It was not until 1967 that the company built its second distillery, Clynelish.

Knockdhu was closed in 1983 and brought back to life six years later by its new owner, Inver House, which has been at pains to preserve the character of the distillery, keeping the wooden washbacks and the old stone-built dunnage warehouses. The traditional worm tubs for condensing the spirit have also been retained; they add a slight sulphury, meaty character to the new make.

ANCNOC VINTAGE 2000

SINGLE MALT: SPEYSIDE 46% ABV
Toffee, vanilla, plums, spicy orange, and chocolate on the nose. Cocoa, vanilla, nutty sherry, nutmeg, and black pepper on the smooth palate.

ANCNOC 12-YEAR-OLD

SINGLE MALT: SPEYSIDE 40% ABV
A relatively full-bodied Speyside malt, with notes of lemon peel and heather-honey on the nose, a fairly luscious mouthfeel, and some length on the finish.

ANCNOC 18-YEAR-OLD

SINGLE MALT: SPEYSIDE 46% ABV
Apples, butterscotch, malt, and honey on the nose, with soft cinnamon spice. Supple on the palate, with stewed fruits, toffee, cinnamon, and developing black pepper notes.

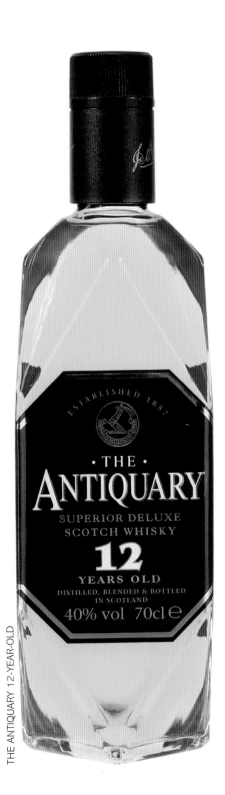

THE ANTIQUARY 12-YEAR-OLD

THE ANTIQUARY 21-YEAR-OLD

THE ANTIQUARY

Owner: Tomatin Distillery
www.tomatin.com

Introduced in 1857 by John and William Hardie, The Antiquary got its name from a novel by Sir Walter Scott. For many years, it was the product of William Sanderson (of VAT 69 fame), but was sold in 1996. Today, it is owned by The Tomatin Distillery Company, itself a subsidiary of Takara Shuzo Co.

Packaged in a decanter-like bottle, The Antiquary was a prized luxury blend in its heyday, but sales gradually ebbed, prompting the sale of the name and the recipe. The current owners offer 12- and 21-year-old expressions, and appear to be making energetic efforts to re-establish the brand. New packaging, reminiscent of the old bottle, has been introduced, and The Antiquary features strongly in Tomatin's marketing. Befitting the blend's deluxe status, The Antiquary has at its heart a very high malt-to-grain ratio, including some of the finest malts from Speyside and Highland distilleries and more than a splash of Tomatin. Islay seems to feature more strongly than previously.

THE ANTIQUARY 12-YEAR-OLD

BLEND 40% ABV

Subtle fruitiness concealing a hint of apples. Outstanding smoothness, depth of flavour, and a long aftertaste. Recent batches may vary somewhat. Other tasters have reported a striking peat influence, new to the blend.

THE ANTIQUARY 21-YEAR-OLD

BLEND 43% ABV

The subtle maltiness with muted peaty notes allows the heather, dandelion, and blackcurrant notes to flourish. A dash of Islay malt creates a truly exceptional dram, as well-balanced as it is rich and smooth. A stand-out blend that deserves to be more widely enjoyed.

ARDBEG 10-YEAR-OLD
SINGLE MALT: ISLAY 46% ABV
*This non-chill filtered malt
has notes of creosote, tar,
and smoked fish on the nose.
Any sweetness on the tongue
quickly dries to a smoky finish.*

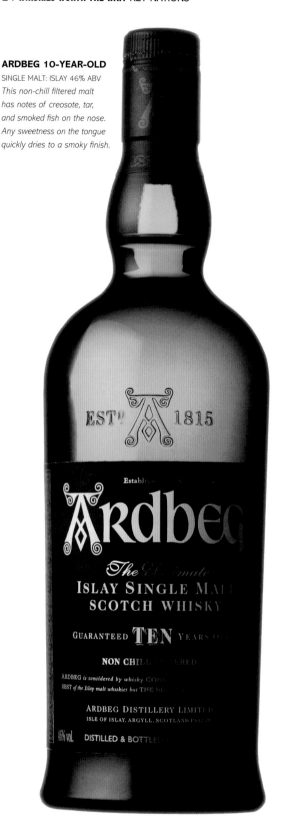

ARDBEG BLASDA
SINGLE MALT: ISLAY 40% ABV
*The Gaelic name translates
as "sweet and delicious", a
reference to a much gentler
style than usual, made from
malt peated at only 8ppm,
one-third Ardbeg's usual levels.*

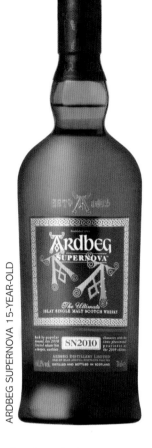

ARDBEG UIGEADAIL

ARDBEG CORRYVRECKAN

ARDBEG PERPETUUM

ARDBEG SUPERNOVA 15-YEAR-OLD

ARDBEG

Port Ellen, Islay
www.ardbeg.com

If Islay is the spiritual home of Scotland's pungent, peat-smoked whiskies, then Ardbeg is undoubtedly one of the island's leading disciples. The distillery was first licensed in 1815 in the parish of Kildalton, on Islay's southern coast just beyond Lagavulin and Laphroaig. "Its isolation tends to heighten the romantic sense of its position," wrote the whisky writer Alfred Barnard in the 1880s. Yet, by then, it was fully part of the whisky industry, supplying "pure Islay malt" to the blenders via Buchanan's in Glasgow.

Reliance on the blending market left Ardbeg in a vulnerable position, however, and when "the whisky loch" became full to the brim in the early 1980s, the distillery was mothballed. Its then owners, Allied Distillers, had decided to mainly concentrate on Laphroaig, which it also owned. The staff, who once numbered 60, were laid off and, despite being cranked back to life at the end of the decade, the distillery had an uncertain future.

In 1997, Ardbeg was rescued by Glenmorangie, who paid a reported £7 million and then spent a further £1.4 million on upgrading the distillery. At first, the years of non-production caused problems but, as the gaps in the

inventory receded, the distillery was finally able to release a standard 10-year-old bottling. Since then, there has been a raft of new bottlings, which have added to Ardbeg's growing cult status among fans of Islay's smoky malt whiskies.

ARDBEG UIGEADAIL

SINGLE MALT: ISLAY 54.2% ABV
Named after Loch Uigeadail – Ardbeg's water source – this has a deep gold colour and a treacle-like sweetness on the nose, with savoury, smoky notes following through on the tongue.

ARDBEG CORRYVRECKAN

SINGLE MALT: ISLAY 57.1% ABV
Peat smoke, tar, freshly dug soil, and medicinal on the nose. A mouth-coating,

silky palate, with rich, sweet peat notes, as well as lemon and salt. Peppery peat in the finish.

ARDBEG PERPETUUM

SINGLE MALT: ISLAY 47.4% ABV
Fragrant, leathery peat smoke on the nose, with white pepper, cinnamon, lime, and milk chocolate. Full and peppery on the palate, with vanilla and orchard fruit sweetness, plus treacle and a hint of contrasting ozone.

ARDBEG SUPERNOVA 15-YEAR-OLD

SINGLE MALT: ISLAY 60.1% ABV
Brine, smoked fish in butter, apricots, ginger, antiseptic, and cigar smoke on the nose. The palate is sweet, with fierce bonfire smoke, lemon, orange peel, oak, almonds, and finally peat ash.

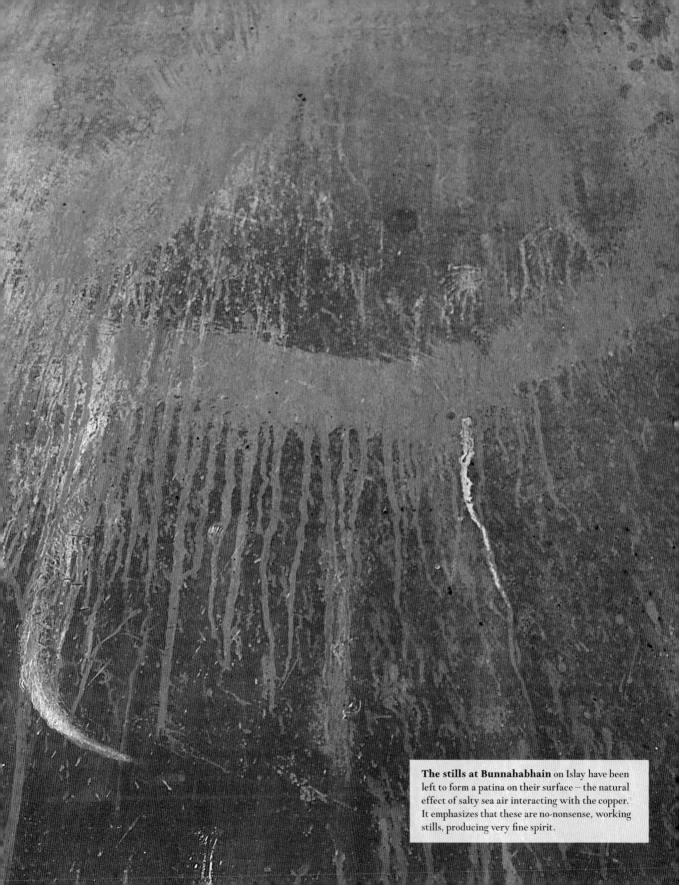

The stills at Bunnahabhain on Islay have been left to form a patina on their surface – the natural effect of salty sea air interacting with the copper. It emphasizes that these are no-nonsense, working stills, producing very fine spirit.

WHISKY STYLES
MALT

The original Scotch whisky – or *uisge beatha* ("water of life" in Gaelic) – from the 15th century or earlier would have been a single malt. That is, a distillation made from barley and the product of just one distillery (or, more likely, pot still on a farm) rather than a blend or vatting of whiskies of different kinds or different provenances. However, it would have been rather different from the malt we know today. It would not have been aged in oak casks but instead drunk almost hot from the still.

The invention of the continuous still in the 19th century created a seismic shift for whisky. It led to the development of blended whisky *(see p.78)*, and the international success of blends all but eclipsed the category of single malt whisky, which became virtually unheard of. The resurrection of single malts was led by Glenfiddich in the 1960s, though the real boom in interest has been far more recent. Today, you can find single malts from many parts of the world, including pretty much every one of the 90 or so active malt distilleries in Scotland. You can also find bottlings from many of the so-called "silent distilleries" – those that are either mothballed and may one day produce again or have closed entirely (stocks can be eked out for decades after a closure). Even in cases where the distillery has yet to bottle its own malt, the whiskies are usually available somewhere thanks to independent bottlers *(see pp.86–87)*, who buy selected casks from distilleries and usually bottle them as single-cask releases.

By law, a single malt can only come from a single distillery, and to protect the category, the Scotch whisky industry has outlawed the use of potentially misleading terms like "pure malt". Today, any vatting of malts from different distilleries has to be called a blended malt *(see p.172)*.

THE ARRAN MALT 10-YEAR-OLD

THE ARRAN MALT 12-YEAR-OLD

THE ARRAN MALT 18-YEAR-OLD

THE ARDMORE

Kennethmont, Aberdeenshire
www.ardmorewhisky.com

Ardmore owes its existence to
Teacher's Highland Cream. The
blend was well-established in
Scotland, particularly in Glasgow,
where it was sold through Teacher's
Dram Shops, and sales were growing
abroad. To keep up with demand,
Adam Teacher decided to build a
new distillery in 1898 and found
the ideal spot near Kennethmont,
beside the main Aberdeen-to-
Inverness railway. Famed for
producing the smokiest malt
on Speyside, Ardmore released
a 12-year-old in 1999 to celebrate
its centenary. The distillery is
now owned by Beam Suntory Inc.

THE ARDMORE LEGACY

SINGLE MALT: HIGHLAND 40% ABV
*Vanilla, caramel, and sweet peat smoke
on the nose, while on the palate vanilla
and honey contrast with quite dry peat
notes, plus ginger, and dark berries.*

THE ARRAN MALT

Lochranza, Isle of Arran
www.arranwhisky.com

Arran lies across the water from
Alloway, Robert Burns' birthplace.
This bond with Scotland's national
bard has been kept alive by the
Isle of Arran Distillery, which has
produced a range of blends in his
honour *(see p.152)*. It was founded
by Harold Currie in 1993, a time
when the mainstream whisky
industry was closing distilleries
as fast as it could. Arran has
survived, however, and in 2006,
released its first official bottling
of a 10-year-old. Since then there
have been various limited editions
and wood finishes. In 2008, the
first 12-year-old expression was
released, with the first bottling
of an 18-year-old following in 2015.

When the distillery opened
in 1993, it marked the return of
distilling on the Isle of Arran after
a hiatus of some 156 years. That's
legal distilling, at least, for there

is thought to have been as many as
50 distilleries quietly going about
their business in an illegal fashion
during much of the 19th century.

Whatever the case, the rebirth
of legal distilling on Arran was
marked by an impromptu fly-past
by two golden eagles during the
opening ceremony, and a pair of
the birds can often be observed
soaring above the distillery today.

Arran's whisky-making
resources are somewhat modest
– four pine washbacks and a
solitary pair of stills – but plans
for expansion are already under
way. A racked warehouse has
recently been added, as an addition
to the original dunnage warehouse,
and a milling machine has been
installed so that the distillery can
now produce its own grist on site
(previously, it had bought in its
malt already ground).

Arran uses water from Loch
na Davie, which is located in the
hills above Lochranza on the north
coast of Arran. The island itself

is positioned right in the Gulf
Stream, and the warm waters
and climate system associated
with it are said to be beneficial
factors in speeding up the period
of maturation at Arran.

THE ARRAN MALT 10-YEAR-OLD

SINGLE MALT: ISLANDS 46% ABV
*Bottled without chill-filtering, this
has fresh bread and vanilla aromas,
with citrus notes that carry through
onto the tongue.*

THE ARRAN MALT 12-YEAR-OLD

SINGLE MALT: ISLANDS 46% ABV
*This expression has an orange peel
and chocolate sweetness and a rich,
creamy texture thanks to the influence
of sherry wood.*

THE ARRAN MALT 18-YEAR-OLD

SINGLE MALT: ISLANDS 46% ABV
*Floral and fragrant on the nose, with
soft fruits and marzipan. Viscous and
full on the palate, with fruit spices, vanilla,
sweet sherry, orange marmalade, and
finally raisins.*

AUCHENTOSHAN
AMERICAN OAK
SINGLE MALT: LOWLANDS 40% ABV
*An initial note of rosewater,
then vanilla, developing musky
peaches, and icing sugar. Spicy,
fresh fruit on the palate, chilli
notes, and more vanilla.*

AUCHENTOSHAN
12-YEAR-OLD
SINGLE MALT: LOWLANDS 40% ABV
*This expression replaced the old
10-year-old and has a dense,
spicy character thanks to the
use of sherry casks.*

AUCHENTOSHAN 18-YEAR-OLD

AUCHENTOSHAN 21-YEAR-OLD

AUCHENTOSHAN SPRINGWOOD

AUCHENTOSHAN THREE WOOD

AUCHENTOSHAN

Dalmuir, Clydebank, Glasgow
www.auchentoshan.com

While Glenkinchie sits among the barley fields of East Lothian just south of Edinburgh, Scotland's other main Lowlands distillery lies west of Glasgow by the Erskine Bridge and the River Clyde.

Auchentoshan stands on the site of a monastery that was dissolved in 1560. Whether the monks moved on from the monastic tradition of making beer to distilling spirits is unknown, but if they did, the roots of Auchentoshan whisky would be very old indeed.

There used to be a distillery called Duntocher here, which was first mentioned in 1800. This may have evolved into Auchentoshan, which was licensed in 1823 by a man called Thorne. With its solitary pair of stills, it produced a modest 225,000 litres (50,000 gallons) a year until it acquired a third still. Ever since, Auchentoshan, with its triple-distilled malt, has been almost unique in Scotland. This being the standard style of Irish whiskey, it soon caught on among the burgeoning Irish community in Glasgow, who arrived seeking work and respite from the potato famine back home.

Having grown up in open countryside, the distillery was gradually swallowed up into a suburb of Clydebank. This area was a key target for the Luftwaffe during World War II and, on 13th and 14th March 1941, up to 200,000 bombs fell on the area, badly damaging the distillery. Since then, Auchentoshan has drawn its cooling water from a pond created in a giant bomb crater. The rest is piped from Loch Katrine in the Highlands.

Auchentoshan joined forces with the Islay distillery Bowmore in 1984, becoming Morrison Bowmore, which is now part of the Japanese Suntory group. In the past decade, the range of single malts has been greatly expanded.

AUCHENTOSHAN 18-YEAR-OLD

SINGLE MALT: LOWLANDS 43% ABV
This is a classic nutty, spicy malt with plenty of age and complexity on the palate and some fruity sherry notes on the nose.

AUCHENTOSHAN 21-YEAR-OLD

SINGLE MALT: LOWLANDS 43% ABV
Despite its age, the oldest standard expression of Auchentoshan is surprisingly crisp and refreshing, with a nutty, honeyed, malty flavour.

AUCHENTOSHAN SPRINGWOOD

SINGLE MALT: LOWLANDS 40% ABV
Matured in bourbon oak casks, its floral nose has tinned peaches and whipped cream. The clean palate starts citric, with emerging fruit, honey, and spice.

AUCHENTOSHAN THREE WOOD

SINGLE MALT: LOWLANDS 43% ABV
This is matured in three different types of cask, and sherry clearly has a big influence on the colour and sweet, candied-fruit flavours.

AULTMORE 12-YEAR-OLD

AULTMORE 18-YEAR-OLD

AUCHROISK

Mulben, Banffshire
www.malts.com

This modern distillery lies on the main road between Craigellachie and Keith. The site was bought by IDV in 1970 for £5 million, and Auchroisk (which means "ford of the red stream" in Gaelic) was up and running four years later. The principal role of the distillery was to supply malt for the J&B blend, but, after a decade, it was decided to release a distillery bottling as well. This was called the Singleton of Auchroisk. The name was soon abandoned, however, and replaced by a 10-year-old in the Flora & Fauna range and occasional Rare Malt series bottlings.

AUCHROISK FLORA & FAUNA 10-YEAR-OLD

SINGLE MALT: SPEYSIDE 43% ABV
An aromatic Speyside with a wisp of smoke and citrus notes, combined with malty flavours that dry on the finish.

AULTMORE

Keith, Banffshire
Owner: John Dewar & Sons (Bacardi)

Alexander Edward was a seasoned distiller who had helped run Benrinnes with his father before establishing the Craigellachie Distillery with Peter Mackie, the whisky baron and founder of the White Horse blend.

In 1895, at the peak of the late-Victorian whisky boom, Edward built a third distillery on the flat farmland between Keith and the sea. It was some distance from the glens but, in good Speyside tradition, he called it the Aultmore-Glenlivet Distillery and promptly doubled its capacity. He also bought Oban and was then in a position to offer the big blenders a choice of Speyside or West Coast malt.

In 1923, Aultmore was sold to John Dewar & Sons. Within three years, it was part of the mighty DCL. Today, there is little trace of its Victorian roots, and Aultmore sits wrapped in its concrete cladding like a light industrial unit from the 1970s, when it underwent a major refurbishment.

In 1991, a 12-year-old bottling of Aultmore was released as part of the Flora & Fauna range. A 21-year-old expression was added in 1996. Two years on, the distillery was one of five sold to the Bacardi drinks company. Over 2014 and 2015 the range was revamped and expanded.

AULTMORE 12-YEAR-OLD

SINGLE MALT: SPEYSIDE 46% ABV
A nose of peaches and lemonade, freshly mown grass, linseed, and milky coffee. Very fruity on the palate, mildly herbal, with toffee and light spices.

AULTMORE 18-YEAR-OLD

SINGLE MALT: SPEYSIDE 46% ABV
Vanilla, new-mown hay, and contrasting lemon notes on the nose, while the nicely textured palate offers more lemon, along with orange and malt.

BALMENACH

Cromdale, Grantown-on-Spey, Morayshire
www.inverhouse.com

In 1824, James McGregor, like many illicit distillers, decided to come in from the cold and take out a licence for his farm distillery near Grantown-on-Spey. It was owned by the family for 100 years until they sold out to DCL. Apart from during World War II, the distillery was in constant production until 1993, when its whisky was available as part of the Flora & Fauna range. In 1997, Balmenach was sold to Inver House, who fired up the stills the following year. A full distillery bottling has had to wait, owing to a dearth of inherited stocks.

BALMENACH GORDON & MACPHAIL 1990

SINGLE MALT: SPEYSIDE 43% ABV
Citrus, grass, and malt on the nose, slight smoke on the palate. Opens up with water.

BALBLAIR 03

BALBLAIR 99

BALBLAIR 90

BALBLAIR

Edderton, Tain, Ross-shire
www.balblair.com

While late-18th-century Scotland was awash with distilleries, both legal and illicit, Balblair is one of only a handful that has survived to this day. It was founded by John Ross in 1790 on the Dornoch Firth, north of Inverness, and sourced its water from the Ault Dearg burn, as it still does today. The first recorded sale was for a gallon of whisky on 25th January 1800.

Balblair remained in family hands for over 100 years. It was then taken over by Alexander Cowan, of Balnagowan, who was forced to close the distillery in 1911. It did not re-open until after World War II, when it was bought by Robert Cumming, who sold it on to the Canadian distiller Hiram Walker in 1970.

Since 1996, the distillery has been owned by Inver House Distillers, who began with a core range called Elements. This was succeeded by a range of vintage malts in a similar style to The Glenrothes bottlings, right down to the bulbous bottle shape.

BALBLAIR 90

SINGLE MALT: HIGHLANDS 46% ABV
The nose is rich, sherried, and spicy, with leather and fruit. Smooth and full on the palate, with honey and spicy sherry. Drying oak in the persistently spicy finish.

BALBLAIR 03

SINGLE MALT: HIGHLANDS 46% ABV
Tinned peaches and apricot jam on the nose, with honey and caramel. Early malt, then zesty lemon on the palate, with freshly cut grass and hazelnuts. Finally, white pepper, and cocoa powder.

BALBLAIR 99

SINGLE MALT: HIGHLANDS 46% ABV
Floral on the nose, with ripe apples, light sherry, and furniture polish. The palate is sweet and rounded, with honey and warm leather.

**BALLANTINE'S
21-YEAR-OLD**

BLEND 43% ABV

*The sought-after older expressions
of Ballantine's are deep in colour,
with traces of heather, smoke,
liquorice, and spice on the nose.
The 21-year-old has a complex,
balanced palate, with sherry,
honey, and floral notes.*

**BALLANTINE'S
30-YEAR-OLD**

BLEND 43% ABV

*Ballantine's flagship 30-year-old is
one of the world's most prestigious
blends. It is characterized by great
depth and range, and has a complex
mix of vanilla and honey.*

BALLANTINE'S FINEST

BALLANTINE'S 12-YEAR-OLD

BALLANTINE'S 17-YEAR-OLD

BALLANTINE'S

www.ballantines.com

Ballantine's is now part of Chivas Brothers, the Scotch whisky arm of Pernod Ricard, the world's number two wines and spirits company after Diageo. The Ballantine's range is arguably the most extensive in the world today, and includes Ballantine's Finest (the standard bottling), as well as Ballantine's 12-year-old, 17-year-old, 21-year-old, and 30-year-old.

Ballantine's was a pioneer in developing aged blends. The flagship 30-year-old was first blended in the late 1920s from special stocks of malt and grain Scotch set aside for many years with the vision of creating a super-premium product.

This remarkable foresight enabled the brand to establish a strong position at the top of the market, which has stood it in good stead despite various changes of ownership.

Relatively hard to find in the UK, Ballantine's Finest has long been popular in Europe, while the older, more premium expressions enjoy huge success in China, Japan, South Korea, and Asian duty-free markets. The range now sells nearly 6.5 million 9-litre (2-gallon) cases a year, making it the world's second biggest Scotch whisky by volume and the top-selling super-premium brand in Asia.

The blend is noted for its complexity, with over 40 different malts and grains being used. The two Speyside single malts Glenburgie and Miltonduff form the base for the blend, but malts from all parts of Scotland are also employed. For maturation, Ballantine's principally favours the use of ex-bourbon barrels, for the vanilla influences and sweet creamy notes they characteristically bring to the blend.

The Glenburgie Distillery has been completely remodelled and modernized and is today Ballantine's spiritual home. Recently, there has been an emphasis on entering the various Ballantine's expressions into international competitions, and a series of major awards suggests the owners have renewed confidence in the quality of this long-established brand.

BALLANTINE'S FINEST
BLEND 40% ABV
A sweet, soft-textured blend, with the Speyside malts giving chocolate, vanilla, and apple notes.

BALLANTINE'S 12-YEAR-OLD
BLEND 40% ABV
Golden-hued, with a honey sweetness on the nose, and vanilla from the oak. Creamy texture and balanced palate, with floral, honey, and oaky vanilla notes. Some tasters detect a hint of salt.

BALLANTINE'S 17-YEAR-OLD
BLEND 43% ABV
A deep, balanced, and elegant whisky with a hint of wood and vanilla. The body is full and creamy, with a vibrant, honeyed sweetness and hints of oak and peat smoke on the palate.

THE BALVENIE DOUBLEWOOD 12-YEAR-OLD

THE BALVENIE PORTWOOD 21-YEAR-OLD

THE BALVENIE CARIBBEAN CASK 14-YEAR-OLD

THE BALVENIE

Dufftown, Keith, Banffshire
www.thebalvenie.com

Having spent 16 years as a book-keeper at Mortlach Distillery in Dufftown, William Grant finally took the plunge to go solo in 1886 and set up Glenfiddich. Within six years, he was converting Balvenie Castle (actually a derelict Georgian pile) next door into another distillery, using second-hand stills from Lagavulin and Glen Albyn. His decision to expand came partly as a result of a request from an Aberdeen blender who desperately needed 1,800 litres (400 gallons) of Glenlivet-style whisky a week. Glenlivet itself was closed at the time, after being damaged by a fire in 1891. People congratulated Grant on his romantic idea of turning a "castle" into a distillery, although one customer in Liverpool warned that he was simply adding to the overproduction in the whisky industry – a warning that proved prescient when a slump hit the trade in the early 20th century.

Despite being physically overshadowed by Glenfiddich, Balvenie is no boutique distillery: it can produce 6.8 million litres (1.5 million gallons) a year and has built up an impressive range of single malts, the first of which was officially released in 1973. One early expression came wrapped in black leatherette with gold lettering. Recent packaging has been much more restrained. This is in keeping with Balvenie's carefully crafted image as an artisan distillery that claims to grow some of its own barley, and in contrast to Glenfiddich. It has also retained its floor maltings to satisfy part of its requirements, and employs a team of coopers and a coppersmith.

The coopers are kept busy by repairing and reconditioning the wide variety of casks employed to mature the varied expressions of Balvenie. Indeed, the distillery's attention to maturation and different wood finishes rivals even that of Glenmorangie.

THE BALVENIE DOUBLEWOOD 12-YEAR-OLD

SINGLE MALT: SPEYSIDE 40% ABV
After a decade in American oak, Doublewood spends two years in ex-sherry casks to give it a smooth, confected, slightly nutty character.

THE BALVENIE PORTWOOD 21-YEAR-OLD

SINGLE MALT: SPEYSIDE 40% ABV
The nose is soft, warming, and creamy, with ripe fruits, vanilla, and a smoky, musky red wine note. Full-bodied, rich, and silk on the palate. Subtly spiced, drying steadily to nutty oak, with fruity wine notes on the finish.

THE BALVENIE CARIBBEAN CASK 14-YEAR-OLD

SINGLE MALT: SPEYSIDE 43% ABV
Toffee, orchard fruits, and white rum on the nose, while the rounded palate yields sugary malt, more fruit, vanilla, and soft oak. The finish is medium in length, with gently spiced oak.

THE BALVENIE SINGLE BARREL 12-YEAR-OLD
SINGLE MALT: SPEYSIDE 47.8% ABV
Maple, honey, vanilla, pine, and oak on the aromatic nose. Vanilla, honey, milk chocolate, newly planed oak, and apple on the full palate, which closes with sweet spices.

THE BALVENIE 30-YEAR-OLD
SINGLE MALT: SPEYSIDE 47.3% ABV
The nose features caramel, nutmeg, figs, Jaffa oranges, and spicy oak, while the rich palate offers honey, spice, ripe plums, and supple oak.

ALL ABOUT...
MALTING

Any cereal grains can be malted, but in whisky-making the term invariably refers to malted barley. It is the sole cereal used in making malt whisky, and a proportion of barley malt is used to produce most types, including grain, rye, and bourbon whiskies. Barley corns are mainly starch. To make alcohol from them, the starch must be converted into sugar and fermented with yeast. Malting prepares the starches in the grain for conversion. It does this by breaking down the tough cell walls and proteins that bind the starch cells, and by activating the enzymes that will later convert the starches into sugar during "mashing" *(see p.8)*.

FROM BARLEY TO MALT ▶
The malting process starts with raw grains of barley (1). The grains are encouraged to germinate and produce shoots, at which point they are called green malt (2). The green malt is kilned to halt the germination when the starch levels are at their maximum; starch in the resulting malt grain (3) is converted into sugar and then into alcohol through the processes known as mashing and fermentation.

FLOOR MALTINGS ▶
Once the barley has been steeped in water over the course of two days, it will begin to germinate. The traditional method is for the damp barley to be spread out on a cement floor, to a depth of about 60cm (2ft). The barley generates heat, so it has to be regularly turned with wooden shovels, to prevent the rootlets matting.

▲ DRUM MALTINGS
These days, most distilleries buy their malt from large industrial maltings. Here, the wet grain is cast into large germination drums *(above)* instead of being laid out on a floor. Cool, humid air is blown through the grain to control the temperature and, every now and again, the drums are turned by motors so the rootlets do not become matted together.

KILNING ▶
Once the barley has begun to germinate, its growth must be stopped. This is done by spreading the green malt over a perforated metal floor above a kiln, and blowing hot air through the grain. It is important that the air is not too hot, or vital enzymes in the malt will be damaged. Moisture is reduced to 4.5 per cent during kilning, which takes about 30 hours.

▲ 1 BARLEY
The most common form used for Scotch malt is plump "two-row" barley.

▲ 2 GREEN MALT
The barley is steeped in water to stimulate germination.

▲ 3 MALT
Once kilned, the grain is more friable and crisp, and rich in starch.

▲ PEAT REEK
If a peaty, smoky flavour is desired in the whisky, peat turfs will be burned during the early hours of kilning. The fragrant peat smoke sticks to the husks of the green malt while it is still damp, so the fires are kept low and cool. *(See also pp.44–45)*

FROM GRAIN TO GLASS ▶
Once malted, the barley will have shrunk slightly; the grains are not as hard as raw barley, and their moisture content will have reduced from 12 to 4%. When you bite into a malted grain, it has a sweet taste. The malt flavour is often not at all obvious in malt whiskies, but in some, such as Knockando and Glenturret, the taste can be more easily discerned.

BELL'S ORIGINAL

BELL'S SPECIAL RESERVE

BELL'S DECANTER

BELL'S

www.bells.co.uk

"Several fine whiskies blended together please the palates of a greater number of people than one whisky unmixed," wrote the first Arthur Bell, and his confidence in his products led him to appoint a London agent as early as 1863.

Bell's acquired the Blair Athol and Dufftown distilleries in 1933, adding Inchgower three years later. Today, the company is owned by Diageo, which has taken a number of steps to consolidate Bell's position. Visitor facilities at the Blair Athol Distillery (the source of the single malt at the heart of the blend) have been enhanced and the blend itself has undergone continuous change and evolution.

After 14 years of being sold as an 8-year-old, Bell's has been non-aged since 2008. But, in keeping with the spirit of Arthur Bell himself, great emphasis is laid on the skill of the blenders, and the company insists that, in blind tests they conducted, experienced drinkers prefer the new version.

The famous and very collectable Bell's decanters are limited-edition releases. They were first produced in the 1930s and a decanter decorated with jolly festive imagery *(see above)* has been released each Christmas since 1988. They are also brought out to commemorate historic moments, such as the marriage of Charles and Diana in 1981.

BELL'S ORIGINAL

BLEND 40% ABV

As well as Blair Athol, Dufftown and Inchgower are important components here, along with Glenkinchie and Caol Ila. Medium-bodied blend, with a nutty aroma and a lightly spiced flavour.

BELL'S SPECIAL RESERVE

BLEND 40% ABV

Special Reserve has smoky hints from the Islay malts, tempered with warm pepper and a rich honey complexity.

BEN NEVIS MCDONALD'S TRADITIONAL

BEN NEVIS SHERRY CASK

BEN NEVIS 10-YEAR-OLD

BEN NEVIS

Lochy Bridge, Fort William
www.bennevisdistillery.com

It is hard to believe that Scotland's most northerly distillery on the west coast once employed 230 people, when it was owned by the MacDonald family in the 19th century. Not all of them were making whisky, as there were workshops and a sawmill too, as well as a farm with 200 head of cattle that fed on the distillery's rich draff. Sitting by Loch Linnhe on the edge of Fort William, Ben Nevis even had its own small fleet of steamers to ferry the whisky down the loch.

It was founded in 1825 by "Long John" MacDonald, who was the inspiration for the once-popular blend of that name. The brewing company Whitbread briefly owned the distillery during the 1980s, before it left the drinks business to concentrate on hotels. Ben Nevis is currently owned by Nikka.

Despite gaps in its inventory due to periodic closures during the 1970s and '80s, a number of older single malts have been released alongside the various Dew of Ben Nevis blends. Since the mid-1990s, the core single malt has been the 10-year-old, augmented in 2011 by the Macdonald's Traditional. Additionally, single cask and wood-finished releases appear occasionally.

BEN NEVIS 10-YEAR-OLD

SINGLE MALT: HIGHLANDS 46% ABV
A big, mouth-filling West Highlands malt with a sweet smack of oak and an oily texture that finishes dry.

BEN NEVIS MCDONALD'S TRADITIONAL

SINGLE MALT: HIGHLANDS 46% ABV
Initial starch on the nose, then buttery smoked haddock, a hint of chilli, sherry, and gentle wood smoke. Spicy on the palate, with hazelnuts, peat, and stewed fruit. Lingering, spicy cigarette ash in the finish.

**BENRIACH CURIOSITAS
10-YEAR-OLD**

SINGLE MALT: SPEYSIDE 40% ABV
*A bitter-sweet whisky
with a dense peaty flavour.
Beneath the smoke, there are
flavours of digestive biscuits,
cereal, and some citrus notes.*

**BENRIACH
12-YEAR-OLD**

SINGLE MALT: SPEYSIDE 40% ABV
*More classically Speyside in
character than the 10-year-
old, with a heathery nose,
creamy vanilla ice cream
flavour, and a hint of honey.*

BENRIACH 16-YEAR-OLD

BENRIACH 20-YEAR-OLD

BENRIACH AUTHENTICUS 21-YEAR-OLD

BENRIACH 30-YEAR-OLD

BENRIACH

Longmorn, Elgin, Morayshire
www.benriachdistillery.co.uk

Of all the Speyside distilleries built on the crest of the great speculative wave that ended the chapter on whisky-making in the 19th century, few crashed so badly as BenRiach.

BenRiach opened in 1897 and, after repossession by the bank two years later, became part of the Longmorn Distilleries Company. It made whisky until 1903 and then shut down for most of the 20th century, although Longmorn, just next door, continued to make use of its floor maltings as well as its warehouses to mature its spirit.

Then, in 1965, after a major refurbishment, its solitary pair of stills was fired up again by its new owners, Glenlivet. It subsequently became part of Seagram, who, having no distillery on Islay, decided to produce a powerful peat-smoked malt at BenRiach in 1983. There were still some stocks of this peated BenRiach left when the distillery's new owners took over in 2004. This led to the Curiositas and Authenticus bottlings – the only commercially available Speyside single malts distilled from peated malted barley.

The new owners were a South African consortium led by Billy Walker, the former head of Burn

Stewart Distillers. They paid Chivas Brothers a reported £5.4 million. The deal included around 5,000 casks dating back to 1970. There were no holes in the inventory due to years of non-production and there were plenty of different casks and different levels of peating to play with. This has allowed Billy Walker and his colleagues to dramatically expand the range of BenRiach malts available.

BENRIACH 16-YEAR-OLD

SINGLE MALT: SPEYSIDE 40% ABV

A nutty, spicy Speysider, with a honeyed texture in the mouth and perhaps the faintest wisp of smoke.

BENRIACH 20-YEAR-OLD

SINGLE MALT: SPEYSIDE 40% ABV

The long years in oak have given this expression a dry, woody flavour, with sharp citrus notes and a clean finish.

BENRIACH AUTHENTICUS 21-YEAR-OLD

SINGLE MALT: SPEYSIDE 46% ABV

The 21-year-old big brother to the 10-year-old Curiositas. A mix of peat, oak, raisins, honey, and spices.

BENRIACH 30-YEAR-OLD

SINGLE MALT: SPEYSIDE 50% ABV

A sumptuous, full-bodied malt, full of raisins, candied fruit, dark chocolate, and spice, which linger on the finish.

ALL ABOUT...
PEAT

Peat is decayed vegetation, decomposed over thousands of years by water and partially carbonized by chemical changes. The vegetation itself varies from place to place, but usually includes mosses, sedges, heather, and rushes. For peat to develop, the climate must be cool and damp, the drainage poor, and the ground poorly aerated. As it decomposes, the vegetation becomes waterlogged and sinks, piling up and being compressed and carbonized. Once the surface turf is cut away, and a trench (or "bank") dug, the peat is revealed. Once dug out, the peat is laid out on the bank to dry.

▲ PEAT WATER
The water on Islay (and in many other places in the Highlands) flows through peat and is the colour of tea.

THE PEATING TRADITION ▶
After the Little Ice Age, which began around 1300, there were few trees left in the Scottish Highlands, but there were huge tracts of peat bog. Peat was the fuel in the Highlands, and remains so to this day in some places, for domestic fires as well as for drying malt and firing stills.

▲ CUTTING TOOLS
All that is needed to "win" peat, as the expression goes, is a peat spade (to cut the turf), a tool called a fal (with a "finger", to cut the peats themselves), and a fork to lift the peats onto the bank where they will dry. A small amount of peat is still dug by hand today, but most is now extracted by machine.

PEAT BOGS ▶
Some peat bogs are thought to be as much as 10,000 years old, and they can be up to 9m (nearly 30ft) deep. Vast swathes of Islay are covered with peat bogs.

◄ PEAT ON THE FIRE
During the kilning of the barley, peat is often burned on the kiln fire. This is best done during the early stages of drying the green malt *(see p.39)*, while it is still damp and sticky.

▲ FRAGRANT SMOKE
The peat smoke adheres to the husks of the grains, which are laid out on a perforated floor above the kiln. It only sticks while the malt is still damp, so the peat fire must be kept cool and smouldering.

SMOKY FLAVOURS ►
The chemicals that impart smoky or medicinal flavours to malt, and the whisky made from it, are called phenols, and are measured in parts per million (ppm). Heavily peated whiskies such as Lagavulin and Laphroaig peat to around 35ppm phenols, and Ardbeg to around 50ppm. Peated to an extraordinary 167ppm phenols, Bruichladdich's limited release Octomore is currently the most heavily peated whisky.

BENROMACH 10-YEAR-OLD

BENROMACH 15-YEAR-OLD

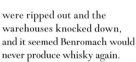

BENROMACH 100 PROOF

BENROMACH

Forres, Morayshire
www.benromach.com

With just a single pair of stills and a maximum production of 500,000 litres (110,000 gallons) of pure alcohol a year, Benromach was always something of a pint-sized distillery. It was founded in 1898 and changed hands no fewer than six times in its first 100 years. At one point, it found itself part of National Distillers of America, sharing a stable with bourbon brands such as Old Crow and Old Grand-Dad. Then, like so many dispossessed distilleries, Benromach became part of the giant DCL who, as UDV, mothballed the distillery in 1983, along with many others. This time the stills were ripped out and the warehouses knocked down, and it seemed Benromach would never produce whisky again.

Luckily, it was not just the whisky industry that was in depression, otherwise some wily property developer would doubtless have snapped up the site. Benromach's saviour was the famous firm of independent bottlers Gordon & MacPhail of Elgin, who bought the distillery in 1993. A new pair of stills was installed, and the first spirit flowed from it in 1998, when Prince Charles officially opened the new Benromach.

In line with many Speyside single malts of old, there is an element of peatiness about the spirit.

BENROMACH PEAT SMOKE

BENROMACH ORGANIC

BENROMACH 35-YEAR-OLD

BENROMACH 10-YEAR-OLD
SINGLE MALT: SPEYSIDE 43% ABV
Smoky on the nose, with wet grass, butter, ginger, and brittle toffee. Mouth-coating, spicy, malty, and nutty on the palate, with citrus fruits, raisins, and soft wood smoke.

BENROMACH 15-YEAR-OLD
SINGLE MALT: SPEYSIDE 43% ABV
Nutty and spicy on the nose, with dried fruits, sherry, and orange. More orange on the palate, with ginger and milk chocolate, leading into smoky, spicy oak.

BENROMACH 100 PROOF
SINGLE MALT: SPEYSIDE 57% ABV
Fragrant sherry, malt, vanilla, chilli, and dried fruits on the nose. Voluptuous in the mouth, with rich malt, smoky sherry, orange, and pepper. Long and smoky finish.

BENROMACH PEAT SMOKE
SINGLE MALT: SPEYSIDE 46% ABV
Sweet peat and cigarette smoke over fresh, fruity notes on the nose. Big-bodied, smoky, fruity, malty, and delightfully balanced on the palate. The long finish tastes of kipper.

BENROMACH ORGANIC
SINGLE MALT: SPEYSIDE 43% ABV
The first single malt officially certified by the Soil Association has a sweet American oak character with notes of toffee and orange zest.

BENROMACH 35-YEARS-OLD
SINGLE MALT: SPEYSIDE 43% ABV
The nose is warm and floral, with sherry, cocktail cherries, and faint smoke in time. Smooth, spicy, and lightly smoky on the palate, with orchard fruits, then orange wine gums, drying to spicy tannins.

BENRINNES

Aberlour, Banffshire
www.malts.com

The original Benrinnes Distillery was founded in 1826 at Whitehouse Farm on lower Speyside by Peter McKenzie, but was swept away in a flood three years later. In 1834, a new distillery called the Lyne of Ruthrie was built a few miles away and, despite bankruptcies and a bad fire in 1896, it has survived as Benrinnes. What you see today is a modern post-war distillery, which was completely rebuilt in the mid-1950s. It has six stills that operate a partial form of triple distillation, with one wash still paired with two spirit stills.

BENRINNES FLORA & FAUNA 15-YEAR-OLD

SINGLE MALT: SPEYSIDE 43% ABV
The only official distillery bottling is fairly sumptuous, with some smoke and spicy flavours and a creamy mouthfeel.

BLACK BOTTLE

Owner: Burn Stewart Distillers
www.blackbottle.com

Black Bottle was created in 1879 by C., D., & G. Grahams, a firm of Aberdeen tea blenders. Grahams ran the company for almost 90 years before it was eventually sold in 1964. The Black Bottle brand changed hands several times before being bought in 2003 by Burn Stewart Distillers as part of their purchase of the Bunnahabhain distillery. In 2013, Burn Stewart relaunched the brand, giving less prominence to malts from Islay by including more Speyside-style characteristics, taking it closer to its north-east roots.

BLACK BOTTLE

BLEND 40% ABV
Fresh oak, light smoke, honey, and a hint of sherry on the nose. Caramel, berry fruits, honey, and more light smoke on the palate, with plain chocolate and drying oak.

BLACK & WHITE

Owner: Diageo

A fondly regarded brand from the Buchanan's stable, Black & White originally went by the name Buchanan's Special. The story goes that, in the 1890s, James Buchanan supplied his whisky to the House of Commons in a very dark bottle with a white label. Apparently incapable of memorizing the name, British parliamentarians simply called for "Black and White". Buchanan adopted the name and subsequently adorned the label with two dogs — a black Scottish terrier and a white West Highland terrier. Today it is marketed by Diageo in France, Brazil, and Venezuela, where it continues to enjoy a popularity long since lost in its homeland.

BLACK & WHITE

BLEND 40% ABV
A high-class, traditional-style blend. Layered hints of peat, smoke, and oak.

BLAIR ATHOL

Pitlochry, Perthshire
www.malts.com

In 1798, John Stewart and Robert Robertson took out a licence for their Aldour Distillery on the edge of Pitlochry. In an area crawling with illicit stills, life was tough for legitimate, tax-paying distilleries, and Aldour soon closed. It was resurrected in 1826 by Alexander Connacher, who re-named it Blair Athol. Within 30 years, some of the malt was being sold to the Perth blender Arthur Bell & Sons, who finally bought the distillery in 1933. Except for the 12-year-old and the occasional rare malt, nearly every drop goes into blends, particularly Bell's.

BLAIR ATHOL FLORA & FAUNA 12-YEAR-OLD

SINGLE MALT: HIGHLANDS 43%
Smooth, well-rounded flavours, with spice and candied fruit, and a trace of smoke on the finish.

BLADNOCH 15-YEAR-OLD

BLADNOCH 18-YEAR-OLD

BLADNOCH

Bladnoch, Wigtown, Wigtownshire
www.bladnoch.com

The most southerly distillery in
Scotland, Bladnoch has a capacity
of just 100,000 litres (22,000
gallons) a year, a figure capped by
its previous owners, UDV. This
classic doll's house distillery was
founded by Thomas and John
McClelland in 1817 on the banks
of the River Bladnoch and remained
in the family's hands until 1911,
when it was bought by an Irish
company. In 1937, it went bust
and was bought and sold six times
over the next few years, spending
long periods lying idle in between.
Finally, it was taken over by
Guinness UDV (now Diageo) in
1985. With the next big whisky
slump, its solitary pair of stills
went cold once more in 1993,
seemingly for good. But just a year
later, it was bought by Raymond
Armstrong from Northern Ireland.
The deal brokered was that
Bladnoch would never produce
whisky again but, by 2000, Diageo
had relented and the distillery
is now allowed to produce the
equivalent of 250,000 bottles
a year. Under the Armstrong
regime, Bladnoch distilled and
bottled both unpeated and
peated expressions at a variety
of ages. In 2015, the distillery
was acquired by Australian
entrepreneur David Prior, after
a six-year period of silence.

BLADNOCH 15-YEAR-OLD

SINGLE MALT: LOWLANDS 55% ABV
*A light, crisp, apertif-style whisky
with a trace of green apples.*

BLADNOCH 18-YEAR-OLD

SINGLE MALT: LOWLANDS 55% ABV
*This smooth Lowlands malt is bottled at
full cask strength without chill-filtration,
but is in short supply.*

BOWMORE LEGEND
SINGLE MALT: ISLAY 40% ABV
*Dry and bracing, with
a faint citrus flavour that
develops into a smoky finish.*

BOWMORE 12-YEAR-OLD
SINGLE MALT: ISLAY 40% ABV
*Gently aromatic, with a mix of
citrus fruits and smoke on the
nose, which carries through to
the tongue, together with some
dark chocolate.*

BOWMORE 15-YEAR-OLD

BOWMORE SMALL BATCH

BOWMORE 18-YEAR-OLD

BOWMORE 25-YEAR-OLD

BOWMORE

Bowmore, Isle of Islay
www.bowmore.com

The oldest surviving distillery on Islay was founded in 1779 by John Simpson, who, as a farmer, distiller, builder, quarry-owner, and part-time postmaster, was a man of many parts. Quite how much time he devoted to Bowmore is unclear, but the distillery remained small for years. When it was bought by the Glasgow firm of W. & J. Mutter in 1837, it was producing just 3,640 litres (800 gallons) a year. Within 50 years, annual production had soared to 900,000 litres (200,000 gallons). This was filled into casks and shipped to Mutter's bonded warehouse beneath Glasgow's Central Station.

After various changes in ownership, including 20 years with DCL, the distillery was bought by another Glasgow-based whisky firm, Stanley P. Morrison. Ever since, it has been the flagship distillery of Morrison Bowmore, now part of the Japanese drinks giant Suntory.

Bowmore stands on the shores of Loch Indaal. With the salty sea breeze blowing right into the warehouses, some of it is bound to seep into the casks. As with most Islay distilleries, the majority of the spirit is tankered off the island to mature on the mainland. The distillery has two pairs of stills, six Oregon-pine washbacks, and its own floor maltings, which can supply up to 40 per cent of Bowmore's needs. Whether using

its own malt, which is peated to around 25 ppm, improves the flavour of Bowmore would be hard to prove, but to see the whole process, from the freshly steeped barley to the peat-fired kiln and its dense blue smoke, certainly makes a visit to the Bowmore Distillery that much more special.

BOWMORE 15-YEAR-OLD

SINGLE MALT: ISLAY 43% ABV
The deep mahogany colour comes from two years in Oloroso casks, which also give a raisin-like sweetness to Bowmore's signature note of smoke.

BOWMORE SMALL BATCH

SINGLE MALT: ISLAY 40% ABV
Floral and delicate, with coconut and vanilla on the nose, then soft peat smoke emerges. Vanilla, honey,

fudge, and sweet smoke on the palate, with a hint of oak towards the close.

BOWMORE 18-YEAR-OLD

SINGLE MALT: ISLAY 43% ABV
A mellow, more autumnal take on the 15-year-old expression, with a waxy, orange-peel flavour mixed with smoke and burnt sugar.

BOWMORE 25-YEAR-OLD

SINGLE MALT: ISLAY 43% ABV
The stewed fruit and treacle flavours from the wood subsume the drier, smokier elements of Bowmore, thanks to a heavy sherry influence.

ALL ABOUT...
POT STILLS

To create an acceptable whisky, the still must be made from copper. The reason for this is that copper purifies the spirit. It acts as a catalyst to extract foul-smelling sulphur compounds, and heavy fusel oils, and it assists in creating desirable fragrant and fruity flavours. It follows that the more contact the alcohol vapour has with copper, the purer and lighter the spirit will be. As the vapour rises during the distillation, much of it condenses in the still and trickles back to be boiled up again. This is called "reflux", and leads to greater purity. The amount of reflux depends upon a number of factors. The size and shape of the still is vital, but so is the depth to which it is filled. Typically, this won't exceed two-thirds of the still's capacity; a high fill makes for less reflux. How fast the stills are operated is another factor, with a speedy operation leading to less reflux. The temperature of the distillate is important too – the warmer the spirit, the greater the copper uptake in the condensers. The pitch of the lyne arms connecting the head of the still to the condenser is also crucial, with different angles affecting the purity of the spirit.

▲ SQUAT STILLS
These act like a reverse boil-ball and create a similarly complex spirit, without the same level of copper contact as onion stills.

▲ ONION OR PLAIN STILL
Large and tall onion-shaped stills afford the greatest copper contact and tend to produce the purest spirit. They are the traditional still shape, and the commonest in Scotch malt distilling.

▲ BOIL-BALL STILL
These generally take longer to complete a distillation, because of condensation in the ball. But such condensation does not lead to increased reflux, so these stills tend to make a heavier, more complex spirit.

▲ LAMP GLASS STILL
The tight neck of the lamp glass still restricts and slows the upward flow of the spirit vapour. It acts like a reverse boil-ball to create a similarly complex spirit, without the same level of copper contact as onion stills.

▲ ASCENDING LYNE ARMS

The more the lyne arm angles upwards, the more reflux is created, making for a lighter spirit. The lyne arms here rise up from the stills to connect to a series of shell-and-tube condensers. Shell-and-tube are the most common form of condensers used in the industry today, and allow more contact between the spirit and copper than traditional "worm tub" condensers.

▲ TALL STILLS

Tall-necked stills make for increased reflux, whereby, part of the spirit vapour condenses on the sides of the still and trickles back down to be re-distilled. The spirit therefore has more contact with copper, which leads to greater purity and delicacy, but to less "character" than the spirit from squat stills.

▲ DESCENDING LYNE ARM

A descending lyne arm encourages the vapour to pass quickly to the condenser, reducing reflux. Where these are found on wash stills, the chance of "carry over" is increased, where liquid rather than vapour makes its way into the condenser, spoiling the spirit.

BRUICHLADDICH

Bruichladdich, Isle of Islay
www.bruichladdich.com

Islay's most westerly distillery stands on the shores of Loch Indaal, across the water from Bowmore. It was built in 1881 by three brothers – Robert, William, and John Gourlay Harvey, who were also the owners of Dundashill in Glasgow, the largest malt distillery in Scotland at the time. Unlike older distilleries on Islay, it was purpose-built and boasted state-of-the-art cavity walls and its own steam generator.

After a promising start supplying blends with a pungent top dressing of Islay malt, Bruichladdich fell into disuse from 1929 to 1937, the first of many closures that have dogged

the distillery. After repeated sales, it passed in the 1970s to the owners of Whyte & Mackay, who closed it down in 1994, seemingly for good. Then, days before Christmas 2000, it was rescued by a private consortium led by the independent bottler Murray McDavid. The old Victorian decor has been lovingly preserved, and no computers are used in the production. The whisky is bottled on site and even uses barley grown on the island.

In recent years, Bruichladdich's core range was joined by a heavily peated whisky, called Port Charlotte after a nearby village, and the intensely smoky Octomore, which took its name from an old Islay distillery that closed in 1852. In 2003, Bruichladdich became

the first distillery on Islay to bottle its whiskies on the island. From the heavily sherried Blacker Still and the pink-hued Flirtation, to 3D, Infinity, and The Yellow Submarine, the range of bottlings has been staggering. To date, over 200, many of them in very limited quantities, have been released.

In 2012, Remy Cointreau acquired the distillery, since which date the number of expressions available has been significantly reduced.

BRUICHLADDICH
THE CLASSIC LADDIE

SINGLE MALT: ISLAY 46% ABV
Chocolate, icing sugar, and contrasting rock salt on the nose, with kiwi fruit and vanilla on the palate, plus spicy, brine notes.

BRUICHLADDICH
PORT CHARLOTTE PC12

SINGLE MALT: ISLAY 58.7% ABV
Apple turnovers, soft caramel, and progressively developing wood smoke on the nose. Sweet peat on the oily palate, with ripe bananas and ultimately liquorice.

BRUICHLADDICH
ISLAY BARLEY 2009

SINGLE MALT: ISLAY 50% ABV
Vanilla, honey, red apples, and an earthy malt note on the nose. Lemon contrasts with vanilla and honey on the gingery palate, closing with cinnamon and dried fruits.

BRUICHLADDICH OCTOMORE 7.1

SINGLE MALT: ISLAY 59.5% ABV
The nose opens with a big hit of peat, followed by brine and orchard fruits. The palate is slick and full, with sweet peat, caramel, ripe apples, and developing oak.

BRUICHLADDICH THE SCOTTISH BARLEY

SINGLE MALT: ISLAY 50% ABV
Baked apples and linseed on the nose after a slightly metallic opening. The body is oily, and rich fruit notes open the palate, with vanilla, spicy hard toffee, and brine.

BUNNAHABHAIN TOITEACH

BUNNAHABHAIN 25-YEAR-OLD

BRAEVAL

Chapeltown of Glenlivet,
Ballindalloch, Banffshire

In the early 1970s, when global
sales of blended Scotch were
booming, the Braeval Distillery was
built to help supply the malt to meet
demand. Edgar Bronfmann, heir
apparent to the Seagram empire,
flew in to cut the turf in 1972 and,
within a year, the distillery was in
production. A century earlier, such
a distillery would have created a
whole community, with houses,
shops, and perhaps even a school.
But today's fully computerized
Braeval needs a staff of one. Only
independent bottlings of the malt
exist. Gordon & MacPhail's goes
by the name of Braes of Glenlivet.

BRAES OF GLENLIVET
GORDON & MACPHAIL 1975

SINGLE MALT: SPEYSIDE 43% ABV
*Floral and vanilla flavours combine
to great effect. The finish offers
a dry, light touch.*

BUCHANAN'S

Owner: Diageo

James Buchanan was one of the
most notable whisky barons –
the Victorian entrepreneurs who
brought Scotch to world attention,
amassing personal fortunes along
the way. Starting as an agent in
1879, he soon began trading on his
own and rapidly saw his whisky
adopted in the House of Commons.
Today the Buchanan's brand is
showing signs of prospering once
again under its owners, Diageo.
Mainly seen in Venezuela, Mexico,
Colombia, and the US, Buchanan's
is positioned as a premium-style
blend. There are two expressions: a
12-year-old and the Special Reserve
at 18 years old.

BUCHANAN'S 12-YEAR-OLD

BLEND 40% ABV
*Rich on the nose, with sherry and
spice. Thinner on the palate, with
bitter, dried-lemon notes. Winey,
with a touch of dry wood.*

BUNNAHABHAIN

Port Askaig, Islay
www.bunnahabhain.com

Before the distilleries of Islay
found fame for the heavily
peat-smoked character of their
single malts, their market was not
the whisky drinker, but the big
blending houses. Many of these
used Islay malts as a top dressing,
to add a smoky intensity to their
blends. The trouble was they only
required limited quantities, as too
much would leave their whiskies
unbalanced. With this in mind,
Bunnahabhain, the most northerly
distillery on the island, used
unpeated or lightly peated malt.

It was founded in 1881 on a
shingle beach near Port Askaig.
Before the distillery was built,
a road had to be laid, along with
a pier, cottages for the workforce,
and a school for their children. The
whole venture cost £30,000, yet
the business was making a profit
of £10,000 by its second year.

The distillery was once part of
Edrington. As a consequence, its
malt was overshadowed by
its stablemates – Macallan and
Highland Park. Since 2003,
however, it has belonged to Burn
Stewart, who are investing heavily
in Bunnahabhain's single malts.

The core range consists of the
12-, 18-, and 25-year-old. Heavily
peated variants are also now
available, and a bottling strength
of 46.3% without chill-filtration
is in place across the range.

BUNNAHABHAIN TOITEACH

SINGLE MALT: ISLAY 46% ABV
*The nose offers hot peat, caramel, and
lively spices, while peat features strongly
on the palate, along with caramel, dried
fruits, brine, and finally, smoky oak.*

BUNNAHABHAIN 25-YEAR-OLD

SINGLE MALT: ISLAY 46.3% ABV
*A relatively fulsome malt with aromas
of polished leather and crème caramel.
On the palate there is ripe European
oak. The texture is luscious and creamy.*

BUNNAHABHAIN
12-YEAR-OLD

SINGLE MALT: ISLAY 46.3% ABV

A clean, refreshing whisky with a scent of ozone and sea spray, which gives way to a nutty, malty sweetness in the mouth.

BUNNAHABHAIN
18-YEAR-OLD

SINGLE MALT: ISLAY 46.3% ABV

With its richer sherry influence, this has less of the malty distillery character than the 12-year-old. Instead, it has a broader texture and woody flavour.

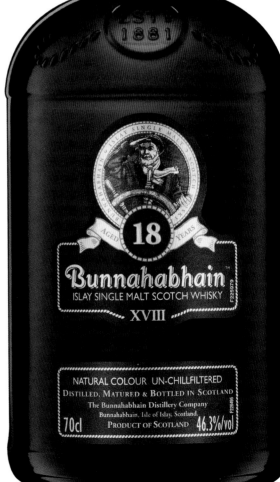

CAOL ILA 12-YEAR-OLD

CAOL ILA CASK STRENGTH

CAOL ILA DISTILLERS EDITION 1995

CAOL ILA

Port Askaig, Islay
www.malts.com

Just as Ardbeg played second fiddle to Laphroaig when both were owned by Allied Domecq, the same was true of Diageo's Caol Ila and Lagavulin. For years the largest distillery on Islay – with a capacity to produce 3.6 million litres (800,000 gallons) of spirit a year – it had a very low profile. This is beginning to change, as its owners are now promoting Caol Ila as a top-quality single malt.

The distillery was built in 1846 by Hector Henderson, who was forced to sell up six years later to Norman Buchanan, the owner of the Jura Distillery across the water. After just five years, he sold out to the big Glasgow blender Bulloch Lade, who reconstructed Caol Ila on a larger scale in 1879.

In 1972, the distillery was effectively demolished. When it re-opened two years later, the only original building still standing was the warehouse. As demand for Lagavulin began to outstrip supply, Caol Ila's malts were finally given the attention they deserved.

CAOL ILA DISTILLERS EDITION 1995

SINGLE MALT: ISLAY 43% ABV
Sweet, smoky, and malty, with aromatic spices (cinnamon), especially in the lingering finish. The most rounded expression of the core range.

CAOL ILA 12-YEAR-OLD

SINGLE MALT: ISLAY 43% ABV
Balancing the scent of tar and peat is a malty sweetness and some citrus aromas. Oily textured, with flavours of treacle and smoke.

CAOL ILA CASK STRENGTH

SINGLE MALT: ISLAY 55% ABV
Paler in colour than other expressions of Caol Ila, the cask-strength version has a strong, assertive character that starts smooth and sweet and dries to a smoky finish.

CARDHU 12-YEAR-OLD

CARDHU AMBER ROCK

CAMERON BRIG

Cameronbridge Distillery,
Winygates, Leven, Fife

Greatly misunderstood, little
drunk in their own right, and sadly
misrepresented, grain whiskies are
Scotch's poor relation. Yet, they
are the essential component and base
of all blends and, when found as
a single grain bottling, the source
of much pleasure. Cameron Brig
is made at Diageo's Cameronbridge
Distillery in Fife, a massive complex
of giant continuous stills. The sheer
scale of grain whisky production
offends some purists but, at its best,
good grain whisky is very good
indeed. You would not expect
anything less from Diageo in its
only offering in this category, and
Cameron Brig won't disappoint.

CAMERON BRIG

SINGLE GRAIN 40% ABV
*Light nose of apples with spicy bourbon
notes. Smooth, fruity palate has grain,
nuts, coffee, and a hint of pepper.*

CARDHU

Knockando, Aberlour, Morayshire
www.malts.com

Having made whisky on the side
for over a decade, John Cumming
decided to take out a licence for
his Cardhu Distillery in 1824. It
remained a small farm distillery
until his daughter-in-law, Elizabeth
Cumming, rebuilt it in the 1880s.
Soon after, it was sold to Johnnie
Walker and became the spiritual
home of the blend.

However, at some point in
the 1990s, a spanner was put in the
works. The owners, Diageo, had
tried to steer Spain's whisky
drinkers on to Johnnie Walker
Black Label as an alternative to
Chivas Regal, but the Spanish, it
seemed, wanted a bottle that had
"malt" on the label. Spanish sales
of Cardhu 12-year-old grew by
100,000 cases between 1997 and
2002, but supply was becoming
a serious issue. Rather than tame
demand by putting up the price,

Diageo took the decision to re-
christen the whisky as Cardhu
Pure Malt, which would allow
them to add in other malts.

Whether Spanish consumers
were bothered is unclear, but the
industry certainly was. After much
outrage, and even questions in
Parliament, Diageo was forced
to withdraw the brand in March
2003 and revert to selling Cardhu
as a genuine 12-year-old single malt.

CARDHU 12-YEAR-OLD

SINGLE MALT: SPEYSIDE 40% ABV
*This heathery, pear-drop-scented
malt is on the lighter side of Speyside,
with a light to medium body and
a malty, slightly nutty flavour that
finishes fairly short.*

CARDHU AMBER ROCK

SINGLE MALT: SPEYSIDE 40% ABV
*Stewed apples, dried fruit, and icing
sugar on the nose. Mouth-coating,
with summer fruits, vanilla, and
peppery spice on the palate. Drying
oak and light liquorice in the finish.*

CATTO'S

Owner: Inver House Distillers
www.cattos.com

James Catto, an Aberdeen-
based whisky blender, set up in
business in 1861. His whiskies
achieved international distribution
on the White Star and P&O
shipping lines.

After the death of James
Catto's son, Robert, in World
War I, the company passed to the
distillers Gilbey's. More recently,
it was acquired by Inver House
Distillers. Catto's is a deluxe, fully
matured, and complex blend. Two
versions are available: a non-age
standard bottling and a 12-year-
old expression with a yellow-gold,
straw-like appearance that belies
its complexity and warm finish.

CATTO'S

BLEND 40% ABV
*The standard Catto blend is aromatic
and well-rounded in character, with
a smooth, mellow finish.*

The Four Ale Bar at the Canny Man's pub in Edinburgh is stocked with several hundred malts as well as numerous objects collected over the course of its nearly 145-year history.

CHIVAS REGAL 25-YEAR-OLD

CHIVAS REGAL 12-YEAR-OLD

CHIVAS REGAL 18-YEAR-OLD

CHIVAS REGAL

Owner: Chivas Brothers
www.chivas.com

Chivas Regal is one of the top five best-selling blends in the world and among the few truly global brands in terms of distribution. Chivas Brothers was founded in the early 19th century and prospered, due in part to some favourable royal connections. The business is owned today by the French multi-national Pernod Ricard.

At the heart of Chivas Regal blends are Speyside single malt whiskies, in particular Strathisla Distillery's rich and full single malt. To safeguard the supply of this critically important ingredient, Chivas Brothers bought the distillery in 1950. It maintains attractive visitor facilities there.

Chivas Regal 18 was launched in 1997 and is a super-premium blend. Strathisla 18-year-old contributes to its memorable, warm finish, but is not available commercially anywhere in the world. Chivas Regal 25 represents a further move upmarket, although supplies of it are strictly limited.

CHIVAS REGAL 25-YEAR-OLD

BLEND 40% ABV

The flagship blend, Chivas Regal 25-year-old is classy and rich. A luxury blend for indulgent sipping. Well-mannered, balanced, and stylish.

CHIVAS REGAL 12-YEAR-OLD

BLEND 40% ABV

An aromatic infusion of wild herbs, heather, honey, and orchard fruits. Round and creamy on the palate, with a full, rich taste of honey and ripe apples and notes of vanilla, hazelnut, and butterscotch. Rich and lingering.

CHIVAS REGAL 18-YEAR-OLD

BLEND 40% ABV

An intense dark amber colour. Multi-layered aromas of fruits, spice, and toffee. Exceptionally rich and smooth, with a velvety chocolate palate, floral notes, and a wisp of mellow smokiness.

CLAN CAMPBELL

Owner: Chivas Brothers

Launched as recently as 1984, Clan Campbell is a million-case-selling brand from Chivas Brothers, the whisky arm of drinks giant Pernod Ricard. It is not available in the UK, but is a leader in the important French market, and may also be found in Italy, Spain, and some Asian countries. Despite its relative youth, its origins are now inextricably entwined with Scottish heritage, thanks to clever marketing and a link to the Duke of Argyll, head of the clan. Indeed, what is claimed to be the oldest whisky-distilling relic in Scotland – a distiller's worm – was by good fortune found on Campbell lands.

CLAN CAMPBELL

BLEND 40% ABV
The malt component of Clan Campbell comes largely from Speyside (Aberlour and Glenallachie especially). A smooth, light whisky with a fruity finish.

CLAN MACGREGOR

Owner: William Grant & Sons
www.williamgrant.com/clanmacgregor.php

This secondary (i.e. budget-priced) blend is sold largely in North America and from Venezuela to the Middle East to Thailand, but not by and large in its Scottish homeland. Sales approach an impressive 1.5 million cases a year and it is one of the world's fastest-growing Scotch whisky brands.

Owned by William Grant & Sons, it is primarily a mix of Grant's own malts (Glenfiddich, Balvenie, and Kininvie) and grain whisky from its substantial Girvan operation. The label proudly carries the badge, motto, and personal crest of the 24th clan chief, Sir Malcolm MacGregor of MacGregor.

CLAN MACGREGOR

BLEND 40% ABV
A blend of grain whiskies and some Speyside malt. Light in style, fragrant, with just a little fruitiness.

THE CLAYMORE

Owner: Whyte & Mackay

A claymore is a Highland broadsword. The name was deemed appropriate by DCL (forerunner of drinks giant Diageo) when, in 1977, it attempted to recover some of the market share it had lost when it withdrew Johnnie Walker Red Label from the UK market. Competitively priced, The Claymore was an immediate success. In 1985, the brand was sold to Whyte & Mackay. It continued to sell well for some time, but in recent years has declined and is now principally seen as a low-priced secondary brand. Dalmore is believed to be the main malt whisky in the blend.

THE CLAYMORE

BLEND 40% ABV
The nose is heavy and full, with silky mellow tones. Well-balanced and full-bodied on the palate. Polished finish.

CLUNY

Owner: Whyte & Mackay

Although it is produced by Whyte & Mackay, Cluny is supplied in bulk to Heaven Hill Distilleries, who have bottled the whisky in the US since 1988. Today, it is one of America's top-selling domestically bottled blended Scotch whiskies.

Cluny contains over 30 malts from all regions of Scotland (Isle of Jura, Dalmore, and Fettercairn single malts among them), along with grain whisky that is almost certainly largely sourced from Whyte & Mackay's Invergordon plant. Cluny is sold primarily on its competitive price. Under Whyte & Mackay's new Indian ownership, it may be a candidate for further international development.

CLUNY

BLEND 40% ABV
Subtle sweet-and-sour nose, with a slight metallic, bitter tang on the palate.

CLYNELISH

Brora, Sutherland
www.malts.com

A large box-shaped distillery dating from 1967, Clynelish has six stills and a capacity of 3.4 million litres (750,000 gallons). Within its grounds is a much older distillery that ran alongside it until 1983. This was Brora, founded in 1819 by the Marquis of Stafford. Known briefly as Old Clynelish, Brora made a heavily peated malt during the 1970s to ensure a supply of Islay-style malts for blends like Johnnie Walker Black Label. In 1983, Brora closed for good, leaving just Clynelish. There have been various rare malts and independent bottlings from Douglas Laing and Caidenheads among others.

CLYNELISH 14-YEAR-OLD

SINGLE MALT: HIGHLANDS 46% ABV
A mouthfilling malt, quite fruity with a creamy texture, a wisp of smoke, and a firm, dry finish.

CRAGGANMORE

Ballindalloch, Morayshire
www.malts.com

When Diageo launched its Classic Malts to showcase the great malt whisky regions of Scotland, deciding which malts to pick must have been challenging, especially on Speyside, where there were so many distilleries to choose from. But most agree that the decision to run with Cragganmore was a good one.

This was a well-conceived distillery from the start. It was built in 1869 by John Smith, a highly experienced distiller who had been involved in Glenfarclas, Macallan, and Glenlivet. He had a reliable source of pure water from the Craggan burn, which also provided the distillery with power. He had nearby access to peat and barley, and he was close to Ballindalloch station. By laying a short stretch of track, Cragganmore became the first distillery in Scotland to have its

own railway siding, to bring in supplies and carry off the freshly filled casks of whisky. It was a model that was widely copied on Speyside, where distilleries sprang up beside the track like farmsteads in the American Midwest.

Part of Cragganmore's famed complexity as a single malt may come from the unusual flat-topped stills and the use of worm tubs to create a heavier spirit.

CRAGGANMORE 12-YEAR-OLD

SINGLE MALT: SPEYSIDE 40% ABV
With its floral, heathery aromas, Cragganmore smells typically Speyside, but there is a robust woody complexity with a trace of smoke on the palate.

CRAGGANMORE DISTILLERS EDITION 1992

SINGLE MALT: SPEYSIDE 40% ABV
This is double-matured, with the final part of its maturation being in a port cask. This results in a cherry and orange sweetness that dies away into a lightly smoky finish.

COMPASS BOX

www.compassboxwhisky.com

Compass Box is the brainchild of ex-Diageo marketing executive John Glaser. The company was formed in 2000 and describes itself as an "artisanal whisky maker", which may seem disingenuous since it isn't a distiller but a blender, albeit a highly innovative and experimental one. From time to time, this brings it into conflict with the industry's establishment. The company's technique of inserting additional oak staves into a barrel to produce Spice Tree led to pressure from the Scotch Whisky Association and the eventual withdrawal of the product. For all this, the company has been highly influential and in its short life has won more than 60 medals and awards. Its limited release "small batch" whiskies sell out quickly.

There are two main ranges: Signature and Limited Release. The former is regularly available and comprises the company's three most popular products: Oak Cross, The Peat Monster, and Asyla. The Limited Release range is indeed very limited: Optimism, for example, was restricted to just 163 bottles.

COMPASS BOX OAK CROSS

BLENDED MALT 43% ABV
Notes of clove and vanilla on the palate accent a sweet maltiness and subtle fruit character.

COMPASS BOX THE PEAT MONSTER

BLENDED MALT: ISLAY / SPEYSIDE 46% ABV
Rich and loaded with flavour: a bacon-fat smokiness, full-blown peat, hints of fruit and spice. A long finish, echoing peat and smoke for several minutes.

COMPASS BOX ASYLA

BLEND 40% ABV
A frequent award-winner. Sweet, delicate, and very smooth on the palate, with flavours of vanilla cream, cereals, and a subtle apple-like character.

ALL ABOUT...
CASKS

"The wood makes the whisky" has long been a saying in Scotland, but it is only over the past 25 years that scientists have discovered why the cask is so important. Oak is the best wood (and incorporated into the legal definition of most whiskies). Most is *Quercus alba* (American white oak), some *Quercus robur* (European oak), and a very small amount of *Quercus mongolica* (Japanese oak). Each type matures its contents slightly differently. The oak cask performs three vital functions: it removes harshness and unwanted flavours (charring plays an important role in this); it adds desirable flavours – vanilla and coconut in the case of American oak, astringency, and dried fruit notes in the case of European oak; and, being semi-porous, it allows the spirit to "breathe" and interact with the surrounding air to oxidize, develop mellowness, increase complexity, and add fruitiness.

▲ INTERACTION WITH WOOD
The vast majority of the character of mature whisky develops during its ageing in oak casks, so the types of casks used are vitally important.

◄ CONSTRUCTION OF A CASK
Stave blanks are cut from the tree trunk in a pattern called "quarter-sawing", which cuts across the grain (so the staves won't leak). The blanks are shaped and jointed so they all fit snugly. Hoops hold them in place while they are heated – traditionally by fire – to bend the wood into the right shape.

AMERICAN BARRELS ▶
By law, to be called bourbon or rye whiskey, the spirit must be matured in new white-oak barrels, which hold 200 litres (44 gallons). Maturation lasts for at least two years. The barrels have a second life in Scotland and other countries where they are exported to be used for maturation. Most Scotch is matured in bourbon casks.

◄ SHERRY BUTTS
Butts and puncheons hold 500 litres (110 gallons) and are usually made from European oak. They are seasoned with sherry for one or two years before being filled with whisky.

▼ MAKING HOGSHEADS
The majority of casks used by the whisky industries of Scotland, Japan, and Ireland began life as American barrels. Having been used to mature American whiskey, the barrels are taken apart and transported in bundles to be "re-made" as hogsheads, which contain around 250 litres (55 gallons) by cannibalizing one barrel in five. A hogshead cask will then be used several times for maturing whisky.

▲ TOASTING AND CHARRING
Burning the inside of the cask causes essential chemical changes within the surface of the wood, without which the spirit will not mature. European oak casks are generally lightly "toasted" to activate the changes; American barrels are more heavily burnt, so the surface blisters.

▲ CASK FINISHING
This is the process in which whisky is aged in one cask, then re-racked into another for the final year or two of its maturation to add an extra layer of flavours. The "finishing cask" is most often a wine, sherry, or – as in the case of the Glenmorangie Quinta Ruban single malt *(right)* – a port cask.

CUTTY SARK 12-YEAR-OLD

CUTTY SARK 18-YEAR-OLD

CRAIGELLACHIE

Craigellachie, Banffshire

Although the name of John Dewar & Sons is writ large above the modern, plate-glass stillhouse that sits on the main road out of Craigellachie, the distillery was originally tied to White Horse. Peter Mackie, the man behind the famous blend, built Craigellachie in 1891 in partnership with Alexander Edward. Of all the Victorian whisky barons, Mackie was the most connected to malt distilling, having served as an apprentice at Lagavulin, whose whisky was also part of White Horse. Since 1998, Craigellachie has been owned by Bacardi.

CRAIGELLACHIE 13-YEAR-OLD

SINGLE MALT: SPEYSIDE 46% ABV

The nose is fresh and fruity, with just a hint of spent matches and a nutty, savoury note. Oily and sweet on the early palate, with more savoury notes coming through in time, plus a hint of charcoal.

CRAWFORD'S

Owner: Whyte & Mackay / Diageo

Crawford's 3 Star was established by Leith firm A. & A. Crawford, and by the time the company joined the Distillers Company (DCL) in 1944, the blend was a Scottish favourite. Although its popularity continued, it was not of strategic significance to its owners, hence the decision to license the brand to Whyte & Mackay in 1986. Whyte & Mackay are today owned by the Indian UB Group, so the future of this venerable label may lie on the subcontinent. Diageo, successors to DCL, retain the rights to the name Crawford's 3 Star Special Reserve outside the UK. Benrinnes single malt (*see p.48*) has been a long-time component in the Crawford's blend.

CRAWFORD'S 3 STAR

BLEND 40% ABV

Spirity, fruity, fresh-tasting blend, with a smack of citrus, a sweet centre, and a dry, slightly sooty finish.

CUTTY SARK

Owner: Berry Bros. & Rudd

Cutty Sark is blended and bottled in Glasgow by Edrington (proprietors of The Famous Grouse). The first very pale-coloured whisky in the world, Cutty Sark was created in 1923 for Berry Bros. & Rudd Ltd, a well-established London wine and spirit merchants who are still the brand owner. The company was looking to innovate with its whisky and decided to produce an original style. The result was a naturally light-coloured blend of quality and character, with a name inspired by the fastest and most famous of all the Scottish-built clipper ships.

One of the acclaimed blended whiskies of the world, Cutty Sark uses some 20 single malt whiskies, many from Speyside distilleries such as Glenrothes and Macallan. Maturation and marriage both contribute to the distinguishing qualities of the blend. The wood for the oak casks is carefully chosen to bring out the characteristic flavour and aroma of each whisky in the Cutty Sark blend and to impart colour gently during the long maturation. There is a non-age expression and a deluxe range at 12, 15, 18, and 25 years old.

CUTTY SARK 12-YEAR-OLD

BLEND 43% ABV

Elegant and fruity, with a subtle vanilla sweetness. Here the malts used are between 12 and 15 years old.

CUTTY SARK 18-YEAR-OLD

BLEND 43% ABV

Balance of vanilla sweetness and bitter and spicy notes – lemon peel, wood, and coal smoke. A dry, wood influence on the finish.

CUTTY SARK ORIGINAL

BLEND 40% ABV

Light and fragrant aroma, with hints of vanilla and oak. Sweet and creamy, with a vanilla note, and a crisp finish.

DAILUAINE

Carron, Banffshire
www.malts.com

Under the shadow of Benrinnes, a local farmer called William Mackenzie built Dailuaine in 1854. His son Thomas later went into partnership with James Fleming to form Dailuaine-Talisker Distilleries Ltd. In 1889, Dailuaine was rebuilt and became one of the biggest distilleries in Scotland. The architect Charles Doig erected his first pagoda roof here, to draw smoke from the kiln through the malt. The idea caught on at other distilleries. With all but 2 per cent of Dailuaine used as fillings, single malt bottlings are relatively rare.

DAILUAINE GORDON & MACPHAIL 1993

SINGLE MALT: SPEYSIDE 43% ABV
Sweet and malty, with spicy notes of liquorice and aniseed. Oaky, toasty notes too. Creamier with a little water.

DALLAS DHU

Forres, Morayshire

This late-Victorian distillery, founded in 1898 by the Master Distiller Alexander Edward, was one of many owned by the Distillers Company (DCL) to be shut down in 1983 to await its fate. With just two stills and a waterwheel that had provided the power right up until 1971, Dallas Dhu never fully embraced the 20th century. However, while its stills have never been fired up again, it has lived on as a museum run by Historic Scotland. Thousands of visitors have taken the tour and tried a drop of the malt in a blend called Roderick Dhu. Rumours of its restart persist.

DALLAS DHU RARE MALTS 21-YEAR-OLD

SINGLE MALT: SPEYSIDE 61.9% ABV
Full-bodied, almost Highland character on the nose, with a trace of smoke and a robust, malty flavour.

**THE DALMORE
12-YEAR-OLD**
SINGLE MALT:
HIGHLANDS 40% ABV
*The well-established
12-year-old has moved
upmarket in its packaging
and price. It has a gentle
flavour of candied peel
and vanilla fudge.*

**THE DALMORE
15-YEAR-OLD**
SINGLE MALT:
HIGHLANDS 40% ABV
*This has the characteristic
rich, fruity sherry
influence, but with rather
more spice – cloves,
cinnamon, and ginger.*

THE DALMORE GRAN RESERVA

THE DALMORE 40-YEAR-OLD

THE DALMORE 1974

THE DALMORE 1263 KING ALEXANDER III

THE DALMORE

Alness, Ross-shire
www.thedalmore.com

While the Whyte & Mackay blend has a long association with Glasgow, its heart lies in the Highlands, in Dalmore on the banks of the Cromarty Firth. The distillery became part of Whyte & Mackay in 1960, and The Dalmore is now the company's flagship single malt.

The name Dalmore is a fusion of Norse and Gaelic and means "the big meadowland". Founded in 1839 by Alexander Matheson, the distillery stands facing the Black Isle, where some of Scotland's best barley is grown. With ample supplies of grain, plenty of local peat, and water from the River Alness, the site was well-chosen.

Matheson soon let others run the distillery for him, among them the Mackenzie brothers, who eventually bought Dalmore in 1891. They were actively involved for a century and today their family motto, "*I shine, not burn*", has been adopted by the brand. According to legend, the Mackenzie clan saved King Alexander III from being gored to death by a stag in 1263. In gratitude, the king granted the Mackenzies the right to bear the head of a 12-point stag on their coat of arms. This has become Dalmore's official crest.

For years, the only distillery bottling of Dalmore was a 12-year-old single malt, but in time a 21- and 30-year-old were added, together with Gran Reserva (formerly known as the Cigar Malt) in 2002. That year also saw a 62-year-old expression bought at auction for a record-breaking £25,877. Since then, the core range has swelled alongside limited-release bottlings. Many of these have played on different cask maturation, a subject that clearly fascinates Whyte & Mackay's Master Blender, Richard Paterson.

THE DALMORE GRAN RESERVA

BLENDED MALT: HIGHLANDS 40% ABV
A blend of Dalmore malts. Subtly smoky, with traces of burnt sugar.

THE DALMORE 40-YEAR-OLD

SINGLE MALT: HIGHLANDS 40% ABV
After years in American oak casks, this Dalmore was poured into second-fill Matusalem Oloroso sherry butts and then Amoroso sherry wood.

THE DALMORE 1974

SINGLE MALT: HIGHLANDS 45% ABV
Smooth and full-bodied, with sherry notes, bananas, dark chocolate, orange, coffee, and walnuts, and a long finish.

THE DALMORE 1263 KING ALEXANDER III

SINGLE MALT: HIGHLANDS 40% ABV
To make this vatting of different-aged Dalmore malts, Richard Paterson used French wine barrels, sherry butts, port pipes, and bourbon casks.

ALL ABOUT...
MATURATION

Whisky consultant Dr Jim Swan likens the change in the character of spirit during maturation to the transformation of a caterpillar into a butterfly: the new-make spirit is the caterpillar, the butterfly is the mature whisky, the cask the chrysalis. The process of ageing in oak wood rounds off, fills out, and mellows the harsh characteristics of the new spirit and develops a huge range of additional aromas and tastes. However, advanced age is not necessarily a good thing: long maturation in an over-active cask can lead to the spirit being dominated by wood-derived flavours. Moreover, a long period in an exhausted cask will not mature the whisky successfully, for the wood will be unable to transform undesirable and immature characteristics of the spirit.

▲ NEW MAKE
Fresh off the still, new make – it cannot be called "whisky" until it has matured for 3 years (2 years in the US) – is crystal clear, fiery, and estery (acetone). It can be quite fruity and drinkable – some is even bottled – but it offers only the merest indication of how the mature whisky will taste.

◄ HOGSHEADS
American whiskey is mostly matured in new oak, while Scotch is always matured in re-used casks. The most commonly used cask for maturing Scotch is an ex-bourbon cask, which is remade into what is known as a hogshead, or a "hoggie" (see p.66).

BUTTS ►
Sherry butts and puncheons are also traditionally used in whisky maturation. They are usually made from European oak – though American oak is used as well – and have previously been used to hold sherry (see p.66).

DUNNAGE WAREHOUSE ►
Cool, damp, earth-floored, and with casks racked three-high, dunnage warehouses are the traditional Scottish warehouse. During maturation in such a warehouse, the spirit's strength reduces but its volume stays high.

▲ RACKED WAREHOUSE

Ubiquitous in North America but also common elsewhere (including Scotland), racked warehouses allow for the storage of casks up to 80-high. In the US, the atmosphere can be warm – even hot – close to the roof, and dry. The volume of liquid in the cask reduces in these conditions, but the strength remains high.

TIME IN CASK ▶

The length of maturation is the single most influential factor in the flavour of the mature whisky. There is no optimum time – this depends on the history of the cask (*see pp.66–67*). Each is unique, and whiskies of the same vintage and distillery are nevertheless still discernably distinct from one cask to the next.

▲ TAKING SAMPLES

Samples are drawn with a simple tubular instrument called a valinch. Some distilleries draw samples intermittently to monitor the progress of the spirit's maturation.

THE WHISKY'S HUE ▶

The whisky draws colour from the wood: the more tannic the wood, the deeper the tint. European oak, being more tannic, gives an umbrageous, "polished mahogany" hue, while American oak (less tannic) tints the liquid golden. The more times a cask has been filled, the less colour it will impart and the less impact it will have on the spirit it carries.

DEWAR'S 12-YEAR-OLD

DEWAR'S 18-YEAR-OLD

DALWHINNIE

Dalwhinnie, Inverness-shire
www.malts.com

Founded in 1897, Dalwhinnie used to claim to be the highest distillery in Scotland, at 327m (1,073ft) above sea level, but it has since been eclipsed by Braeval. Its other claim to fame holds good, however: with a mean annual temperature of just 6°C (43°F), Dalwhinnie remains the coldest distillery in the country. In 1905, it became Scotland's first American-owned distillery, bought by the New York company Cook & Bernheimer, and the Stars and Stripes were raised above the owners' warehouse in Leith. Since 1926, it has been part of DCL (now Diageo), supplying blends such as Black & White.

DALWHINNIE 15-YEAR-OLD

SINGLE MALT: HIGHLANDS 43% ABV
Sweet, aromatic, and subtly infused with smoke, this complex malt is thick on the tongue.

DEANSTON

Deanston, Perthshire
www.deanstonmalt.com

Many distilleries evolved from illicit stills on the farm, others from breweries or malt mills, but only Deanston is a former cotton mill. It was founded in 1785 by Richard Arkwright, one of the great pioneers of the Industrial Revolution. The conversion to whisky-making took place in 1965, in a joint venture with Brodie Hepburn, who also owned Tuillibardine. Deanston was soon producing a single malt – Old Bannockburn was released in 1971. Having spent most of the 1980s in mothballs, the distillery was bought by Burn Stewart, now owned by South African Distell Group, in 1990.

DEANSTON 12-YEAR-OLD

SINGLE MALT: HIGHLANDS 40% ABV
Non-chill filtered and relatively light-bodied, it has a nutty, vanilla flavour.

DEWAR'S

www.dewars.com

When it was bought by Bacardi in 1988, the whole Dewar's enterprise was reinvigorated. The brand was repackaged, with considerable investment made throughout the business, from distilling to warehousing and bottling. New products were developed to augment the standard White Label – one of the biggest selling Scotch blends in the US. First of these was a 12-year-old expression, Special Reserve, followed by the 18-year-old Founder's Reserve bottling, and finally an ultra-premium non-age style known as Signature.

The main single malt in the Dewar's blends is Aberfeldy (a visitor's centre at the latter distillery celebrates the firm's long history), although the group's other single malts – Aultmore, Craigellachie, Royal Brackla and, to a lesser extent, MacDuff *(see Glen Deveron, p.80)* – are also used.

Dewar's is not widely available in the UK, but is a dominant presence in the US. It is also important in some European markets and is developing a following in Asia. Bacardi has expanded global distribution for Dewar's and greatly expanded its profile through increased advertising and marketing. Standards of production have been kept high, and some would say that the blend quality has improved, especially in the new products.

DEWAR'S 12-YEAR-OLD

BLEND 40% ABV
Sweetish and floral. A full and rich blend, with honey and caramel, and liquorice notes in the long finish.

DEWAR'S 18-YEAR-OLD

BLEND 43% ABV
In the 18-year-old expression, the Dewar's nose is more delicately perfumed, with notes of pear and lemon zest. Soft on the palate, but drying, with a slightly spicy finish.

DEWAR'S WHITE LABEL
BLEND 40% ABV
Sweet and heathery on the nose. Medium-bodied, fresh, malty, and vaguely spicy, with a clean, slightly dry finish.

DEWAR'S SIGNATURE
BLEND 43% ABV
A limited-edition blend, with a heavy share of old Aberfeldy malt. Silky textured and mellow, with rich fruit and dark honey to the fore.

DIMPLE 12-YEAR-OLD

DIMPLE 15-YEAR-OLD

DIMPLE

Owner: Diageo

Launched to marked success in 1890, Haig's Dimple brand is today part of the Diageo stable. However, despite its long and distinguished history, it is rarely seen in the UK, and is sold mainly in Korea, Greece, Germany, the US, and Mexico.

John Haig began operations in 1627, when there are records of distilling on the family's farm in Stirlingshire. The family united through marriage with the powerful Stein family, also distillers on a prodigious scale, and eventually founded a large grain distillery at Cameronbridge, which is still in business today.

Dimple has always been a deluxe blend, noted for its distinctive packaging introduced by G.O. Haig in the 1890s. It stood out in particular for the wire net over the bottle, originally applied by hand and intended to prevent the cork popping out in warm climates or during sea transport. It was the first bottle of its type to be registered as a trademark in the United States, although this was done only in 1958.

Shortly after World War I, the British military leader Field Marshal Douglas Haig returned to head the family firm. Years spent dominating the UK followed thanks to strong but simple advertising ("Don't be vague, ask for Haig"). Today, there are three expressions – at 12-, 15-, and 18-year-old.

DIMPLE 12-YEAR-OLD

BLEND 40% ABV

Aromas of fudge, with woody notes. Hints of mint, and an initial richness on the palate, with toffee apples and caramel; spiciness and dried fruits too.

DIMPLE 15-YEAR-OLD

BLEND 43% ABV

In this blend, there are hints of smoke, chocolate, and cocoa, completed by a long, rich finish.

DUFFTOWN

Dufftown, Keith, Banffshire
www.malts.com

This epicentre of Speyside whisky-making was bound to have a distillery named after it, although it took until 1896, by which point there were already five distilleries in town. Within a year, Dufftown was owned outright by Peter Mackenzie, who also owned Blair Athol. He was soon selling whisky to the blender Arthur Bell & Sons, who eventually bought Dufftown in 1933. Now part of Diageo, Dufftown continues to supply malt for the Bell's blend and, until recently, had produced little in the way of its own single malt.

SINGLETON OF DUFFTOWN

SINGLE MALT: SPEYSIDE 40% ABV

A sweet and eminently drinkable, introductory malt. If this recently launched 12-year-old takes off, there should be plenty available – it comes from one of Diageo's biggest distilleries.

EDRADOUR

Pitlochry, Perthshire
www.edradour.com

With a production of just 95,000 litres (21,000 gallons) of pure alcohol a year, this picturesque distillery would have been one of many farm distilleries in the Perthshire hills when it was founded in 1825. Today, it feels much more special, and a world apart from the large-scale malt distilleries of Speyside. It became part of Pernod Ricard in 1975 but, as the French group expanded to become a huge global player in the whisky industry, tiny Edradour began to look increasingly out of place. In 2002, it was finally sold to Andrew Symington, owner of independent bottler Signatory.

EDRADOUR 10-YEAR-OLD

SINGLE MALT: HIGHLANDS 40% ABV

Clean peppermint nose, with a trace of smoke. Richer, nutty flavours and a silky texture on the tonuge.

THE FAMOUS GROUSE
MELLOW GOLD

BLEND 40% ABV

Subtle sherry, vanilla, almonds, and dried fruits on the nose. Vanilla, brittle toffee, sultanas, figs, and mildly spicy sherry on the palate, which closes with Jaffa oranges and ginger.

THE FAMOUS GROUSE ORIGINAL

THE FAMOUS GROUSE SMOKY BLACK

THE FAMOUS GROUSE

Owner: Edrington
www.thefamousgrouse.com

The best-selling blend in Scotland was created by the Victorian entrepreneur Matthew Gloag in 1896. At first, it was known simply as The Grouse Brand, but it evolved to become The Famous Grouse. The company was passed down through the generations until 1970, when death duties forced the family to sell to Highland Distillers, today part of Edrington. Sales developed well ahead of the market over the next 20 years and The Famous Grouse increased its visibility. Today, with sales of nearly 3 million cases a year, it is firmly established in the top ten global brands.

Edrington also owns some of Scotland's finest single malt distilleries – Highland Park, Macallan, and Glenrothes among them. Naturally, there are high proportions of these fine whiskies in The Famous Grouse blend.

The last decade has seen a number of interesting innovations, including The Black Grouse, now rebranded as "Smoky Black". It contains more strongly flavoured Islay malt in the blend. Snow Grouse is a grain whisky, sold initially in duty-free outlets. The company recommends it is drunk cold from the freezer, like vodka. A creamy mouth-coating effect results.

THE FAMOUS GROUSE ORIGINAL

BLEND 40% ABV

Oak and sherry on the nose, well balanced with a citrus note. Easy-going, and full of bright Speyside fruit. Clean and medium-dry finish.

THE FAMOUS GROUSE
SMOKY BLACK

BLEND 40% ABV

Cream teas, peaches, apples, and jammy aromas. Soft peat and smoke notes on the palate (more so with water), plus vanilla, pepper, and spices, then a gentle finish.

WHISKY STYLES
BLENDS

A blended whisky (usually called simply a "blend") is a mixture of one or more single malts and one or more single grain whiskies. The advent of blending in the mid-19th century proved to be the making of the Scotch whisky industry. Drinkers rapidly adopted the lighter, cheaper, and more palatable blends over the then highly variable and strongly flavoured "single whiskies" and Irish whiskey.

Today, more than 90 per cent of all Scotch whisky is a blend, with brands such as Johnnie Walker, Chivas Regal, Dewar's, Ballantines, and Cutty Sark dominating world markets. In the UK, The Famous Grouse and Bells vie for top spot. Blending was made possible by the invention of the continuous still by Aeneas Coffey and by legislative changes that permitted blending under bond (that is, before the payment of tax on the alcohol). The growth in the popularity of blends was also greatly assisted by the collapse of France's brandy production, following the phylloxera infestation of European vineyards in the 1880s. As a result, whisky was increasingly drunk instead of brandy.

The first blends were produced in about 1853 by Andrew Usher, an Edinburgh whisky merchant. His Old Vatted Glenlivet is often cited as the first blend, and it achieved rapid popularity. Charles Mackinlay and W.P. Lowrie were also early pioneers, as were many well-known whisky houses in the industry today, such as Johnnie Walker, Dewar's, and Buchanan's.

The master blenders are important figures in the distilling business. They are responsible for the selection of the whiskies for a blend – a process described by Whyte & Mackay's Richard Paterson as "90 per cent down to instinct and a 'feel-good' factor".

FETTERCAIRN

Fettercairn, Laurencekirk, Kincardineshire

While the northeastern flank of the Grampians is full of distilleries spilling down to the Spey, the southern slopes are now depleted. Fettercairn stands as their sole survivor. The distillery was established in 1824 as a farm distillery on the Fasque Estate, which was soon bought by Sir John Gladstone, father of the Victorian prime minister William Gladstone. It remained in family hands until 1939, since when it has been bought, sold, and mothballed several times. Today, Fettercairn is part of Whyte & Mackay, but their main priorities are in the shape of Dalmore and Jura.

FETTERCAIRN FIOR

SINGLE MALT: HIGHLANDS 43% ABV
Weighty, smoky nose of sherry, ginger, orange, and toffee. Palate has smoke, treacle, orange, chocolate, and nuts.

GIRVAN

Grangestone Industrial Estate, Girvan, Ayrshire

The distillery at Girvan was established in 1964 by William Grant & Sons in response to a perceived threat to their grain-whisky supplies. Today, it includes a grain-whisky distilling complex, a gin distillery, and the Ailsa Bay single malt distillery. Until 2013, Girvan was rarely bottled by the proprietors as a single grain, but now several expressions of Girvan Patent Still are available. Older expressions are generally dominated by the maize component and are greatly softened by age to provide a delicate and refined whisky of some subtlety and delightful complexity.

GIRVAN PATENT STILL NO.4 APPS

SINGLE GRAIN 42% ABV
The nose yields citrus fruit and brittle toffee, while the palate is glossy, with spicy fruit. Faint spice and watery toffee in the finish.

GLENALLACHIE

Aberlour, Banffshire

This modern gravity-flow distillery was established by a subsidiary of the giant Scottish & Newcastle Breweries in 1967. The architect was William Delmé-Evans, who had earlier designed and part-owned Tullibardine and Jura. With the capacity to produce 2.8 million litres (615,000 gallons) of pure alcohol a year, there should be plenty available for a single malt. And yet, so far there have only been a few independent bottlings and a 16-year-old cask strength expression from the distillery's current owners, Chivas Brothers (Pernod Ricard).

GLENALLACHIE 16-YEAR-OLD 1990

SINGLE MALT: SPEYSIDE 56.9% ABV
A dark, heavily sherried whisky matured in first-fill Oloroso casks, which can be hard to find.

GLENBURGIE

Glenburgie, Forres, Morayshire

Glenburgie began life as the Kilnflat Distillery in 1829. It was renamed Glenburgie in 1878 and, after various changes in ownership, became part of Canada's Hiram Walker in the 1930s. From then on, the primary role of this distillery was to supply whisky for Ballantine's Finest. Yet, as early as 1958, long before most of Speyside began thinking of single malt, Glenburgie released its own bottling under the name Glencraig. In 2004, its then owners, Allied Distillers, demonstrated their faith in Glenburgie by investing £4.3 million. The distillery was completely rebuilt. Only the stills and milling equipment were kept.

GLENBURGIE 10-YEAR-OLD

SINGLE MALT: SPEYSIDE 40% ABV
The nose offers fudge, vanilla, honey, malt, and soft oak. Creamy mouthfeel.

GLENDRONACH 12-YEAR-OLD

GLENDRONACH 18-YEAR-OLD

GLENCADAM

Brechin, Angus
www.glencadamdistillery.co.uk

With the demise of Lochside in
2005, Glencadam became the
only distillery left in Angus. It was
founded in 1825 by George Cooper
and, despite various changes in
ownership, remained in private
hands until 1954, when it became
part of Hiram Walker and later
Allied Distillers. While there was
some safety in numbers on Speyside,
Glencadam looked increasingly
isolated. When it shut down in
2000 – a victim of overproduction
in the industry – its prospects
looked bleak. But it slipped back
into independent hands in 2003
when bought by Angus Dundee.

GLENCADAM 10-YEAR-OLD

SINGLE MALT: HIGHLANDS 46% ABV
*The nose is fresh and grassy, with
citrus notes and a trace of spicy oak.
Rounded on the palate, citrussy and
crisp. Well-balanced, with a long finish.*

GLEN DEVERON

Macduff Distillery, Banff, Aberdeenshire

While the single malt is Glen
Deveron (named after the water
source – the River Deveron in
eastern Speyside), the distillery is
called Macduff. It was founded in
1962 by a consortium led by the
Duff family. Much of the malt
was used in blends, particularly
William Lawson, whose owners
bought the distillery in 1972.
Since then, it has changed hands
twice, increased its number of
stills to five, and now belongs to
Bacardi. Various age statements
are produced, and, just to confuse
matters, there are occasional
independent bottlings under
the name Macduff.

GLEN DEVERON 10-YEAR-OLD

SINGLE MALT: HIGHLANDS 40% ABV
*Although it is described as a "Pure
Highland Single Malt" on the bottle's
label, in style this is a classic, clean,
gentle Speyside whisky.*

GLENDRONACH

Forgue, Huntly, Aberdeenshire

This distillery is the spiritual sister
to Ardmore, and fellow contributor
to the Teacher's blend. Although
William Teacher & Sons did not
buy Glendronach until 1960, the
firm had sourced Glendronach
malts for years. After Teacher's was
swallowed up by Allied Distillers,
Glendronach was picked, in 1991,
to be one of the "Caledonian Malts"
– the company's belated riposte
to UDV's Classic Malts. A decade
later, after five years in mothballs,
the distillery re-opened. In 2008, the
BenRiach Distillery Co. acquired
Glendronach, and set about
restoring the single malt to its
former sherried glory.

Accordingly, some £3 million was
invested over a five-year period in
ex-sherry casks, sourced directly
from Spain, and a three-year
programme was undertaken to
re-rack around 50 per cent of the
entire inventory into fresh, Oloroso
sherry casks. Today, all spirit
distilled is filled into either ex-
Pedro Ximinez or ex-Oloroso casks.

Cask-finished variants have
been added to the portfolio along
with a peated edition, and vintage
and single cask bottlings have
become a regular part of the
Glendronach release strategy.

In April of 2016, Glendronach
was acquired by Brown-Forman. It
remains to be seen what marketing
and production changes may be in
store with the new ownership.

GLENDRONACH 12-YEAR-OLD

SINGLE MALT: SPEYSIDE 40% ABV
*This dense, heavily sherried malt
replaced the 15-year-old and is
best suited to after-dinner sipping.*

GLENDRONACH 18-YEAR-OLD

SINGLE MALT: SPEYSIDE 46% ABV
*A medium-bodied single malt with
redcurrants, soft fudge, and a hint
of cinnamon on the nose. Cedar
spice and red berry fruit on the
palate. Long, oaky spice finish.*

Macallan still has in use 16 traditional dunnage warehouses with earth floors and thick stone walls. The atmosphere is cool and damp all year round, and the air is rich with aromas of whisky and oak.

The landscape of Islay is low-lying and boggy, with
plenty of peaty earth and peaty rivulets. Like much of
Scotland's coastal peat, Islay's has a slightly sandy texture
and sweet, citrus, and maritime characteristics from the
mix of sphagnum moss and bog myrtle that produced it.

GLENFARCLAS 10-YEAR-OLD

GLENFARCLAS 105

GLENFARCLAS 12-YEAR-OLD

GLENFARCLAS 15-YEAR-OLD

GLENFARCLAS 21-YEAR-OLD

GLENFARCLAS 25-YEAR-OLD

GLENFARCLAS 30-YEAR-OLD

GLENFARCLAS

Ballindalloch, Banffshire
www.glenfarclas.co.uk

The oldest family-owned distillery in Scotland has belonged to the Grants since 1865, when John Grant and son George took over the tenancy of Rechlarich farm, near Ballindalloch. The small distillery on site was immediately sublet to John Smith of Glenlivet. Five years later, when Smith left to set up Cragganmore, it was back with the Grants. It gradually assumed importance in the family business, and went on to become the Glenfarclas-Glenlivet Distillery Company in partnership with the Pattison Brothers of Leith, whose bankruptcy at the end of the 19th century almost dragged the distillery down with it.

Surrounded by 32 large dunnage warehouses, Glenfarclas is no boutique distillery. It boasts a modern mill and six stills. It also claims to be the first malt distillery to have offered a cask strength expression – Glenfarclas 105 was released in 1968. At the time, the industry doubted that single malts, let alone something that was 60 per cent pure alcohol, would catch on.

Since 2007, single cask bottlings from as early as 1952 have been offered in the Family Casks range. The house style is a robust, outdoors take on Speyside, with a greater affiliation to sherry butts than bourbon barrels.

GLENFARCLAS 10-YEAR-OLD

SINGLE MALT: SPEYSIDE 40% ABV
This rich, malty whisky with a smoky, aromatic nose is a nod to the Highlands.

GLENFARCLAS 105

SINGLE MALT: SPEYSIDE 60% ABV
A cask strength 10-year-old. Water dampens the fiery edge and brings out a sweet, nutty-spicy character.

GLENFARCLAS 12-YEAR-OLD

SINGLE MALT: SPEYSIDE 43% ABV
A distinct sherry nose, with spicy flavours of cinnamon and stewed fruit.

GLENFARCLAS 15-YEAR-OLD

SINGLE MALT: SPEYSIDE 46% ABV
The 15-year-old expression was once described by writer Dave Broom as "George Melly in a glass", for its fruity, over-the-top exuberance. *It is intensely perfumed, sherried, and powerful.*

GLENFARCLAS 21-YEAR-OLD

SINGLE MALT: SPEYSIDE 43% ABV
A ripe, truffly nose. There is plenty of sherry influence on this earthy, leathery malt.

GLENFARCLAS 25-YEAR-OLD

SINGLE MALT: SPEYSIDE 43% ABV
A fruity, toffee-scented whisky with a smooth, spicy character and a taste of ginger and burnt sugar.

GLENFARCLAS 30-YEAR-OLD

SINGLE MALT: SPEYSIDE 43% ABV
The wood is more obvious here: oaky, spicy, and nutty. Slight peatiness in the long finish.

ALL ABOUT...
INDEPENDENT BOTTLERS

Whisky is either bottled by the brand owner (proprietary bottlings) or by other companies, clubs, or individuals – these are known as independent bottlings. The former are subject to rigorous quality controls; the latter may be more variable, although the "indies" mentioned here all have high reputations for the quality of their goods. Proprietors also have huge stocks to draw from, while independents select and buy individual casks from distilleries or brokers, and sometimes have their own casks filled by distillers.

GORDON & MACPHAIL Established in Elgin in 1895, Gordon & MacPhail has been bottling single malts for longer than any other company. The business is still family owned and managed, and still operates from the original shop (*see p. 93*). The Connoisseur's Choice range was launched in 1956, and the company currently offers around 300 bottlings.

SIGNATORY Based in Leith, the port of Edinburgh, and founded in 1988 by Andrew and Brian Symington, Signatory lists some 50 single malts from operating, mothballed, and closed distilleries, which they bottle at natural strength and at 43% ABV. Andrew Symington bought Edradour Distillery in 2002.

ADELPHI The original Adelphi Distillery was in Glasgow, and ceased production in 1902. Ninety years later, the name was revived by the great-grandson of the last owner, to select and bottle around 50 top-quality single cask malt whiskies each year.

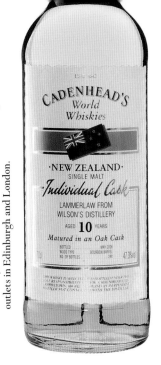

CADENHEAD Established in Aberdeen in 1842, Cadenhead is Scotland's oldest firm of independent bottlers. In 1972, the business was bought by J. & A. Mitchell, owners of Springbank Distillery, and Cadenhead is now based in Campbeltown, with outlets in Edinburgh and London.

DUNCAN TAYLOR The company has been filling its own casks and laying down whisky since the 1960s. When Euan Shand bought the company and its stocks in 2001, he acquired one of the world's largest privately held collections of rare Scotch casks.

NUMBER ONE DRINKS COMPANY This company was founded in 2006 to select and bottle casks of distinguished Japanese single malt whisky, and to distribute them throughout Europe via specialist retailers and bars.

DEERSTALKER The Deerstalker independent bottling brand is owned by Glasgow-based Aberko Ltd. The company offers 10- and 12-year-old single malts from unspecified Speyside distilleries, as well as single cask bottlings in its Limited Release range. To date, these have included Allt-a-Bhainne, Braeval, and Auchroisk single malts.

GLENFIDDICH

Dufftown, Keith, Banffshire
www.glenfiddich.com

It was no impulsive decision when William Grant decided to abandon a 16-year career at Mortlach Distillery in 1886 to go it alone. With a wife and nine children to support on a salary of £100 a year, plus the £7 he received as the precentor of the Free Church of Dufftown, he had to scrimp and save until he raised the funds to start Glenfiddich. Using stones from the bed of the River Fiddich, and second-hand stills from neighbouring Cardhu, he was able to produce his first spirit on Christmas Day 1887. From these humble beginnings, Glenfiddich has grown into the biggest malt distillery in the world.

In 1899, the distillery almost collapsed when its biggest customer, Pattison Brothers of Leith, went bankrupt. The fact that it survived engendered a spirit of self-reliance in William Grant & Sons. By the time William Grant died in 1923, his firm was already producing its own blends, which were sold as far afield as Australia and Canada. In the same spirit, the company pioneered today's market for single malts in the 1960s. Such whiskies existed, but there was no big brand before Glenfiddich.

To meet demand, Glenfiddich underwent a dramatic expansion in 1974, when 16 new stills were added. Today, it has no fewer than 31 stills and a capacity of 14 million litres (3.1 million gallons) of pure alcohol a year. This makes it the most productive malt distillery in Scotland, with significantly greater capacity than Diageo's new Roseisle Distillery (the main purpose of which is to supply malt for blending). Having enjoyed the status of being the world's best-selling single malt since 1963, Glenfiddich was finally overtaken by The Glenlivet in 2014.

The Glenfiddich range includes expressions from a soft 12-year-old up to a luscious, creamy 30-year-old with a trace of ginger.

GLENFIDDICH 12-YEAR-OLD

SINGLE MALT: SPEYSIDE 40% ABV
A gentle aperitif-style whisky with a malty, grassy flavour and a little vanilla sweetness. Quite soft.

GLENFIDDICH 15-YEAR-OLD SOLERA RESERVE

SINGLE MALT: SPEYSIDE 40% ABV
After 15 years in American oak, this is finished off in Spanish casks for an extra-soft layer of fresh fruit and spice.

GLENFIDDICH 18-YEAR-OLD SOLERA RESERVE

SINGLE MALT: SPEYSIDE 40% ABV
A big step up from the 12-year-old, with ripe tropical fruit flavours, a pleasant oaky sweetness, and a trace of sherry.

GLENFIDDICH 21-YEAR-OLD CARIBBEAN RUM CASK

SINGLE MALT: SPEYSIDE 40% ABV
Rich, toffee-flavoured malt with flavours of bananas, caramel, spice, and chocolate orange.

GLENFIDDICH 15-YEAR-OLD SOLERA RESERVE

GLENFIDDICH 18-YEAR-OLD SOLERA RESERVE

GLENFIDDICH 21-YEAR-OLD CARIBBEAN RUM CASK

GLEN ELGIN 12-YEAR-OLD

GLEN ELGIN 16-YEAR-OLD

GLEN GARIOCH FOUNDER'S RESERVE

GLENDULLAN

Dufftown, Keith, Banffshire
www.malts.com

There were already six distilleries
in Dufftown when the Aberdeen-
based blenders William Williams
& Sons decided to build a seventh.
Work on Glendullan began in 1897,
and within five years its whisky
had secured a royal warrant from
the new king, Edward VII. The
distillery has been in almost
continual production ever since.
In the 1960s, a modern distillery
was erected next door. Although
both facilities continued in
tandem for 20 years, now the
modern distillery carries on
alone. Since 2007, Singleton of
Glendullan bottlings have been
available in the US.

GLENDULLAN FLORA & FAUNA 12-YEAR-OLD

SINGLE MALT: SPEYSIDE 43% ABV
A crisp, aperitif-style malt with a
sweeter palate than you would expect.

GLEN ELGIN

Longmorn, Morayshire
www.malts.com

Although Cragganmore's position
as the Speyside among the original
Classic Malts is well-deserved,
Glen Elgin must have been a
strong contender. It has always
been considered a top-rated malt
by blenders, and has long been a
key component of White Horse.

The distillery was founded in
1898 by James Carle and William
Simpson, a former manager of
Glenfarclas, when demand for
Speyside malt from the blenders
was at its peak. It was the last
distillery to be built on Speyside
for 60 years. Within two years,
however, the speculative boom had
turned to bust and the industry
entered a prolonged slump.

During its first three decades,
production at Glen Elgin was
intermittent, as the distillery
passed from one owner to the
next. Since 1930, Glen Elgin

has been part of what is now
Diageo. In the 1960s, the number
of stills was increased from two
to six. The old worm tubs, which
add weight and body to the new
make, were retained. In 1977,
a first distillery bottling of Glen
Elgin was released. The stills at
Glen Elgin were fired up again
in May 1990, only to go cold five
months later. Production resumed
once again in September 1995.

GLEN ELGIN 12-YEAR-OLD

SINGLE MALT: SPEYSIDE 43% ABV
This is one of the most floral and
perfumed Speyside malts, with a nutty,
honey-blossom aroma and a balanced
flavour that goes from sweet to dry.

GLEN ELGIN 16-YEAR-OLD

SINGLE MALT: SPEYSIDE 58.5% ABV
A recent limited edition, the 16-year-
old is a non-chill filtered, cask-strength
malt with a deep mahogany colour
and a ripe, fruitcake flavour from its
years in European oak.

GLEN GARIOCH

Oldmeldrum, Inverurie, Aberdeenshire
www.glengarioch.com

Three centuries old and still going
strong – quite an achievement for
this small Aberdeenshire distillery
on the road between Banff and
Aberdeen. It was founded by
Thomas Simpson in 1797, yet the
first distillery bottling of Glen
Garioch (pronounced *glen geerie*)
as a single malt was not until
1972. It survived the long years in
between thanks to its popularity
among blenders.

One such was William
Sanderson of Aberdeen, who
came across Glen Garioch when
it belonged to a firm of blenders
in Leith. In 1886, he bought a
half share in the distillery, and by
1921, his son, together with other
investors, had full control of the
business. After numerous changes
in ownership since, and extended
periods of lying idle, Glen Garioch
is now part of Morrison Bowmore,

GLEN GARIOCH 12-YEAR-OLD

GLEN GARIOCH VIRGIN OAK

which bottles most of the distillery's limited production as a single malt.

GLEN GARIOCH FOUNDER'S RESERVE

SINGLE MALT: HIGHLANDS 48% ABV

Pears, peaches, and apricots on the nose, plus butterscotch and vanilla. Relatively full-bodied, with a palate of vanilla, malt, melon, and subtle smoke.

GLEN GARIOCH 12-YEAR-OLD

SINGLE MALT: HIGHLANDS 48% ABV

The nose yields peaches, pineapple, malt, vanilla, and light sherry. Full-bodied with orchard fruits on the palate, plus spicy toffee and ultimately drying oak.

GLEN GARIOCH VIRGIN OAK

SINGLE MALT: HIGHLANDS 48% ABV

Ripe peaches on the nose, spicy oak, vanilla, and developing floral notes. The palate yields malt, milk chocolate, nougat, orange, and a hint of cloves.

GLENGLASSAUGH

Portsoy, Banffshire
www.glenglassaugh.com

Glenglassaugh was founded by Aberdeenshire entrepreneur James Moir in the 1870s at a cost of £10,000. Although it was also renovated and expanded, it was sold for only £15,000 20 years later, when it was bought by blender Robertson & Baxter, now called Edrington. The distillery has had periodic bursts of production, but has spent much of its life in mothballs. When its stills went cold before the millennium, many feared that Glenglassaugh was doomed. It was rescued by a private consortium, however, and was reopened in 2008. Glenglassaugh is now owned by Brown-Forman.

GLENGLASSAUGH EVOLUTION

SINGLE MALT: HIGHLANDS 57.2% ABV

The nose offers toffee, ginger, peaches, and vanilla. Orchard fruits, caramel, and coconut on the palate.

WHISKY TOUR: SPEYSIDE

Speyside boasts the greatest concentration of distilleries in the world and thus is a "must see" for all whisky lovers. The concept of the distillery tour was also pioneered here, when William Grant & Sons first opened Glenfiddich to the public in 1969. Its competitors laughed – but soon opened their own centres. Today, Speyside hosts two whisky festivals each year, in May and September, with special events and tastings. Subsidized bus and taxi travel is available during festival times. Two accommodation options favoured by whisky fans are the Highlander Inn in Craigellachie and The Mash Tun in Aberlour.

SCOTLAND

TOUR STATISTICS		
DAYS: 3	**LENGTH:** 90 miles (145 km)	**DISTILLERIES:** 5
TRAVEL: Car, or bus and taxi	**REGION:** Banffshire and Moray, Scotland	

DAY 1: GLENFIDDICH, THE BALVENIE

1 Begin at Dufftown's **Glenfiddich**, the ultimate home of whisky tourism. The makers of the world's most popular single malt offer a free tour or – like a number of their competitors – an option with extended tastings at extra cost. You need to pre-book for the extended tour, which lasts for two and a half hours. *(www.glenfiddich.com)*

GLENFIDDICH STILLS

2 After lunch at the Glenfiddich café, you can stroll down the hill to sister distillery **The Balvenie** *(www.thebalvenie. com)*. The three-hour guided tour here, which must also be pre-booked, includes the floor maltings and tastings of exclusive vintages. You can also bottle your own whisky straight from the cask. If time permits after the tour, head to Dufftown's well-stocked Whisky Shop.

THE BALVENIE

FORRES

NAIRN

A96

A96

A940

MILL BUIE

A939

CÀRN NA LÒINE

A939

B9007

A95

GRANTOWN-ON-SPEY **7**

A9

Spey

A95

A939

NETHY BRIDGE

A95

BOAT OF GARTEN

AVIEMORE

CAIRNGORMS NATIONAL PARK

DAY 2: COOPERAGE, ABERLOUR, THE MACALLAN, CARDHU

3 Start the day at the **Speyside Cooperage**. There you can watch a film about cask-making and see the the coopers at work from a viewing gallery. *(www.speysidecooperage.co.uk)*

4 **Aberlour** Distillery is the next stop and, again, pre-booking is advisable. The tour culminates in a tasting and the chance to bottle your own. *(www.aberlour.com/distillery)*

ABERLOUR CASKS

5 Head over the Spey, pausing to admire the Thomas Telford bridge (1812), then take the B9102 to **The Macallan**. Its "Precious Tour" is the one to pre-book for its tutored nosing and tasting of a range of Macallan whiskies. *(www.themacallan.com)*

6 **Cardhu** Distillery is further along the B9102, which you can visit without pre-booking. The malt made here is used in Johnnie Walker blends. *(www.discovering-distilleries.com/cardhu)*

DAY 3: GRANTOWN-ON-SPEY, THE WHISKY CASTLE, THE GLENLIVET, GORDON & MACPHAIL

7 **Grantown-on-Spey** is the gateway to the Cairngorms National Park. It's a handy place to pick up provisions, and has a good little whisky shop on the High Street called the Wee Spey Dram.

8 Head east from Grantown to get to Tomintoul, where **The Whisky Castle** shop has an excellent selection of Scotch malts. *(www.whiskycastle.com)*

SHOP SIGN

9 Pre-register on **The Glenlivet** website as a "Guardian" to gain access to a secret room where you can enjoy some unusual drams. The free tour is a good introduction to the oldest legal distillery in Speyside; better still is its three-day Whisky School. *(www.theglenlivet.com)*

10 The final stop on this tour is a place of pilgrimage for serious whisky fans: the **Gordon & MacPhail** shop in Elgin. Here you'll find all your favourites, some rare bottles, and exceptional value in G&M's own bottlings from their vast stock of whiskies laid down over many years. *(www.gordonandmacphail.com)*

GORDON & MACPHAIL

Map labels

LOSSIEMOUTH

FINISH

10 GORDON & MACPHAIL

A96

A98

Spey

A941

A96

MORAY

A95

THE MACALLAN

CRAIGELLACHIE

B9102

5

3 SPEYSIDE COOPERAGE

2 THE BALVENIE

1 GLENFIDDICH

6 CARDHU

4 ABERLOUR

A95

DUFFTOWN

START

A920

BANFFSHIRE

A941

9 THE GLENLIVET

B9008

CAIRNGORMS NATIONAL PARK

8 THE WHISKY CASTLE

A939

THE WHISKY CASTLE

miles
0   5

0   5
kilometres

GLENGOYNE 10-YEAR-OLD

GLENGOYNE 18-YEAR-OLD

GLENGOYNE 21-YEAR-OLD

GLENGOYNE 12-YEAR-OLD CASK STRENGTH

GLENGOYNE

Drumgoyne, Stirlingshire
www.glengoyne.com

The Campsie Fells were once a
hotbed of whisky smuggling. Before
the Excise Act of 1823, there were
at least 18 illicit distillers in this
corner of Stirlingshire. Among
them was probably George Connell,
who finally took out a licence for
his Burnfoot Distillery in 1833. It
went on to become Glenguin and
eventually Glengoyne in 1905.

By then the distillery was
owned by the blending house of
Lang Brothers, who were bought
out in the 1960s by Robertson &
Baxter, now Edrington. In 2001,
it released a novel expression of
Glengoyne, involving the first
ever use of Scottish oak casks.

Two years later, the distillery
was sold to the blender and bottler
Ian MacLeod & Co. The number of
single malts has grown dramatically
and includes single cask bottlings
alongside the core range.

GLENGOYNE 12-YEAR-OLD CASK STRENGTH

SINGLE MALT: HIGHLANDS 57.2% ABV
*Non-chill filtered and bottled
at cask strength, it has a lightly
sweet nose, with notes of heather,
pear drops, and marzipan. Malty,
cereal palate, seasoned with
black pepper.*

GLENGOYNE 10-YEAR-OLD

SINGLE MALT: HIGHLANDS 40% ABV
*This unpeated whisky has a clean,
grassy aroma, with a nutty sweetness
that comes through on the palate.*

GLENGOYNE 18-YEAR-OLD

SINGLE MALT: HIGHLANDS 43% ABV
*Milk chocolate, vanilla, melon, and
grapefruit on the nose. The palate
is rich, with cinnamon and ginger,
almonds, and orange marmalade.*

GLENGOYNE 21-YEAR-OLD

SINGLE MALT: HIGHLANDS 43% ABV
*This is a rich, after-dinner malt, with
notes of brandy butter, cinnamon,
and sweet spice.*

The Spey gives its name to Scotland's best-known and most productive whisky region, Speyside. Winter is traditionally the season for whisky-making here.

GLEN GRANT 10-YEAR-OLD

GLEN GRANT 12-YEAR-OLD NON-CHILL FILTERED

GLEN GRANT 18-YEAR-OLD

GLEN GRANT

Rothes, Morayshire
www.glengrant.com

There is something solid and baronial about the Glen Grant Distillery on Speyside. It was the first of the five distilleries in the town of Rothes, built in 1840 from red sandstone, with a pair of pepperpot turrets.

It was founded by James Grant, a solicitor in Elgin, and his brother, John, a grain merchant who is said to have learnt about whisky-making from supplying all the illicit distillers in the area.

It was a very good site for a distillery, with the Glen Grant burn supplying water for the mash and to power the machinery. There were plentiful supplies of grain too, from the barley fields of nearby Moray. And, from 1858, when the first train steamed into Rothes, there was also the railway to carry off the filled casks and bring back the empties.

In 1872, James Grant's son took over the business. Known to all as "The Major", permanently clad in tweed and with a bristling walrus moustache, he was very much the quintessential Victorian gent. After dining, he would take guests to a narrow ravine in the garden and unlock a safe secreted in the rock to produce a tray of glasses and a bottle of Glen Grant. For anyone requiring water, they had only to dip their glass into the fast-flowing waters of the nearby stream.

The distillery remained in family hands until 1977 when it was sold to Seagrams. Soon afterwards, an Italian visitor persuaded the owners to sell him some cases of Glen Grant 5-year-old, which went on to become Italy's biggest-selling brand of Scotch. Having passed through the hands of Pernod Ricard in 2001–2006, it is now with the Italian Campari drinks group. Though it receives little attention at home, it is one of the top five best-selling malts in the world.

GLEN GRANT 10-YEAR-OLD

SINGLE MALT: SPEYSIDE 40% ABV
A relatively dry nose with the scent of orchard fruit. Light to medium body with a cereal, nutty flavour.

GLEN GRANT 12-YEAR-OLD NON-CHILL FILTERED

SINGLE MALT: SPEYSIDE 48% ABV
Malt, caramel, and bright, fresh fruits on the vibrant nose. The palate is nicely textured, with sweet apple, more caramel, and light spices.

GLEN GRANT 18-YEAR-OLD

SINGLE MALT: SPEYSIDE 43% ABV
The nose is fresh and fruity, but with added depth and greater fragrance compared to younger expressions. Full and rich on the fruity palate, with milk chocolate, sweet spices, brittle toffee, and a hint of creamy oak.

GLEN KEITH

Keith, Banffshire

Having bought Strathisla in 1950, Seagram built Glen Keith on the site of an old corn mill seven years later. Both are in Keith and were part of Seagram's whisky arm, Chivas Brothers (now part of Pernod Ricard). Both also shared a simple function – to supply the company's best-selling brands. Glen Keith began life using triple distillation and later pioneered the use of computers in its whisky-making at a time when some distilleries had only recently joined the national grid.

Glen Keith was mothballed in 2000, but re-opened in 2013 after major refurbishment.

GLEN KEITH 19-YEAR-OLD CASK STRENGTH

SINGLE MALT: SPEYSIDE 56.3% ABV
Banoffee pie, ginger, and raisins on the nose. The viscous palate yields sherry, fudge, and white pepper.

GLENKINCHIE 12-YEAR-OLD

GLENKINCHIE 20-YEAR-OLD

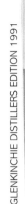

GLENKINCHIE DISTILLERS EDITION 1991

GLENKINCHIE

Pencaitland, Tranent, East Lothian
www.malts.com

Robert Burns described the rolling farmland south of Edinburgh as "the most glorious corn country I have ever seen", and it was here at Pencaitland that John and George Rate founded Glenkinchie in 1825. It was originally the Milton Distillery and struggled in its early years, spending much of the second half of the 19th century as a saw mill. In 1881, it was rescued by an Edinburgh brewer and a couple of wine merchants, who transformed it into a highly efficient whisky-making machine, with everything from mechanical rakes in the mash tun to its own railway siding. The grain came from the surrounding fields, and the draff was fed to the Aberdeen Angus cattle on site.

In modern times, the most important date was probably 1988, when the Glenkinchie 10-year-old was picked as one of the original Classic Malts by Diageo.

GLENKINCHIE 12-YEAR-OLD

SINGLE MALT: LOWLANDS 43% ABV
The nose reveals a sweet, grassy aroma with a faint wisp of smoke. In the mouth, it has a firm, cereal flavour and a touch of spice at the end.

GLENKINCHIE 20-YEAR-OLD

SINGLE MALT: LOWLANDS 58.4% ABV
Aged in bourbon casks and then re-racked into brandy barrels, the 20-year-old has a luscious, mouth-coating texture and plenty of spicy, stewed fruit flavours.

GLENKINCHIE DISTILLERS EDITION 1991

SINGLE MALT: LOWLANDS 43% ABV
The malty flavour of digestive biscuits is well balanced by the drier, oaky flavours from the wood, and these linger to a long, slow finish.

THE GLENLIVET XXV
SINGLE MALT: SPEYSIDE 43% ABV
This 25-year-old is a sumptuous after-dinner malt of real complexity, with flavours of candied orange peel and raisins and an intense nutty, spicy character.

THE GLENLIVET FOUNDER'S RESERVE
SINGLE MALT: SPEYSIDE 40% ABV
The nose is fresh and floral, with ripe pears, pineapple, tangerines, honey, and vanilla. Medium-bodied, with ginger nuts, soft toffee, and tropical fruit on the smooth, softly spiced palate.

THE GLENLIVET FRENCH OAK RESERVE 15-YEAR-OLD

THE GLENLIVET 18-YEAR-OLD

THE GLENLIVET ARCHIVE 21-YEAR-OLD

THE GLENLIVET

Ballindalloch, Banffshire
www.theglenlivet.com

In the early 19th century, before the Excise Act lured so many distillers to come in from the cold and take out a licence, Glenlivet was a one-industry glen dedicated to making moonshine after the harvest. It was said that there were at least 200 illicit stills in this small corner of Speyside. Doubtless among them was George Smith, who made whisky on the side at his Upper Drummin farm. In 1824, he established Glenlivet as a licensed distillery there. But breaking ranks with the smuggling fraternity meant

that, from then on, Smith had to carry hair-trigger revolvers for his protection.

Smith began supplying Andrew Usher in Edinburgh, who bottled a prototype blend, Old Vatted Glenlivet, in 1853. As blended Scotch took off towards the end of the 19th century, demand for "Glenlivet-style" malts to feed the blends also soared. This encouraged distillers all down the Spey to bolt the magic name "Glenlivet" to their distillery and hope the blenders beat a path to their door.

Glenlivet's current owner – the French giant Pernod Ricard, who bought it from Seagram in 2001, along with Chivas Regal and a host of other whisky brands and

distilleries – set about restoring its good name: although always strong in the US, Glenlivet had been somewhat neglected in other markets.

The core range of malts has been dusted down, expanded, and repackaged, while new expressions such as Nadurra Cask Strength Glenlivet have been launched in retail and duty-free markets.

During 2009 and 2010, the capacity of Glenlivet was dramatically increased to 10.5 million litres (2.3 million gallons) per annum as Pernod's whisky division, Chivas Brothers, sought to overtake Glenfiddich as the world's best-selling single malt. That ambition was finally achieved in 2014.

THE GLENLIVET FRENCH OAK RESERVE 15-YEAR-OLD

SINGLE MALT: SPEYSIDE 40% ABV

A smoother, richer take on the 12-year-old, with a malty, strawberries-and-cream flavour laced with a little spice.

THE GLENLIVET 18-YEAR-OLD

SINGLE MALT: SPEYSIDE 43% ABV

Far more depth and character than the standard 12-year-old. Honeyed, fragrant, and dries to a long, nutty finish.

THE GLENLIVET ARCHIVE 21-YEAR-OLD

SINGLE MALT: SPEYSIDE 43% ABV

A distinctly smooth and richly fruity whisky. Malty, toasty flavours, an almond sweetness, and a touch of fresh orange. A long, slightly smoky finish.

GLENLOSSIE

GLENMORANGIE ORIGINAL

GLENMORANGIE 18-YEAR-OLD

GLENMORANGIE 25-YEAR-OLD

GLENLOSSIE

Elgin, Morayshire
www.malts.com

Glenlossie was built in 1876 by John Duff, the former manager of Glendronach. For a century, it was a single entity, and part of DCL from 1919. Its role was simply to pump out malt whisky for blends. Yet, within the industry, the quality of Glenlossie was appreciated and it was one of only a dozen to be designated "top class". It now shares its site with Mannochmore, a new distillery built in 1971.

Glenlossie has produced a 10-year-old since 1990, although there have been a fair number of independent bottlings from Gordon & MacPhail among others.

GLENLOSSIE FLORA & FAUNA 10-YEAR-OLD

SINGLE MALT: SPEYSIDE 43% ABV
Grassy, heathery, with a smooth, mouth-coating texture and a long spicy finish.

GLENMORANGIE

Tain, Ross-shire
www.glenmorangie.com

The "Glen of Tranquillity", to use the single malt's old strapline, has been bustling with activity since the French luxury goods group LVMH bought Glenmorangie for £300 million in 2004. The distillery started life as an old farm distillery, but was taken over and licensed in 1843 by William Matheson, who was already involved with Balblair. It remained a rustic operation for years. In the 1880s, Alfred Barnard described Glenmorangie as "the most ancient and primitive we have seen" and "almost in ruins".

Outside investors were brought in just in time and the distillery was rebuilt. For much of the 20th century, its key role was to supply malt for blends such as Highland Queen and James Martin's. In the 1970s, though, Glenmorangie started laying down casks for a 10-year-old single malt. In hindsight, it

was the best decision the company ever took – by the late 1990s, this had become the best-selling single malt in Scotland. Glenmorangie's stills are tall and thin, and produce a light, very pure spirit. The real skill of the distillery has been in the way it has combined this elegant spirit with wood – indeed, Glenmorangie has been a pioneer of wood finishes. After endless experiments with increasingly exotic barrels, it became an expert in how a particular cask could twist and refocus a mature malt before bottling.

GLENMORANGIE ORIGINAL

SINGLE MALT: HIGHLANDS 40% ABV
This is the ever-popular 10-year-old, dressed up in new packaging. It has honeyed flavours with a hint of almonds.

GLENMORANGIE 18-YEAR-OLD

SINGLE MALT: HIGHLANDS 43% ABV
A rich, well-rounded whisky, with dried fruit notes and a distinctive nuttiness from its finishing in sherry butts.

GLENMORANGIE 25-YEAR-OLD

SINGLE MALT: HIGHLANDS 43% ABV
Packed with flavour, this produces dried fruit, berries, chocolate, and spice. An intense and complex whisky.

GLENMORANGIE NECTAR D'OR

SINGLE MALT: HIGHLANDS 46% ABV
Here, the Glenmorangie honeyed floral character is given a twist of spice and lemon tart from Sauternes casks.

GLENMORANGIE QUINTA RUBAN

SINGLE MALT: HIGHLANDS 46% ABV
The slight reddish-amber tint and Portuguese name are a clue: this malt is finished off in port pipes to give it a fruity, mint-chocolate character.

GLENMORANGIE LASANTA

SINGLE MALT: HIGHLANDS 46% ABV
The facelift and fancy Latin name were not the only changes Glenmorangie made to its finely balanced sherry finish: it is now bottled non-chill filtered.

GLENMORANGIE NECTAR D'OR

GLENMORANGIE QUINTA RUBAN

GLENMORANGIE LASANTA

GLEN MORAY CLASSIC

GLEN MORAY 12-YEAR-OLD

GLEN MORAY CLASSIC PEATED

GLEN MORAY

Bruceland Road, Elgin
www.glenmoray.com

The trouble with being the little brother of two far more famous siblings is that you are liable to feel unloved at times. Being in the same family as Glenmorangie and Ardbeg must have been tough for the small distillery of Glen Moray. Even its lead role in the premium blend of Bailie Nicol Jarvie went unnoticed. So, when Glenmorangie's parent company, LVMH, announced it was selling Glen Moray to the French group La Martiniquaise, no one was surprised.

Glen Moray began life as a brewery and was converted into a distillery in 1897. It struggled for the first couple of decades, until it was bought by the blenders Macdonald & Muir, who were the owners until 2004, when it was sold to LVMH. Before then, Glen Moray followed the lead of Glenmorangie and released a range of special wine finishes, including Chenin Blanc and Chardonnay. These have since been abandoned and replaced with three or four core expressions and a raft of limited releases.

GLEN MORAY CLASSIC PEATED

SINGLE MALT: SPEYSIDE 40% ABV
Light-bodied, with fruity peat, vanilla, and black pepper. Drying in the medium-length finish, with citrus fruit and a hint of liquorice.

GLEN MORAY CLASSIC

SINGLE MALT: SPEYSIDE 40% ABV
The distillery also produces this introductory single malt without an age statement. It has a pale straw colour and some light grassy notes.

GLEN MORAY 12-YEAR-OLD

SINGLE MALT: SPEYSIDE 40% ABV
This is a classic light Speyside malt, with candyfloss aromas and notes of heather honey. There is a faint taste of dried fruit and orange peel on the tongue.

Traditional methods persist in the cooperage, and straw remains the best material for creating a watertight seal for the ends of the casks.

THE GLENROTHES 1975

THE GLENROTHES 1978

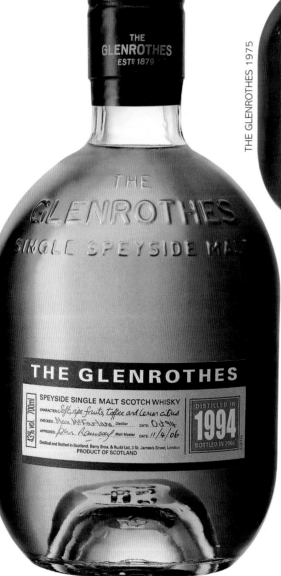

THE GLENROTHES 1994

THE GLENROTHES

Rothes, Morayshire
www.theglenrothes.com

After Dufftown, Rothes is the second busiest whisky town on Speyside. Not that you would know it, driving through this small town by day: the distilleries are tucked discreetly out of sight, including Glenrothes, which sits quietly in a dip beside the Rothes burn.

The distillery was built in 1878 as a joint venture between James Stuart of Macallan and two local bankers – Robert Dick and Willie Grant. Before building finished, Stuart had pulled out and a banking crisis that year almost scuppered the plans entirely.

After this shaky start, Glenrothes began to build a reputation among blenders for the quality of its malt, and became a key filling in Cutty Sark, which, for a brief period, was the best-selling Scotch whisky in

the US. It was also supplying other blends, and it seemed as if there was never any to spare – until 1987, when the first single malt, a 12-year-old, was released. At first, Glenrothes failed to stand out from the crowd: it had entered the 12-year-old stakes late in the day and there was plenty of competition, particularly on Speyside.

This all changed with the launch of the highly acclaimed Glenrothes Vintage malt in 1994. The brand owners, wine merchants Berry Bros. & Rudd, realized that if vintage variation was appreciated by wine-lovers, the same might be true of malt-whisky-lovers. In 2004, Glenrothes Select Reserve was released to provide continuity between vintages.

To date, the oldest vintage released has been the 1972, and the core range now includes the Select Reserve and the Alba

THE GLENROTHES 1987

THE GLENROTHES 1991

THE GLENROTHES SELECT RESERVE

Reserve, along with the Vintage Single Malt, which contains a vatting of ten different vintages from 1989 to 2007.

THE GLENROTHES 1994

SINGLE MALT: SPEYSIDE 43% ABV

A satisfyingly complex malt with a fruity, toffee-scented bouquet that leads to a soft citrus flavour and long, gentle finish.

THE GLENROTHES 1975

SINGLE MALT: SPEYSIDE 43% ABV

Increasingly hard to find, this vintage offers big, rich flavours – stewed fruits, toffee, bitter chocolate, and orange peel. Medium-sweet satisfying finish.

THE GLENROTHES 1978

SINGLE MALT: SPEYSIDE 43% ABV

A very rare expression, released in 2008, with a concentrated plum pudding and treacle character, a silky, honeyed texture and great length.

THE GLENROTHES 1987

SINGLE MALT: SPEYSIDE 43% ABV

Fruit, vanilla, and floral notes hit the nose. The palate is juicy, with an orange zestiness balancing the sweetness, and a long, sweetish finish.

THE GLENROTHES 1991

SINGLE MALT: SPEYSIDE 43% ABV

A nose of ripe berry fruits and vanilla, with some butterscotch and coconut flavours that last long on the palate.

THE GLENROTHES SELECT RESERVE

SINGLE MALT: SPEYSIDE 43% ABV

Like non-vintage Champagne, this is a vatting of different ages to produce a complex whisky with notes of barley sugar, ripe fruit, vanilla, and spice. Sweeter on the nose than in the mouth.

GLEN ORD

Muir of Ord, Ross-shire

Despite its name, Glen Ord is not in a valley, but on the fertile flatlands of the Black Isle, north of Inverness. It was founded in 1838, close to the alleged site of the Ferintosh Distillery, which was established in the 1670s. In 1923, Glen Ord was bought by John Dewar & Sons, shortly before they joined the DCL.

With 14 stills and an 11-million-litre (2.4-million-gallon) production, it has plenty to spare for a single malt. Confusingly, this has been called Ord, Glenordie, and Muir of Ord at various times. Recent bottlings are The Singleton of Glen Ord, aiming at the Asian market.

THE SINGLETON OF GLEN ORD 12-YEAR-OLD

SINGLE MALT: HIGHLANDS 40%ABV
The nose is nutty, with honey, milk chocolate, and Turkish delight. Relatively light-bodied, with cinnamon, sherry, toffee, apples, and a hint of milky coffee.

GLEN SCOTIA

Campbeltown, Argyll
www.glenscotia.com

Strung-out at the far end of the Mull of Kintyre, Campbeltown's rise and fall as "whiskyopolis" has been well-documented – as has the story of the Springbank Distillery's survival and subsequent cult status. Meanwhile, the much lesser known Glen Scotia also survived. With its single pair of stills, Campbeltown's "other" distillery was founded in the 1830s by the Galbraith family, who retained control for the rest of the century. After various owners followed, it was bought by Loch Lomond Group, part of Exponent Private Equity, in 2014.

GLEN SCOTIA DOUBLE CASK

SINGLE MALT: CAMBELTOWN 46% ABV
Sweet on the nose, with brambles, redcurrants, vanilla, and toffee. More vanilla on the smooth palate, with ginger, spicy sherry, and finally a suggestion of sea salt.

GLEN SPEY

Rothes, Aberlour, Banffshire
www.malts.com

James Stuart was an established distiller with Macallan and the key partner in building the Glenrothes Distillery in 1878, although he quickly pulled out of that venture. A few years later, he decided to convert an oat mill he owned into Glen Spey, on the opposite bank of the Rothes Burn from Glenrothes. The project inevitably led to disputes over water rights. In 1887, Glen Spey was sold to the London-based gin distiller Gilbey's, who later merged with Justerini & Brooks. Its J&B blend has contained Glen Spey ever since. The current owners, Diageo, have just one malt bottling in their Flora & Fauna range.

GLEN SPEY FLORA & FAUNA 12-YEAR-OLD

SINGLE MALT: SPEYSIDE 43% ABV
A light, grassy nose and brisk, nutty flavour. Very dry, with a short finish.

GLENTAUCHERS

Mulben, Keith, Banffshire

Many late-Victorian distilleries sprang up in the hope of finding a market among whisky blenders but, in 1897, Glentauchers was built to supply Buchanan's blend, which evolved into the top-selling Black & White. The distillery was a joint venture between James Buchanan and the Glasgow-based blender W.P. Lowrie. They chose an ideal site, right by a main road that connected to the east-coast rail line from Aberdeen to Inverness. Now owned by Pernod Ricard, Glentauchers has the same principal role it always had – supplying malt for blends.

GLENTAUCHERS GORDON & MACPHAIL 1991

SINGLE MALT: SPEYSIDE 43% ABV
This 16-year-old Gordon & MacPhail bottling has a sweet, sherried character, with a subtle smoky flavour.

THE GLENTURRET 10-YEAR-OLD

THE GLENTURRET PEATED

GRAND MACNISH ORIGINAL

GRAND MACNISH 12-YEAR-OLD

THE GLENTURRET

Crieff, Perthshire
www.theglenturret.com

This small Perthshire distillery, first licensed in 1775, claims to be the oldest working distillery in Scotland. It was certainly one of the first local farm distilleries to go legal, and this must have made life tough for the first few decades, given that most of the competition would have been untaxed.

Today, Glenturret is known as the spiritual home of The Famous Grouse *(see p. 77)*. This fact is hard to escape as a 5m (17ft) sculpture of the bird stands in the car park of the distillery.

Though Glenturret malt may have gone into the Grouse blend for years, most visitors would have been unaware of the fact until fairly recently. The only animal they would have been told about was Towser, the distillery cat, who won a place in *The Guinness Book of Records*

for killing nearly 30,000 mice between 1963 and 1984.

All changed when Glenturret's owners, Edrington, built a visitor centre at the distillery, from which a number of tour options are available. On top of that, the last couple of years have seen a concerted effort to re-establish Glenturret as a premium single malt in its own right. Glenturret single malt is promoted using the slogan "By Hand and by Heart" – the distillery is the last in Scotland with a hand-operated mash tun.

THE GLENTURRET 10-YEAR-OLD

SINGLE MALT: HIGHLANDS 40%
Replacing the 12-year-old, this floral, vanilla-scented malt is now the main Glenturret expression.

THE GLENTURRET PEATED

SINGLE MALT: HIGHLANDS 46% ABV
Furniture polish, pineapple, and rosehip on the nose. Smooth, fruity palate of chocolate, vanilla, and allspice, finishing with slightly bitter orange.

GRAND MACNISH

Owner: MacDuff International
www.macduffint.co.uk

The long history of this brand dates back to Glasgow and 1863, when the original Robert McNish (an "a" crept into the brand name some time later), a grocer and general merchant, took up blending. The pioneering family firm was driven forward by his two sons, who greatly expanded the business and developed sales in the whisky boom of the 1890s.

Things grew harder after World War I, and the family eventually sold out to Canadian Industrial Alcohol (later Corby Distilleries) in 1927. Further changes of ownership ensued, but today, the Grand Macnish has returned to Glasgow in the custody of MacDuff International, which appears to be developing an international profile for the brand and its distinctively "retro" dimpled bottle.

Two blended expressions are available: Grand Macnish Original, which still uses up to 40 whiskies in the blend, as was Robert McNish's practice, and a 12-year-old, described by the company as "more mature, fruity, and malty" than its younger sibling. The distinctive bottle gives Grand Macnish splendid "on shelf" presence, and the label is graced by the McNish clan motto, *"Forti nihil difficile"* ("To the strong, nothing is difficult").

GRAND MACNISH ORIGINAL

BLEND 40% ABV
Old leather and ripe fruits, giving way to a brandy-like aroma. Noticeably sweet on the palate, with strong vanilla (wood) influences. A sustained and evolving finish, with some gentle smoke.

GRAND MACNISH 12-YEAR-OLD

BLEND 40% ABV
The extra age shows here in a fuller, rounder flavour with greater intensity and a more sustained finish.

GRANT'S SIGNATURE

GRANT'S ALE CASK RESERVE

GRANT'S SHERRY CASK RESERVE

GRANT'S

Owner: William Grant & Sons
www.grantswhisky.com

This staunchly independent company has prospered on Speyside since 1887, when the original William Grant and family opened the Glenfiddich Distillery. Grant had served a long apprenticeship in rival distilleries and shrewdly applied his knowledge when setting up his own business.

The company remains in private hands and is renowned for its focus on whisky and its determination to pass this down the generations. Today, it is famous for Glenfiddich and its sister single malt, Balvenie, but it also produces a third malt, Kininvie, which is reserved for blending. In addition, it built a grain distillery at Girvan in 1963. Chosen for ease of access to North American maize supplies, the site has been expanded massively, and, in 2008, a new single malt distillery, Ailsa Bay, was opened there. A number of distinct styles of spirit are produced, though its output was primarily intended for blending purposes.

The first Ailsa Bay single malt was released in 2016, and it is a heavily peated whisky, comprising spirit matured in four different types of cask, namely refill American oak, first-fill bourbon, new oak, and Baby Bourbon casks from the Hudson Distillery in New York State.

Grant's Family Reserve blend broke through the 1 million case barrier as long ago as 1979 and, since then, has continued to grow at an exceptional rate, keeping up with demand from the world's Scotch whisky drinkers. Grant's now sells around 4 million cases of whisky a year and is one of the world's top five Scotch whisky brands, enjoyed in over 180

GRANT'S FAMILY RESERVE

GRANT'S 25-YEAR-OLD

HAIG GOLD LABEL

HAIG CLUB

countries. The fact that the company is privately owned, and therefore not subject to pressures from shareholders, has enabled Grant's blenders to work with a remarkable depth of mature stock, some dating back as far as 40 years or more.

The blended range of whiskies continues to evolve, while still remaining true to the distinctive triangular bottle that marks out the products of this respected firm.

GRANT'S SIGNATURE

BLEND 40% ABV

Soft citrus fruits, barley, vanilla, and almonds on the nose. Nutty spices, milky coffee, and caramel shortcake on the palate. Coffee turns to cocoa powder in the finish, accompanied by light oak notes.

GRANT'S ALE CASK RESERVE

BLEND 40% ABV

Grant's has ventured into special wood finishes with great success. This is the only Scotch whisky to be finished in barrels

that have previously held beer, and the ale casks give the whisky a uniquely creamy, malty, and honeyed taste.

GRANT'S SHERRY CASK RESERVE

BLEND 40% ABV

Prepared in the same way as the ground-breaking ale cask version, but here the whisky is finished in Spanish Oloroso sherry casks instead, giving it a distinctively warm, rich, and fruity palate.

GRANT'S FAMILY RESERVE

BLEND 40% ABV

An unmistakably Speyside nose, with fluting malty notes. A firm mouthfeel, with banana-vanilla sweetness balancing sharper malty notes. Clean, but very complex with a long, smooth finish.

GRANT'S 25-YEAR-OLD

BLEND 40% ABV

Mellow on the nose; warm, floral, and peachy, with butter, vanilla, worn leather, and a whiff of smoke. Fresh fruits, spice, discreet vanilla, ginger, and oak on the palate.

HAIG

Owner: Diageo
www.haigwhisky.com

The distinguished name of Haig can trace its whisky-making pedigree back to the 17th century, when distilling began on the family farm. The first record that the Haigs were making whisky dates from 1655, when Robert Haig was obliged to appear before the local church council for the serious misdemeanour of distilling on a Sunday. The company developed extensive interests in grain whisky distilling and was an early pioneer of blending. By 1919, however, it was absorbed into the DCL, where it continued to be a powerful force. The company's Dimple brand *(see p. 76)* was a highly successful deluxe expression, and Haig was once the best-selling whisky in the UK. But its glory days are far behind it: today, under the control of Diageo, it is found mainly in

Greece and the Canary Islands. During its heyday, the ubiquitous blend was advertised for many years with the strapline "Don't be vague – ask for Haig".

HAIG GOLD LABEL

BLEND 40% ABV

Some sweetness on the nose, with faint smoky notes. Light and delicate, with soft wood notes and some spice on the finish, where a hint of smoke returns.

HAIG CLUB

SINGLE GRAIN 40% ABV

Gentle on the early nose, with apricots, hot metal, and subtle spices. Relatively viscous and fruity on the palate, with toffee, honey, gingerbread, and a hint of cloves.

ALL ABOUT...
WHISKY COCKTAILS

When it comes to whisky, cocktails can be a thorny subject, with some traditionalists condemning them as an "adulteration" of the finest of all drinks. They're missing out: the interplay of flavours from the whisky and its accompanying ingredients can be sublime. What's more, a decent whisky has the strength and character to maintain its identity in the mix, and delicate layerings of flavours can be achieved. Bartenders today are experimenting with big, characterful malts – even peaty expressions from Islay have their place. Balance of flavours is key, but the results can be astounding. Here are seven, using whiskies from around the globe.

MINT JULEP Roughly tear 12–15 mint leaves and place in a julep glass. Add some crushed ice, 25ml Buffalo Trace bourbon, 12.5ml sugar syrup, and stir well. Add 5 more torn mint leaves, another 25ml bourbon, and stir well. Add 5 more torn mint leaves, fill the glass with crushed ice, and stir well. Top with more crushed ice, garnish with a sprig of mint, and serve with two short straws.

PEAT COLLINS Chill a collins glass with ice cubes. Put 50ml Laphroaig 10-year-old into the mixing glass, add 20ml freshly squeezed lime juice, 12.5ml sugar syrup, a dash of orange bitters, and shake well. Double-strain the Peat Collins into the collins glass, add a couple of dashes of soda water, and stir well. Top with crushed ice and a twist of orange zest.

RYE MANHATTAN Chill a martini glass with crushed ice. Half-fill a mixing glass with ice cubes, add a dash of Angostura bitters, 50ml Sazerac rye whiskey, and 25ml Antica Formula sweet red vermouth. Fill with more ice cubes and stir for 20 seconds. Discard the crushed ice from the martini glass and double-strain the Rye Manhattan into it. Garnish with a maraschino cherry.

ROB ILA Chill a coupette glass with crushed ice. Fill the mixing glass with ice cubes, add 50ml Caol Ila Distillers Edition, 12.5ml Muscat de Beaumes de Venise, a dash of orange bitters, 10ml Drambuie, and stir well for 30 seconds. Discard the ice and double-strain the Rob Ila into it. Run a piece of lemon zest round the rim and garnish with a twist of zest.

BLACK SOUR Put three cardamom seeds in the mixing glass and crush well. Add half a cored Williams' pear and mash to a pulp. Add 37.5ml Bushmills Black Bush, 12.5ml crème de pêche, 2 good dashes of Angostura bitters, 25ml freshly squeezed lemon juice, 12.5ml sugar syrup, a dash of egg white, and shake well. Double-strain into a chilled old-fashioned glass, top with crushed ice, and garnish with fanned Williams' pear.

YAMAZAKI MARTINI Chill a small martini glass with crushed ice. Fill the mixing glass with ice cubes, add 50ml Yamazaki 12-year-old, a dash of Angostura bitters, 20ml orgeat syrup, 5ml sugar syrup, 12.5ml freshly squeezed lime juice, a dash of egg white, and shake well. Discard the ice from the martini glass and double-strain the Yamazaki Martini into it.

ALBANNACH RENAISSANCE Fill a mixing glass with ice cubes, add 37.5ml Ardbeg Renaissance, 12.5ml Aperol, 20ml lime juice, 12.5ml sugar syrup, and dashes of orange bitters, grapefruit juice, and egg white. Cover and shake till frothy. Double-strain into a chilled rocks glass, squeeze in the juice from a small piece of orange zest, and garnish with a twist of orange zest.

**HIGHLAND PARK
12-YEAR-OLD**

SINGLE MALT: ISLANDS 40% ABV
*This whisky has been praised
for its all-round quality. There
are soft heather-honey
flavours, some richer spicy
notes, and an enveloping
wisp of peat smoke that
leaves the finish quite dry.*

**HIGHLAND PARK
15-YEAR-OLD**

SINGLE MALT: ISLANDS 40% ABV
*Sweetly aromatic, with ripe
fruits and almond notes.
The fruit is more caramelized
on the palate, which fades to
a dry, smoky finish.*

HIGHLAND PARK 18-YEAR-OLD

HIGHLAND PARK 21-YEAR-OLD

HIGHLAND PARK 25-YEAR-OLD

HIGHLAND PARK 30-YEAR-OLD

HIGHLAND PARK

Kirkwall, Orkney
www.highlandpark.co.uk

Unless, and until, a distillery is built on Shetland, Highland Park will remain Scotland's most northerly distillery. Today, its far-flung island location is a great asset for the marketing of Highland Park whiskies but, for much of its history, the distance from its core market – the big blenders on the mainland – represented a major challenge for the distillery. It survived, and now produces a Highland malt that is highly regarded. Highland Park was first licensed to David Robertson in 1798 and stands near the island's capital,

Kirkwall, on the site of an illicit distillery run by Magnus Eunson, a notorious smuggler. Eunson was finally arrested by John Robertson, an excise officer, who took over the distillery in 1826. In 1895, it was bought by James Grant of Glenlivet, who expanded the number of stills to four. Since 1937, it has been part of Highland Distilleries (now Edrington), which began to invest seriously in single malts from Highland Park in the late 1970s. To this day, a proportion of the barley is malted using the distillery's original floor maltings. The malt is then dried in a kiln, using local peat, which has a slightly sweeter aroma than that from Islay.

The range starts with the no-age-statement (NAS) Dark Origins and stretches to a 50-year-old. There have also been many limited edition and travel retail-exclusive releases in recent years.

HIGHLAND PARK 18-YEAR-OLD

SINGLE MALT: ISLANDS 43% ABV
This is a touch sweeter than the 12-year-old, with notes of heather, toffee, and polished leather. The flavour of peat smoke comes through stronger on the finish than on the palate.

HIGHLAND PARK 21-YEAR-OLD

SINGLE MALT: ISLANDS 47.5% ABV
The nose offers brittle toffee, spicy malt, and contrasting heather and smoke notes. Rich and full-bodied in

the mouth, with caramel, stewed fruits, and milk chocolate, plus a hint of gentle smoke.

HIGHLAND PARK 25-YEAR-OLD

SINGLE MALT: ISLANDS 48.1% ABV
As suggested by its deep amber colour, this whisky had plenty of contact with European oak. In fact, half of it was matured in first-fill sherry butts. Despite its age, it has a rich, nutty flavour, with dried fruits and scented smoke.

HIGHLAND PARK 30-YEAR-OLD

SINGLE MALT: ISLANDS 48.1% ABV
The flagship of the range. Caramel sweetness, aromatic spices, dark chocolate, and orange notes. A long, drying, smoky finish, tinged with salt.

HANKEY BANNISTER

Owner: Inver House Distillers

Messrs Hankey and Bannister went into partnership in 1757 and were wine merchants to the great and the good, including the Prince Regent and William IV. Today, the company is owned by Inver House Distillers, giving it access to a range of single malts from some of Scotland's distinguished but lesser-known distilleries, such as Balblair, Balmenach, and Knockdhu. Although managed in Scotland, Inver House is owned by Thai Beverage, and key markets for Hankey Bannister include Latin America, Australia, and South Africa, but it is exported to a total of 47 countries worldwide.

The 12-year-old was awarded a silver medal at the 2007 International Wine and Spirit Competition while, in June 2008, the 40-year-old received the coveted accolade of World's Best Scotch Blended Whisky at the World Whiskies Awards. This rare blend is characterized by the presence of whiskies such as Glen Flagler, Garnheath, and Killyloch, whose distilleries are no more.

HANKEY BANNISTER 21-YEAR-OLD

BLEND 43% ABV

A fresh and quite youthful nose. Soft and smooth, creamy toffee, with the vanilla house style coming through. Greater depth on the palate, with malty overtones and a warm finish.

HANKEY BANNISTER ORIGINAL BLEND

BLEND 40% ABV

Light on the nose, with grain and hints of lemon and pepper. Creamy mouthfeel, with more grain, lemon, and soft toffee.

HANKEY BANNISTER 21-YEAR-OLD

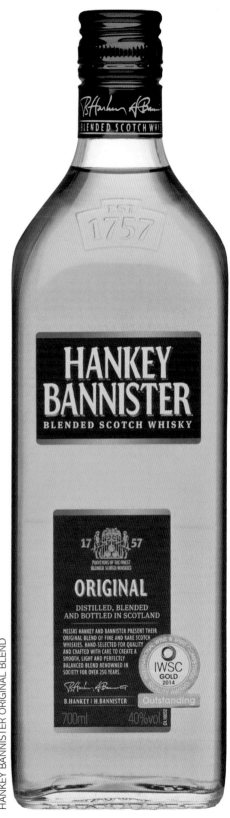

HANKEY BANNISTER ORIGINAL BLEND

HAZELBURN

Well Close, Campbeltown
www.springbankwhisky.com

Springbank Distillery is the great survivor of the Campbeltown whisky boom, which saw a staggering 34 distilleries in town in the 19th century. Today, Springbank is a miniature malt-whisky industry on its own, with three separate distillations under one roof: Springbank itself, the pungently smoky Longrow, and the light, gentle Hazelburn. As well as using no peat in its malt, Hazelburn – which was named after an old, abandoned distillery in Campbeltown – is triple-distilled. The first spirit was produced in 1997 and bottled as an 8-year-old in 2005. The oldest expression currently available is a 12-year-old.

HAZELBURN 8-YEAR-OLD

SINGLE MALT: CAMPBELTOWN 46% ABV
Lowland in style, clean and refreshing, with a subtle, malty flavour.

INCHGOWER

Buckie, Banffshire
www.malts.com

This is Speyside, but only just – the Inchgower Distillery sits near the mouth of the Spey and the fishing port of Buckie. It was established in 1871 by Alexander Wilson, using equipment from the disused Tochieneal Distillery, which had been founded in 1824 by his father, John Wilson, a short distance down the coast at Cullen. It remained a family business until 1930, when the stills went cold. Six years on, the local town council bought it for just £1,000, selling it on to Arthur Bell & Sons in 1938. Bell's blends swallow up most of the malt.

INCHGOWER FLORA & FAUNA 14-YEAR-OLD

SINGLE MALT: SPEYSIDE 43% ABV
Brisk and fresh, with a floral nose, sweet-and-sour flavour, and quite a short finish.

INVER HOUSE GREEN PLAID

Owner: Inver House Distillers

Controlled today by Thai Beverage, Inver House is one of the smaller but more dynamic Scotch whisky companies and, in 2008, was named International Distiller of the Year by Whisky Magazine. Its Green Plaid label was originally launched in 1956 in the US, where it remains among the top ten best-selling whiskies. More than 20 malts and grains are used to blend Green Plaid, which is available as a competitively priced non-aged version and as 12- and 21-year-olds. Inver House's Speyburn, anCnoc, Balblair, Old Pulteney, and Balmenach single malts undoubtedly feature strongly in the blend.

INVER HOUSE GREEN PLAID

BLEND 40% ABV
A light, pleasant, undemanding dram, with notes of caramel and vanilla.

INVERGORDON

Cottage Brae, Invergordon, Ross-shire
www.whyteandmackay.com

Located on the shores of the Moray Firth, the Invergordon grain distillery is owned by Whyte & Mackay. It was established in 1961 and expanded in 1963 and 1978. The distillery issued its pioneering official bottling of Invergordon Single Grain as a 10-year-old in 1991, but this was subsequently withdrawn. As a consequence, the only supplies now available are independent bottlings, many of which are very highly regarded by independent tasters.

INVERGORDON WEMYSS APPLEWOOD BAKE 1988

SINGLE GRAIN 46% ABV
Cider-like notes on the nose, with grapes and walnuts. Pears, vanilla, and milk chocolate on the palate, which is quite short with peppery oak finish.

ISLAY MIST

Owner: MacDuff International

Created in 1922 for the 21st birthday of the son of the Laird of Islay House, Islay Mist is a highly awarded blend of single malts from the Hebridean island. The strongly flavoured Laphroaig is predominant, but is tempered with Speyside and Highland malts. Naturally, Islay Mist is favoured by lovers of peat-flavoured whiskies, but it also offers an excellent alternative to less characterful blends. It is produced by MacDuff International, and is available in Peated Reserve, Deluxe, 12-, and 17-year-old.

ISLAY MIST DELUXE

BLEND 40% ABV

A great smoky session whisky that some will find easier to drink than full-on Islay malt. Sweet and complex under all the peat.

J&B RARE

J&B JET

J&B

Owner: Diageo

A Diageo brand widely sold in Spain, France, Portugal, Turkey, South Africa, and the US, J&B is one of the world's top-selling blended whiskies. In fact, nearly two bottles are sold every second.

The founding firm dates from 1749. In 1831, it was bought by the entrepreneurial Alfred Brooks, who renamed it Justerini and Brooks. The company began blending in the 1880s, and developed J&B Rare in the 1930s, when the end of Prohibition in the US created a demand for lighter-coloured whisky with a more delicate flavour. It was an immediate success, achieving sales in excess of 3 million cases a year by the 1970s.

J&B has long been a favourite with writers and film stars: Truman Capote, Graham Greene, and Bret Easton Ellis have all been connected with the brand. J&B have attempted several innovative expressions,

J&B ULTIMA

JAMES MARTIN'S 20-YEAR-OLD

JAMES MARTIN'S 30-YEAR-OLD

inluding the -6°C in 2006, an almost clear blend aimed at younger vodka drinkers, and the Urban Honey "spirit drink" launched in 2014.

J&B RARE
BLEND 40% ABV

Top-class single malts such as Knockando, Auchroisk, and Glen Spey are at its heart; delicate smokiness suggests an Islay influence. Apple and pear sweetness, vanilla notes, and honey hint against a background of restrained peat. A highly distinctive blend.

J&B JET
BLEND 40% ABV

A very mellow, smooth whisky, with Speyside malt at its core.

J&B ULTIMA
BLEND 43% ABV

With a blending of whiskies from no fewer than 128 malt and grain distilleries, this is about as rich and complex a blend as it's possible to get. Increasingly rare, though, as J&B has discontinued this bottling.

JAMES MARTIN'S
Owner: Glenmorangie

This brand exhibits something of a split personality: Martin's VVO (very, very old – a generous description of the blend) remains a low-price contender in parts of the US, where it was once a significant seller; in Portugal, however, the older expressions of Martin's are highly regarded as a prestigious, premium style.

The name relates to the Leith blenders MacDonald Martin Distillers (now Glenmorangie, and thus part of the French luxury goods house LVMH) and dates back to 1878, when the original James Martin set up in business. Given LVMH's influence over Glenmorangie, and its wish to concentrate on prestige products, the future of the VVO style may be in some doubt. It is certainly years since it received any meaningful marketing, trading largely on price. In their stylish

Art Deco bottles, the older expressions may have brighter prospects. They are certainly better suited to the new corporate strategy, and the product was always highly regarded, as it contained a healthy proportion of Glenmorangie single malt with some richer components.

Currently there are 12- and 20-year-old versions of James Martin's. The 30-year-old version appears to have been withdrawn – presumably owing to a shortage of aged stocks – but bottles can still be bought from specialist retailers.

JAMES MARTIN'S 20-YEAR-OLD
BLEND 40% ABV

Citrus on the nose initially, then honey, vanilla, and a rich mead liqueur. With water, hints of coconut and vanilla appear. Very soft on the palate at the start, with cereal (grain) notes to the fore. Complex, lively spice and soft, sweet grain notes. Well-balanced with a soft finish.

JOHN BARR
Owner: Whyte & Mackay

Introduced into the UK by DCL to compensate for its withdrawal of Johnnie Walker (the result of a spat with the EU over pricing), John Barr was intended to make up for lost sales. The range echoes Johnnie Walker quite shamelessly, with Red, Black, and Gold being the main variants. Today, the brand is owned by Whyte & Mackay and is seen principally in the US, where it competes largely on price. The Whyte & Mackay single malts Jura, Tamnavulin, and Fettercairn appear to play a large part in the blend, along with a good measure of Invergordon grain.

JOHN BARR
BLEND 40% ABV

The nose is firm, with luscious, creamy, round tones. Positive and full-flavoured, with an almost spicy richness.

JOHNNIE WALKER BLACK LABEL

JOHNNIE WALKER GREEN LABEL

JOHNNIE WALKER GOLD LABEL

JOHNNIE WALKER BLUE LABEL

JOHNNIE WALKER

Owner: Diageo

While the original firm, then called simply "Walker's", can be traced back to the purchase of a Kilmarnock grocery store in 1820, it did not enter the whisky business in a serious way until the 1860s. Then, with the legalization of blending, John Walker's son and grandson progressively launched and developed their range of whiskies. These were based around the original Walker's Old Highland blend, which was launched in 1865 and is the ancestor of today's Black Label. Having been renamed

"Johnnie Walker" in 1908, the firm joined DCL in 1925 and, by 1945, was the world's best-selling brand of Scotch.

Total sales of Johnnie Walker whiskies amount to around 19 million cases a year, and its Red Label is the most successful brand of Scotch whisky in the world. There has been significant growth in Scotch's developing markets (China, Asia, and Russia), where the brand is seen as a symbol of Western affluence and success.

The range comprises Johnnie Walker Red, Black, Double Black, Gold, Platinum, and Blue. From time to time the firm also releases a number of one-off, limited, or regional expressions, including

Swing, Quest, Honour, Excelsior, Old Harmony, and 1805.

From the early 1990s, the brand positioned itself upmarket. Blue Label, launched in 1992, set new price records for blended whisky. The King George V Edition followed, costing three times more than the Blue, then the ultra-exclusive 1805, sold at £1,000 a glass.

JOHNNIE WALKER BLACK LABEL

BLEND 40% ABV
The flagship, classic blend, recognizable by the smoky kick contributed by Talisker and Diageo's Islay malts, Caol Ila and Lagavulin. Glendullan and Mortlach add some Speyside malt; the grain component is from Cameron Brig.

JOHNNIE WALKER GREEN LABEL

BLENDED MALT 43% ABV
Complex, rich, and powerful. Pepper and oak, fruit aromas, a malty sweetness, and some smoke.

JOHNNIE WALKER GOLD LABEL

BLEND 40% ABV
Honey, fresh fruit, and toffee notes, with smoke in the background. Diageo recommends chilling this in the freezer before serving.

JOHNNIE WALKER BLUE LABEL

BLEND 40% ABV
Smooth and mellow, with traces of spice, honey, and the signature hint of smoke.

**JOHNNIE WALKER
PREMIER**

BLEND 43% ABV

*A complex blend of 28
different single malt and
grain whiskies. Rich, with
a subtle oak finish. Sweet
and dark, with dried fruits,
treacle toffee, and chocolate.*

**JOHNNIE WALKER
SWING**

BLEND 43% ABV

*Notes of sherry wood
and vanilla, with an almost
perfumed sweetness. Fresh,
light, smooth, and intensely
fruity, with traces of oak
and a hint of smoke.*

JURA SUPERSTITION

JURA 10-YEAR-OLD

JURA 16-YEAR-OLD

JURA

Isle of Jura, Argyllshire
www.jurawhisky.com

When the Indian tycoon Vijay Mallya bought Whyte & Mackay in May 2007, part of the appeal was sentimental: included in the sale was Jura – an island distillery off the northeast tip of Islay, which his father found irresistible. "I remember hearing the name 40 years ago," Mallya told reporters. "It was his favourite whisky and now it's part of Whyte & Mackay. I hope he would be proud." In 2014, Whyte & Mackay Distillers and the Jura brand were acquired by Emperador Inc.

The original Jura Distillery was licensed in 1831 and later leased to James Ferguson, who rebuilt it in

1875. However, the terms of the lease were so harsh that his family abandoned Jura in 1901, ripping out the equipment as they did so. For the next 20 years, the landlord – the local laird, Archibald Campbell – pursued them in the courts, while removing the distillery roof to avoid paying rates.

In the late 1950s, two estate owners on Jura resurrected the distillery in a joint venture with Scottish & Newcastle breweries. They hired the leading distillery architect of his day, William Delmé-Evans, and his design, completed in the early 1960s, still stands today.

The profile of the whisky also changed when the distillery was resurrected. Gone was the strong, phenolic malt of the past, and in came something more Highland

in style, with less peat and a more subtle touch. Employing large stills (nearly as tall as those at Glenmorangie) to create a cleaner style of spirit, Jura was able to produce a softer malt whisky – one that would be distinct from those of its peaty neighbours, over on Islay.

Having said that, in recent years Jura has produced an interesting array of limited-edition bottlings, some of which have used various sherry cask finishes and some of which have actually been quite heavily peated. A whisky called Earth (from the Elements series) was one such bottling.

Jura's core range consists of 10-year-old, Origin, 16-year-old, Diurach's Own, Superstition, and the peated Prophecy.

JURA SUPERSTITION

SINGLE MALT: ISLANDS 43% ABV
A mix of heavily peated, young Jura with older whisky, to produce an intensely smoky, smooth-textured malt.

JURA 10-YEAR-OLD

SINGLE MALT: ISLANDS 40% ABV
A lightly peated island malt that seems to have improved in recent years.

JURA 16-YEAR-OLD

SINGLE MALT: ISLANDS 40% ABV
A slightly spicy, cereal nose with a nutty flavour that dries on the finish.

KILKERRAN WORK IN PROGRESS 6 BOURBON MATURED

KILKERRAN WORK IN PROGRESS 6 SHERRY MATURED

KILKERRAN

Glengyle Road, Campbeltown
www.kilkerransinglemalt.com

Glengyle is Campbeltown's newest distillery in the sense that it first produced spirit during 2004. However, the original Glengyle operated between 1872 and 1925 — a period when Campbeltown was still a major player in the Scotch whisky world. The malt whisky it produces is named Kilkerran, as "Glengyle" was already registered as a blend by Loch Lomond. It is named after an early settlement that would later become Campbeltown.

Glengyle was revived by Springbank owner Hedley Wright, and features a pair of modified stills formerly used by the Ben Wyvis malt distillery at Invergordon in the late '70s. The first permanent expression of Killkeran will be a 12-year-old, but since 2009, the distillery has released annual limited batches of "Work in Progress". In 2014, "Work in Progress 6" featured both sherry cask-matured and bourbon cask-matured bottlings.

KILKERRAN WORK IN PROGRESS 6 BOURBON MATURED

SINGLE MALT: CAMPBELTOWN 46% ABV
Lemongrass, a pinch of salt, wood smoke, and ginger snaps on the nose. Tropical fruits on the soft, oily palate, with a slight underpinning of nutty, spicy smoke. Drying in the mellow finish.

KILKERRAN WORK IN PROGRESS 6 SHERRY MATURED

SINGLE MALT: CAMPBELTOWN 46% ABV
Initially savoury on the nose, slightly earthy, with sherry, new leather, and a hint of chlorine. Spicy and zesty, with developing stewed fruits, dark chocolate, and deep sherry notes on a mildly smoky palate.

WHISKY TOUR: ISLAY

"Peat freaks" adore the Islay taste, and tourism to this Hebridean island is booming, particularly during the annual Feis Ile (the Islay Malt and Music Festival) at the end of May. The easiest way to reach Islay is to fly from Glasgow, but you will need to hire a car to get around; the Caledonian MacBrayne ferry from Kennacraig allows you to bring your own vehicle but is a longer journey (four hours). For accommodation, there are converted distillery cottages at Bowmore and Bunnahabhain available to rent, hotels in Bowmore and Port Charlotte, and plenty of B&B and self-catering options too. A four-day itinerary should take in all eight distilleries.

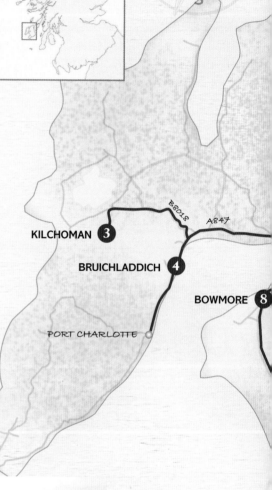

TOUR STATISTICS		
DAYS: 4	**LENGTH:** 60 miles (96 km)	**DISTILLERIES:** 8
TRAVEL: Car, walking	**REGION:** Islay, Scotland	

DAY 1: CAOL ILA, BUNNAHABHAIN

1 Arriving in Port Askaig by ferry, the logical place to stay is the charming, family-run Port Askaig Hotel on the coast (*www.portaskaig.co.uk*). From there you can walk to **Caol Ila**, a large Diageo distillery that is the most highly productive on the island. (*www.discovering-distilleries.com/caolila*)

2 It's a car trip or hike along the coastal path from Port Askaig to **Bunnahabhain**. This distillery makes the most lightly peated of all Islay whiskies. It is possible to rent one of the distillery cottages and soak up the tranquillity of Bunnahabhain Bay, with its captivating views of Jura. (*www.bunnahabhain.com*)

WASHBACKS AT CAOL ILA

BUNNAHABHAIN DISTILLERY

BUNNAHABHAIN ②

JURA

CAOL ILA ①

PORT ASKAIG

FEOLIN FERRY

Port Askaig - Colonsay ferry

START

FINISH

A846

A846

BRIDGEND

Port Askaig - Kennacraig ferry

ISLAY

B8016

KILDALTON

Port Ellen - Kennacraig ferry

⑦ ARDBEG

⑤ ⑥ LAGAVULIN

PORT ELLEN LAPHROAIG

miles
0   2

0   2
kilometres

DAY 2: KILCHOMAN, BRUICHLADDICH

③ Tiny **Kilchoman** is Islay's newest and smallest distillery. It's also a farm with a friendly café. Like other Islay distilleries, it sells special bottlings that may not be available elsewhere. This is a great spot for lunch and the dishes use locally sourced ingredients. Alternatively, in good weather, you can picnic at nearby Machir Bay. *(www.kilchomandistillery.com)*

④ A short drive back over the hill brings you to **Bruichladdich** *(www.bruichladdich.com)*, which produces a huge array of whiskies. The distillery is just outside Port Charlotte, where you can learn about illicit whisky production in the Museum of Islay Life *(www.islaymuseum.org)*, then enjoy dinner at the Port Charlotte Hotel *(www.portcharlottehotel.co.uk)*.

BRUICHLADDICH

DAY 3: LAPHROAIG, LAGAVULIN, ARDBEG

⑤ Spend today taking in three distilleries and some ancient history. The Kildalton distilleries, as these three are known, are renowned for their strong peaty character, and **Laphroaig** is reputedly Prince Charles's favourite dram. The distillery tour includes the splendidly maintained maltings. *(www.laphroaig.com)*

⑥ From Laphroaig, take a five-minute stroll to **Lagavulin** to compare these two strongly peated single malts with their assertive flavours. *(www.discovering-distilleries.com/lagavulin)*

⑦ The last distillery of the day is **Ardbeg** *(www.ardbeg.com)*, where lunch at the Old Kiln Café is not to be missed. If you're interested in history, drive a few miles further on the tiny road to Kildalton where there's a very fine 8th-century cross.

MODEL IN LAGAVULIN'S DRAM ROOM

DAY 4: BOWMORE

⑧ Spend your last morning in the little town of Bowmore, where you can visit the floor maltings, history of distillery exhibition, and visitor centre at **Bowmore** Distillery *(www.bowmore.com)*. Repair to the Harbour Inn *(www.harbour-inn.com)* for a final lunch of local produce before catching the afternoon ferry from Port Askaig back to the mainland.

BOWMORE WAREHOUSE

KILCHOMAN

Rockside Farm, Bruichladdich, Islay
www.kilchomandistillery.com

Whisky-making began here in 2005, and this is as quintessential a farm distillery as you'll find. The barley is grown on Rockside Farm, and malting, fermenting, distilling, and maturing all take place on-site; a dam on the farm creates a supply of fresh water.

Having started out selling new-make spirit, Kilchoman released its first 3-year-old single malt in 2009, followed by several limited bottlings before the first "core" expression – Machir Bay – appeared in 2012. Loch Gorm and 100% Islay are also regularly produced.

KILCHOMAN MACHIR BAY

SINGLE MALT 46% ABV
A nose of sweet peat and vanilla, undercut by brine, wood smoke, kelp, and black pepper. Smooth on the palate, with citrus fruit, peat smoke, and antiseptic, leading to a long, sweet, chilli, and nut finish.

KNOCKANDO 12-YEAR-OLD

KNOCKANDO 18-YEAR-OLD

KNOCKANDO

Knockando, Morayshire
www.malts.com

Knockando was launched as a single malt in the late 1970s and had some success in Spain, although most of the production went into J&B. The name is an anglicized version of Cnoc-an-Dhu, which is Gaelic for the "dark hillock" that stands close by the distillery, guarding a bend in the Spey.

The distillery was set up by John Thomson in 1898 close to Cardhu, on the old Strathspey railway line, where it had its own station. Although it was one of the first to have electric light, it was only run on a seasonal basis and soon fell victim to the speculative crash that hit the industry at the beginning of the 20th century. Knockando was snapped up by London gin distillers Gilbey's, who, via a series of acquisitions, became part of what is now Diageo. In 1968, the floor maltings were

KNOCKANDO 21-YEAR-OLD

LANGS SUPREME

LANGS 12-YEAR-OLD

stopped and the old malt barns converted to host meetings for J&B salesman around the world.

As a single malt, Knockando was originally sold not by age statement, but by vintage in all its markets except the US. It has proved popular in Spain and France.

KNOCKANDO 12-YEAR-OLD

SINGLE MALT: SPEYSIDE 43% ABV

This very gentle, grassy malt has a cereal character and a light, creamy texture.

KNOCKANDO 18-YEAR-OLD

SINGLE MALT: SPEYSIDE 43% ABV

A slightly more fulsome expression of this gentle Speyside malt, with a smooth, mellow texture.

KNOCKANDO 21-YEAR-OLD

SINGLE MALT: SPEYSIDE 43% ABV

Sweet on the nose, with oak and nuts (almonds) on the palate, matched by berry fruits, leading on to a smoky, oaky finish.

LABEL 5

Owner: La Martiniquaise

The Label 5 brand is owned by La Martiniquaise, a French producer with significant blending and distilling facilities in Scotland, as well as interests in rum and other spirits. Founded in 1934 as a blending house, the company now owns Glen Moray single malt and is building new grain and single malt facilities at its central Scotland base.

Label 5 is its leading brand, and sells well over 1 million cases in the price-competitive "value" category, mainly in France, although it is available in more than 50 countries worldwide. A 12-year-old deluxe version is also available.

LABEL 5 CLASSIC BLACK

BLEND 40% ABV

Delicate, malty, and smoky, with hints of flowers and fruit. Smooth, robust, and balanced on the palate, with subtle oak notes.

LANGS

Owner: Ian MacLeod
www.ianmacleod.com

At the heart of this long-established blend is Glengoyne single malt, from the distillery just outside Glasgow. This was bought in 1876 by two local merchants, Alexander and Gavin Lang. In 1965, the brand and distillery were sold to their rivals, Robertson & Baxter, who invested in the distillery and developed the brand with some success. Sales also grew steadily in Europe and the Far East and, in 1984, HM The Queen Mother awarded Langs her royal warrant.

But in 2003, Robertson & Baxter decided they could take Langs no further. The sale to Ian MacLeod marked an important transition for that business, from blender and bottler to full-blown distiller.

Since the acquisition, Ian MacLeod has invested in both

the Glengoyne Distillery, with its range of alternative visitor experiences, and in presenting Langs in new packaging. Today, the principal Langs products are Langs Select 12-year-old and Langs Supreme, both blends noted for their relatively high malt content. Langs Select was awarded a gold medal by *Scottish* Field magazine's Merchants' Challenge, beating some very well-known names.

LANGS SUPREME

BLEND 40% ABV

A rich malt aroma on the nose, well-matured, with just a hint of sherry. A full-flavoured, medium-sweet blend, with the Glengoyne heart evident.

LANGS SELECT 12-YEAR-OLD

BLEND 40% ABV

Rhubarb and cooking apples on the nose, with a good helping of vanilla. Sweet, soft, and delicate. Richer on the palate, with lots of fruity notes and a lemon-tart sweetness that build towards a spicy finish with hints of peat smoke.

LAGAVULIN 16-YEAR-OLD

LAGAVULIN 12-YEAR-OLD

LAGAVULIN 21-YEAR-OLD

LAGAVULIN

Port Ellen, Isle of Islay
www.malts.com

Lagavulin is said to have evolved into a distillery from various illicit smuggling botheys in 1816. In 1836, its lease was taken over by Alexander Graham, who sold the island's whiskies through his shop in Glasgow. Peter Mackie, the nephew of Graham's partner, worked for the business and went on to create the famous White Horse blend based on Islay malt. When neighbouring Laphroaig refused to supply him, he decided to build Malt Mill Distillery in the grounds of Lagavulin, which he inherited after his uncle's death. Malt Mill was demolished in the 1960s, but Lagavulin rode on the back of the White Horse until its iconic 16-year-old became a founding member of the "Classic Malts" in 1988.

During the slump in demand for Scotch in the 1980s, Lagavulin was working a two- to three-day week. Sixteen years down the line, the managers were having to juggle the short supply with booming demand. Having been the top-selling Islay malt, low stocks pushed it into third place behind Laphroaig and Bowmore. To try and meet demand, production at Lagavulin was cranked up to a seven-day week, and less and less was made available for blends. It is said that over 85 per cent of Lagavulin is now bottled as a single

LAGAVULIN 25-YEAR-OLD

LAGAVULIN 1976 37-YEAR-OLD

LAGAVULIN DISTILLERS EDITION

malt. The core range comprises the 12-year-old Cask Strength, 16-year-old, and Pedro Ximinez sherry cask-finished Distillers Edition. In recent years, 21- and 37-year-olds have also been bottled as limited editions.

LAGAVULIN 16-YEAR-OLD

SINGLE MALT: ISLAY 43% ABV

The long-time stalwart of the "Classic Malts" has an intensely smoky nose with the scent of seaweed and iodine and a sweetness in the mouth that dries to a peaty finish.

LAGAVULIN 12-YEAR-OLD

SINGLE MALT: ISLAY 56.4% ABV

An initial sweetness gives way to scented smoke and a malty, fruity flavour ahead of the dry, peaty finish.

LAGAVULIN 21-YEAR-OLD

SINGLE MALT: ISLAY 56.5% ABV

Pungent and smoky on one hand, with a sherried, golden-syrup warmth on the other. The two sides live in harmony.

LAGAVULIN 1976 37-YEAR-OLD

SINGLE MALT: ISLAY 51% ABV

Earthy, savoury, and smoky on the nose, with old leather, sea salt, almonds, and honey. Oak, brine, more leather, and earthy notes on the palate, with kelp, dried fruits, and lingering sweet peat smoke.

LAGAVULIN DISTILLERS EDITION

SINGLE MALT: ISLAY 43% ABV

A richer, fuller-flavoured take on the 16-year-old, still with plenty of dense smoke and seaweed.

LAPHROAIG 10-YEAR-OLD CASK STRENGTH

LAPHROAIG 18-YEAR-OLD

LAPHROAIG 25-YEAR-OLD

LAPHROAIG SELECT

LAPHROAIG

Port Ellen, Isle of Islay
www.laphroaig.com

In June 2008, Prince Charles returned to visit the home of his favourite Islay malt after 14 years. This time, he came with his wife, Camilla, and did not crash-land on Islay's tiny airstrip, as he had the last time (he made the mistake of landing with a strong tail wind, and the plane came to a halt nose-down in the peat bog).

Laphroaig has always revelled in its pungent smokiness – a mix of hemp, carbolic soap, and bonfire that is about as a far from the creamy, cocktail end of whisky as it is possible to get. Its intense medicinal character is said to be

one reason it was among the few Scotch whiskies allowed into the US during Prohibition – it was accepted as a "medicinal spirit", and could be obtained on prescription from a doctor.

Laphroaig was founded in 1810 by Alexander and Donald Johnston, although official production did not begin for five years. Living beside the equally famous Lagavulin has not always been easy, and there were the usual fights over water access, but today, the feeling is more one of mutual respect.

Laphroaig is one of the very few distilleries to have retained its floor maltings, which supply about a fifth of its needs. The reason may be more to do with

marketing than anything else, but it makes for an interesting distillery visit.

Although Allied Distillers could appear ambivalent about its commitment to Scotch, there were never any doubts about its proud flagship distillery. Just before Allied was bought out in 2005, and Laphroaig became part of Fortune Brands, it released its first Quarter Cask expression: by increasing the proportion of wood to whisky for the final seven months before bottling, the whole process of maturation is speeded up.

Quarter Cask is now offered alongside 10-year-old, 10-year-old Cask Strength, Select, Triple Wood, and 18- and 25-year-old expressions.

LAPHROAIG 10-YEAR-OLD CASK STRENGTH

SINGLE MALT: ISLAY 57.3% ABV
Tar, seaweed, and salt, and some sweet wood too. Iodine and hot peat rumble through a long, dramatic finish.

LAPHROAIG 25-YEAR-OLD

SINGLE MALT: ISLAY 50.9% ABV
A spicy, floral character, with smoke and sea spray taking over only in the finish. Also available in cask strength.

LAPHROAIG SELECT

SINGLE MALT: ISLAY 40% ABV
Nose of pipe tobacco, peat, and, in time, a medicinal note and smoky peaches. Thin on the peaty palate, with dark berries and contrasting hints of vanilla.

LAPHROAIG
QUARTER CASK

SINGLE MALT: ISLAY 48% ABV
The Quarter Cask is at the heart of Laphroaig's core range. Small casks speed up the maturation process and lead to a sweet, woody taste that succumbs to a triumphal burst of peat smoke.

LAPHROAIG
10-YEAR-OLD

SINGLE MALT: ISLAY 40% ABV
The 10-year-old is also very popular. Beneath the dense peat smoke and salty sea spray is a refreshing, youthful malt with a sweet core.

THE SECRETS OF...
LAPHROAIG

The malt from this great Islay distillery delights in its tough, uncompromising image, and for years it was promoted as a whisky that people would either love or hate.

Laphroaig is one of the smokiest, most pungent malts around, and, as a result, you almost expect the distillery to be perched on a cliff-top, battered by the ocean waves. It is a coastal distillery, but its position is a little more serene, in a quiet bay on the southern shore of the island.

The signature note of Laphroaig is apparent before you step inside. As one of the very few distilleries to have retained its floor maltings, you can see and smell the plumes of peat smoke wafting from the pagoda roof above the kiln. While the maltings provide only some of the malt needed, they do make visiting the distillery particularly interesting. Until 50 years ago, this was how all malt whisky was made.

Other factors that make Laphroaig special include the long years in wood and a unique set of stills. The dominant note remains the same today as it was in the 19th century. Then, when the whisky writer Alfred Barnard asked about the influence of the sea air, he was told it had no effect whatsoever. It was all down to peat.

▲ A SEASIDE LOCATION
It is tempting to relate the maritime character of Laphroaig to the distillery's dramatic position by the sea. Though hard to prove, the whisky does have a distinct taste of seaweed.

▼ SOFT, PEATY WATER
An abundant supply of water is vital for any distillery, yet many believe the character of the water has a minimal effect on the whisky's flavour. Laphroaig's whisky-makers disagree, and say the soft, peaty water from Loch Kilbride is an important factor.

▲ TURNING THE WET BARLEY
Having been steeped in water, the wet barley is spread across a stone floor, about 15cm (6in) deep. It is turned regularly with wooden shiels (broad shovels) to prevent the shoots matting together as the barley starts to germinate. After six days this "green" malt is ready for the kilns.

▼ A UNIQUE SET OF STILLS

Laphroaig has three wash stills and four spirit stills in two different sizes, which is very unusual. Another uncommon feature of the stills is the way the lyne arms slope upwards rather than downwards. This increases reflux during the long, slow distillation.

▼ PEATING BEFORE KILNING

The green malt is spread on a wire mesh suspended 5m (15ft) above a kiln, filled with peat. The kiln is fired up, and dense smoke immediately begins to impregnate the grains of malt. Unlike any other Scotch malt distillery, Laphroaig peats the malt first and then dries it afterwards. It is maintained that this gives the whisky a much wider range of smoke flavours.

◄ CASKING STRENGTH

The middle cut from the spirit stills comes in at a strength of 68% ABV which is then reduced to 63.5% ABV before filling into casks. This is thought to be the most desirable strength for the maturation process.

LONG YEARS IN WOOD ►

The casks used at Laphroaig are almost entirely from Maker's Mark (see pp.244–245), its sister distillery in the US. Maturation is said to account for a third of the character of the whisky. Recently, the distillery began using quarter casks to increase the ratio of wood to whisky and speed up the process.

LINKWOOD FLORA & FAUNA 12-YEAR-OLD

THE LAST DROP

www.lastdropdistillers.com

This unusual super-premium blend is the brainchild of three industry veterans – Tom Jago, James Espey, and Peter Fleck. Allegedly, a random discovery of very old whiskies pre-vatted at 12 years of age and then allowed to mature for a further 36 years in sherry casks, The Last Drop would appear to have been something of an accident and cannot be repeated. Included in the blend are whiskies from long-lost distilleries, the youngest reputed to have been distilled in 1960. Savour the tasting notes – at £1,000 or so a bottle and with only 1,347 bottles available, it may be the closest you'll get to tasting it.

THE LAST DROP

BLEND 54.5% ABV
Exceptionally complex nose, with figs, chocolate, and vanilla. An unusual combination of new-mown hay, dried fruit, herbs, and buttery biscuits.

LAUDER'S

Owner: MacDuff International

Between 1886 and 1893, Lauder's Royal Northern Cream scooped up a total of six gold medals in international competitions – a tribute to the meticulous research and repeated trials undertaken by the original proprietor, Archibald Lauder, a Glasgow publican. The development of the blend is said to have taken him two years. Today, Lauder's is once again blended in Glasgow, by MacDuff International, and Lauder's Bar on Sauchiehall Street remains to commemorate Lauder himself. His blend has largely slipped from public view in its homeland, but is imported by Barton Brands of Chicago to the US, where it remains popular among value-conscious consumers.

LAUDER'S

BLEND 40% ABV
A light and fruity blend designed for session drinking and mixing.

LEDAIG

Tobermory Distillery,
Tobermory, Isle of Mull

Tobermory, the capital of Mull and the island's main port, was originally called Ledaig, and this was the name chosen by John Sinclair when he began distilling here in 1798. Quite when the Ledaig Distillery became Tobermory is unclear, as it has had an incredibly interrupted life, spending more time in mothballs than in production. In recent years, the distillery adopted a similar approach to Springbank, producing a heavily peated robust West Coast malt called Ledaig and a lightly peated malt called Tobermory. At present, 10- and 18-year-old expressions of Ledaig are available, along with 10- and 15-year-old Tobermorys *(see p.170).*

LEDAIG 10-YEAR-OLD

SINGLE MALT: ISLANDS 43% ABV
Slightly medicinal, but full of dry, slightly dusty peat smoke.

LINKWOOD

Elgin, Morayshire
www.malts.com

From the outset, Linkwood was a well-conceived, almost self-sufficient distillery. It was named after Linkwood House on the Seafield Estate, where the estate manager, Peter Brown, decided to build a distillery in 1821. It was surrounded by barley fields to supply the grain, and cattle to feed on the spent draff. What you see today, dates back to the 1870s, when Brown's son William demolished the original Linkwood and built a new distillery on the same site. It remained in private hands until 1933, when it became part of DCL. As a supplier of a "top dressing" malt used in many blends, Linkwood was highly regarded, and DCL paid a hefty £80,000 for it, around £4.3 million in today's money.

In 1960, the number of stills was tripled to six, with the new stills

LINKWOOD RARE MALTS 26-YEAR-OLD

LOCH FYNE PREMIUM SCOTCH

LOCH FYNE LIVING CASK

housed in a separate building. Between 2011 and 2013, much of the existing distillery was demolished, and replaced with new structures housing six stills. Linkwood now has a capacity of 5.6 million litres (1.2 million gallons) of spirit per annum.

LINKWOOD FLORA & FAUNA 12-YEAR-OLD

SINGLE MALT: SPEYSIDE 43% ABV
This standard expression is on the lighter side of the Speyside style, with a fresh, grassy, green-apple fragrance and faint notes of spice. In the mouth, it has a delicate sweet-and-sour flavour and a slow finish.

LINKWOOD RARE MALTS 26-YEAR-OLD

SINGLE MALT: SPEYSIDE 56.1% ABV
Bright and breezy for a 26-year-old. Lightly smoky with caramelized sugar notes. Spicy and warm in the finish.

LOCH FYNE

Owner: The Whisky Shop
www.lochfynewhiskies.com

Created by Professor Ronnie Martin, a former production director at United Distillers (now Diageo), Loch Fyne is the exclusive and eponymous house blend of Loch Fyne Whiskies of Inverary. It is blended and bottled under licence for this famous Scottish whisky specialist. The label, incidentally, honours the long-lost Highland distillery Glendarroch.

Slightly sweet and smoky, Loch Fyne is an easy-drinking, well-flavoured blend, which the proprietors describe as "one to drink and enjoy rather than concentrate on". It has been praised by leading critics and won awards in international competitions.

Also available is a full-strength 12-year-old liqueur, which comes in a 70cl decanter. Created for whisky-lovers on the look-out for a sophisticated and complex

alternative, it can be enjoyed on its own, but is notably successful as a mixer or cocktail ingredient.

In addition to this, Loch Fyne has an ongoing whisky project in the shape of the Living Cask. Inspired by the way whisky was kept and drunk prior to the ubiquity of bottles, this is a cask used simultaneously for maturing and serving. The cask is filled with a vatting of malt whiskies, and tapped halfway down for drawing off bottlings. When about half the contents has been used, it is filled to the top again, so creating an everchanging blended malt, which can be bought in 20cl sample bottles at cask strength.

LOCH FYNE PREMIUM SCOTCH

BLEND 40% ABV
Apple dumplings on the nose, enlivened by orange and tangerine notes. Subtle, with nutty, oil-related aromas and hints of smoke. The palate is smooth and well-balanced: acidic, salty, sweet, and dry. The finish is surprisingly warming.

LOCH LOMOND

Alexandria, Dumbartonshire
www.lochlomondgroup.com

Within the confines of the Loch Lomond Distillery, on the southern end of Loch Lomond, all manner of Scotch whiskies are produced, although originally it was just malt. The distillery was built in 1965 as a joint venture between Barton Brands of America and Duncan Thomas. Twenty years later, it was bought by Glen Catrine Bonded Warehouse Ltd. and is now owned by Exponent Private Equity. Today, grain whisky is produced alongside the malt. The distillery's stills have rectifying columns that can be adjusted to produce a lighter or heavier spirit.

LOCH LOMOND

SINGLE MALT: HIGHLANDS 40% ABV
With no age statement and a competitive price, this is likely to be a fairly young single malt. It has a light, fresh flavour and no great influence of wood.

LONGMORN 16-YEAR-OLD

LONGMORN CASK STRENGTH

LONGMORN BITTER SWEET BARLEY 1997 (WEMYSS)

LONG JOHN

Owner: Chivas Brothers

Despite reasonably healthy sales in France, Scandinavia, and some Spanish-speaking markets, Long John appears very much the poor relation in the Chivas Brothers' stable, dominated as it is by Chivas Regal and Ballantine's. The brand has passed through a number of owners since it was founded in the early 19th century by the eponymous Long John MacDonald.

In the past, Long John has produced and marketed 12- and 15-year-old expressions, but today, the concentration is on the standard non-age version.

LONG JOHN 12-YEAR-OLD

BLEND 40% ABV
A deluxe blend, Long John 12-year-old is a dark, traditional style of whisky, noted for its distinctive character. The blend is said to contain 48 different malts, including Laphroaig and Highland Park.

LONGMORN

Elgin, Morayshire

John Duff was 52 when he went into partnership with George Thomson and Charles Shirres in 1894. Together, they built Longmorn, in a village of the same name just south of Elgin. The distillery occupies the site of an old chapel (Longmorn means "place of the holy man" in Gaelic) and, with its four stills, it was conceived on a grand scale at a cost of £20,000 (around £2 million in today's money). Yet, within five years, Duff had bought out his partners and built another distillery, BenRiach, next door. While BenRiach has often struggled, Longmorn has been in almost continuous production since the start. It seems this classic, floral Speyside malt was just what the blenders wanted.

In 1970, Longmorn formed a small group with Glenlivet and Glen Grant, which had become part of Seagram by the end of the decade. Aside from independent expressions, a distillery bottling appeared in Seagram's Heritage Selection of malts in 1994.

Since 2000, Longmorn has been owned by Chivas Brothers, the whisky arm of drinks giant Pernod Ricard, which has replaced the existing 15-year-old with one a year older and clearly aimed at the super-premium category of malts.

Meanwhile, its valuable blending role sees it feated in several of Chivas Brothers' high-end blends, including the Royal Salute range and Chivas Regal 18-year-old.

In 2012, Longmorn underwent major expansion work, with a new lauter mash tun being fitted, along with three additional stainless steel washbacks. The four pairs of stills have been adapted to save energy in line with Chivas Brothers' overall policy in that area, and capacity has been extended by around 30 per cent to 4.5 million litres (990,000 gallons) per year.

LONGMORN 16-YEAR-OLD

SINGLE MALT: SPEYSIDE 48% ABV
Its cereal aroma is sweetened with coconut from ageing in bourbon casks. The mouthfeel is smooth and silky and dries on the tongue to give a crisp, slightly austere finish.

LONGMORN CASK STRENGTH

SINGLE MALT: SPEYSIDE 56.9% ABV
The nose is floral, with rose water, soft toffee, lemon, and sweet oak. Rich on the palate, with more rose and lemon, plus milk chocolate. Creamy and sweet in the finish.

LONGMORN BITTER SWEET BARLEY 1997 (WEMYSS)

SINGLE MALT: SPEYSIDE 46% ABV
Notably fruity on the nose, with sweet barley notes, figs, and hazelnuts. Vanilla, ripe peach, and coconut feature on the warming palate, closing with spicy biscuits.

LONGROW PEATED

LONGROW RED

LONGROW 18-YEAR-OLD

LONGROW

Springbank Distillery,
Well Close, Campbeltown, Argyll
www.springbankwhisky.com

After being Scotland's most famous whisky town, Campbeltown suffered a swift and brutal demise. As blenders began to source their malt from Speyside, it turned to the US, until Prohibition shut that market down in 1919. From over a dozen distilleries, only Springbank and Glen Scotia were left by 1935.

In 1973, Springbank decided to distil a pungent, heavily smoked whisky alongside its main malt. The new whisky was christened Longrow after a distillery that had once stood next door. It was released as an experiment in 1985 and finally became a regular fixture in 1992.

Today, the core range includes Longrow, Longrow Red, and Longrow 18-year-old, the last released in small amounts from time to time. Various limited-

release expressions have been added, including one finished in old Barolo casks.

LONGROW PEATED

SINGLE MALT: CAMPBELTOWN 46% ABV
The nose offers vanilla, brine, and peat smoke, while the relatively light palate features early orchard fruits and milk chocolate before more brine and smoke appear and really make their presence felt.

LONGROW RED

SINGLE MALT: CAMPBELTOWN 52.9% ABV
Smoked fish, coal tar soap, citrus fruit, and new leather on the peaty nose. Mouth-coating, with rich peat on the palate, plus fruity spice, redcurrants, and liquorice, leading into a long finish.

LONGROW 18-YEAR-OLD

SINGLE MALT: CAMPBELTOWN 46% ABV
The nose is oily, with sherry, brine, figs, and spicy peat. Citrus fruit and earthy peat on the full, oily, palate, with smoked fish and barbecue notes.

THE MACALLAN

Easter Elchies, Craigellachie, Morayshire
www.themacallan.com

The Macallan stands on the west bank of the Spey, just across the river from Craigellachie and well beyond the bustle of Dufftown and the Speyside whisky trail. The signpost to the distillery is discreet, and visitors tend to come privately, by appointment.

It was first licensed in 1824 as the Elchies Distillery by Alexander Reid, a tenant farmer on Easter Elchies farm. It was a small-scale operation, run as a sideline to the main business of farming. At certain times of year, however, there would have been a good passing trade of cattle drovers on their way to and from the big markets to the south. Being close to a ford through the river, the farm became a good stopping place for them to rest, swap stories, and buy whisky.

Annual production at Macallan was still only 180,000 litres (40,000 gallons) when it was sold to Roderick Kemp in 1892. The distillery was expanded and remained in family control until 1996, when it was bought by Highland Distillers (now part of Edrington), for £180 million. Ironically, Highland had made an unsolicited bid for Macallan back in 1898. Its offer then was a modest £80,000, which was turned down flat.

In the intervening years, the distillery was rebuilt in the 1950s and the number of stills grew to 21. More importantly, The Macallan 10-year-old, launched in 1978, established itself as one of the leading single malts on Speyside.

The distillery had always made a virtue of its use of sherry casks, which were carefully selected and shipped in from Spain. A deep amber colour and fruitcake character came to symbolize the whisky. So the launch of the Fine Oak series in 2004, which uses bourbon casks alongside sherry butts, marked a radical departure.

In 2012, Macallan began to phase in a new core range to replace Sherry Oak and Fine Oak, all expressions being without age statements. They are Gold, Amber, Sienna, and Ruby.

THE MACALLAN GOLD

SINGLE MALT: SPEYSIDE 40% ABV
The nose offers apricots and peaches, fudge, and a hint of leather. Medium-bodied, with malt, walnuts, and spices on the palate. Quite oaky in the medium-length finish.

THE MACALLAN FINE OAK 10-YEAR-OLD

SINGLE MALT: SPEYSIDE 40% ABV
With less sherry influence than the standard 10-year-old, more of the fresh, brisk, malty distillery character comes through.

THE MACALLAN 25-YEAR-OLD

SINGLE MALT: SPEYSIDE 43% ABV
Spicy citrus notes accompany the ripe dried-fruit character from the sherry casks, which lead to a little wood-smoke on the tongue.

THE MACALLAN 30-YEAR-OLD

SINGLE MALT: SPEYSIDE 43% ABV
A big, post-prandial malt with a sweet, sherried nose and spicy flavours of orange peel, cloves, and dates that linger on the finish.

THE MACALLAN FINE OAK 10-YEAR-OLD

THE MACALLAN 25-YEAR-OLD

THE MACALLAN 30-YEAR-OLD

THE SECRETS OF...
MACALLAN

Of everything that goes into making malt whisky, the greatest impact comes from wood, and this is something that Macallan understood and appreciated long before many of its rivals.

Maturation is something that the Speyside distillery has always taken very seriously, and the insistence on expensive sherry butts rather than far cheaper bourbon barrels goes way back. The rich, nutty flavour from the sherry casks remains the signature tune to The Macallan, though The Fine Oak range, launched in 2004, now provides a partly bourbon-matured alternative.

Yet, while maturation may be the biggest single influence on the whisky, the casks can only work their magic on what the distillery provides in terms of new make spirit. The unique character of this is determined by a host of factors – from the choice of barley, to the shape of the stills, to the speed of distillation.

Among the most important choices is selecting the final "cut" – that part of the spirit between the foreshots and the feints that is kept. The Macallan prides itself on taking one of the finest cuts of any distillery in Scotland. Typically, just 16 per cent of what flows from the spirit still is filled into casks.

▲ A FARM DISTILLERY
Long before the distillery was founded in 1824, local farmers were distilling whisky from the barley in surrounding fields. This would have been offered to the drovers who stopped here on their way to market.

▲ DOUGLAS FIR WASHBACKS
Macallan has used stainless-steel washbacks for many years, but, as part of a recent expansion, a new set of six Douglas fir washbacks were built, so now fermentation is carried out in both wood and metal.

SQUAT STILLS ▶
The seven wash stills at the distillery work in tandem with 14 spirit stills – these being the smallest on Speyside. Their unique shape and size helps maximize the contact between the liquid and the copper. This strips out some of the heavier sulphur compounds, leaving the new make spirit clean and fruity.

◀ THE LONG SLEEP

Having been diluted to a strength of 69.8% ABV with water from the estate, the spirit is filled into casks and left to slumber. A quarter of the 140,000 casks are stored in Macallan's 16 traditional dunnage warehouses, which are cool and damp, with earth floors and stone walls. The rest of the casks are kept in five modern-racked warehouses that have recently been built on site.

▲ SHERRY AND BOURBON

Although most of the casks in Macallan's warehouses are sherry butts, you can also find puncheons, barrels, and ex-bourbon hogsheads shipped over from Kentucky. The sherry casks are a mixture of European and American oak.

▲ THE FLAVOUR PROFILE

The key flavours of The Macallan can be explored in an interactive display at the distillery's visitor centre. Traditional Macallan takes a floral, quite fruity Speyside spirit and coats it with a rich layer of spicy sherry flavours. The relatively new Fine Oak range has a fresher, more delicate flavour, with the distillery character more pronounced

MANNOCHMORE FLORA & FAUNA 12-YEAR-OLD

MANNOCHMORE RARE MALTS 22-YEAR-OLD

MACARTHUR'S

Owner: Inver House Distillers

The MacArthur clan of Argyllshire fought nobly alongside Robert the Bruce in the struggle for Scottish independence and subsequently gave their name to this standard blend. Like so many others, it has its roots in the upsurge of blending from independent merchants in the late-Victorian era and can be traced to the 1870s. Today, it is owned by Inver House Distillers, who describe it as having a "light, smooth flavour with toffee and vanilla from cask ageing". MacArthur's is not to be confused with single malts bottled independently under the label James MacArthur.

MACARTHUR'S

BLEND 40% ABV

Fragrant, barley-malt nose with sweet, citrus aftertones. A medium-bodied, uncomplicated whisky, softly aromatic, with a smooth, mellow palate and a fresh, lingering finish.

MAC NA MARA

Owner: The Gaelic Whisky Co.
www.gaelicwhisky.com

Despite its Irish-sounding name, which means "son of the sea" in Gaelic, Mac Na Mara hails from the Isle of Skye whisky company Pràban na Linne (also known as the Gaelic Whisky Company).

A lighter blended whisky with some West Coast character, it was first introduced in 1992 and became popular in France, where the company enjoys its strongest following. A Rum Finish version is also offered from time to time. Unusually for a blended whisky, this is non-chill filtered and aged for a further 12 months in Guyanan rum casks for a sweet finish.

MAC NA MARA

BLEND 40% ABV

A light and essentially undemanding blended whisky with a biscuit-like nose, a citrus tang, and a creamy finish.

MANNOCHMORE

Elgin, Morayshire
www.malts.com

This modern distillery was part of the Haig empire – a separate fiefdom within the Distillers Company Limited. It was built in 1971 as one of a cluster of distilleries between Elgin and Rothes. Nearby are Longmorn and BenRiach, while almost next door is Glenlossie, which has operated in tandem with Mannochmore from the start, sharing the same workforce and warehouses.

From conception, Mannochmore's simple role in life was supplying malt for Haig, then the top-selling blend in the UK. Fourteen years later, it fell victim to the chronic oversupply in the industry and was mothballed, as the big distillers sought to drain the whisky loch. It was back in production by 1989 and launched its first official malt as part of the Flora & Fauna range three years later.

Mannochmore is famous for launching Loch Dhu in 1996. With its distinctive dark colour, it was only produced for four years, but has become something of a cult since, particularly in Denmark. There has been the odd independent bottling, including, in 2014, a 1994 distillation from Gordon & MacPhail, and a 1999 14-year-old from Douglas Laing.

MANNOCHMORE FLORA & FAUNA 12-YEAR-OLD

SINGLE MALT: SPEYSIDE 43% ABV

This is very much an aperitif-style malt, with a light, floral nose but, in the mouth, a more luscious, spicy character, with hints of liquorice and vanilla, comes through.

MANNOCHMORE RARE MALTS 22-YEAR-OLD

SINGLE MALT: SPEYSIDE 60.1% ABV

Distilled in 1974, this limited edition exudes fragrant, flowery aromas. Herbaceous and peppery, with a touch of peat in the mix.

MCCLELLAND'S LOWLAND

MCCLELLAND'S HIGHLAND

MCCLELLAND'S SPEYSIDE

MCCLELLAND'S ISLAY

MCCLELLAND'S

Owner: Morrison Bowmore
www.mcclellands.co.uk

The range of McClelland's single malts offers a chance to explore Scotland and four of its key whisky-distilling regions. It was first launched in 1986, with a Highland, Lowland, and Islay expression. These proved so successful that a Speyside expression was introduced in 1999. According to the company, each one is carefully selected to reflect the true essence and character of the region in which it is produced.

The brand currently claims to be number four in the US market, where it competes against the likes of Glenlivet, Glenfiddich, and The Macallan. McClelland's is also distributed to global markets, including Taiwan, Austria, South Africa, Japan, Canada, France, Russia, and the Netherlands.

MCCLELLAND'S LOWLAND

SINGLE MALT: LOWLANDS 40% ABV
A richly floral nose with hints of nutmeg, ginger, and citrus fruits. Very clean and delicate on the palate, with floral notes.

MCCLELLAND'S HIGHLAND

SINGLE MALT: HIGHLANDS 40% ABV
Delicate wood notes on the nose, with sweet buttercream and fresh vanilla. Some initial sweetness, giving way to fresh fruit and lime hints.

MCCLELLAND'S SPEYSIDE

SINGLE MALT: SPEYSIDE 40% ABV
Fresh mint, cut pine, hints of dark chocolate, and sweet malt on the nose. Initially sweet, developing nutty flavours and floral hints.

MCCLELLAND'S ISLAY

SINGLE MALT: ISLAY 40% ABV
The nose is unmistakably Islay: wood smoke and cinders, tar, vanilla, and citrus hints. Forceful sea salt, burnt oak, and peat smoke, with vanilla undertones on the palate.

MILLBURN

Inverness, Inverness-shire

It was Millburn's misfortune to be located on the outskirts of Inverness on the road to Elgin. When the whisky industry suffered one of its big periodic downturns in the 1980s, the distillery was in the wrong place at the wrong time – not remote enough to simply be mothballed when there was the prospect of redevelopment instead. And so, it shut down for good in 1985 and was turned into a steakhouse; today, it's a hotel and restaurant called The Auld Distillery. Brand owner Diageo released several expressions in its Rare Malts series.

MILLBURN RARE MALTS 25-YEAR-OLD

SINGLE MALT: SPEYSIDE 61.9% ABV
This Rare Malts bottling is a big, meaty whisky that is dry and chewy in the mouth, with damp wood, smoke, and orange skins.

MILTONDUFF

Miltonduff, Elgin, Morayshire

Miltonduff was one of supposedly more than 50 illicit stills in Elgin until it took out a licence in 1824. In 1936, it was bought by George Ballantine & Son. From 1964 until 1981, the distillery had a pair of Lomond stills, allowing it to produce different styles of whisky, such as the single malt Mosstowie. These are now increasingly rare. Pernod Ricard bought Miltonduff in 2005, and uses much of the 5.8 million-litre (1.3 million-gallon) production to supply malt for its Ballantine's Finest blend. An official 16-year-old cask strength malt is now available, with several more bottlings existing among independents.

MILTONDUFF 16-YEAR-OLD CASK STRENGTH

SINGLE MALT: SPEYSIDE 52.9% ABV
Soft nose, with vanilla and citrus, continuing through the cinnamon and toffee palate. Lengthy finish.

MONKEY SHOULDER

Owner: William Grant & Sons

The name may seem contrived, but this blended malt from William Grant & Sons refers to a condition among workers in the maltings – turning the damp grain by hand, they often incurred a repetitive strain injury.

Three metal monkeys decorate the shoulder of the bottle and just three single malts go into the blend – Glenfiddich, Balvenie, and Kininvie. At the launch, great play was made of the whisky's mixability, and you're as likely to encounter it on a cocktail menu as you are in your local off-licence.

MONKEY SHOULDER

BLEND 40% ABV
Banana, honey, pears, and allspice on the nose. Vanilla, nutmeg, citrus hints, and generic fruit on the palate. A dry finish, then a short burst of menthol.

MORTLACH

Dufftown, Keith, Banffshire
www.mortlach.com

Long before the distillery building boom on Speyside, James Findlater became the first licensed distiller in Dufftown in 1823. By the end of the century, the town had no fewer than six distilleries. Mortlach changed hands at regular intervals, and was briefly a brewery and even a temporary home for the Free Church of Scotland at one point. In 1897, the number of stills was doubled to six, making this one of the largest distilleries in the Highlands. It became part of DCL (now Diageo) in 1925, which used its malt in blends, especially Johnnie Walker. The first official bottling as a single malt was not until 1995, when a 22-year-old Rare Malts was released.

The six stills are configured in a uniquely complex manner, with a fifth of the spirit being triple-distilled in an intermediate

MORTLACH 25-YEAR-OLD

OBAN 14-YEAR-OLD

OBAN DISTILLERS EDITION 1992

SINGLE MALT: HIGHLANDS 43% ABV
A 15-year-old malt, aged in different casks during maturation. Spicy and oaky flavours dominate from the strong sherry-wood effect – the result of finishing in Montilla Fino casks.

still called "Wee Witchie". This process is intended to add richness and depth to the spirit, which is then condensed in traditional worm tubs outside, to create a more robust style of whisky.

Mortlach is ever-popular with blenders, but 2014 saw the single malt given a greatly enhanced profile, with the release of four new expressions, namely Rare Old, Special Strength, 18-year-old, and 25-year-old.

MORTLACH RARE OLD

SINGLE MALT: SPEYSIDE 43.4% ABV
Fresh on the nose; with peaches and apricots, milk chocolate, and finally caramel. Fruit carries over from the nose to the nutty palate, with cinnamon spice.

MORTLACH 25-YEAR-OLD

SINGLE MALT: SPEYSIDE 43.4% ABV
A hint of fresh soil on the nose, with apples, and a slight meatiness. Malt, muted spices, and interplay between sweet and savoury on the palate. Gentle oak finish.

OBAN

www.malts.com

Oban distillery dates back to 1793, when Oban itself was a tiny West Coast fishing village. The town (dubbed "Gateway to the Isles") now surrounds the distillery and prevents any expansion. Due to its small capacity of 700,000 litres (150,000 gallons), Oban was never closed during periods of overproduction, and so it has been in almost continuous production since it was built.

Oban has been one of Diageo's "Classic Malts" since 1990, and is only sold in selected markets. Alongside the official no-age Little Bay and 14-year-old statements, double-matured Distillers Edition malts are released from time to time.

OBAN 14-YEAR-OLD

SINGLE MALT: HIGHLANDS 43% ABV
The brisk, maritime distillery character is mellowed by the years in wood. It has a rich, dried-fruit character.

ALL ABOUT...
BOTTLES

It was only in the late 1880s, with the invention of mechanical glass-blowing, that whisky began to be filled into glass bottles. Prior to this, it was sold in bulk, by the small cask, or the stoneware jar. The advantage of the sealed bottle – until 1913, the seal was always a driven cork, requiring a cork-screw – was that it prevented, or at least discouraged, adulteration. Such bottles, as were used for whisky prior to the 1880s, were recycled wine bottles, made from dark glass – clear glass was taxed at 11 times the rate of dark glass.

STANDARD LIQUOR BOTTLE This shape became the standard bottle for Scotch whisky in the 1890s, although earlier bottles tend to be heavier and of very dark green glass.

PETARD In its shape and use of a small, hand-written label, The Glenrothes petard derives its look from a lab sample bottle. The colour of the liquid is allowed to shine through, and this design embodies integrity. Introduced in 1994, it quickly became known as the "petard" or "grenade".

EMBOSSED Heavily embossed bottles speak of luxury and are especially popular in Asia. Crown Royal was introduced to mark the State Visit of Britain's King George VI to Canada in 1939. The bottle is further "ennobled" by coming in a purple velvet bag.

PINCH George Ogilvy Haig introduced this unusual shape in 1893 for his Dimple brand of Scotch. In the US, it was sold as Pinch, and the bottle shape was the first to be patented under US law, in 1958.

CERAMIC Such vessels hark back to the stoneware jars of the late 19th century. Arthur Bell & Sons have been issuing commemorative bell-shaped Christmas decanters annually since 1988. They have become collectors' items, and some are now very valuable.

SWING Sir Alexander Walker, Johnnie Walker's grandson, created the deluxe blend Swing specifically for luxurious transatlantic liners. The bottle has a rounded base, so it "swings" with the motion of the ship and remains perpendicular!

TRIANGULAR William Grant & Sons introduced this supremely ergonomic shape for their brand Standfast in the mid-1950s, and adopted it in 1964 for Glenfiddich. The innovative shape was created by the modernist designer Hans Schleger.

WAX-SEALED MAKER'S MARK In the late 19th century, some blenders dipped the neck of the bottle in sealing wax, having driven home the cork. This was common practice with port, and made the bottle "tamper-proof". Marge Samuels, wife of the owner of Maker's Mark, applied it to this brand in the 1950s.

DISTILLED, BLENDED & BOTTLED IN SCOTLAND JOHN WALKER & SONS

ESTD 1820

JOHNNIE WALKER®

Swing

EXCEPTIONALLY SMOOTH
SCOTCH WHISKY

Johnnie Walker

KILMARNOCK 43%vol 70cl KA1 1HD SCOTLAND

Grant's
BLENDED SCOTCH WHISKY
THE FAMILY RESERVE
SINCE 1887

William Grant & Sons

1887

Maker
S IV
Ma

KENTUCKY STRAIGHT
WHISKY
HANDMADE

Distilled, aged and bottl
Maker's Mark Distille
Star Hill Farm, Loretto
750mL 45%alc

OLD PARR

Owner: Diageo

"Keep your head cool by temperance and your feet warm by exercise. Rise early, go soon to bed, and if you want to grow fat [prosperous], keep your eyes open and your mouth shut." So said the original "Old Parr", one Thomas Parr, who lived from 1483 to 1635, making him 152 years old when he died. If that seems improbable, his tomb can be inspected in Poets' Corner, Westminster Abbey.

In 1871, Old Parr's name was borrowed by two famous blenders of their day, the Greenlees brothers, for their deluxe whisky. Now under the stewardship of industry giants Diageo, the brand has gone on to success in Japan, Venezuela, Mexico, and Colombia. The square brown bottle appears unchanged in years, and Old Parr whisky has a loyal band of followers who appreciate its distinctive, old-fashioned style.

Old Parr 18-year-old was awarded the title of "World Whisky of the Year" by one popular guide in 2007. By tradition, Cragganmore is the mainstay of the blend.

A few years ago, Old Parr launched a limited edition series that it called the Four Seasons. Comprising blends of carefully selected casks to obtain four styles of whisky with very different characteristics, the series has become something of a collector's item, with the Autumn expression in particular having become extremely rare.

GRAND OLD PARR 12-YEAR-OLD

BLEND 43% ABV

Pronounced malt, raisin, and orange notes on the nose, with some apple and dried-fruit undertones, and perhaps a hint of peat. Forceful on the palate, with flavours of malt, raisin, burnt caramel, and brown sugar.

OLD PULTENEY 12-YEAR-OLD

OLD PULTENEY 17-YEAR-OLD

OLD PULTENEY 21-YEAR-OLD

OLD PULTENEY

Pulteney Distillery, Wick, Caithness
www.oldpulteney.com

Wick, in the far northeast corner of Scotland, is just a short distance from John o'Groats, commonly regarded as Britain's most northerly point. Wick was a tiny village when Sir William Johnstone Pulteney decided to turn it into a major fishing port in the early 1800s. In 1826, with the trade in herring booming, James Henderson built Pulteney in his honour.

The business of fishing, gutting, and packing the herring into barrels was thirsty work, and the town's only distillery thrived. The setting appeared perfect, but dwindled the herring fleet gradually and, in 1922, at the high-water mark of the temperance movement, the town voted to go dry. The distillery closed in 1930 and did not re-open until 1951 – by which time the town was no longer a haven of sobriety.

The solitary wash still comes with a giant ball, to increase reflux, and a truncated top, supposedly lopped off to fit the still room. Pulteney's malts are marketed today as "Old Pulteney".

OLD PULTENEY 12-YEAR-OLD

SINGLE MALT: HIGHLANDS 40% ABV
Launched by Inver House in 1997, two years after buying the distillery, this is a brisk, salty, maritime malt with a woody sweetness from ageing in bourbon casks.

OLD PULTENEY 17-YEAR-OLD

SINGLE MALT: HIGHLANDS 46% ABV
The non-chill filtered big brother of the 12-year-old is partly matured in sherry wood, to add fruity, butterscotch notes to the flavour, which is long with a medium-full body in the mouth.

OLD PULTENEY 21-YEAR-OLD

SINGLE MALT: HIGHLANDS 46% ABV
The sherry influence comes from the American oak used in the cask. The result is a rich, creamy, honey-scented malt that dries on the finish.

OLD SMUGGLER

Owner: Gruppo Campari

Reputedly, and appropriately, a big favourite during Prohibition, Old Smuggler was first developed by James and George Stodart in 1835. Although the firm is today largely forgotten, history records that it was the first to marry its whisky in sherry butts. The brand is now owned by Gruppo Campari, who acquired it along with its sister blend Braemar and the flagship Glen Grant Distillery from Pernod Ricard in 2006. It continues to hold a significant position in the US and Argentina, where it is the second-best-selling whisky, and is reported to be developing strong sales in Eastern Europe.

OLD SMUGGLER

BLEND 40% ABV
Decent Scotch with no offensive overtones and some smoke hints. Blended for value, and for drinking with a mixer.

PASSPORT

Owner: Chivas Brothers

Passport was developed by Seagram and acquired by Pernod Ricard in 2002. Like many brands that are invisible in the UK, it enjoys conspicuous success elsewhere: Passport's main strongholds are the US, South Korea, Spain, and Brazil, where its fruity taste lends itself to being served on the rocks, in mixed drinks and in cocktails. Packaged in a distinctive retro, rectangular green bottle, Passport is "a unique Scotch whisky, inspired by the revolution of 1960s Britain, with a young and vibrant personality". Such distinguished and famous malts as Glenlivet are found in the blend.

PASSPORT

BLEND 40% ABV
A fruity taste and a deliciously creamy finish. It can be served straight or, more usually, mixed over ice. Medium-bodied, with a soft and mellow finish.

PIG'S NOSE

Owner: Spencerfield Spirits
www.spencerfieldspirit.com

Should you visit one of the UK's many agricultural or county fairs, you may well encounter this whisky being sold from the back of an old horse box. Do not walk away: Pig's Nose has been re-blended by Whyte & Mackay's superstar master blender, Richard Paterson, and launched back on to the market in smart new livery. Brother to the better-known blended malt Sheep Dip *(see p.155)*, Pig's Nose is a full-flavoured and drinkable blend that more than lives up to the claim that "our Scotch is as soft and smooth as a pig's nose".

PIG'S NOSE

BLEND 40% ABV
The nose is delicate and refined, with soft and sensual floral notes supported by complex fruit flavours. On the palate, there is a forceful array of malty flavours from Scotland's four distilling regions.

PINWINNIE ROYALE

Owner: Inver House Distillers

Pinwinnie Royale stands out from the crowd, its label hinting at an early ecclesiastical manuscript and regal connections, though there is little to support these romantic suppositions. Given its place in the Inver House stable, it would seem likely that Old Pulteney, Speyburn, anCnoc, and Balblair single malts are to be found in the blend, with the emphasis on the lesser-known names. As well as the standard expression, there is a 12-year-old version, which mixes a light Speyside fruitiness with drier background wood notes, and a buttery texture.

PINWHINNIE ROYALE

BLEND 40% ABV
Young, spirity fruitiness on the nose, smooth-textured but spicy in the mouth, with burnt, sooty notes in the finish.

POIT DHUBH

Owner: The Gaelic Whisky Co.
www.gaelicwhisky.com

Pràban na Linne (known also as the Gaelic Whisky Co.) was established by Sir Iain Noble in 1976 to create employment in the south of Skye. The business has grown steadily since. Poit Dhubh (pronounced *Potch Ghoo*) is a non-chill filtered blended malt supplied as 8-, 12-, and 21-year-olds. A limited edition 30-year-old was bottled for the company's 30th anniversary. Poit Dhubh makes much play of the possible bootleg nature of its whisky, stating, "We are unwilling either to confirm or deny that Poit Dhubh comes from an illicit still." This is, of course, complete fantasy.

POIT DHUBH 8-YEAR-OLD

BLENDED MALT 43% ABV
Dried fruits and a light spiciness give a bitter-sweet character, with dry, woody notes and a trace of peat.

PORT ELLEN

Port Ellen, Isle of Islay

Of all Islay malts, Port Ellen has possibly the largest cult following, owing to its rarity, which has increased every year since the distillery shut down in 1983. It was founded in 1825 by Alexander Kerr Mackay, and remained in family hands until the 1920s, when it became part of DCL (Distillers Company Ltd). Its misfortune was to be part of the same stable as Laphroaig and Caol Ila: when the downturn came, it was the weakest link. Today, it remains active as a maltings plant, supplying Islay's distilleries with most of their malt.

PORT ELLEN DOUGLAS LAING 26-YEAR-OLD

SINGLE MALT: ISLAY 50% ABV
Matured in refill bourbon casks, this bottling has a sweet and fruity nose, with some new leather. Sweetness on the palate, but overwhelmed by peat smoke. A long, tarry finish, with a dab of salt.

PRIME BLUE

Owner: Morrison Bowmore

Prime Blue is a blended malt available largely in Taiwan, where the market has developed in sensational style during the last decade. The colour blue is said to convey nobility and royalty, and the brand name was reputedly chosen to reflect sophistication in the whisky's taste. At their peak, sales exceeded 1 million cases a year, although the market for this style in the Far East has declined somewhat in recent years and competition in Taiwan and elsewhere has intensified.

PRIME BLUE

BLENDED MALT 40% ABV
Aromas of vanilla and malted barley are soon followed by light cocoa, and then heathery, floral notes. Initially fruity on the palate, followed by a malty sweetness, and a long finish.

QUEEN ANNE

Owner: Chivas Brothers

A good example of an "orphan brand" that has found its way into the portfolio of a larger company and appears to lack any clear role and purpose, Queen Anne was once a leading name from the distinguished Edinburgh blenders Hill, Thomson & Co. It was first produced in 1884 and blended by one William Shaw. Today, it belongs to Chivas Brothers. Like so many once-famous and proud brands, Queen Anne has been left bereft and isolated by consolidation in the Scotch whisky industry, steadfastly clinging on in one or more regions where once it was loved and popular.

QUEEN ANNE

BLEND 40% ABV
Not especially characterful, as the flavours are so tightly integrated that it is difficult to discern individual aromas or tastes. A standard blend for mixing.

Hogsheads are assembled from the broken down staves of bourbon barrels. They are about 20 per cent bigger than barrels and, once reassembled, are steam heated to expand the oak and make the joints watertight.

ROBERT BURNS BLEND

ROBERT BURNS SINGLE MALT

ROBERT BURNS

Owner: Isle of Arran Distillers
www.arranwhisky.com

With the Scotch whisky industry
generally apt to employ Scottish
imagery and heritage associations
at the drop of a tam-o'-shanter, it
is a surprise to find that no one
had previously marketed a brand
named after Scotland's national
bard. Independent distiller Isle of
Arran has worked with the World
Burns Federation to fill this gap,
and now produces an officially
endorsed Burns Collection of
blended whiskies and malts.

Naturally, the Robert Burns
brand contains a significant
proportion of Arran single malt,
and is claimed by the company
to "capture the character of our
beautiful island of clear mountain
water and soft sea air". Sadly, it
seems that the poet never actually
visited the Isle of Arran, although
he would have been able to see it
from his Ayrshire home.

Isle of Arran Distillers *(see The
Arran Malt, p.29)* is one of
the few remaining independent
distilleries in Scotland. It was
set up in 1995 by Harold Currie,
who was previously managing
director of Chivas Brothers.

ROBERT BURNS BLEND

BLEND 40% ABV
*Hints of oak on the nose give way
to sherry, almonds, toffee, and ripe
fruits. Plenty of toffee, cake, and
dried fruits on the palate, with a
light to medium, spicy finish.*

ROBERT BURNS SINGLE MALT

SINGLE MALT 40% ABV
*A nose of green apples, the acidity
tempered by a note of vanilla. Apple
and citrus notes on the palate, balanced
by vanilla again. An aperitif whisky
that is light in style and finish.*

ROSEBANK

Camelon, Falkirk

Few distilleries have managed
to stay in continuous production.
Many closed during the 1980s and
'90s when the industry was dealing
with over-supply. Whether a
distillery survived when demand
picked up depended largely on
location. Rosebank, near Falkirk,
was mothballed in 1993 and has
since been redeveloped into offices
and flats. Founded in 1840, it was
chosen to be part of The Ascot Malt
Cellar in 1982. Unfortunately for
Rosebank, when this became the
'Classic Malts' series, Glenkinchie
was picked to represent the
Lowlands rather than Rosebank.

ROSEBANK DOUGLAS LAING 16-YEAR-OLD

SINGLE MALT: LOWLANDS 50% ABV
*This independent bottling from
Douglas Laing is part of its Old Malt
Cask collection. Despite its strength
and age, it is fresh and citrussy.*

ROYAL BRACKLA

Cawdor, Nairn, Nairnshire

Brackla was founded between the
River Findhorn and the Murray
Firth by Captain William Fraser
in 1812. He was soon complaining
that, although he was surrounded
by whisky-drinkers, he could only
sell 450 litres (100 gallons) a year.
By way of compensation, he
secured the first royal warrant
for a distillery in 1835. Whether
he would recognize Royal Brackla
today seems unlikely: it was fully
modernized in the 1970s and 1990s
and now belongs to Bacardi, who
launched 12-, 16-, and 21-year-old
expressions in 2015.

ROYAL BRACKLA 12-YEAR-OLD

SINGLE MALT: HIGHLANDS 40% ABV
*Ripe peaches, spice, walnuts, malt,
honey, vanilla, and a slightly herbal
note on the nose. Spice, sweet sherry,
and mildly smoky orchard fruit on
the full palate, closing with cocoa
and ginger.*

ROYAL LOCHNAGAR 12-YEAR-OLD

ROYAL LOCHNAGAR SELECTED RESERVE

ROYAL LOCHNAGAR DISTILLERS EDITION 2000

ROYAL LOCHNAGAR

Ballater, Aberdeenshire
www.malts.com

This charming distillery sits alone on Deeside as the only whisky-making business in the area. It was founded by John Begg in 1845 as New Lochnagar, to distinguish it from a distillery of the same name that had stood on the other bank, only to be washed away in the great Muckle Spate of 1829. Begg wasted no time in asking his new neighbours at Balmoral – Queen Victoria and Prince Albert – to look round his distillery in 1848. By the end of the year, Lochnagar had become Royal Lochnagar.

Begg prospered until he sold out to John Dewar & Sons in 1916, by which point the malt had become a key component in VAT 69.

With a production of just 400,000 litres (90,000 gallons) from its single pair of stills, it is a fairly pocket-sized distillery and, being so far from any others, it must have felt vulnerable at times. Yet, in recent years, its owner, Diageo, has lavished lots of money and attention on Royal Lochnagar. A Distillers Edition expression featuring a Moscatel finish was launched in 2008, and, in 2013, a Triple Matured bottling was released exclusively to Friends of the Classic Malts.

ROYAL LOCHNAGAR 12-YEAR-OLD

SINGLE MALT: HIGHLANDS 40% ABV
A subtle, leathery nose with a flavour that becomes drier and more acidic before a spicy, sandalwood finish.

ROYAL LOCHNAGAR DISTILLERS EDITION 2000

SINGLE MALT: HIGHLANDS 48% ABV
Pears poached in dessert wine on the malty, gingery nose. The rich palate offers ripe peaches, figs, ginger, and cloves, closing with nutty spice.

ROYAL SALUTE 21-YEAR OLD

ROYAL SALUTE, THE HUNDRED CASK SELECTION

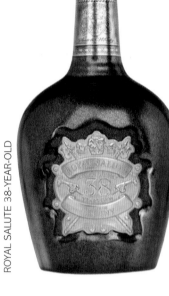

ROYAL SALUTE 38-YEAR-OLD

ROYAL SALUTE

www.royalsalute.com

Originally produced by Seagram in 1953 to commemorate the coronation of Queen Elizabeth II, Royal Salute claims to be the first super-premium whisky. Today, it remains market leader in the over 21 years category.

Historically, Chivas Brothers were noted for their exceptional stocks of rare, aged whiskies, and these formed the basis for the Royal Salute expressions. The company is now controlled by Pernod Ricard, whose blenders, led by the highly respected Colin Scott, have access to single malts from such well-known distilleries as Glenlivet, Aberlour, Strathisla, and Longmorn.

Given the veneration and respect accorded to age by consumers in the Far East, it is no surprise that Royal Salute is particularly successful in Asia, especially in China (where Chivas has invested much effort), Taiwan, Korea,

and Vietnam. Duty-free shops also provide a major source of sales.

The various expressions have won an impressive range of medals, including major awards at the International Wine and Spirit Competition.

ROYAL SALUTE 21-YEAR-OLD

BLEND 40% ABV

Soft, fruity aromas balanced with a delicate floral fragrance and mellow, honeyed sweetness.

ROYAL SALUTE, THE HUNDRED CASK SELECTION

BLEND 40% ABV

Elegant, creamy, and exceptionally smooth, with a mellow, oaky, slightly smoky finish.

ROYAL SALUTE 38-YEAR-OLD

BLEND 40% ABV

Rich notes of cedarwood and almond, with a sherried oakiness. Dried fruits linger with an assertive spiciness. An experience, even for the connoisseur.

SCAPA

St Ola, Orkney
www.scapamalt.com

Founded in 1885 on the "Mainland", as Orcadians call the largest of the Hebridean islands, Scapa kept going more or less continuously until 1994, when it was shut down. Although production resumed three years later, it was only on a seasonal basis, using staff from its neighbour, Highland Park. For years it seemed there was only room for one viable distillery on Orkney – that being Highland Park – but Scapa's rescue came in the form of Allied Domecq, and over £2 million was lavished on it in 2004. The company has since been bought by Chivas Brothers.

SCAPA 16-YEAR-OLD

SINGLE MALT: ISLANDS 40% ABV
The nose offers apricots and peaches, nougat, and mixed spices. Medium-bodied, with caramel and spice notes on the palate, leading to a gingery, buttery finish.

SCOTTISH LEADER

Owner: Burn Stewart Distillers
www.scottishleader.com

The owner describes Scottish Leader as "An international award-winning blend with a honey rich smooth taste profile. It has a growing presence in a number of world markets". The blend's heart is Deanston single malt, from the Perthshire distillery of the same name. Although it was initially targeted at the value-conscious supermarket buyer, Scottish Leader has subsequently been repackaged and moved somewhat upmarket. Today, there are Original, Signature, Supreme, and 12-year-old expressions.

SCOTTISH LEADER

BLEND 40% ABV
A standard blend in which the flavour characteristics are tightly integrated. Not much to mark it out, but okay for mixing or drinking on the rocks.

SHEEP DIP

Owner: Spencerfield Spirits
www.spencerfieldspirit.com

Sheep Dip is one of the better blended malts. The brand has been around since the 1970s but, under the ownership of Whyte & Mackay, was largely ignored. In 2005, it was taken on by Alex and Jane Nicol, who aim to rebuild the former glory of so-called "orphan brands". Since then, they've introduced new packaging, appointed a global network of agents and, most important of all, reformulated the whisky under the guidance of master blender Richard Paterson. It seems to be working. The whiskies are aged between 8 and 12 years in quality first-fill wood, producing a great dram.

SHEEP DIP

BLENDED MALT 40% ABV
The nose is delicate and refined. Great finesse on the palate, then a majestic assertion of pure malty flavours.

SOMETHING SPECIAL

Owner: Chivas Brothers

It's quite a name to live up to, but "something special" is a justifiable claim for this premium blend, which, with sales of over half a million cases, is the third best-selling whisky in South America. The blend dates back to 1912, when it was created by the directors of Hill Thompson & Co. of Edinburgh. The primary component is drawn from Speyside malts, especially the highly regarded Longmorn, which is at the heart of the blend. A 15-year-old version was launched in 2006. The distinctive bottle is said to have been inspired by an Edinburgh diamond-cutter.

SOMETHING SPECIAL

BLEND 40% ABV
A distinctive blend of dry, fruity, and spicy flavours, with a subtle, smoky, sweetness on the palate.

ALL ABOUT...
WHISKY GLASSES

The traditional whisky glass is a cut crystal "Old-fashioned" glass. It was invented for drinking brandy and soda (with ice) in the 1840s, and was adopted 30-odd years later for drinking blended Scotch (with soda and ice) or an "old-fashioned" cocktail, which consists of sugar syrup, Angostura bitters, ice cubes, and bourbon or rye whiskey. Fine for drinking long, it is hopeless for appreciating the aroma and taste of malt whisky – or indeed of any whisky worthy of consideration. For this, you need a glass that will present the aroma to the best advantage.

COPITA Also known as a *catavino* – and adopted and adapted from sherry glasses – the copita is the industry standard glass for the organoleptic assessment of whisky. It has a bowl, so you can swirl the liquid and release its aroma, and the rim narrows, so the aroma is presented to the nose extremely well.

THE RIEDEL "GLAS" Founded in Austria in 1756, and still managed by descendants of the founder, Riedel is the world's leading manufacturer of glasses designed specifically for wines and spirits. Georg Riedel, the current president of the company, created this glass in 1992, but now admits that it was his one failure. Its straight sides do not gather the aroma, although the lip presents the spirit nicely on the palate.

THE GLENCAIRN GLASS The malt whisky industry wanted something more robust than a copita, so Glencairn Crystal in Glasgow came up with a stocky glass, reminiscent of a pot still. It is widely used in the whisky world.

THE SINGLE MALTS OF SCOTLAND GLASS Developed by The Whisky Exchange, London, to showcase their range of malts of the same name, this glass is good for both nosing and tasting.

OLD-FASHIONED GLASS Often made of crystal, an old-fashioned glass is designed for a long drink with lots of ice. Since the liquid will "sweat", coasters should be provided. A smaller version is called a "jigger" and is used as a measure.

THE GLENMORANGIE GLASS This small, elegant glass was first adopted and promoted by Glenmorangie. It is standard practice in the whisky trade to place a cover on the glass, to hold in the aromas – usually a watch glass is used. Glenmorangie went further with this charming little lid.

QUAICH The Celtic *quaich* ("koo-ayk") is a very ancient drinking vessel. The shape is thought to have evolved from that of a scallop shell. Early examples are wooden, but today, they are typically of silver or pewter. The Scotch whisky industry's most exclusive club is The Keepers of the Quaich.

SPRINGBANK 10-YEAR-OLD

SPRINGBANK 15-YEAR-OLD

SPEY

Glen Tromie, Kingussie, Inverness-shire
www.speysidedistillery.co.uk

With a production of just 600,000 litres (130,000 gallons), the Speyside distillery, named after Scotland's biggest malt whisky region, is no giant. Nor is it all that old. Despite its rustic appearance – only a discreet modern smoke stack belies its youth – Speyside was commissioned in 1962 by the blender and bottler George Christie. Built stone-by-stone, it was not finished until 1987. In 2012, the distillery was acquired by Harvey's of Edinburgh, and, since 2015, its single malt has been marketed as Spey.

SPEY 12-YEAR-OLD

SINGLE MALT: SPEYSIDE 40% ABV
Fresh and relatively light on the nose, with roasted barley, cooking apples, and nutty vanilla. More vanilla on the palate, along with walnuts, dried fruit, and brittle toffee.

SPEYBURN

Rothes, Aberlour, Morayshire
www.speyburn.com

Whether she knew it or not, Queen Victoria's loyal subjects at the newly built Speyburn Distillery near Rothes laboured through the night to produce a whisky for her Diamond Jubilee of 1897. It was mid-December and, though the windows were not yet in place and snow was swirling in from outside, the distillery manager ordered the stills to be fired up. Speyburn has retained its Victorian charm and, since 1991, has been owned by Inver House.

SPEYBURN 10-YEAR-OLD

SINGLE MALT: SPEYSIDE 40% ABV
Despite older expressions, including a recently released 25-year-old Solera, the core expression remains the 10-year-old, which has a flavour of vanilla fudge and a sweet, lingering finish.

SPRINGBANK

Campbeltown, Argyll
www.springbankwhisky.com

Springbank was officially founded in 1828, at a time when there were no fewer than 13 licensed distillers in Campbeltown. Although this end of the Mull of Kintyre stills feels pretty cut off by car, it was always a short hop across the Firth of Clyde to Glasgow by ship. And, as the second city of the empire boomed, distilleries like Springbank were on hand to quench its ever-growing thirst. In the other direction there was the US but, when that went dry during Prohibition, and the big blenders turned ever more to Speyside, Campbeltown's demise was swift.

Yet Springbank survived. Much of this must have been down to its continuity: the distillery was originally owned by the Reid family, who sold out to their in-laws, the Mitchells, in the mid-19th century. The Mitchells are still in charge, and have built up a real cult following for their innovative range of single malts.

The distillery itself is quirky in the extreme, and Springbank malts all its own barley requirements in house on a traditional malting floor. It then mashes in a cast iron open mash tun, and the wash still is both directly fired and internally steam-heated. Finally, the mature spirit is bottled on site.

SPRINGBANK 10-YEAR-OLD

SINGLE MALT: CAMPBELTOWN 46% ABV
A complex cocktail of flavours, from ripe citrus fruit to peat smoke, vanilla, spice, and a faint underlying salty tang.

SPRINGBANK 15-YEAR-OLD

SINGLE MALT: CAMPBELTOWN 46% ABV
Sweet toffee and candied peel on the nose give way to more exotic sweet-and-sour flavours in the mouth.

**SPRINGBANK 12-YEAR-OLD
CASK STRENGTH 2014 RELEASE**
SINGLE MALT: CAMPBELTOWN 54.3% ABV
*Christmas cake aromas, with vanilla
and sherry on the nose, plus a maritime
note. The palate is viscous and earthy,
with soft peat smoke, plus spice, ginger,
caramel, and light sherry.*

SPRINGBANK 18-YEAR-OLD
SINGLE MALT: CAMPBELTOWN 46% ABV
*The nose is rich, with sweet sherry,
angelica, and apricots, while the
palate is rounded and confident,
offering fresh fruit, smoke, molasses,
and liquorice, leading into a slowly
drying finish.*

Standing on the shore of Loch Indaal, Bowmore is Islay's oldest distillery. It was founded in 1779 by a local farmer *(see p. 51)*, who in its early years complained of having an insufficient supply of barley due to the number of illicit distillers on the island.

STEWARTS CREAM OF THE BARLEY

Owner: Chivas Brothers

First produced around 1831, this old-established brand is today a bestseller in Ireland. For many years, it enjoyed great popularity in Scotland, too, not least because of its widespread distribution in public house chain of Allied, the owner at the time. Single malt from Glencadam used to be at the heart of the blend. With changes in ownership, Glencadam is now in other hands, but the blend reputedly still contains a healthy proportion of up to 50 different single malts.

STEWARTS CREAM OF THE BARLEY

BLEND 40% ABV

A malty, sweet, soft, and slightly spirity nose. The fruitiness of a young spirit on the palate – spicy, raw, and a little smoky. Peppery, drying, charred-wood finish.

STRATHCLYDE

Owner: Chivas Brothers

Strathclyde first opened in the Gorbels district of Glasgow in 1928, constructed by Long John blended whisky owners Seager Evans & Co. The distillery eventually passed to Allied Domecq, whose investment in the facility increased capacity to 39 million litres (8.6 million gallons) a year. The facility uses two of its column stills for grain whisky, and the other five for grain neutral spirit. Very little Strathclyde is bottled as grain whisky, although a 2001 13-year-old Cask Strength is now available. Strathclyde is considered the most "meaty" of the grain whiskies.

STRATHCLYDE CASK STRENGTH 13-YEAR-OLD

SINGLE GRAIN 64.4% ABV

Citrus, toffee, and banana, on the nose. Fudge and brandy on the palate, before drying rapidly.

STRATHISLA

Keith, Banffshire
www.maltwhiskydistilleries.com

In 1786, Alexander Milne and George Taylor founded the Milltown Distillery in Keith. The whisky it produced was known as Strathisla and, in 1951, this was adopted as the name for the distillery. Over the years, Strathisla has survived fires, explosions, and bankruptcy, to become the oldest and possibly most handsome distillery in the Highlands, with a high-gabled roof and two pagodas. Bought by Chivas Brothers in 1950, it has been the spiritual home of Chivas Regal ever since.

STRATHISLA 12-YEAR-OLD

SINGLE MALT: SPEYSIDE 43% ABV

A rich, sumptuous nose and a spicy, fruitcake character, thanks to the influence of sherry. It is medium-bodied, with a slight smoky note on the finish.

STRATHMILL

Keith, Banffshire
www.malts.com

With its twin pagoda roof, this handsome late-Victorian distillery was built in 1891 as the Glenisla-Glenlivet Distillery. Four years later, it was bought by Gilbey's, the London-based gin distiller, and re-christened Strathmill – a reference to the fact that it stood on the site of an old corn mill. A single malt expression was released as early as 1909, but Strathmill's long-term role in life was – and is – to supply malt for blended Scotch, particularly J&B.

STRATHMILL FLORA & FAUNA 12-YEAR-OLD

SINGLE MALT: SPEYSIDE 43% ABV

On the lighter, more delicate side of Speyside, Strathmill has a nutty, malty character with notes of vanilla from the wood. It is quite soft and medium-sweet on the tongue.

WHISKY STYLES
GRAIN WHISKY

Unlike malt whisky, which is made in pot stills, grain whisky is made using a continuous still (also known as a Coffey or Patent still). It is distilled from a mixture of malted barley and other unmalted cereals, such as wheat or corn (maize). Barley is malted in the conventional way *(see pp.38–39)* and mixed with hot water in a mash tun with the unmalted cereals, which have been cooked under pressure to soften the starch and make it soluble. The resulting sugary liquid (or wort) is then fermented with yeast to produce the wash, ready for distilling.

In the continuous still, the wash passes through two columns fitted with metal plates. Heated wash is pumped into the top of the first column (the analyser), where it meets steam rising up through the column. As alcohol boils at a lower temperature than water, the alcohol can be extracted as vapour. It is then pumped to the base of the second column (the rectifier). The temperature of the column is highest at the base and coolest at the top, so the higher the vapour rises, the greater its alcohol content. The distiller can draw off the resulting grain whisky at the desired strength from one of the plates, where the vapour condenses. Virtually pure alcohol (about 96% ABV) is collected at the top of the column and water discharged at the base. This kind of still can be operated for several weeks continuously.

Like malt whisky, grain whisky is filled into oak casks and matured in warehouses for many years. It tends to be milder in flavour and aroma than malt, and is predominantly used in blending *(see p.78)*. However, a tiny amount is sold as grain whisky. Cameron Brig bottles a single grain 12-year-old and Compass Box sells a delicately flavoured blended grain, called Hedonism.

TALISKER 10-YEAR-OLD
SINGLE MALT: ISLANDS 45.8% ABV
An iconic West Coast malt
with a pungent, slightly peaty
character that has a peppery
catch on the finish.

TALISKER 18-YEAR-OLD
SINGLE MALT: ISLANDS 45.8% ABV
Age has softened the youthful
vigour of the 10-year-old,
and given it a scent of leather
and aromatic smoke and a
creamy, mouth-filling texture.

TALISKER DISTILLERS EDITION 1996

TALISKER 57° NORTH

TALISKER 25-YEAR-OLD

TALISKER 30-YEAR-OLD

TALISKER

Carbost, Isle of Skye
www.discovering-distilleries.com

The Scotch Whisky Industry Record of 1823 lists seven licensed distilleries on Skye, of which none has survived. There were doubtless many illicit stills in operation, but these have all long gone, leaving only Talisker, founded in 1830 by Hugh and Kenneth MacAskill, still going strong. Given Skye's size and proximity to the mainland, it seems odd that it has only one distillery when Islay has so many.

Talisker struggled through the 19th century, being sold in 1857 for just £500. Things picked up when Aberdeen entrepreneur

Roderick Kemp became a co-partner in 1880. As demand from the blenders increased, small steamers began to call at the distillery to discharge grain and load up with casks.

In 1898, Talisker teamed up with Dailuaine, then the largest distillery in the Highlands. In 1916, the venture was bought by a consortium involving Dewar's, the Distillers Company, and John Walker & Sons. Ever since, Talisker has been a key component in Johnnie Walker Black Label.

Until 1928, Talisker was triple-distilled, like an Irish whiskey, which explains why two-wash stills are paired to one-spirit still. The lyne arms have a unique

U shape to increase reflux and produce a cleaner spirit, although the fact that this is then condensed in worm tubs seems contradictory — worm tubs tend to produce a heavier, more sulphurous spirit. Whatever the rationale, it seems to work, and Talisker has won countless awards. The owners have delighted fans by releasing a whole raft of ages and special editions — more than any other Diageo malt.

TALISKER DISTILLERS EDITION 1996

SINGLE MALT: ISLANDS 45.8% ABV
With a maturation that ends in Amoroso sherry casks, it has a peppery, spicy character, softened by a luscious, dried-fruit richness in the mouth.

TALISKER 57° NORTH

SINGLE MALT: ISLANDS 57% ABV
Named in reference to the latitude of the distillery, this is rich, fruity, smoky, peppery, and spicy, with a long finish.

TALISKER 25-YEAR-OLD

SINGLE MALT: ISLANDS 54.2% ABV
A brooding, complex malt, with notes of seaweed and smoke giving way to a leathery, more fruity richness.

TALISKER 30-YEAR-OLD

SINGLE MALT: ISLANDS 49.5% ABV
A highly sophisticated Talisker that's sweet, spicy, fruity, and floral, with understated peat smoke and leather.

THE SECRETS OF...
TALISKER

Distilling whisky on Skye never took off as it did on Islay, possibly because it was always too wet and infertile to grow the barley to kick-start a whisky industry on the island.

In Talisker's case, there was also the local minister to contend with and his weekly sermon on the evils of strong drink. In the 1850s, his prayers were answered when the distillery was sold for a pittance – half what it cost to build.

From this shaky start, Talisker has risen to cult status among its devotees. Its single malts, with their brooding, pungent character that seems to explode with a peppery catch on the finish, have grown evermore popular and garnered many prestigious awards.

Somehow the physical isolation of Talisker, on the shores of Loch Harport, must play a part in its distinctive taste. Unlike on Speyside, where there were always neighbouring distilleries to learn from, Talisker had to work things out for itself. One can imagine early distillers playing with the shape of the lyne arms, adjusting the peating of the barley, the shape of the stills, and the speed of distillation to achieve a desired effect. The result is the Talisker we can taste today, a whisky like no other in Scotland.

▲ SWEET ISOLATION
Though Skye is connected to the mainland by a bridge, Talisker still feels cut off. It sits by the shore of Loch Harport, beneath the blackened, serrated peaks of the Cuillins.

▼ THE WASH STILLS SET-UP
In 1960, Talisker almost burnt down when the door to a wash still was left open, and the volatile liquid ignited. They were replaced with stills of exactly the same shape and size. Quite what their unique shape, with their curious U-shaped lyne arms, give to the final character of the whisky is hard to gauge, but the master distiller at the time did not take any chances.

▲ SUGAR LEVELS IN THE WASH
Samples are taken to find the specific gravity of the wash before fermentation. By checking sugar levels before the yeast enzymes have started their work, the distiller can predict the final alcoholic strength of the wash. The other, less scientific, check is simply to sniff the air and make sure it is sweet and malty.

INCREASED REFLUX ▶
Having three spirit stills for just two wash stills is said to be a hangover from the old days, before 1928, when Talisker was triple distilled, like an Irish whiskey. This must have stripped out much of its character. The lyne arms are flat, rather than tilting down, to increase reflux.

▼ OLD-STYLE WORM TUBS
There is no doubt that having traditional, old-style worm tubs to condense the spirit impacts on the character of the new make. Though the famous U-shaped lyne arms will have increased the amount of copper contact, the use of worm tubs works the other way, ensuring a heavier, more sulphurous spirit. It may appear counter-intuitive, but it certainly seems to work.

▲ THE DUNNAGE WAREHOUSE
While much Talisker is shipped off the island for maturation on the mainland, some casks are matured on site. The old-fashioned dunnage warehouses have a glorious musty smell of damp earth, wood, and sweet, spirity vapours. How much the scent of sea air and seaweed actually penetrates the casks is hard to say, but Talisker does have an unmistakable maritime character

TAMDHU 10-YEAR-OLD

TAMDHU BATCH STRENGTH (BATCH 1)

THE TALISMAN

Tomatin Distillery, Inverness-shire
www.talismanwhisky.co.uk

The Talisman is the house
blend from Tomatin Distillery
(see p.170). As you might
expect, given this, there is
a high proportion of Tomatin
malts in what is a superior blend.
It offers surprises, too: there are
complex and smooth aromas,
with subtle peaty and savoury
overtones, and the grain marries
well with the malt. If you like
your blend smooth but with
a bit of bite, this could be the
one for you.

THE TALISMAN

BLEND 40% ABV

*A complex aroma on the nose: fruits
and maltiness with some pleasing
grain or cereal highlights. Honey
and vanilla with hints of apple on
the palate. Subtle peaty notes linger
to give a long finish.*

TAMDHU

Knockando, Aberlour, Morayshire
Owner: Ian Macleod Distillers
www.tamdhu.com

For all the misty-eyed romance
about Speyside's early roots as
a region teeming with smugglers
and illicit stills, the railways,
which arrived in the second
half of the 19th century, had
a far greater impact. Before the
opening of the Strathspey line
in 1863, the region was simply
too cut-off to flourish. But once
the rails were laid, distilleries
began popping up. One such
was Tamdhu, founded in 1896
between Cardhu and Knockando.
In fact, Knockando's old station
was used as the reception centre
of Tamdhu Distillery.

Tamdhu is a large setup, with
nine pine washbacks, three pairs
of stills, and a mix of dunnage and
racked warehousing on site. The
former Saladin maltings, which
were an interesting feature of

Tamdhu, are now disused. The
distillery was closed in 2010,
and, in 2011, owners Edrington
sold the mothballed distillery
to Ian Macleod Distillers, with
production resuming the following
year. A 10-year-old with a strong
sherry cask maturation influence
is now the principal expression.

TAMDHU 10-YEAR-OLD

SINGLE MALT: SPEYSIDE 40% ABV

*Soft sherry notes on the nose, new
leather, almonds, marzipan, and a
hint of peat. Citrus fruit, gentle spice,
and more sweet sherry on the leathery
palate, which closes with black pepper.*

TAMDHU BATCH STRENGTH (BATCH 1)

SINGLE MALT: SPEYSIDE 58.8% ABV

*Vanilla, toffee, milk chocolate, and
sweet sherry on the nose. The
palate offers orange marmalade,
vanilla, malt, cinnamon, and pepper,
finishing with sherry and nutmeg.*

TAMNAVULIN

Ballindalloch, Banffshire

In 1966, Invergordon Distillers,
now part of Whyte & Mackay,
decided to build a big new
distillery in a picturesque corner
of Upper Speyside by the River
Livet. Its six stills could pump
out as much as 4 million litres
(880,000 gallons) of pure alcohol
a year. Yet, in 1995, Tamnavulin
closed down – the owners, it
seemed, had decided to focus
their attention on their other
distilleries, Dalmore and Jura
in particular. The UB Group
bought Whyte & Mackay in
2007, and now Tamnavulin is
back up and running.

TAMNAVULIN 12-YEAR-OLD

SINGLE MALT: SPEYSIDE 40% ABV

*A light, aperitif-style malt, with
a dry, cereal character and minty
nose. This standard release of the
so-called "Stillman's Dram" is joined
by occasional older expressions.*

TEANINICH FLORA & FAUNA 10-YEAR-OLD

TEANINICH GORDON & MACPHAIL 1991

TEACHER'S

Owner: Beam Suntory
www.teacherswhisky.com

This venerable brand can be dated to 1830, when William Teacher opened a grocery shop in Glasgow. Like other whisky entrepreneurs, he soon branched out into the spirits trade. His sons took over, and blending became increasingly important. In 1884, the trademark Teacher's Highland Cream was registered, and this brand eventually came to dominate the business. The whisky was always forceful in character, built around single malts from Glendronach and Ardmore. Today, it continues to be popular in South America.

TEACHER'S HIGHLAND CREAM

BLEND 40% ABV
Full-flavoured, oily, with fudge and caramel notes on the nose, toffee and liquorice on the palate. A well-rounded, smooth texture and quite a quick finish that leaves the palate refreshed.

TEANINICH

Alness, Ross-shire
www.malts.com

Distillery visitors to the Highland village of Alness, just north of Inverness, rarely notice Teaninich as they make their way to its more famous neighbour Dalmore. And yet Teaninich has been quietly distilling away with barely a break since 1817, when it was set up by Captain Hugh Munro, who named it after his Highland estate beside the River Alness.

Teaninich, it seems, was run as a hobby until 1852, when it was leased out to Robert Pattison of Leith, whose family firm almost brought down the entire whisky industry when it collapsed in 1899. Despite this, the distillery has been in almost continual production, stopping during World War II and briefly again in the 1980s. By then, there were two still rooms working in tandem. These were known as Side A and Side B – not the most

poetic of names, but then no one was interested in marketing Teaninich as a single malt to whisky-drinkers – its role was to supply the spirit for blending.

In 1992, Teaninich's owners, UDV (now Diageo), released a 10-year-old expression. Seven years later, it decommissioned Side B. The distillery crushes its malted barley with an Asnong hammer mill, as opposed to the more traditional roller mills. Whether this affects the flavour of the malt is hard to say.

TEANINICH FLORA & FAUNA 10-YEAR-OLD

SINGLE MALT: HIGHLANDS 43% ABV
The only official distillery bottling is polished and grassy, with a predominantly malty flavour.

TEANINICH GORDON & MACPHAIL 1991

SINGLE MALT: HIGHLANDS 46% ABV
A deep amber, fruitcake-flavoured malt, with notes of mint, tobacco, cloves, and wood smoke.

TÉ BHEAG

Owner: The Gaelic Whisky Co.
www.gaelicwhisky.com

Although it is blended and bottled elsewhere in Scotland, this is another brand from the Pràban na Linne company on Skye (The Gaelic Whisky Company). Té Bheag (pronounced *Chey Vek*) means "the little lady" and is the name of the boat in the logo. It is also colloquial Gaelic for a "wee dram". The blend is popular in France and has won medals in international competition. Té Bheag is non-chill filtered, and Islay, Island, Highland, and Speyside malts aged from 8–11 years are used in the blend.

TÉ BHEAG

BLEND 40% ABV
The nose is fresh, with a citrus note, good richness, a delicate peatiness, and a touch of cereal. Weighty on the palate, with a good touch of liquorice, a toffee-like richness, and some peat.

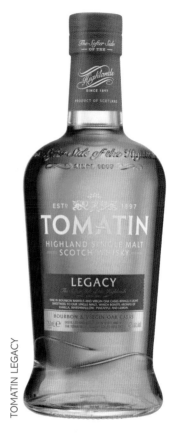

TOBERMORY

Tobermory, Isle of Mull
www.tobermorydistillery.com

If Islay to the south can boast eight working distilleries (at the last count), it seems only fair that Mull should have at least one. And yet, the very survival of Tobermory has been something of a miracle, given that it has spent much of its life lying idle.

Tobermory was founded as the Ledaig Distillery by John Sinclair in 1798. For Sinclair, whisky was a sideline to his main business of dealing in kelp, and, when he died in 1837, the distillery died with him, remaining shut for the next 40 years. It was bought by the Distillers Company in 1916, but became an early casualty of the Depression and closed in 1930.

Once the place had been gutted, few believed whisky would ever be made here again. Then, in 1972, the site was bought and restored by a consortium that included a

shipping company and the famous sherry house of Domecq. The new Ledaig distillery company soon collapsed but, having installed new stills and other whisky-making equipment, Tobermory's future was finally made secure. Production resumed in 1989 and, in 1993, the distillery was bought by its current owner, Burn Stewart.

TOBERMORY 10-YEAR-OLD

SINGLE MALT: ISLANDS 46.3% ABV
This fresh, unpeated, maritime malt claims to have a slight smoky character, thanks to the water from Mull's peat lochans. If true, the effect is subtle.

TOBERMORY 15-YEAR-OLD

SINGLE MALT: ISLANDS 46.3% ABV
The nose has rich fruitcake notes and a trace of marmalade, thanks to ageing in sherry casks. The spicy character comes through on the tongue. It is non-chill filtered.

TOMATIN

Tomatin, Inverness-shire
www.tomatin.com

With 23 stills and a capacity of 12 million litres (2.6 million gallons) of pure alcohol, Tomatin was the colossus of the malt whisky industry in 1974 at the time of its expansion.

Founded in 1897, it took a while to reach its super-size status. Its two stills were increased to four as recently as 1956; thereafter expansion was rapid until it peaked in the 1970s, just in time for the first big post-war slump. Tomatin struggled on as an independent distillery until 1985, when the liquidators arrived. A year later, it was sold to two of its long-standing customers – Takara Shuzo and Okara & Co. – thus becoming the first Scottish distillery in Japanese hands.

With 11 fewer stills, production has been cut back to 5 million litres (1.1 million gallons), which

still allows plenty of capacity for bottling as a single malt. Tomatin's principal bottlings include 12-, 18-, and 30-year-olds, and Legacy, the no-age-statement, while several expressions of peated Tomatin have been released since 2013 under the Cù Bòcan label.

TOMATIN LEGACY

SINGLE MALT: HIGHLANDS 43%ABV
The fragrant nose offers malt, honey, pepper, and faint treacle. The palate is fresh and fruity, with pineapple, pepper, and a suggestion of chilli in the drying finish.

TOMATIN 30-YEAR-OLD

SINGLE MALT: HIGHLANDS 49.3% ABV
A voluptuous after-dinner dram with a big, sherried nose and impressive legs.

TOMATIN 12-YEAR-OLD
SINGLE MALT: HIGHLANDS 40% ABV
A mellow, soft-centred Speyside-style malt, which replaced the old core 10-year-old expression back in 2003.

TOMATIN 18-YEAR-OLD
SINGLE MALT: HIGHLANDS 43% ABV
The deep amber hue betrays a strong sherry influence that brings out a fruity, cinnamon flavour in the malt.

WHISKY STYLES
BLENDED MALT

In 1853, Andrew Usher, an Edinburgh-based wine and spirit merchant, launched the world's first modern brand of Scotch whisky – Old Vatted Glenlivet. Assuming there was no grain spirit in the mix, this would now be called a "Blended Malt", defined by the Scotch Whisky Association (SWA) as "a blend of Single Malt Scotch Whiskies which have been distilled at more than one distillery".

This definition was hammered out when Diageo decided to relaunch the Speyside whisky as a "Pure Malt" in 2002. No longer a "single malt", it meant other malts could be added to Diageo's Cardhu to satisfy surging demand in Spain and perhaps challenge Glenfiddich for poll position among malts. Glenfiddich's owners, William Grant & Sons, were alarmed and led a campaign that provoked the biggest storm in the whisky industry in recent years. There were cries of betrayal, questions in Parliament, and eventually an embarrassing climbdown by Diageo in March 2003.

While Cardhu reverted to being a single malt, the industry had to decide what to call such whiskies in the future. Within the trade they had always been known as vatted malts, though this was thought to have industrial connotations. "Pure malt" sounded better to marketing folk, though it was no longer politically acceptable within the industry. Eventually, having studied Roget's Thesaurus for many months, the committee responsible came up with "blended malt", though many still question whether this will only confuse consumers even more.

TOMINTOUL 10-YEAR-OLD

TOMINTOUL 16-YEAR-OLD

TOMINTOUL PEATY TANG

TOMINTOUL

Kirkmichael, Ballindalloch, Grampian
www.tomintoulwhisky.com

Of all the Speyside distilleries that bolted the magic word "Glenlivet" on to their names in the hope of added lustre, Tomintoul-Glenlivet has the best case, being a virtual next-door neighbour. Tomintoul stands 350m (1,165ft) up, beside the River Avon, the largest tributary of the River Spey. It opened in 1964 – a time of great confidence in the industry, with booming sales of blended Scotch, particularly in export markets such as the US. Tomintoul's role in life was simply to supply malt for these blends. This role continues under Angus Dundee who bought the distillery in 2000 when it was in need of malt for its own blends. And yet, while single malts account for a small fraction of the 3.3 million litres (600,000 gallons) produced each year, the number of expressions has increased greatly. Peaty Tang,

for example, is a vatting of young unpeated malt and even younger peated malt. The distillery's oldest expression is a 40-year-old released in 2015.

TOMINTOUL 10-YEAR-OLD

SINGLE MALT: SPEYSIDE 40% ABV
First launched in 2002, this delicate, aperitif-style malt has some vanilla from the wood and a light cereal character.

TOMINTOUL 16-YEAR-OLD

SINGLE MALT: SPEYSIDE 40% ABV
The extra years give this expression a more nutty, spicy character, with notes of orange peel on the nose, as well as more depth and a more rounded texture.

TOMINTOUL PEATY TANG

SINGLE MALT: SPEYSIDE 40% ABV
The peaty character of this malt comes through on the nose, though not so much as to set off the smoke alarm or swamp the underlying cereal character.

ALL ABOUT...
LIQUEURS

The earliest way of drinking whisky was probably to mix the spirit with honey, herbs, and fruits. From as early as the late 14th century, and increasingly during the 16th century, recipe books were available for preparing medicines at home, which involved distilled spirits compounded with many varieties of herbs. An alfresco hunting feast enjoyed by James V, King of Scots, in 1531 includes, among many other drinks, *Hippocras aquavitae* – a mix of spirits with sugar and spices, strained through a "Hippocrates sleeve", named after the patron of physicians. By the 18th century, when whisky drinking was more widespread, it was commonly served as a "toddy" or a "punch", mixed with sugar, lemons, and spices such as cloves and cinnamon – no doubt to cover the variable quality of the whisky itself.

DRAMBUIE Supposedly made from a recipe gifted by Bonnie Prince Charlie to Captain John McKinnon in 1746, Drambuie began to be made commercially in the 1880s. The recipe is still a family secret, handed down through the female line. It has a honeyed sweetness, a floral heathery note, and a little spiciness.

BAILEYS Launched in 1974, this mix of Irish whiskey and cream has for many years been the best-selling liqueur (and one of the top selling premium spirits) in the world. It is the single most successful spirit to be launched anywhere in the world in the last 50 years. As well as whiskey and cream, there's a touch of vanilla and chocolate in the blend of this silky liqueur.

GLAYVA Created by Ronald Morrison before World War I, and named by his Gaelic-speaking warehouseman (*gle mhath*, pronounced "glay-va", is Gaelic for "very good"). Almond essence and tangerine are discernable in the flavour, and some mildly warming spices. The liqueur makes a good base for fruity cocktails.

IRISH MIST Claiming to be made to an ancient recipe for a drink known as "heather wine", and using Irish whiskey, honey, and herbs in the blend, Irish Mist is now sold in 60 countries.

JACQUIN'S ROCK AND RYE Made with rock candy, Kentucky Rye whiskey, and candied oranges (which are suspended in the bottle), this liqueur was first introduced in Philadelphia in the 1930s. The flavour is caramel-like, with hints of cherry.

SOUTHERN COMFORT This blend of whiskey, sugar, and assorted fruits was invented by New Orleans bar tender Martin Wilkes Heron in 1874. He later patented the drink in Memphis, Tennessee, in 1889. It is produced at various strengths.

ORANGERIE Created by John Glaser, the talented and passionate owner of Compass Box, this is an "infusion" of Navalino orange zest, cassia bark, cloves, and blended Scotch. Clean and fresh on the palate, Orangerie is not as sweet as most liqueurs.

TULLIBARDINE 225 SAUTERNES FINISH

TULLIBARDINE 228 BURGUNDY FINISH

TULLIBARDINE SOVEREIGN

TULLIBARDINE

Blackford, Perthshire
www.tullibardine.com

With its box shape, corrugated roof, and tall metal chimney, Tullibardine is no homely Victorian distillery. It was designed in 1949 by William Delmé-Evans, and survived through various changes in ownership until it was bought by Whyte & Mackay in 1993. The company promptly mothballed the distillery a year later and, as each year passed, the chances of resuscitation appeared to fade.

Then, in 2003, a rescue package was agreed, and Tullibardine was bought by an independent consortium that began distilling again. The new owners released a wide range of expressions, including many cask finishes, and, in 2011, the French family drinks company Picard Vins & Spiritueux purchased Tullibardine, going on to launch an entirely new product range in 2013. Two years later, the oldest cask of whisky in the Tullibardine warehouse – dating from 1952 – was bottled as the first release in the Custodian Collection.

TULLIBARDINE 225 SAUTERNES FINISH

SINGLE MALT: HIGHLANDS 43% ABV
Citrus fruits, vanilla, white pepper, and a slightly herbal note on the nose. Citrus fruits carry over onto the malty palate, with orange, milk chocolate, and enduring spice.

TULLIBARDINE 228 BURGUNDY FINISH

SINGLE MALT: HIGHLANDS 43% ABV
A hint of charred oak on the nose, with vanilla, milk chocolate, and sweet chilli. Sweet and spicy on the palate, with hazelnuts, apples, and allspice, leading to a lengthy finish.

TULLIBARDINE SOVEREIGN

SINGLE MALT: HIGHLANDS 43% ABV
The floral nose features fudge, vanilla, and freshly cut, sweet grass, while the palate is fruity and malty with cocoa, vanilla, and a spicy finish.

TORMORE

Advie, Grantown-on-Spey, Morayshire
www.tormoredistillery.com

Built on a grand scale in 1958, Tormore symbolizes the whisky industry's self-confidence at a time when global demand for blended Scotch was growing strongly.

With its copper-clad roof and giant chimney stack, the distillery towers up beside the A95 in Speyside. It seems no expense was spared by the architect, Sir Albert Richardson, a past president of the Royal Academy.

Tormore is now owned by Chivas Brothers (Pernod Ricard) who released 14- and 16-year-old variants in 2014.

TORMORE 14-YEAR-OLD

SINGLE MALT: SPEYSIDE 43% ABV
Tangy berry fruits, vanilla, spice, and almonds on the nose. The palate is smooth and citric, with toffee, ginger, and a closing note of pepper.

VAT 69

Owner: Diageo

At its peak, VAT 69 was the tenth-best-selling whisky in the world, and references to it crop up in films and books from the 1950s and 60s. It was launched in 1882 and was once the flagship brand of the independent South Queensferry blenders William Sanderson & Co., its name coming from the fact that VAT 69 was the finest of 100 possible blends tested. Today, its current owner, Diageo, gives precedence to Johnnie Walker and J&B, and it might not be unreasonable to suggest that – despite sales of more than 1 million cases a year in Venezuela, Spain, and Australia – VAT 69's glory days are behind it.

VAT 69

BLEND 40% ABV
A light and well-balanced standard blend with a noticeably sweet impact of vanilla ice cream initially and a pleasantly malty background.

WHITE HORSE

Owner: Diageo

In its heyday, White Horse was one of the world's top ten whiskies, selling more than 2 million cases a year.

Its guiding genius was "Restless Peter" Mackie, described in his day as "one-third genius, one-third megalomaniac, and one-third eccentric". He took over the family firm in 1890 and established an enviable reputation as a gifted blender and entrepreneur.

White Horse is still marketed in more than 100 countries. A deluxe 12-year-old version, White Horse Extra Fine, is occasionally seen.

WHITE HORSE

BLEND 40% ABV
Complex and satisfying, White Horse retains the robust flavour of Lagavulin, assisted by renowned Speysiders such as Aultmore. With its long finish, this is a stylish, intriguing blend of crisp grain, clean malt, and earthy peat.

WILLIAM LAWSON'S FINEST

WILLIAM LAWSON'S SCOTTISH GOLD 12-YEAR-OLD

WINDSOR 12-YEAR-OLD

WINDSOR 17-YEAR-OLD

WILLIAM LAWSON'S

Owner: John Dewar & Sons (Bacardi)

Although the brand name of Lawson's dates back to 1849, the "home" distillery today is Macduff, built in 1960 by a consortium of blenders in northeast Scotland and subsequently sold to Martini.

Lawson's is managed alongside its big brother, Dewar's, and, although dwarfed by it and virtually invisible in the UK, the brand sells well over 1 million cases a year in France, Belgium, Spain, and parts of South America. It is well-known in Europe for its iconoclastic advertising and provocative TV commercials.

Glen Deveron single malt from Macduff features heavily in the blend. Macduff employs the highest percentage of sherry wood of any whisky in the Dewar's group, and this contributes to the Lawson house style – a full flavour and rich golden colour. In recent years, the standard expression, William

Lawson's Finest, has been moved into line with other standard blends and is competitive on price while remaining good value for money. The range also comprises the 12-year-old Scottish Gold and two premium styles: an 18-year-old Founder's Reserve and limited quantities of the 21-year-old Private Reserve.

WILLIAM LAWSON'S FINEST

BLEND 40% ABV

The nose is slightly dry, with delicate oak notes. The palate is well-balanced, with hints of a crisp toffee-apple flavour. A medium- to full-bodied whisky that punches above its weight.

WILLIAM LAWSON'S SCOTTISH GOLD 12-YEAR-OLD

BLEND 40% ABV

Fuller-flavoured than the standard Lawson's expression, suggesting a higher malt content.

WINDSOR

Owner: Diageo

According to its owner Diageo, Windsor is "the largest selling super premium Scotch whisky in the world". As such, the brand has fallen prey to counterfeiting in the highly competitive South Korean market. Drinkers here look for a small, bar-shaped weight that signals the whisky's authencity – once the cap is twisted and opened, the weight is separated and falls into the bottle.

The name Windsor is an overt link to the British royal family, and the packaging strongly confirms the brand's luxury position. Although Windsor was originally developed in a partnership between Seagram and local producer Doosan, Diageo acquired the Seagram interest and launched Windsor 17 as the first super premium whisky in 2000. The Korean market at the time was dominated by 12-year-old premium products. Windsor 17's sweeping

popularity posed a strong threat to its competitors, many of whom have since emulated the older style.

Buoyed by the success of Windsor 17, Diageo recently unveiled a 21-year-old variant, aimed at encouraging further trading up to even more premium blends. The company currently supplies Windsor products to China and Japan, and has plans to expand into other Asian countries.

Do not confuse Windsor with its Canadian namesake (see p.277).

WINDSOR 12-YEAR-OLD

BLEND 40% ABV

Vanilla, wood, and light fresh fruit on the nose. Green apples on the palate, with honey, more vanilla, and spiciness that mellows into a smooth finish.

WINDSOR 17-YEAR-OLD

BLEND 40% ABV

A rich vanilla crème brûlée nose, with fruit and a background layer of malt. Fresh fruit and honey on the palate, with creamy vanilla oak notes.

Quarter casks like these at the Speyside Cooperage accelerate the rate of maturation through increased interaction between the wood and the spirit. Laphroaig uses them to good effect to bottle a relatively young whisky.

**WHYTE & MACKAY
30-YEAR-OLD**

BLEND 40% ABV

*The flagship of the Whyte &
Mackay range is a big, rich, oaky
whisky with a deep mahogany
hue. The sherry influence is strong,
with a pepperiness mellowed by
the sweeter flavours.*

**WHYTE & MACKAY
OLD LUXURY**

BLEND 40% ABV

*A rich bouquet, with malty
notes and a subtle sherry
influence. It all blends
smoothly on the palate.
Mellow and silky textured.
Warming finish.*

WHYTE & MACKAY SPECIAL

WHYTE & MACKAY THE THIRTEEN

WHYTE & MACKAY SUPREME

WHYTE & MACKAY

www.whyteandmackay.com

The Glasgow-based firm of Whyte & Mackay started blending in the late-19th century. Its flagship Special brand quickly established itself as a Scottish favourite, and remains so to this day among value-conscious consumers. Having been through a bewildering number of owners and a management buy-out in recent years, the company was acquired in May 2007 by the Indian conglomerate UB Group, which sold it to Emperador Inc. in 2014.

One constant through all these changes has been Whyte & Mackay's highly regarded master blender, Richard Paterson, who joined the firm in 1970 and has received a great number of awards. As well as creating the "new" 40-year-old, Paterson has overseen several aged innovations. The range today includes the Special (which is actually the standard blend) and five expressions aged at 13, 19, 22, 30, and 40 years old. The company defends the unusual age declarations on the grounds that "the extra year gives the whisky a chance to marry for a longer period, giving it a distinct graceful smoothness". A number of own-label customers are also supplied by Whyte & Mackay.

Historically, the company's main market has been the UK, although the older styles, especially the 13-year-old, are popular in Spain, France, and Scandinavia. Sales in India are expected to grow since the launch of the locally bottled Whyte & Mackay range in 2008.

The backbone of the blends emanates from Speyside and the Highlands, although small amounts from Islay, Campbeltown, and the Lowlands are also used. Dalmore and – to a lesser extent – Isle of Jura are the company's flagship single malts, and Dalmore's influence can be clearly felt in the premium blends. Great stress is laid on marrying, the company having long been an adherent to this time-consuming process. All the blends are noticeably smooth and well-balanced.

WHYTE & MACKAY SPECIAL

BLEND 40% ABV

The nose is full, round, and well-balanced. On the palate, honeyed soft fruits in profusion; smooth and rich, with a long finish.

WHYTE & MACKAY
THE THIRTEEN

BLEND 40% ABV

Full, firm, and rich nose, with a slight hint of sherry wood. "Marrying" for a full year before bottling gives great backbone. A well-integrated blend.

WHYTE & MACKAY SUPREME

BLEND 40% ABV

Aged for 22 years, the Supreme is velvet textured, with a soft maltiness and sherry wood notes on nose and palate.

TULLAMORE D.E.W.

Bushmills

LONDONDERRY

Northern
Ireland

BELFAST

OMAGH

Echlinville

DOWNPATRICK

SLIGO

Cooley

The Shed

IRELAND

WESTPORT

Kilbeggan
(used by Cooley)

DUBLIN   Teeling

Tullamore D.E.W.   TULLAMORE
Clonminch

GALWAY

Glendalough   WICKLOW

CARLOW

LIMERICK

CLONMEL

WATERFORD

Dingle

CORK   Midleton

West Cork
Distillers

miles
0   25
0   25
kilometres

TYRCONNEL – COOLEY

POWERS – MIDLETON

Until comparatively recently, modern-day whiskey-making in Ireland centred on just three producers: Bushmills, Midleton, and Cooley. Now, however, we are seeing the development of a vibrant craft distilling movement, with several new entrants to the distilling ranks, while William Grant & Sons Ltd have constructed an entirely new, large-scale distillery in which to produce its Tullamore D.E.W. brand. Bushmills and Midleton have a long history and are the only distilleries to have survived from Ireland's golden age of whiskey distilling in the 19th century. Other famous whiskey names from the 19th century, such as Jameson and Powers, which used to be made at distilleries in Dublin, were closed as independent operations, but live on as brands from Midleton. The modern Midleton plant, near Cork in the Republic of Ireland, has been in operation since the mid-1970s and produces a wide range of whiskeys. By contrast, the Bushmills Distillery, in Northern Ireland, makes only single malt whiskey – this is mixed with grain whiskey bought in from Midleton for Bushmills blends. Cooley dates only from 1987, and has revived the Locke's and Tyrconnel names in its whiskey ranges.

LOCKE'S – COOLEY

CONNEMARA – COOLEY

GREEN SPOT – MIDLETON

BUSHMILLS

JAMESON – MIDLETON

BUSHMILLS ORIGINAL

BLEND 40% ABV

A fruity, easy-to-drink, vanilla-infused mouthful. Its clean, clear character makes it very approachable. A lovely entry to the world of Irish whiskey.

BUSHMILLS BLACK BUSH

BLEND 40% ABV

A living legend, Black Bush is the lovable rogue of the family. It is a very classy glassful of honey nut scrumptiousness with an extremely silky mouthfeel. The benchmark for Irish blends.

BUSHMILLS MALT 10-YEAR-OLD

BUSHMILLS MALT 16-YEAR-OLD

BUSHMILLS MALT 21-YEAR-OLD

BUSHMILLS

2 Distillery Road, Bushmills,
County Antrim
www.bushmills.com

Old Bushmills has the amazing ability to be all things to all men: a thoroughly modern distillery housed in a beautiful Victorian building; a boutique distillery that nevertheless produces global brands; and a working distillery that welcomes the public.

Bushmills produces only malt whiskey, so the grain used in its blends is made to order in the Midleton Distillery. Unusually, Old Bushmills doesn't have a problem selling single malts and blends under the same name: it is a distillery that isn't afraid to push the boundaries. An example of this is the whiskey Bushmills produced to celebrate the 400th anniversary of its original licence to distil. Only a company as quixotic as Bushmills would choose a blended whiskey for such an occasion – and one bottled at 46% ABV too. Bushmills 1608 was the result, and at the heart of this limited-edition whiskey was spirit made using crystal malt – the kind of malt mostly found only in breweries. Its effect on the blend was to give it an almost spicy intensity, which was complemented by some fine sherry notes from the Oloroso casks.

BUSHMILLS MALT
10-YEAR-OLD

SINGLE MALT 40% ABV

As you'd expect from a triple-distilled, peat-free whiskey, this charmer appeals to just about everyone. There's a hint of sherry wood, but it is the classy malt that's showcased here – sweet with hints of fudgy chocolate. A classic and very approachable Irish malt.

BUSHMILLS MALT
16-YEAR-OLD

SINGLE MALT 40% ABV

This malt isn't just a straight ageing of the classic 10-year-old. Instead, it's a pretty much half-and-half mix of bourbon- and sherry-cask-matured malt, married for a further nine months in port pipes. The three woods bring their own magic to bear, and produce a riot of dried-fruit flavours cut with almonds and the ever-present honey.

BUSHMILLS MALT
21-YEAR-OLD

SINGLE MALT 40% ABV

This is the rarest of all Bushmills whiskeys – only 900 cases of the 21-year-old malt are produced each year, and then only when stocks of suitably matured whiskey become available.

This bottling is made from sherry- and bourbon-matured whiskey, which is then finished for another two years in Madeira drums. As you'd expect after 21 years, the malt is almost chewy, with chocolate notes and a sweetness that has mellowed almost to raisin pastry. Delicious.

THE SECRETS OF...
BUSHMILLS

Old Bushmills has been around for a very long time. Distilling on this site goes back to 1608 and possibly even further, though the current distillery was built in the Victorian period.

With its twin pagoda roof, the Victorian distillery is a classic of its type. What is really remarkable about Bushmills, though, is that, while production here has expanded time and again, somehow the place has never lost its charm.

Bushmills has survived for this long because it does what it does very well indeed. The equipment may change over time, but the distillery's attention to consistency means that the single malt produced today doesn't taste much different from what was being made here when America was still a colony.

Over the centuries, various people and companies have owned this little corner of County Antrim; while they have come and gone, the whiskey has kept on going. In a world of change, this place is truly remarkable.

▲ THE WATER SOURCE
The picturesque lake in front of the distillery nicely frames the buildings. More importantly, however, it is where St Columb's Rill is pooled. This is the distillery water source, and so this water will one day get turned into whiskey.

▲ REVITALIZED MASH HOUSE
Bushmills' mash house was refitted with a new stainless-steel mash tun and washbacks in 2007. This is part of Diageo's investment in the distillery, with a view to greatly increasing sales of Bushmills over the forthcoming years. The mash house is full of wonderful yeasty and malty aromas; in the stills house, the aromas are more fruity.

◀ CASK SELECTION

Bushmills mostly uses a mix of bourbon and sherry casks for maturation, and the master blender takes regular trips to Spain and Portugal to select casks being seasoned with sherry. Once the new oak has been mellowed by the sherry and has absorbed some of its fruity flavours, it is ready to mature Bushmills whiskey.

▼ WOOD FINISHES

Bushmills was one of the pioneers of exotic wood finishes. The light style of the spirit produced here lends itself nicely to ageing in Port, Madeira, or Oloroso sherry casks. This is best experienced by sampling the 16- and 21-year-old malts. Bushmills 16 is finished in port pipes for the final months of maturation; Bushmills 21 is finished in Madeira casks for about two years.

◀ TRIPLE DISTILLATION

Bushmills has four wash stills and five spirit stills, and uses triple distillation to produce a very light and pure spirit — the traditional Irish way. The distillery produces two kinds of spirit: one is unpeated; the other is given a light peating. The two types of spirit are matured in separate casks, and can be used in combination to produce the final whiskey.

MALTS AND BLENDS ▶

Bushmills is highly regarded for the quality of its single malts, but it also pays close attention to the standard of its blends. Grain whiskey from Midleton Distillery is used for Bushmills blends, and, significantly, the malt and grain are "married" in casks for a period so that the flavours fully integrate.

CLONTARF

www.clontarf1014.com

Clontarf is owned by Castle Brands Inc. The name commemorates the battle of Clontarf in 1014, when Irish high king Brian Boru achieved a remarkable victory for the Irish over Viking raiders. There is no distillery in Clontarf (near Dublin), and so Castle Brands source their spirit from third-party distillers.

CLONTARF SINGLE MALT

SINGLE MALT 40% ABV

Sweet and thin with some nice mouthfeel. Cereal notes with hints of honey, but a bit one-dimensional.

COLERAINE

Coleraine Distillery Ltd, Hawthorn Office Park, Stockman's Way, Belfast

Never underestimate the selling power of nostalgia: the sole reason this blend is still produced is because whiskey drinkers are very brand loyal, and the name Coleraine still has resonance some three decades after the distillery fell silent. It once produced a single malt of some repute, then in 1954, it started to make grain whiskey for Bushmills, before it was eventually wound down in the 1970s. The reputation of the distillery was such, however, that customers still look out for the name, and so a brand and blend were created to fill a niche. Though the company is called Coleraine Distillery, the whiskey is produced elsewhere.

COLERAINE

BLEND 40% ABV

Light, sweet, and grainy. Probably best suited to drinking with a mixer.

CONNEMARA

Cooley Distillery, Riverstown, Cooley, County Louth
www.kilbeggandistillingcompany.com

Connemara is one of the few whiskeys the Cooley Distillery produces that has no heritage. Names like Millars, Tyrconnell, and Locke's have been around in one form or another for a century or more, but here a totally new brand was created for a totally new whiskey. So what's new? Well, it's a peated malt. Nothing too radical if this were Scotland, but in Ireland it caused quite a stir. In the eyes of the Irish whiskey industry — and many a traditionalist beside — Irish whiskey was a triple-distilled and unpeated drink. Then along came Cooley's John Teeling, who started making Irish whiskey that was double-distilled and peated.

It's not surprising that when Irish Distillers tried to take over Cooley a few years back, IDL boss Richard Burrows was adamant that brands such as Connemara would have no future. Yet, Connemara has gone from being a curiosity to winning gold medals. In December 2011, Beam Inc. acquired Cooley from the Teeling family, and early in 2014, Suntory took over Beam, creating Beam Suntory Inc., with the Irish operation being renamed the Kilbeggan Distilling Company. Several expressions of Connemara have been offered, but today, only the flagship Original variant is produced.

CONNEMARA ORIGINAL

SINGLE MALT 40% ABV

A smouldering turf fire on the nose, with marshmallows, honey, and floral notes. Spicy malt, sweet smoke, and peppery, drying oak on the palate.

KILBEGGAN 8-YEAR-OLD (SEE P.198)

KILBEGGAN WHISKEY (SEE P.198)

THE TYRCONNELL
Single Malt
IRISH WHISKEY

*Centuries of craftsmanship
have produced this soft, elegant
and sophisticated Single Malt
Irish Whiskey*

Estd 1762 Since

DISTILLED MATURED AND BOTTLED IN IRELAND BY
Andrew A. Watt & Co.
RIVERSTOWN DUNDALK IRELAND.
70cl   PRODUCT OF IRELAND   40%vol

TYRCONNELL WHISKEY (SEE .P.214)

COOLEY

Riverstown, Cooley, County Louth
www.kilbeggandistillingcompany.com

In the 1930s, the Irish Government went into the distilling business. It wasn't out to make whiskey; it was simply looking for a way of using up blighted potatoes. Five industrial alcohol factories were built to produce power methylated spirit (PMS), which was then mixed with petrol to make it go further.

By the 1980s, PMS was a thing of the past, and the last of these distilleries on the Cooley Peninsula was being sold for scrap. In 1988, Dr John Teeling bought the Cooley Distillery unseen: he reckoned the scrap value alone was greater than the £106,000 the government wanted. But Teeling didn't do the sensible thing and sell off the scrap – instead he opened a distillery.

On 17 July 1992, as the first cask of Cooley whiskey was tapped, Teeling's dream of taking on Irish Distillers had turned into a nightmare: the company was strapped for cash, and Teeling was looking to offload the loss-making distillery. But the only interested buyers were arch-rivals Irish Distillers, who intended to close the place down. Not surprisingly, its offer was blocked by Ireland's Competition Authority, which ruled that any take-over by Irish Distillers would be anti-competitive. By 1994, Teeling was stuck with a distillery that he couldn't sell and neither could afford to run.

How he, Master Distiller Noel Sweeney, and his team turned Cooley around is nothing short of remarkable. They pre-sold whiskey to the American and German markets, and expanded into the retailer own-brand business. Eventually, with the launch of the Tyrconnell single malt and Kilbeggan blend, Cooley started to sell whiskey under its own label. Today, the Cooley operation is in the hands of Beam Suntory Inc.

WHISKY STYLES
IRISH WHISKEY

Ireland produces four different styles of whiskey, and it is a unique combination. Pure pot still is the style of whiskey that is as Irish as leprechauns. You just don't get it anywhere else. Pot still whiskey is made from both malted and unmalted barley in a pot still. It's a full-flavoured whiskey, which in the Victorian era accounted for just about all the whiskey made in the country.

Nowadays, it is only produced in Midleton and there are just two expressions of pure pot still currently produced, Redbreast and Green Spot. However, it can be found in the make up of the most popular Irish whiskeys, including Jameson, Paddy, and most obviously in Powers Gold Label.

Single malt whiskey is made purely from malted barley. It's a popular style that is produced everywhere from Japan to Scotland. In Ireland, it is made by Bushmills and Cooley, and both companies market it at various different ages. Bushmills 10-year-old or The Tyrconnell would be good examples. Most Irish single malts are unpeated, but Connemara bucks the trend, with a classic Irish peated malt.

Produced in a continuous still, grain whiskey is usually made from corn (maize) in Ireland. It is lighter in flavour than either malt or pot still whiskey. Midleton and Cooley both make grain whiskey. The former uses grain in Jameson and Paddy for example; Cooley blends its grain. Irish whiskey brands like Jameson, Powers, Paddy, Black Bush, and Kilbeggan are blends. In Ireland, that means a mixture of grain with either or both pot still and single malt.

CRAOI NA MONA

Cooley Distillery, Riverstown,
Cooley, County Louth
Owner: Berry Bros. & Rudd

Craoi na Mona is Gaelic for "heart of peat". Produced by Cooley, though not one of its own brands, this whiskey can be found in places as diverse as Moscow and London, but so far, it hasn't been spotted in Dublin. Given the huge rise in the popularity of Irish whiskey recently, it's not surprising that so many drinks companies are trying to cut themselves a slice of the action. The Craoi Na Mona brand is owned by leading London wine merchants Berry Bros. & Rudd, and at 10 years of age, is part of their Berrys' Own Selection range.

CRAOI NA MONA

SINGLE MALT 40% ABV
Sweet and young, this is a decidedly immature peated malt.

CRESTED TEN

Midleton Distillery, Midleton,
County Cork

Launched in 1963, Crested Ten was Jameson's first venture into distillery bottling. The fact that it came at least a century after the Scots started branding and distillery bottling shows how far behind the times the Irish industry was and how close it came to vanishing entirely. Crested Ten is a whiskey you'll see lurking on a top shelf in many Irish pubs. It's never on an optic, probably because it's no good with mixers. Instead, you'll have to ask for it by name. It will soon be re-branded as "Jameson Crested".

CRESTED TEN

BLEND 40% ABV
An old-fashioned Irish whiskey with plenty of pot-still character and its Oloroso maturation in evidence. This is a great big hug of a drink that will reward those brave enough to take it from the top shelf. Have it neat, cut with just a splash of water.

DUNGOURNEY 1964

Midleton Distillery, Midleton,
County Cork

No one is quite sure how, but for 30 years, some of the last pot still to be produced at the old Midleton Distillery lay undiscovered in the corner of a warehouse at Dungourney. In 1994, the remarkable survivor was bottled and named after the river it had come from some three decades before.

Dungourney 1964 is a time machine: one sniff and you are transported back to the days when Jameson, Powers, and Paddy came from competing distilleries.

DUNGOURNEY 1964

IRISH POT STILL WHISKEY 40% ABV
The mushroom edge to the nose gives a hint of age, but the body is still firm. They made whiskey differently back then, which is why this tastes slightly oily, but the tell-tale, almost minty, kick of pure pot still whiskey is still evident.

DUNVILLE'S

Echlinville Distillery, Kircubbin,
County Down
www.echlinville.com

Echlinville became the first new Northern Irish distillery in over 125 years when it opened in 2013. The plan is to produce spirit for use in the Feckin Irish Whiskey blends, founded by distillery owner Shane Braniff, who has also revived the old Dunville's brand. At one time, Dunville's Royal Irish Distillery was the biggest in Belfast, but Dunville & Co. went into liquidation in 1936.

DUNVILLE'S VERY RARE
10-YEAR-OLD

SINGLE MALT 46% ABV
Finished in Pedro Ximénez sherry casks, this expression has cut grass, orchard fruits, and vanilla on the nose, with a soft, sweet, lightly spiced palate.

FECKIN IRISH WHISKEY

www.feckinirishwhiskey.com

As Irish whiskey sales continue to buck the trend and sail upwards, it's not surprising that bright entrepreneurs continue to pour new products onto the market. From its name to the label, this offering is aimed at the younger end of the spectrum, and there's not a tweed jacket in sight. "Feck", by the way, is a very mild and very Irish swear word that was popularized on the TV show *Father Ted*.

FECKIN IRISH WHISKEY

BLEND 40% ABV
Made using whiskey from the Cooley Distillery, this is light, approachable, and totally inoffensive. It's clearly a young whiskey and lacks much in the way of depth.

GLENDALOUGH

Glendalough Distillery,
Glendalough, County Wicklow
www.glendaloughdistillery.com

Glendalough distillery was established in 2013, purchasing a still made in Germany's Black Forest region. The company had actually already been trading for two years at that point, offering a range of poteen and whiskeys sourced from other distillers.

Glendalough currently markets 7- and 13-year-old single malts, and an innovative single grain whiskey, matured initially for three years and six months in ex-Bourbon barrels, and then finished for six months in Spanish Oloroso sherry casks.

GLENDALOUGH SINGLE GRAIN DOUBLE BARREL

SINGLE GRAIN 42% ABV
Light on the nose, with Christmas pudding aromas. The palate features honey, vanilla, dried fruit, and a hint of pepper. Ginger and almonds in the finish.

GREEN SPOT

Midleton Distillery, Midleton,
County Cork

In the days before distillers in Ireland spent millions on building brands, they simply used to make the stuff, leaving the filthy job of selling the whiskey to bonders like Mitchell's. This, of course, was a terrible business plan: it allowed the Scots to build global brands, while the Irish were obsessed with an ever-shrinking domestic market. By the time the Irish got back into the race in the 1960s, Irish whiskey had a miserable 1 per cent of the global whiskey market. Green Spot is the last bonder's own label. Owned by Mitchell's of Dublin, it's a pure pot still whiskey, made in Midleton.

GREEN SPOT

PURE POT STILL 40% ABV
Green Spot is matured for just six to eight years, but a glass of this is still bracing stuff, with a wonderful lightly sherried finish. One of a kind.

INISHOWEN

Cooley Distillery, Riverstown,
Cooley, County Louth
www.kilbeggandistillingcompany.com

Inishowen is the kind of concept an accountant would come up with. It's brand economics by numbers. The Scotch industry is worth billions, with blended Scotch making up 90 per cent of sales. So if an Irish brand could create a similar product, it would have to be a sure-fire success – wouldn't it? There's nothing much wrong with Inishowen – it is well-made and nicely blended – it's just that it will never be… well, Scotch.

INISHOWEN

BLEND 40% ABV
You won't find any other blended Irish whiskey that has a nose like this: it's both peaty and floral. However, it's the fine grain whiskey and not the malt that gives Inishowen some real charm.

THE IRISHMAN SINGLE MALT

THE IRISHMAN CASK STRENGTH

THE IRISHMAN FOUNDER'S RESERVE

THE IRISHMAN

Walsh Whiskey Distillery
Royal Oak, County Carlow
www.irishmanwhiskey.com

The Irishman whiskey was launched in 2007 by Bernard and Rosemary Walsh, who had previously specialized in bottling an Irish coffee recipe under the Hot Irishman label. Whiskey was supplied by Irish Distillers, but, in 2013, the Walshes revealed plans to build their own distillery at Royal Oak, County Carlow.

The Irishman range now includes the Single Malt, the 12-year-old Single Malt, the Founder's Reserve, and The Irishman Rare Cask Strength.

THE IRISHMAN FOUNDER'S RESERVE

BLEND 40% ABV
Cooking apples, vanilla, and black pepper on the nose. Rich mouthfeel, with cinnamon, peaches, caramel, and spicy oak.

THE IRISHMAN SINGLE MALT

SINGLE MALT 40% ABV
Bushmills tends to keep all the best whiskey for itself, which means the Irishman malt has great cereal character but will never be anything outstanding. There is a hint of sherry on the palate.

THE IRISHMAN CASK STRENGTH

PURE POT STILL/MALT BLEND 56% ABV
A limited-release, cask-strength version of the Irishman 70. The whiskey has a rich, sherried nose. Chocolate notes are in evidence here, alongside rum and raisin, and dark brown sugar. The blend is fresh and vigorous on the palate, with chilli spice and notes of orange zest. The chilli heat creates a lingering finish.

The old Jameson Distillery at Bow Street in Dublin is where the famous Irish whiskey was made until the mid-1970s, when production moved to the new Midleton Distillery. Today, it is a visitor centre.

JAMESON
STANDARD BLEND
BLEND 40% ABV

This whiskey has a malty smell, which is promising, but the drink itself is a major let-down. The grain is unruly and overwhelms the pot still, leaving some citrus notes. There is a gentle buzz of sherry, but nothing more.

JAMESON GOLD RESERVE
BLEND 43% ABV

This is a viscous, oily, syrupy mouth-coater of a whiskey. Finer, lighter flavours find it hard to fight their way through the fug of sugars. The finish is buzzy and long, in rather the same way as a cough medicine.

JAMESON SPECIAL RESERVE 12-YEAR-OLD

JAMESON LIMITED RESERVE 18-YEAR-OLD

JAMESON RAREST VINTAGE RESERVE

JAMESON

Midleton Distillery,
Midleton, County Cork
www.jamesonwhiskey.com

This is the biggest selling Irish whiskey of them all. Jameson is a global brand and can be found in just about every bar in the world. However, if the founder of the company, John Jameson, was around today, he certainly wouldn't recognize the whiskey that now bears his name. The modern standard blend is a 50:50 blend of medium-bodied pot still and grain whiskey. It's a light, approachable spirit that lacks character. Beyond the standard bottling, though, are some cracking

whiskeys. Gold Reserve was originally launched as a premium, duty-free blend, but it is now widely available. Some of the whiskeys used in it are more than 20 years old, but they are cut with younger pot still whiskey, matured in first-fill oak casks. This is the only Irish whiskey to feature virgin wood, and it lends the blend a really sweet, vanilla-like flavour.

Jameson's Special Reserve 12-year-old is a full-bodied whiskey, with plenty of malt from the whiskey and spicy oak after 12 years in Oloroso sherry butts. This whiskey has won several awards and collected Gold at the San Francisco World Spirits Competition in 2007.

Six extra years in the cask doesn't change the flavour profile of the 18-year-old premium offering too much, but what it does do is double the price. The Limited Reserve blend is hand-picked by a Jameson master blender from a limited, but excellent selection of sherry casks.

JAMESON SPECIAL RESERVE 12-YEAR-OLD

BLEND 40% ABV

This world-beating whiskey tweaks the nose firmly with hints of leather and spice. It has an incredible, silky quality, quite unlike the monotone, regular Jameson. Dried fruits wrapped in milk chocolate round off a master-class in how to make a great whiskey.

JAMESON LIMITED RESERVE 18-YEAR-OLD

BLEND 40% ABV

The pot still here has taken old age well. The body of the whiskey is firm and yielding and the Oloroso wood has to be very fine not to dominate a blend this old. Sweet almond and spiced fudge notes compliment the oiliness of the pot still.

JAMESON RAREST VINTAGE RESERVE

BLEND 40% ABV

An exceptional blending of choice, aged grain, pot still from bourbon wood, and some pot still aged in port pipes. Sweet fruits on the nose, coupled with pot still spice. Rich fruit, oak, and caramel flavours, and a long fruity, spicy finish.

KILBEGGAN

BLEND 40% ABV

This whiskey has improved over the past decade. It is a grainy blend, with strong notes of honey and porridge. The end note is a pleasing combination of coffee and dark chocolate. Pound for pound, Kilbeggan is one of the best Irish whiskeys that money can buy.

KILBEGGAN 8-YEAR-OLD

KILBEGGAN

The Old Kilbeggan Distillery, Main Street, Kilbeggan, County Westmeath
www.kilbeggandistillingcompany.com

Kilbeggan has been home to many distilleries, and if you visit the town you can understand why: there's plenty of fresh water (and plenty of rain), and County Westmeath is good barley-growing country. Yet, in the mid-1950s, the most famous of the distilleries, John Locke & Sons, fell silent. Although the two remaining Locke family members – sisters Flo and Sweet – had warehouses full of raw ingredients, they had no interest in whiskey-making. With post-war whiskey prices on the rise, they decided to sell the distillery to an international consortium. However, when the deposit of £75,000 never materialized, questions began to be asked. It was rumoured that various members of the government were involved in a shady deal to sell the distillery to foreigners. Accusations of bribery went as high as the Taoiseach, Eamon de Valera, but nothing was ever proven. In the end, the sale fell through, but a year later, the Locke scandal was a factor in the government's subsequent downfall.

Having been part of the Teeling family's Cooley-centred operation for some years, Kilbeggan is now owned by Beam Suntory Inc., and a Kilbeggan blend and a Kilbeggan 8-year-old single grain are currently available.

KILBEGGAN 8-YEAR-OLD

SINGLE GRAIN 40% ABV

Lemon and vanilla on the nose, with a smooth palate of vanilla and honey, which ultimately becomes drier.

KNAPPOGUE CASTLE

Bushmills Distillery, 2 Distillery Road, County Antrim

After World War II, the owner of Knappogue Castle, near the city of Limerick, took to buying casks of Irish whiskey – particularly from the Tullamore Distillery – which he'd store in a cellar in the family pile. These whiskeys would then be bottled and given away to family and friends over time. The last of these original casks filled with Tullamore whiskey was bottled in 1987, when the spirit was 36 years old.

This particular whiskey is obviously extremely rare now. It is not only its age that makes it rather special, though. It is also that this bottling perfectly captures the flavour of a dying age and a whiskey industry that then looked to be heading the same way. However, fast-forward to the 1990s, and the story begins to take on a more upbeat air, when the son of the castle's owner, Mark Andrews, decides to follow in his father's footsteps and bottle single vintages of his own, also labelled Knappogue Castle.

The range now includes a 12-year-old (triple-distilled single malt) and 14- and 16-year-old Twin Wood expressions.

KNAPPOGUE CASTLE 1995

SINGLE MALT 40% ABV

This whiskey clearly originates from a Bushmills malt, and a seriously classy one to boot. There are strong notes of toasted nuts here, while a juicy, honey sweetness lingers on the palate. However, like many of the independent Bushmills offerings, the whiskey is still a bit too young to display the full potential of its characteristics.

WHISKEY TOUR: IRELAND

In 1887, when the Victorian travel and drinks writer Alfred Barnard visited Ireland, he had 28 different distilleries to visit. Nowadays, the range is markedly more limited, but every bit as enjoyable. Several historic whiskey distilleries have facilities for tourists, and there are other attractions along with the beautiful Irish landscape to further entice the visitor on a whiskey tour of the country.

TOUR STATISTICS

DAYS: 4	**LENGTH:** 375 miles (600 km)	**DISTILLERIES:** 1 working, 3 converted
TRAVEL: Car, tram, walking	**REGION:** Northern Ireland and Republic of Ireland	

DAY 1: GIANTS CAUSEWAY, BUSHMILLS

1 The North Antrim coast is stunning. Start your journey at the magnificent **Giants Causeway**, a World Heritage Site near the town of Bushmills, where extraordinary hexagonal basalt columns stretch out along the rugged coast.

2 Of all the distilleries in Ireland that are open to the public, **Bushmills** (*www.bushmills.com*) is the only one that is still in production. Enjoy the tour, sample some fine whiskeys, then stroll to the nearby Bushmills Inn (*www.bushmillsinn.com*) for some superb food and a good night's sleep. Rooms in the Mill House are best.

GIANTS CAUSEWAY

COOLEY DISTILLERY

DAY 2: COOLEY, OLD JAMESON DISTILLERY

3 Although **Cooley** Distillery is not open to the public, the hilly Cooley Peninsula and its attractive seaside town of Greenore are worth taking in on the way to Dublin.

4 Avoid the Dublin traffic by taking the LUAS tram from Junction 9 of the M50 to Smithfield in the city centre. This is near the **Old Jameson** Distillery, which offers guided tours and the chance to sample Jameson whiskey. (*www.jamesonwhiskey.com*)

GALWAY

LIMERICK

CORK **7** **8**
THE JAMESON
EXPERIENCE

FINISH

GIANTS CAUSEWAY **1**
2 BUSHMILLS
START

NORTHERN IRELAND

A37

A6

BELFAST

A5 A29

A28

N54

N3

IRELAND

M1

N4

3 COOLEY

M1

M50

M4 M4

5 KILBEGGAN **4** OLD JAMESON

6 TULLAMORE D.E.W.

N80 N78 N81 N11

N8 N9

N24

N25 WATERFORD

miles
0   25
0   25
kilometres

DAY 3: KILBEGGAN, TULLAMORE D.E.W.

5 Take Junction 7 of the M50 and head west out of Dublin to the old Locke's building at **Kilbeggan**. The original distillery fell silent in 1957, but the site has been revived by locals and now houses the Kilbeggan micro-distillery and a whiskey museum with working waterwheel, restaurant, shop, and whiskey bar. Cooley leases warehouses at this site and brings casks of its whiskey here for maturation. (*www.kilbeggandistillery.com*)

KILBEGGAN

6 The vibrant town of Tullamore is home to the **Tullamore D.E.W.** visitor centre. This building used to be a bonded warehouse for storing whiskey casks before they were shipped downstream to Dublin. It is now the setting for an exhibition about traditional whiskey-making. Although now distilled at Clonminch, on the outskirts of the town, Tullamore whiskey is, of course, available for tasting and purchase at the visitor centre. (*www.tullamoredew.com*)

TULLAMORE D.E.W.

DAY 4: CORK, THE JAMESON EXPERIENCE AT MIDLETON

7 The cross-country trip from Tullamore to Cork traverses the boggy heart of Ireland – a bleak landscape that is strangely beautiful at any time of the year. The city of **Cork** is a food haven, where you can visit the historic English Market to buy a picnic lunch and eat it in nearby Bishop Lucey Park. Alternatively, the Market Café is a great place to try local specialities such as tripe, pigs' feet, and Irish Stew. For a drink, stop at the South County Bar & Café (*www.southcounty.com*), in Douglas Village, a suburb of Cork. It's a traditional, family-run pub, with its own "whiskey corner" to celebrate Irish whiskey.

POT STILL AT MIDLETON

8 **The Jameson Experience** (*www.jamesonwhiskey.com*) is set in the beautifully restored 18th-century distillery at Midleton, and boasts the world's largest pot still, which now stands outside the buildings. For refreshment, try the restaurant at nearby Ballymaloe House, which is overseen by Darina Allen, the doyen of Irish foodies. (*www.ballymaloe.ie*)

KNOCKEEN HILLS POTEEN – FARMER'S STRENGTH

KNOCKEEN HILLS POTEEN – GOLD STRENGTH

LOCKE'S 8-YEAR-OLD

LOCKE'S BLEND

KNOCKEEN HILLS

www.irish-poteen.com

Poteen (or poitín) is a clear spirit that was traditionally distilled in homemade pot stills throughout Ireland. It was originally made with malted barley or any other available grain, though potatoes were also used. Poteen is synonymous with illegal spirit, and the reason for this can be traced back to the 1660s. This was when the English government in Ireland first started taxing the ancient art of distilling. *Uisce beatha* became the legal, duty-paid whiskey; *uisce poitín* the illegal version. Over the intervening 300 years, its love-hate relationship with the law has been celebrated in story and song. This is a rich folk heritage for drinks companies to draw upon.

In 1997, the Revenue removed their previous objection to the term being used to describe a white spirit on which duty had been paid. Hackler from Guinness

was soon out of the trap and it quickly went the way of Guinness Light. One of the few to survive – and indeed to thrive – is Knockeen Hills. Its spirit is bottled at three strengths: triple-distilled at 60% and 70% ABV, and quadruple-distilled at 90% ABV. It should not be drunk neat.

KNOCKEEN HILLS POTEEN – FARMER'S STRENGTH

POTEEN 60% ABV

Clean, fresh, and fruity on the nose. Creamy textured, with tantalizing sweet and juicy fruit notes on the palate. Crisp, mouth-cleansing finish.

KNOCKEEN HILLS POTEEN – GOLD STRENGTH

POTEEN 70% ABV

Stronger on the nose than the 60. With a large measure of water (almost 50-50), it becomes fruity, with tangerine-skin aromas and a sweet perfumed note. Warming in the mouth, sweet-and-sour on the palate, with a dry, fruit-tinged finish.

LOCKE'S

Cooley Distillery, Riverstown, Cooley, County Louth
www.kilbeggandistillingcompany.com

Locke's Distillery in the town of Kilbeggan is an oasis of calm in the Irish midlands. The ancient stone walls filter what traffic noise there is, while the inner courtyard still echoes to the sound of a blacksmith and the trickle of whiskey-making.

It's hard to believe that, just 25 years ago, this truly remarkable distillery was almost derelict. Since the early 1950s, when the Locke's whiskey business initially folded, the abandoned distillery buildings had been used to house pigs and farm machinery. In the late 1970s, the local community got together and restored the distillery. Shortly after the renovation was completed, fate decided to smile upon Kilbeggan. John Teeling was setting up a new distillery in County Louth and wanted to age his maturing stocks at Locke's. A deal was done in

which Cooley bought the rights to the Locke's brand, leased the buildings and, after decades of dusty silence, whiskey barrels once more trundled into the stone warehouses.

In 2007, to celebrate the distillery's 250th anniversary, a micro-distillery was opened at Locke's. The first of its spirit came of age in 2010.

LOCKE'S 8-YEAR-OLD

SINGLE MALT 40% ABV

This malt is a vatting of Cooley's unpeated malt, with a top dressing of peated malt. It is not a bad whiskey; but it's just a bit dull. More Daniel O'Donnell than Shane McGowan, as it were.

LOCKE'S BLEND

BLEND 40% ABV

This is a pleasant enough dram. It would be particularly good in a hot whiskey, where its limited range doesn't have to sing out. Taken neat, Locke's can be a tad monosyllabic, in that it only really has a malty note.

MICHAEL COLLINS SINGLE MALT

MICHAEL COLLINS BLEND

MICHAEL COLLINS

Owner: Beam Suntory

General Michael Collins was one of the founding fathers of the modern Irish state. Numerous movies have been made about his life, with everyone from Brendan Gleeson to Liam Neeson playing "the big fellow", as he was known. Almost everyone in Ireland knows just about everything there is to know about Collins, and yet most people have never heard of this whiskey.

The reason for this is that the whiskey was initially formulated for the American market by Cooley Distillery in conjunction with US importer Sidney Frank. However, it can now be bought on both sides of the Atlantic.

Unusually for an Irish whiskey, the Michael Collins malt is double-distilled and has a light peating too. The blend is a mix of the malt and a younger grain whiskey, which is subsequently put into bourbon casks for maturation.

MICHAEL COLLINS SINGLE MALT

SINGLE MALT 40% ABV

This is like a cream soda for adults – but in a good way. It is soft and drinkable, with plenty of biscuity flavours. Vanilla notes emerge, as a result of the bourbon casking, with a hint of light smoke. This is a vatting of peated and unpeated malt, and a really classy one at that.

MICHAEL COLLINS BLEND

BLEND 40% ABV

The blend is a lot less impressive than the malt. It is thin, with the scent of woody embers at its core, but it lacks a decent finish.

Bushmills in County Antrim is the only working distillery in Ireland that is open to the public. It is also the world's oldest surviving distillery, dating back to 1608.

YELLOW SPOT 12-YEAR-OLD

GREEN SPOT CHÂTEAU LÉOVILLE BARTON

MIDLETON

Midleton, County Cork
www.irishdistillers.ie

Midleton is Ireland's largest distillery. It is home to Jameson, Powers, Paddy, and all of the Irish Distillers' portfolio of whiskeys, as well as their gins and vodkas. The place looks like an enormous petrochemical plant, but it can still make some sublime spirits.

The history of distilling on this site goes back as far as 1825, when the Murphy brothers went into the drinks business. One branch of the family started to make a stout, which still bears their name, and the other side of the family went into the whiskey business.

With its proximity to fine fields of barley and a large harbour on its coast, County Cork enjoys a long tradition of distilling. In 1867, five of the local operations joined forces to form Cork Distilleries Company (CDC) and, gradually, all production was centralized at the Midleton plant.

In 1966, CDC, along with Jameson and Powers, were among the founding members of Irish Distillers. As before, all production was eventually moved over to Midleton Distillery. But by 1975, the old Victorian building could no longer cope with the demands of production, and a new state-of-the-art plant was built to the rear of the original Victorian buildings.

The company also produces the only regular bottlings of pure pot still whiskey in the world. Having

MIDLETON VERY RARE

MIDLETON MASTER DISTILLER'S PRIVATE COLLECTION 1973

MIDLETON DAIR GHAELACH GRINSELL'S WOOD

POWER'S JOHN'S LANE 12-YEAR-OLD

previously offered only Redbreast and Green Spot pure pot still malts, Irish Distillers set out to raise the profile of what it termed "single pot still whiskeys" on a grand scale, launching a number of new expressions and building a dedicated new pot still stillhouse at Midleton. The result is that Power's Signature Release and John's Lane Release have been bottled, along with a Green Spot Château Léoville Barton (finished in ex-Bordeaux wine casks), a 12-year-old Yellow Spot, and, most radical of all, Midleton Dair Ghaelach, the first Irish whiskey to be finished in virgin Irish oak casks. The Redbreast range has also been expanded.

Among all the spirits produced at Midleton, there is just one regularly appearing whiskey that carries the actual Midleton moniker. Launched in 1984,

Midleton Very Rare is aimed at the premium market and the price reflects whatever that market can bear. A new vintage is released late every year and, although they vary slightly, the house style is essentially the same. The constituent whiskeys are aged for between 12 and 25 years in seasoned bourbon casks. The spirit in these bottlings was mostly distilled at the new plant, but the oldest vintages were made at the old Midleton Distillery — now beautifully restored to house the Jameson Experience (see p.209).

YELLOW SPOT 12-YEAR-OLD
SINGLE POT STILL 46% ABV
Sweet and oily on the nose, with vanilla and peaches in syrup, icing sugar, and Madeira. Very spicy on the palate, mouth-coating, with citrus fruits, roasted coffee beans, and toasted oak.

GREEN SPOT CHÂTEAU LÉOVILLE BARTON
SINGLE POT STILL 46% ABV
Fragrant on the nose, with caramel, rose petals, apple pie, and white pepper. Smooth and oaky on the palate, with cereal, plums, berry fruits, vanilla, honey, and hot spices.

MIDLETON VERY RARE
BLEND 40% ABV
The nose is a skilful balancing act; classy oak and bold cereal notes dance on a high wire made of pure beeswax. The body is full and yielding, and the finish breaks on the tongue in waves of silky, walnut whip. You get a classy ball of malt for your money, and so you should. Note that there is a little variation in the whiskey from year to year.

MIDLETON MASTER DISTILLER'S PRIVATE COLLECTION 1973
PURE POT STILL 56% ABV
Even rarer than Midleton Very Rare, this whiskey was distilled in 1973 and

is a bottling of pure pot still whiskey from the old Midleton Distillery. It was produced as a 30-year-old in an edition of 800 bottles, and its taste is said to be spicy, fruity, and honeyed, with some dry, sherry nuttiness.

MIDLETON DAIR GHAELACH GRINSELL'S WOOD
SINGLE POT STILL 58.2% ABV
Oily on the nose, with freshly sawn timber, bananas, cinnamon, nutmeg, and ginger. Viscous and spicy on the palate, nutty, with pineapple, cloves, and tingling oak. Very spicy in the drying finish.

POWER'S JOHN'S LANE 12-YEAR-OLD
SINGLE POT STILL 46% ABV
Vanilla, new leather, nougat, and carnations on the slightly salty nose. Sunflower oil and, ultimately, a whiff of molasses. Full-bodied in the mouth, with an oily texture. Palate of dried fruits, spices, and nuts.

THE SECRETS OF...
MIDLETON

The town of Midleton is an easy 30-minute drive from Cork city. It's a pleasant market town and on a clear day, with the wind in a certain direction, comes the curious scent of whiskey.

Set back slightly from the main thoroughfare, hugging the bank of the River Dungourney, lie the imposing Victorian buildings of Midleton Distillery. This is the original Cork Distilleries Company (CDC) plant that ceased production in the early 1970s. Nowadays, it houses an impressive visitor centre, the Jameson Experience.

Behind the old distillery, lies the new one. In 1966, the remaining Irish distilleries – Powers and Jameson in Dublin, and CDC in Cork – came together to form Irish Distillers. When the two Dublin-based distilleries closed, all production shifted to the new state-of-the-art plant at Midleton. This is now where everything from Jameson whiskey to Cork Dry Gin are produced. You shouldn't be put off by its industrial scale, though, for Midleton has exacting standards and produces fantastic whiskeys, including bottlings of the two remaining Irish pot still whiskeys, Redbreast and Green Spot. It all comes down to the basics: a good water source and local barley.

◄ LOCAL BARLEY

Midleton uses locally grown barley for its malt. The malt used to produce its great whiskeys is dried by warm air and not with peat smoke, as is common in Scotland. This means that there is nothing to mask the wonderful malty, biscuity taste of fine Irish barley.

THREE MASH PROCESS ►

The malt (or a mixture of malt and barley if pot still whiskey is being produced) is ground into a coarse flour called grist and dumped into a large tub known as a mash tun, or locally as a kieve. Hot water is added, and the mixture is stirred to help convert the starch in the grain into sugar. At Midleton, this process is repeated three times, with the barley water being drained off after each mashing. The final barley water is held and used in the first mashing of the next batch of grist. This ensures a certain continuity between batches.

▲ **THE WHISKEY'S SOURCE**
Dungourney River runs right past the distillery. In fact the river is the reason the factory is sited where it is. The old Midleton distillery was powered by a giant waterwheel *(see bottom right)*. That may have changed, but the new distillery still uses the Dungourney for its whiskey.

◄ **CHOICE WOOD**

Midleton has a very strict wood policy: only the finest American oak barrels are used, while the sherry wood comes from oak butts that are built and seasoned to order in Jerez, Spain. They will be used to mature sherry for one or two years before being brought over to Midleton to age the whiskey. The distillery is currently building new warehousing to cope with its maturing stocks.

◄ **BOTTLING**

Jameson is the biggest-selling whiskey that Midleton produces, and the vast majority of it is bottled near Dublin. But there is a second line close to Midleton, at the old North Mall Distillery in the heart of Cork. This old distillery no longer produces whiskey, but does at least keep a connection to the industry by bottling some of the output from Midleton.

▼ **THE JAMESON EXPERIENCE**

The old Midleton Distillery now houses a visitor centre, where you can be taken on a tour of the buildings and the grounds, sample some whiskeys, and become an expert on the characteristics of Irish whiskey *(see also p.201)*.

▲ **PRODUCTION VARIATIONS**

There isn't a distillery in the world that can produce the range of whiskeys that comes out of Midleton. Many pure pot still, malt, and grain variations are stored in tanks under the plant. These can then be combined in different quantities and matured in different woods to produce myriad whiskey types and styles.

Without barley, there would be no whiskey; it's as simple as that. Midleton Distillery in County Cork sits among scenic, rolling fields of barley. The distillery makes great use of this local supply.

POWERS GOLD LABEL

POWERS GOLD LABEL 12-YEAR-OLD

PADDY

Midleton Distillery, Midleton,
County Cork
www.paddy.ie

There was a time when Irish whiskey was sold anonymously from casks in pubs. What whiskey a pub stocked was down to the owner and his relationship with the agent for the distillery.

Paddy Flaherty was an agent for the Cork Distilleries Company of Midleton in the 1920s and '30s. You knew when he was in town, as he'd stand everyone free drinks at the bar, and the whiskey he sold – the CDC's Old Irish Whiskey – became so synonymous with the man himself that it was simply known as Paddy's whiskey.

PADDY

BLEND 40% ABV
This is a malty dram, which is both solid and well matured. It offers a satisfying, spicy, peppery kick.

THE POGUES

West Cork Distillers, Market Street,
Skibbereen, County Cork
www.thepoguesirishwhiskey.com

The official Irish whiskey of legendary band The Pogues, this blend is produced by West Cork Distillers in Skibereen. It was launched during 2015, and, according to the whiskey's promoters, it is "Sunlight and barley held together with water and left in an oak barrel for three years and a day. This whiskey is a measure of who we are, made with the sole intention of spreading that same raucous joy."

THE POGUES

BLEND 40% ABV
The nose is floral and nutty, with almonds and malt. Sweet, smooth, and malty on the palate, with milk chocolate, spice, and citrus fruit.

POWERS

Midleton Distillery, Midleton,
County Cork
www.irishdistillers.ie

For longer than anyone could remember, Jameson and Powers used to stare each other down across the narrow strip of Dublin water they call the Liffey. The Powers family (on Dublin's south side) had been in the business since 1817, and a member of the family sat on the board of Irish Distillers until it was incorporated into the Pernod Ricard group, some 171 years later.

The Powers family had always embraced innovation. They pioneered the production of Irish gin and vodka, and moved into distillery bottling before anyone else in the country. They also invented the miniature, or, as it is known, the "baby Powers".

Incidentally, the picture of the three swallows on the Powers label is an example of typical Dublin wit.

It has long been held that the only way to enjoy a Powers is not to sip it slowly, but to lower the glass in "three swallows". As well as the famous blends, Powers John's Lane Release *(see p.207)* and Signature Release pot still whiskeys are now available.

POWERS GOLD LABEL

BLEND 40% ABV
This whiskey is something really special. Powers Gold Label is an upfront, take-no-prisoners experience. This isn't another bland, global brand; this is a real, solid whiskey. The nose is classically Irish – at once bracing and brittle. At its core, this whiskey is pure pot still, cut with just enough good grain. Powers Gold Label is an utterly captivating blend.

POWERS GOLD LABEL 12-YEAR-OLD

BLEND 40% ABV
An older, more layered expression of the same Powers formulation. Spice, honey, crème brûlée, with soft wood tones and sweet, fresh fruits.

TEELING SINGLE GRAIN

TEELING SINGLE MALT

TEELING SMALL BATCH

REDBREAST

Midleton Distillery, Midleton,
County Cork
www.irishdistillers.ie

Redbreast was the name that
wine merchants Gilbey's gave
to the Jameson whiskey that they
matured and bottled. The bonder
trade was finally phased out in 1968,
but Redbreast was so popular that
it was allowed to continue well
into the 1980s. In the 1990s, Irish
Distillers bought the brand from
Gilbey's and re-launched the drink
as a 12-year-old pure pot still,
part-matured in sherry wood.
There are also now 12-year-old
cask strength and 15- and
21-year-old versions.

REDBREAST 12-YEAR-OLD

PURE POT STILL 40% ABV
*This is, without doubt, one of the world's
finest whiskeys. Flavours range from
ginger to cinnamon, peppermint to
linseed, and liquorice to camphor. A
sherry note sets off an elegant finish.*

TEELING

Teeling Distillery,
13-17 Newmarket, Dublin 8
www.teelingwhiskey.com

When the €10 million Teeling
Distillery opened for business on
St Patrick's Day (17th March) 2015,
it was the first time since 1974 that
whiskey had been produced in the
city of Dublin. The venture is
headed by brothers Jack and
Stephen Teeling, whose father John
established the Cooley distillery
in County Louth in 1987. In 2011,
the family sold the Cooley to Beam
Inc. for $16 billion. However, the
Teeling siblings wanted to continue
in the Irish Whiskey business, and
their new Dublin distillery is the
ultimate result.

Teeling is situated in The
Liberties, a historic district of the
city. This area was home to no fewer
than 37 distilleries during the early
19th century, but is now best-
known for the vast St James's Gate
Guinness Brewery and adjacent

Storehouse – named Europe's
leading tourist attraction in 2015.

The Teelings wanted to create
a modern, city-based distillery,
and were inspired by Anchor
Distilling in San Francisco and
the London Distillery Company.
The Teeling Distillery in Dublin
occupies two adjoining converted
warehouses and is equipped with
a four-tonne Steinecker full-lauter
mash tun, six washbacks, two pine
and four stainless steel, holding a
combined total of 110,000 litres
(24,000 gallons), and three pot
stills fabricated by Frilli. The
annual output is currently 200,000
to 250,000 litres (44,000 to
55,000 gallons).

Although primarily producing pot
still single malt whiskey, the Teelings
want to devote 25 per cent of their
distilling time to experimentation.
They may, in time, produce an Irish
rye and a heavily-peated single malt.
In addition to their Single Grain,
Single Malt, and Small Batch
expressions, all based on spirit

sourced from Cooley, the Teelings
also offer The Revival – a limited
edition, 15-year-old single malt
specially selected to celebrate the
opening of the new distillery – and
a 21-year-old single malt finished
in Sauternes casks.

TEELING SINGLE GRAIN

SINGLE GRAIN 46% ABV
*Sweet on the nose, with spicy fruit
notes. Notably spicy in the mouth,
with red berries and drying tannins.*

TEELING SINGLE MALT

SINGLE MALT 46% ABV
*This expression comprises a vatting
of five different wine cask-finished
Irish malt whiskeys. Lemon, toffee, and
melon on the lively nose, with a palate
of vanilla, spicy dry fruits, and cloves.*

TEELING SMALL BATCH

BLEND 46% ABV
*Finished in ex-rum casks, it has vanilla
and spice on the nose, with sweet rum
in the background. Smooth and sweet,
with light, spicy wood notes.*

TULLAMORE D.E.W.

TULLAMORE D.E.W. 10-YEAR-OLD

TULLAMORE D.E.W. 12-YEAR-OLD

TULLAMORE D.E.W.

www.tullamoredew.com

Tullamore is a sizeable market town. It is situated pretty much smack-bang in the middle of Ireland. Although Tullamore itself is largely built on bogland, some great barley-producing counties lie nearby that once provided the grain for both this distillery and the operation at Locke's Distillery in nearby Kilbeggan.

In 1901, the worldwide sales of Irish whiskey peaked at 10 million cases, and two years later, the Williams family gained control of Tullamore Distillery. In fact, D.E. Williams is the man whose name is still associated with whiskey in Tullamore; as in Tullamore D.E.W.illiams.

In 1954, the distillery closed and the brand was sold to Powers. It was then absorbed by Irish Distillers and ultimately ended up in the hands of William Grant & Sons Ltd in 2010. Grant's reunited the brand with its original home, building a large new distillery on the outskirts of Tullamore. After Jameson, Tullamore D.E.W. is the world's second-best-selling Irish whiskey.

TULLAMORE D.E.W.

BLEND 40% ABV

This whiskey is fairly one-dimensional. It has a characteristic bourbon burn, with not much else to recommend it.

TULLAMORE D.E.W. 10-YEAR-OLD

BLEND 40% ABV

There's malt, spice, and vanilla on the nose, and a hint of oakiness and spice on the palate. The finish is long and dry, with a citric tang.

TULLAMORE D.E.W. 12-YEAR-OLD

BLEND 40% ABV

A considerable step up from the other Tullamore blends, the 12-year-old is reminiscent of a premium Jameson. The precious trinity of pot still, sherry, and oak is very much in evidence.

TULLAMORE D.E.W.

TYRCONNELL
SINGLE MALT

SINGLE MALT 40% ABV

Cooley's best-selling malt and it's easy to see why. This has the loveliest nose of any Irish whiskey, releasing jasmine, honeysuckle, and malted milk biscuits.

TYRCONNELL 10-YEAR-OLD PORT CASK

THE TYRCONNELL

www.kilbeggandistillery.com

Once very popular in the US, the original Old Tyrconnell whiskey is now remembered by few. In 1925, civil unrest in Ireland and Prohibition in the US pushed the Watt Distillery, where Old Tyrconnell was produced, into the hands of the Scottish United Distillers Company. UDC closed the many Irish distilleries it bought to protect its core Scotch brands, bringing the Irish industry to its knees. However, Tyrconnell was the first brand Cooley's John Teeling brought back to life when he bottled his first single malt in 1992. The brand is now owned by Beam Suntory Inc.

TYRCONNELL 10-YEAR-OLD
PORT CASK

SINGLE MALT 46% ABV

Port changes the nose slightly, spicing things up. The body has aromas of fig rolls and plum pudding.

WRITERS TEARS

Walsh Whiskey, Equity House, Deerpark Business Park, Dublin Rd, Co. Carlow
www.walshwhiskey.com

Writers Tears is a pot still-blended Irish whiskey produced by the Walsh family, which is also responsible for The Irishman range. It was introduced in 2009, and contains only pot still whiskey and malt whiskey, with no grain whiskey component.

The Walsh family is currently engaged in the construction of a new distillery in County Carlow, which will be equipped with both pot and column stills, and will have the capacity to distil up to 8 million bottles of whiskey per year.

WRITERS TEARS
POT STILL BLEND

BLEND 40% ABV

Soft on the nose, with honey and citrus fruits. Mellow and easy-drinking, with malt, caramel, and apple notes on the long, warming palate.

THE WILD GEESE RARE IRISH

THE WILD GEESE SINGLE MALT

THE WILD GEESE CLASSIC BLEND

THE WILD GEESE

www.thewildgeese-irishwhiskey.com

With victory at the Battle of Kinsale, the English crown finally wrestled power from the native Gaelic chieftains, and in 1608, these Irish nobles fled the country. However, this didn't end the conflict in Ireland. The term "Wild Geese" refers to those Irish nobles and soldiers who left to serve in continental European armies from the early 17th century to the dawn of the 20th century. Most of those families remained in Europe. Some, like the Hennessys, started producing cognac. Others, such as the Lynchs, went on to make wine.

The name "Wild Geese" has come down through history to embrace all the men and women who left Ireland in the last 400 years – not just the nobles. The idea of diaspora and immigration has, of course, been a poignant theme in Irish culture and remains so today. Wild Geese raises a glass to this part of Irish history, and they've certainly produced a good whiskey for the job.

THE WILD GEESE CLASSIC BLEND

BLEND 40% ABV

A boiled-sweet nose. The malt doesn't have much impact here, leaving the grain to carry things to the finish.

THE WILD GEESE RARE IRISH

BLEND 43% ABV

A rich and malty blend, with some spiciness and lemon notes in the body. You'll find a little dry oak in the finish.

THE WILD GEESE SINGLE MALT

SINGLE MALT 43% ABV

This whiskey is predominantly malty, with a caramel sweetness. There is also a little oakiness and a hint of spice.

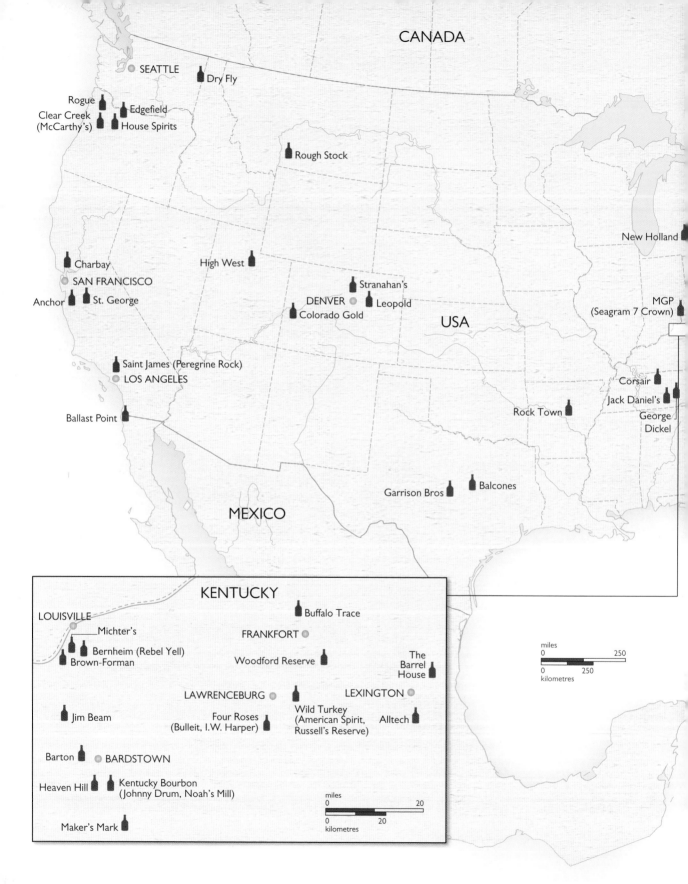

CANADA

SEATTLE ● 🍾 Dry Fly

Rogue 🍾
Clear Creek 🍾 🍾 Edgefield
(McCarthy's) 🍾 🍾 House Spirits

🍾 Rough Stock

Charbay 🍾
● SAN FRANCISCO
Anchor 🍾 🍾 St. George

High West 🍾

Stranahan's 🍾
DENVER ● 🍾 Leopold
Colorado Gold 🍾

USA

New Holland 🍾

MGP
(Seagram 7 Crown) 🍾

Saint James (Peregrine Rock) 🍾
● LOS ANGELES

Corsair 🍾 🍾
Jack Daniel's 🍾

Rock Town 🍾

George
Dickel

Ballast Point 🍾

MEXICO

Garrison Bros 🍾 🍾 Balcones

miles
0 ———— 250
0 ———— 250
kilometres

KENTUCKY

LOUISVILLE ●
Michter's
Bernheim (Rebel Yell) 🍾 🍾
Brown-Forman

🍾 Buffalo Trace

FRANKFORT ●

Woodford Reserve 🍾

The
Barrel 🍾
House

Jim Beam 🍾

LAWRENCEBURG ●

Four Roses 🍾
(Bulleit, I.W. Harper)

Wild Turkey 🍾
(American Spirit,
Russell's Reserve)

LEXINGTON ●

Alltech 🍾

Barton 🍾 ● BARDSTOWN

Heaven Hill 🍾 🍾 Kentucky Bourbon
(Johnny Drum, Noah's Mill)

Maker's Mark 🍾

miles
0 ———— 20
0 ———— 20
kilometres

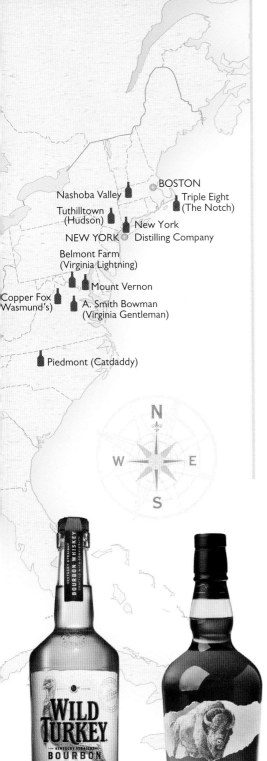

Nashoba Valley

BOSTON

Triple Eight
(The Notch)

Tuthilltown
(Hudson)

New York
Distilling Company

NEW YORK

Belmont Farm
(Virginia Lightning)

Mount Vernon

Copper Fox
Wasmund's

A. Smith Bowman
(Virginia Gentleman)

Piedmont (Catdaddy)

The limestone soil of Kentucky yields rich crops of corn, and it is no coincidence that Kentucky and the surrounding whiskey-producing states of the US partly overlie the same limestone shelf. Kentucky is the heartland of American whiskey, and is where most of the US's large-scale commercial distilleries are located, including Jim Beam, Buffalo Trace, Heaven Hill, Barton, and Brown-Forman. To the south, Tennessee has its own legally defined whiskey style and is the home of two other big names in American whiskey: Jack Daniel's and George Dickel. Today, international spirit companies own many of these major distilleries and brands. Besides this core of large-scale distillers, however, the US has seen an explosion of craft distilling during the last couple of decades, with 769 distilleries now operational across the country at the last count. They are often eager to experiment with recipes and production practices, injecting new and dynamic life into the exciting world of American whiskey.

WILD TURKEY

BUFFALO TRACE

CATDADDY

OLD POTRERO

MELLOW CORN

1776

www.jamesepepper.com

1776 was the year the US declared its independence, and the year in which Elijah Pepper of Culpeper, Virginia, settled at Old Pepper Springs in Kentucky. By 1780, he was a well-established distiller, and today the site where he began distilling is home to the Woodford Reserve Distillery. Three generations of the Pepper family were involved in distilling, and in more recent years, the Georgetown Trading Co. has been custodian of the Pepper distilling legacy. Both 1776 Bourbon and 1776 Rye are available.

1776 STRAIGHT BOURBON WHISKEY

BOURBON 50% ABV

Vanilla, spicy rye, and citrus fruit on the nose. Honey and vanilla on the palate, with chocolate, tangerines, and then cinnamon in the lengthy finish.

AMERICAN SPIRIT

Wild Turkey Distillery, US Highway 62 East, Lawrenceburg, Kentucky
www.wildturkeybourbon.com

American Spirit is distilled at the Wild Turkey Distillery *(see p.262)* by Austin Nichols & Co., and was introduced in September 2007. According to Eddie Russell, who developed this expression with his father, Master Distiller Jimmy Russell, the name "American Spirit" seemed to suggest itself.

AMERICAN SPIRIT 15-YEAR-OLD

BOURBON 50% ABV

Richly aromatic and characterful on the nose, silky smooth in the mouth, with vanilla, brittle toffee, molasses, stewed fruits, spice, and a little mint. The finish is lengthy and spicy, with gentle oak and a final menthol note.

ANCIENT AGE

Buffalo Trace Distillery, 1001 Wilkinson Boulevard, Frankfort, Kentucky
www.buffalotrace.com

Ancient Age was, from 1969 to 1999, the name of what is now the Buffalo Trace Distillery *(see p.223).* The brand was introduced in the 1930s shortly after the end of Prohibition, initially being distilled in Canada. After World War II, it was reformulated as a straight Kentucky-made bourbon, and went on to become one of the best-known brands produced by its proprietors.

ANCIENT AGE 10-YEAR-OLD

BOURBON 40% ABV

This 10-year-old bourbon is complex and fragrant on the nose, with spices, fudge, oranges, and honey. Medium-bodied and, after a slightly dry opening, the oily palate sweetens with developing vanilla, cocoa, and a lightly charred note.

BAKER'S

Jim Beam Distillery, 149 Happy Hollow Road, Clermont, Kentucky
www.jimbeam.com

Baker's is one of three whiskeys that were introduced in 1992 as Beam's Small Batch Bourbon Collection. It is named after Baker Beam, the former Clermont Master Distiller and grand-nephew of the legendary Jim Beam himself. He is also a cousin of the late Booker Noe, the high-profile distiller who instigated small-batch bourbon distilling.

Baker Beam's namesake whiskey is distilled using the standard Jim Beam formula, but is aged for longer and offered at a higher bottling strength.

BAKER'S 7-YEAR-OLD

BOURBON 53.5% ABV

Baker's is a fruity, toasty expression of the Jim Beam formula: medium-bodied, mellow, and richly flavoured, with notes of vanilla and caramel.

BALCONES

Balcones Distilling,
212 S 17th Street, Waco, Texas
www.balconesdistilling.com

Balcones was established in 2008
by Chip Tate, but he has since
parted company with the venture
and plans to create a new distillery
in the near future. From the outset,
Balcones was synonymous with
the more experimental side of
micro-distilling, producing products
such as the "Texas Scrub Oak
Smoked" corn whiskey Brimstone,
and Baby Blue, made from roasted
heirloom blue corn. The innovative
company's best-seller is its Texas
Single Malt whiskey.

BALCONES TEXAS SINGLE MALT

SINGLE MALT 53%

*Toffee, honey, and creamy vanilla on the
nose. Malt, honey, apples, and cinnamon
on the palate, with closing spicy oak.*

BARTON

300 Barton Road, Bardstown, Kentucky
Owner: Sazerac

Very Old Barton is distilled in the
Barton 1792 distillery at Bardstown,
and the brand is now owned by
Sazerac Company Inc. of New
Orleans. Bardstown is in the true
heartland of bourbon, and once
boasted more than 20 distilleries.
Barton's whiskeys are typically
youthful, dry, and aromatic.

In addition to the Barton-
named brands, the company also
owns Kentucky Gentleman (*see
p.242*), Kentucky Tavern (*p.242*),
Ridgemont (*p.252*), Ten High
(*p.256*), and Tom Moore (*p.256*).

VERY OLD BARTON

BOURBON 43% ABV

*The nose is rich, syrupy, and spicy, with
a prickle of salt. Big-bodied in the mouth,
it is fruity and spicy, with spices and
ginger in the drying finish.*

BASIL HAYDEN'S

Jim Beam Distillery, 149 Happy Hollow
Road, Clermont, Kentucky
www.basilhaydens.com

Basil Hayden's was one of the
three whiskeys that made up
Beam's pioneering Small Batch
Bourbon Collection, introduced
in 1992. Basil Hayden was an early
Kentucky settler from Maryland
who began making whiskey in the
late 18th century near Bardstown,
and it is claimed that the recipe for
this particular expression dates
from that period.

BASIL HAYDEN'S 8-YEAR-OLD

BOURBON 40% ABV

*The nose is light, aromatic, and spicy, with
flavours of soft rye, wood polish, spices,
pepper, vanilla, and a hint of honey on
the comparatively dry palate. The finish
is long, with notes of peppery rye.*

BERNHEIM

Heaven Hill Distillery, 1701 West
Breckinridge Street, Louisville, Kentucky
www.bernheimwheatwhiskey.com

The Bernheim brand takes its
name from Heaven Hill's Bernheim
Distillery in Louisville, Kentucky,
where Heaven Hill whiskeys have
been produced since the plant was
acquired in 1999.

Launched in 2005, Bernheim
is the only straight wheat whiskey
on the US market.

Heaven Hill father and son,
Master Distillers Parker and Craig
Beam, developed the wheat formula
with a minimum of 51 per cent
winter wheat, and the recipe also
includes corn and malted barley.

BERNHEIM ORIGINAL

WHEAT WHISKEY 45% ABV

*Bernheim exhibits light fruit notes on
the spicy nose, with freshly sawn wood,
toffee, vanilla, sweetish grain, and a hint
of mint on the palate. A long, elegant,
honeyed, and spicy finish.*

EARLY TIMES *(SEE P.224)*

OLD FORESTER *(SEE P.248)*

BLANTON'S

Buffalo Trace Distillery, 1001 Wilkinson Boulevard, Frankfort, Kentucky
www.buffalotrace.com

Colonel Albert Bacon Blanton worked for no fewer than 55 years at what is now the Buffalo Trace Distillery, starting as office boy in 1897 and graduating to distillery manager in 1912. When he retired in 1955, the distillery was renamed Blanton's in his honour. This single barrel expression was created in 1984 by Master Distiller Elmer T. Lee, who worked with Blanton during the 1950s.

BLANTON'S SINGLE BARREL

BOURBON 46.5% ABV

The nose of Blanton's is soft, with toffee, leather, and a hint of mint. Full-bodied and rounded on the palate, this is a notably sweet bourbon, embracing vanilla, caramel, honey, and spices. The finish is long and creamy, with a hint of late spice.

BOOKER'S

Jim Beam Distillery, 149 Happy Hollow Road, Clermont, Kentucky
www.bookersbourbon.com

A brand created by the global Jim Beam company, Booker's is named after Jim Beam's grandson, Booker Noe. Booker was a sixth generation Master Distiller and the man credited with the introduction of "small batch" bourbon in 1992. On their website, Booker's declare that of the few batches they release every year, "each varies in age and proof because reaching Booker's standards is a mix of art, science and Mother Nature. It tells us when it's ready, and then we'll let you know."

BOOKER'S 2015 BATCH 06 NOE'S SECRET

BOURBON 64.05% ABV

Richly aromatic nose of vanilla, corn, and cinnamon. Caramel and more vanilla on the palate, with big spice notes, char, oak, and raspberries.

BROWN-FORMAN

850 Dixie Highway,
Louisville, Kentucky
www.brown-forman.com

The Brown-Forman Distillery is situated in the area of Louisville known as "Distillery Row". Half a dozen once operated here, but today, only Brown-Forman and Bernheim *(see p.219)* survive.

The Brown-Forman Corporation has its origins in a blending and bottling operation established by George Garvin Brown and his half-brother John Thompson Street Brown in 1870. Their practice of selling whiskey in sealed bottles was a major innovation that overcame problems of adulteration, but the Browns were also forward-thinking in acquiring whiskeys from a variety of distillers and blending them to achieve ongoing consistency. Their whiskey brand was originally called Old Forrester (later changed to Forester). When John Brown left the company he was replaced

by accountant George Forman, whose name was added to the company title in 1890.

The firm's Louisville facility was established in 1935 as the Old Kentucky Distillery. Brown-Forman acquired it in 1940 and subsequently rebuilt the plant, renaming it the Early Times Distillery. Brown-Forman's other distillery in Louisville, Old Forester Distillery, closed in 1979, after which production of Old Forester bourbon was moved to the Early Times Distillery.

Today, it is simply the Brown-Forman Distillery. Early Times Kentucky Whisky *(see p.224)* and Old Forester Kentucky Straight Bourbon Whisky *(p.248)* are now its principal output (Brown-Forman favours the Scottish spelling of "whisky" for some of its output). The Brown-Forman Corporation also owns the Jack Daniel's *(p.236)* and Woodford Reserve distilleries *(p.264)*.

WHISKY STYLES
BOURBON

Bourbon enjoys a global reputation as the quintessential US whiskey, and boasts a long and colourful heritage. It takes its name from Bourbon County in Kentucky, which in turn was named in honour of the French royal House of Bourbon when the former Western Virginian county of Kentucky was subdivided in the 1780s.

Distilling probably began in the area when settlers of Scottish, Irish, and German origin arrived during the late 18th century. The "invention" of bourbon is often credited to the Baptist minister, entrepreneur, and distiller Elijah Craig, who is said to have pioneered the use of charred casks for maturation at the distillery he founded in 1789. In reality, however, no one person created bourbon, which evolved from the distilling practices of many individuals. It is also a common misconception that bourbon must be distilled in Kentucky. In fact, it can be produced anywhere in the United States where it is legal to distil spirits. However, in practice, some 95 per cent of all bourbon is distilled and matured in its "home" state.

The legally-binding modern definition of bourbon dates from May 1964, when the US Congress recognized it as a "distinctive product of the United States", and created the Federal Standards of Identity for Bourbon. By law, the whiskey type must be produced from a mash of not less than 51 per cent corn grain, and is usually made using between 70 and 90 per cent corn, with some barley malt plus rye and/or wheat in the mashbill. It has to be distilled to no more than 80% ABV and casked at 62.5% ABV or less. Legally, bourbon must be matured in new, charred, white-oak barrels for a minimum of two years.

Among the most notable bourbon brands on the market are Jim Beam *(see p.240)*, Buffalo Trace *(p.223)*, Maker's Mark *(p.244)*, Wild Turkey *(p.262)*, and Woodford Reserve *(p.264)*.

A misty morning dawns at Buffalo Trace in Frankfort, Kentucky. The distillery's water towers are an iconic landmark in the heartland of Bourbon Country.

BUFFALO TRACE KENTUCKY STRAIGHT BOURBON

BUFFALO TRACE EXPERIMENTAL COLLECTION

BUFFALO TRACE

Buffalo Trace Distillery,
1001 Wilkinson Boulevard,
Frankfort, Kentucky
www.buffalotrace.com

Formerly known as Ancient Age (*see p.218*), Buffalo Trace is located at a crossing point where, in the past, herds of migrating buffalo forded the Kentucky River. The trail they followed was known as the Great Buffalo Trace.

A distillery was first established here in 1857 by the Blanton family. Later, it was run by "bourbon aristocrat" Edmund Haynes Taylor and the pioneering George T. Stagg. Then Albert Bacon Blanton steered and grew the company through flood, Prohibition, and war. He and Stagg have exclusive bourbons named after them (*see pp.220 and 231*).

Buffalo Trace boasts the broadest age-range of whiskey in the US (from 4 to 23 years) and is the only US distillery using five recipes – a wheat whiskey, a rye whiskey, two rye bourbons, and a barley. The Buffalo Trace Experimental Collection of cask strength, wine-barrel-aged whiskeys was launched in 2006. It included a "Fire Pot Barrel" for which the barrel was heated to 39°C (102°F) prior to filling, to give a greater "burn" than usual. Subsequent releases in the Experimental Collection have included a 10-year-old Chardonnay, a 14- and a 16-year-old Cabernet Franc, and a 6-year-old Zinfandel.

BUFFALO TRACE KENTUCKY STRAIGHT BOURBON

BOURBON 45% ABV

Aged a minimum of nine years, it has aromas of vanilla, gum, mint, and molasses. Sweet, fruity, and spicy on the palate, with emerging brown sugar and oak. The finish is long, spicy, and fairly dry, with developing vanilla.

BULLEIT

Four Roses Distillery, 1224 Bonds Mill Road, Lawrenceburg, Kentucky
www.bulleit.com

Bulleit Bourbon originated in the 1830s with tavern-keeper and small-time distiller Augustus Bulleit, but production ceased after his death in 1860. However, the brand was revived, using the original recipe, in 1987 by his great-great-grandson Tom Bulleit. Seagram subsequently took over the label and from there it passed to Diageo. Although it is distilled by Four Roses (*see p.229*), brand owner Diageo has created the Bulleit Experience at the silent Stitzel-Weller Distillery in Louisville. (*www.bulleitexperience.com*)

BULLEIT BOURBON

BOURBON 40% ABV

Rich, oaky aromas lead into a mellow flavour, focused around vanilla and honey. The medium-length finish features vanilla and a hint of smoke.

CATDADDY

Piedmont Distillers, 203 East Murphy Street, Madison, North Carolina
www.catdaddymoonshine.com

Piedmont is the only licensed distillery in North Carolina, and its Catdaddy Moonshine celebrates the state's great heritage of illicit distilling. In 2005, ex-New Yorker Joe Michalek established Piedmont in Madison. It is the first legal distillery in the Carolinas since before Prohibition. "According to the lore of moonshine, only the best moonshine earns the right to be called the Catdaddy," says Joe Michalek. "True to the history of moonshine, every batch of Catdaddy is born in an authentic copper pot still."

CATDADDY CAROLINA MOONSHINE

CORN WHISKEY 40% ABV

Triple-distilled from corn in small batches, Catdaddy is sweet and spicy, with notes of vanilla and cinnamon.

CHARBAY

Domaine Charbay, 4001 Spring
Mountain Road, St Helena, California
www.charbay.com

The father-and-son partnership
of Miles and Marko Karakasevic
are 12th and 13th generation wine-
makers and distillers. Charbay
whiskeys are distilled in a 3,750-
litre (1,000-US-gallon) copper
alembic Charentais pot still. Many
innovative whiskeys have emerged
from the still, including R5 Lot
No. 3, double-distilled from Bear
Republic IPA, and Whiskey S
(Lot 211A), produced from Bear
Republic Stout. Whiskey Release
III was distilled using Pilsner.

CHARBAY WHISKEY RELEASE III
6-YEAR-OLD

AMERICAN WHISKEY 66.2% ABV
*This "hop-flavoured whiskey" offers
a herbal, lager-like nose, with lemon
and cloves, plus a note of vanilla. Big
fruit, spice, and herbal notes on the
full palate, with developing oak.*

EAGLE RARE

Buffalo Trace Distillery, 1001 Wilkinson
Boulevard, Frankfort, Kentucky
www.eaglerare.com

The Eagle Rare brand was
introduced in 1975 by Canadian
distilling giant Joseph E. Seagram
& Sons Inc. In 1989, it was acquired
by the Sazerac company of New
Orleans. In its present incarnation,
Eagle Rare is part of Sazerac's
Buffalo Trace Antique Collection,
which is updated annually.

In addition to the popular 10-
year-old expression, Eagle Rare
also releases small quantities of
a 17-year-old variant in the
autumn of each year.

EAGLE RARE 10-YEAR OLD

BOURBON 45% ABV
*Stewed fruits, spicy oak, new leather,
brittle toffee, and orange on the nose.
Rounded on the palate, with dried
fruits, spicy cocoa, almonds, and
a lengthy finish.*

EARLY TIMES

Brown-Forman Distillery, 850 Dixie
Highway, Louisville, Kentucky
www.earlytimes.com

Early Times takes its name from
a settlement near Bardstown
where it was created in 1860. It
cannot be classified as a bourbon
because some spirit is put into used
barrels, and bourbon legislation
dictates that all spirit of that name
must be matured in new barrels.

This version of Early Times was
introduced in 1981 to compete with
the increasingly popular, lighter-
bodied Canadian whiskies. The
Early Times mashbill is made up
of 79 per cent corn, 11 per cent
rye, and 10 per cent malted barley.

EARLY TIMES

KENTUCKY WHISKEY 40% ABV
*Quite light on the nose, with nuts
and spices. The palate offers more
of the same, together with honey
and butterscotch notes, leading into
a medium-length finish.*

EDGEFIELD

2126 Southwest Halsey Street,
Troutdale, Oregon
www.mcmenamins.com

Operated by the McMenamin's
hotel and pub group, Edgefield
Distillery is located in a former
dry store for root vegetables on the
beautiful Edgefield Manor Estate
at Troutdale. The distillery has
been in production since February
1998 and features a 4-m (12-ft)
tall copper and stainless-steel
still. According to Mcmenamin's,
it resembles a hybrid of a 19th-
century diving suit and oversized
coffee urn, a design made famous
by Holstein of Germany, the world's
oldest surviving still manufacturer.

EDGEFIELD HOGSHEAD

OREGON WHISKEY 46% ABV
*Hogshead whiskey has banana and
malt on the sweet, floral nose, with
vanilla and caramel notes on the
palate, plus barley, honey, and oak
in the medium-length finish.*

EVAN WILLIAMS BLACK LABEL

EVAN WILLIAMS SINGLE BARREL 1998 VINTAGE

ELIJAH CRAIG

Heaven Hill Distillery, 1701 West Breckinridge Street, Louisville, Kentucky
www.heavenhill.com

The Reverend Elijah Craig (1743–1808) was a Baptist minister who is widely viewed as the "father of bourbon", having reputedly invented the concept of using charred barrels to store and mature the spirit he made. There seems to be no hard evidence that he was the first person to make bourbon, but the association between a "man of God" and whiskey was seen as a useful tool in the struggle against the temperance movement.

ELIJAH CRAIG 12-YEAR-OLD

BOURBON 47% ABV

A classic bourbon, with sweet, mature aromas of caramel, vanilla, spice, and honey, plus a sprig of mint. Rich, full-bodied, and rounded on the mellow palate, with caramel, malt, corn, rye, and a hint of smoke. Sweet oak, liquorice, and vanilla dominate the finish.

ELMER T. LEE

Buffalo Trace Distillery, 1001 Wilkinson Boulevard, Frankfort, Kentucky
www.buffalotrace.com

Elmer T. Lee is a former Master Distiller at Buffalo Trace *(see p.223)*, having joined what was then the George T. Stagg Distillery in the 1940s. During his time there, the name changed first to the Albert B. Blanton Distillery (1953), then to the Ancient Age Distillery (1962), and finally to the Buffalo Trace Distillery in 2001.

Lee is credited with creating the first modern single barrel bourbon in 1984.

ELMER T. LEE SINGLE BARREL

BOURBON 45% ABV

Aged from six to eight years, this expression offers citrus, vanilla, and sweet corn merging on the fragrant nose, with a full and sweet palate, where honey, lingering caramel, and cocoa notes are also evident.

EVAN WILLIAMS

Heaven Hill Distillery, 1701 West Breckinridge Street, Louisville, Kentucky
www.evanwilliams.com

The second biggest-selling bourbon after Jim Beam, Evan Williams takes its name from the person considered by many experts to be Kentucky's first distiller.

Evan Williams was born in Wales but emigrated to and settled in Virginia, moving to what would become Kentucky (but was then Fincastle County of Virginia) in around 1780. Subsequently, he set up a small distillery on the Ohio River at the foot of what is now Fifth Street in Louisville.

According to an article in the *Louisville Courier-Journal* for 29 April 1889, Williams was a member of the early Board of Trustees of Louisville, and tradition says he never attended a meeting of the board without bringing a bottle of his whiskey, and that what he brought was

always drunk by the members before the meeting adjourned. He was apparently censured every time for doing so, but still he never left with a full jug.

EVAN WILLIAMS BLACK LABEL

BOURBON 43% ABV

The nose is quite light, yet aromatic, with vanilla and mint notes. The palate is initially sweet, with caramel, malt, and developing leather and spice notes.

EVAN WILLIAMS SINGLE BARREL 1998 VINTAGE

BOURBON 43.3% ABV

This is the world's only vintage-dated single barrel bourbon, selected by Master Distillers Parker and Craig Beam. The latest release, distilled in 1998, offers an aromatic nose of cereal, dried fruit, caramel, and vanilla. The palate comprises maple, molasses, cinnamon, nutmeg, and berry notes. There is a whiff of smoke, plus almonds and honey in the spicy finish.

WHISKEY TOUR: KENTUCKY

The state of Kentucky is the bourbon-producing heartland of the US and home to many of the best-known names in American whiskey. Most of the state's distilleries offer visitor facilities, allowing guests to study the production and maturation of this historic spirit. A tour embracing these distilleries and associated attractions not only provides an opportunity to make a real connection with bourbon and its fascinating heritage, but also offers a great way to experience the beauty of Kentucky and its hospitality.

USA

TOUR STATISTICS

DAYS: 5	LENGTH: 85 miles (137 km)	DISTILLERIES: 8
TRAVEL: Car	REGION: Northern Kentucky, US	

DAY 1: BUFFALO TRACE, WOODFORD RESERVE

BARRELS AT WOODFORD RESERVE

1 Frankfort, the state capital, has a range of hotels and restaurants, and is the home of **Buffalo Trace**. The distillery has a large visitors' centre and offers tours throughout the year. (*www.buffalotrace.com*)

2 **Woodford Reserve** lies near the attractive town of Versailles, in Kentucky's famous "blue grass" horse-breeding country. Its copper pot stills are the highlight of the distillery tour. (*www.woodfordreserve.com*)

DAY 2: WILD TURKEY, FOUR ROSES

3 Spectacularly situated on a hill above the Kentucky River, **Wild Turkey**'s Boulevard Distillery allows visitors into its production areas at most times of the year. (*www.wildturkeybourbon.com*)

4 **Four Roses** Distillery is a striking structure, built in the style of a Spanish Mission. Tours are available from autumn to spring (the distillery is closed throughout the summer). You can also pre-arrange to visit Four Roses' warehouse at Cox's Creek. (*www.fourrosesbourbon.com*)

LOUISVILLE

KENTUCKY

FINISH

9 JIM BEAM

OSCAR GETZ

7

6

BARTON

BARDSTOWN

5

HEAVEN HILL

Loretto Rd

8

MAKER'S MARK

WILD TURKEY EMBLEM

DAY 3: HEAVEN HILL, BARTON, OSCAR GETZ

5 Bardstown is renowned as the "World Capital of Bourbon", and makes an excellent base for visiting the distilleries in the area. Book a room at the Old Talbott Tavern *(www.talbotts. com)*, which is set in a building dating back to the late 1700s and offers a well-stocked bourbon bar. Then head out to the **Heaven Hill** Bourbon Heritage Center, which includes a tour of a bourbon-ageing rackhouse and the chance to taste two Heaven Hill whiskeys. *(www.heavenhill.com)*

HEAVEN HILL, BARDSTOWN

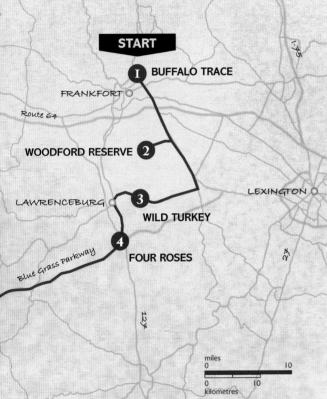

START

1 BUFFALO TRACE

FRANKFORT

Route 64

I 75

2 WOODFORD RESERVE

LAWRENCEBURG

3 WILD TURKEY

LEXINGTON

4 FOUR ROSES

Blue Grass Parkway

127

27

miles
0 — 10
0 — 10
kilometres

JIM BEAM'S CLERMONT DISTILLERY

6 The **Barton 1792 Distillery** in downtown Bardstown traditionally maintained a low profile compared to its neighbours, but nowadays comprehensive tours of the production areas are available, together with a state-of-the-art visitor centre. *(www.1792bourbon.com)*

7 A few blocks from Tom Moore, the **Oscar Getz** Whiskey Museum houses a collection of whiskey artefacts, including rare antique bottles, a moonshine still, advertising art, novelty whiskey containers, and Abraham Lincoln's original liquor licence. *(www.whiskeymuseum.com)*

DAY 4: MAKER'S MARK

8 The historic **Maker's Mark** Distillery stands on the banks of Hardin's Creek, near Loretto, in Marion County. The distillery grounds are notable as they act as an arboretum, being home to some 275 species of trees and shrubs. Guided tours of the distillery are available daily. *(www.makersmark.com)*

MAKER'S MARK

DAY 5: JIM BEAM

9 **Jim Beam's** Clermont Distillery offers tours of the site grounds, a working rackhouse and the Hartmann Cooperage Museum. The American Outpost is an on-site visitors' centre, with a film about the bourbon-making process at Jim Beam and displays of whiskey memorabilia that take in more than two centuries of bourbon history. *(www.jimbeam.com)*

WHISKY STYLES
TENNESSEE WHISKEY

Whiskey-making in Tennessee dates back at least as far as the 18th century. During the late 19th century, there were said to be some 700 stills in operation in the state, but Tennessee went "dry" in 1910 and distilling remained illegal until 1938.

Tennessee whiskeys are essentially bourbon-style spirits that undergo filtration through a thick layer of sugar-maple charcoal before the spirit is casked. The same legal criteria that apply to bourbon, in terms of strength and maturation period *(see p.221)*, also apply to Tennessee whiskey, but formal adoption of the classification of Tennessee whiskey as a distinct style can be dated to 1941, when the charcoal filtration process was recognized in a United States tax authority letter to Jack Daniel Distillers. This defining aspect is known as the Lincoln County Process in reference to Lincoln County, Tennessee, where Jack Daniel was founded.

Jack Daniel's *(see p.236)* is undoubtedly the best-known Tennessee whiskey. The distillers like to emphasize that their product has the distinctive classification of Tennessee whiskey – it is not a bourbon, although it has some of the characteristics of bourbon. The difference, according to Jack Daniel's, is that their whiskey is trickled very slowly through 3 metres (10 feet) of hard maple charcoal, right after distillation. The company claims that this extra step in the whiskey-making process provides the special character known only to Tennessee Whiskey. The charcoal mellowing process is said to remove some of the congeners and harsh fusel oils that are present in any grain alcohol.

The use of charcoal leaching was actually pioneered in 1825 by Alfred Eaton of Tullahoma, close to where the George Dickel Distillery operates today. Along with Jack Daniel, George Dickel *(see p.230)* is the only surviving, licensed, full-scale distillery left in Tennessee.

EZRA BROOKS

www.ezrabrooks.com

The Ezra Brooks brand was introduced in 1957 by Frank Silverman to take advantage of a shortage of Jack Daniel's (and its early presentation was markedly similar). The whiskey is sourced from the Hoffman Distilling Co. in Lawrenceburg, Kentucky, though the Ezra Brooks website claims it is from the Medley Distillery set up during 1901 in Owensboro, Kentucky. David Sherman Coporation (now Luxco Inc.) acquired the brand in 1993. The signature sour mash bourbon is produced at the Heaven Hill distillery, and an Ezra Brooks cinnamon liqueur is also now available.

EZRA BROOKS BOURBON

BOURBON 40% ABV

Sweet nose of vanilla, corn, and coconut. The palate offers stewed fruit, cream, and hint of oak. Milky coffee finish.

FOUR ROSES

1224 Bond Mills Road,
Lawrenceburg, Kentucky
www.fourrosesbourbon.com

Built to a striking Spanish Mission-style design in 1910, Four Roses Distillery near Lawrenceburg takes its name from the brand first trademarked by Georgia-born Paul Jones Jr in 1888. Legend has it that the southern belle with whom he was in love wore a corsage of four red roses to signify her acceptance of his marriage proposal, hence the name he gave to his bourbon.

In 2002, after a period of almost 60 years under the ownership of the Seagram organization, when it had become a bestseller in the booming European and Asian market, the Four Roses trademark brand, production, bottling, and warehousing facilities were bought by Tokyo-based Kirin Brewery Company. In addition to its own Four Roses whiskeys, the distillery now produces a number of other well-known brands, including Bulleit Bourbon *(see p.223)* and I.W. Harper President's Reserve Bourbon.

FOUR ROSES SINGLE BARREL

BOURBON (VARIABLE ABV)

Offers a rich, complex nose, comprising malt, fruits, spices, and fudge. Long and mellow in the mouth, with vanilla, oak, and a hint of menthol. The finish is long, spicy, and decidedly mellow.

FOUR ROSES SMALL BATCH

BOURBON 45% ABV

Mild and refined on the nose, with nutmeg and restrained honey. Bold and rich on the well-balanced palate, with spices, fruit, and honey flavours. The finish is long and insinuating, with developing notes of vanilla.

GARRISON BROTHERS

Garrison Brothers Distillery,
1827 Hye Albert Road, Hye, Texas
www.garrisonbros.com

The oldest legal distillery in Texas, Garrison Brothers has produced nothing but bourbon since it opened in 2005. The distillery uses organic yellow corn from the Texas Panhandle, organic winter wheat from the Garrison ranch, and two-row winter barley from the Pacific Northwest and Canada. Grain is ground daily, and the sweet mash is cooked one batch at a time. The distillery receives many visitors, and its whiskey has won several major awards.

GARRISON BROTHERS TEXAS STRAIGHT BOURBON

BOURBON 47% ABV

Rich aromas of honey and vanilla on the nose, continuing onto the palate of apple, cinnamon, and black pepper.

GEORGE DICKEL NO. 12

GEORGE DICKEL BARREL SELECT

GEORGE DICKEL NO. 8

GEORGE DICKEL

1950 Cascade Hollow Road,
Normandy, Tennessee
www.georgedickel.com

Along with Jack Daniel's, George
Dickel is the last licensed, full-scale
distillery in the state of Tennessee,
though a century ago there were
around 700 operating there.

The distillery uses the spelling
"whisky" because founder George
A. Dickel insisted that the spirit he
made was as smooth as the finest
Scotch. Dickel was German by
birth and a Nashville merchant
before founding his Cascade
Hollow distillery in the 1870s.
He used pure water from the
nearby Cascade Springs source.

The year 1910 saw the arrival
of Prohibition in Tennessee, and
the Dickel operation was moved
to Kentucky, subsequently being
acquired by Schenley Distilling
Co. In 1958, Schenley decided
that George Dickel should return
to its roots, and a new distillery

was built close to the original
Cascade Hollow location and
using recipes from Dickel's own
notes. Dickel is now owned by
the Diageo group.

GEORGE DICKEL NO. 12

TENNESSEE WHISKY 45% ABV
*The nose is aromatic, with fruit, leather,
butterscotch, and a whiff of charcoal
and vanilla. The palate is rich, with rye,
chocolate, fruit, and vanilla. The finish
offers vanilla toffee and drying oak.*

GEORGE DICKEL BARREL SELECT

TENNESSEE WHISKY 43% ABV
*Aromas of rich corn, honey, nuts, and
caramel lead into a full body with soft
vanilla, spices, and roast nuts. The long,
creamy finish boasts almond and spices.*

GEORGE DICKEL NO. 8

TENNESSEE WHISKY 40% ABV
*Sweet on the nose, with chocolate,
cocoa, and vanilla. The palate is quite
sweet and well rounded, with fresh
fruit and vanilla notes. The short
finish features spices and charcoal.*

GEORGE T. STAGG

Buffalo Trace, Sazerak Company Inc., Frankfort, Kentucky
www.buffalotracedistillery.com

Part of the Buffalo Trace Antique Collection, George T. Stagg takes its name from the one-time owner of what is now the Buffalo Trace Distillery. In the early 1880s, the distillery was owned by Edmund Haynes Taylor Jr. During tough economic times he obtained a loan from his friend Stagg – who later foreclosed on Taylor, taking over his company in the process.

GEORGE T. STAGG 2008 EDITION

BOURBON 72.4% ABV
Distilled in the spring of 1993, this high-strength whiskey boasts a rich nose of butterscotch, marzipan, sweet oak, and glacé cherries. The palate features corn, roasted coffee beans, leather, spice, and mature oak, with a long toffee and spice finish.

GEORGIA MOON

Heaven Hill Distillery, 1701 West Breckinridge Street, Louisville, Kentucky
www.heavenhill.com

Corn whiskey is distilled from a fermented mash of not less than 80 per cent corn, and no minimum maturation period is specified. One of the best-known examples is Heaven Hill's Georgia Moon. With a label that promises the contents to be less than 30 days old, and available bottled in a mason jar *(see p.233)*, Georgia Moon harks back to the old days of moonshining.

GEORGIA MOON

CORN WHISKEY 40% ABV
The nose commences with an initial tang of sour liquor, followed by the smell of sweet corn. The palate suggests cabbage water and plums, along with developing sweeter, candy-corn notes. The finish is short. Drinkers should not expect anything sophisticated.

HANCOCK'S RESERVE

Buffalo Trace Distillery, 1001 Wilkinson Boulevard, Frankfort, Kentucky
www.buffalotrace.com

This whiskey, which is usually created from barrels of spirit aged for around 10 years, takes its name from Hancock Taylor, great-uncle of US president Zachary Taylor, and an early surveyor of Kentucky. He was shot and killed by Native Americans in 1774, and it is said that his deathbed will was one of the first legal documents executed in the region.

HANCOCK'S RESERVE PRESIDENT'S SINGLE BARREL

BOURBON 44.45% ABV
Oily on the nose, with liquorice, caramel, and spicy rye. Sweet in the mouth, with malt, fudge, and vanilla notes. Drying in the finish, with notable oak notes, but the whiskey's residual sweetness remains to the end.

I.W. HARPER

Four Roses Distillery, 1224 Bond Mills Road, Lawrenceburg, Kentucky
www.iwharper.com

The historic and once best-selling I.W. Harper brand was established by Jewish businessman Isaac Wolfe Bernheim (1848–1945), a major figure in the bourbon business at the turn of the 20th century. It was made at the Bernheim Distillery *(see p.219)* in Louisville. It is now produced in no-age-statement (NAS) and 15-year-old formats for current owners Diageo by Four Roses Distillery and is one of the leading bourbons in the Japanese market.

I.W. HARPER

BOURBON 43% ABV
A big-bodied bourbon in which pepper combines with mint, oranges, caramel, and quite youthful charring on the nose, while caramel, apples, and oak feature on the elegant palate. The finish is dry and smoky.

HEAVEN HILL

BERNHEIM ORIGINAL *(SEE P.219)*

PARKER'S HERITAGE *(SEE P.249)*

HEAVEN HILL

1701 West Breckinridge Street,
Louisville, Kentucky
www.heavenhill.com

Heaven Hill is the US's largest independent producer of distilled spirits to remain in family ownership, and the last family-owned distillery in Kentucky. A Heaven Hill distillery had been built in 1890, but the present one was established in 1935, soon after the repeal of Prohibition, by five Shapira brothers, who built their distillery just south of Bardstown, and whose descendants control the firm to this day.

The Shapira brothers were experts in the dry-goods business, but had no practical knowledge of bourbon distillation. However, they employed Joe Beam, a cousin of legendary Jim Beam, who proved adept at making fine spirit.

More recently, Parker Beam has flown the flag for Heaven Hill as a high-profile Master Distiller,

starting work at the distillery in 1960, and succeeding his father, Earl, as Master Distiller in 1975. Parker's son, Craig, is a seventh-generation Master Distiller, following in the footsteps of his now-retired and hugely respected father.

On 7 November 1996, the distillery and warehouses were almost completely destroyed by fire, and over 350,000 litres (90,000 US gallons) of maturing spirit was lost. As a result, the company purchased Diageo's technologically advanced Bernheim Distillery in Louisville, and all production was moved to that site. For most of its existence, Heaven Hill has concentrated on its flagship bourbon labels, Evan Williams *(see p.225)* and Elijah Craig *(p.225)*. Its speciality is older, higher proof bourbons, traditional in character, full-bodied, and complex. As part of its notably diverse portfolio, Heaven Hill also produces

Bernheim Original *(see p.219)*, Pikesville *(p.252)*, Parker's *(p.249)*, and Rittenhouse Rye *(p.253)*. Additionally, it is the only remaining national producer of corn whiskeys such as Mellow Corn *(see p.246)* and Georgia Moon *(p.231)*. Heaven Hill is also a major supplier of "own-label" whiskey to other customers.

HEAVEN HILL
BOURBON 40% ABV
An excellent and competitively priced "entry-level" bourbon, with a nose of oranges and corn bread, a sweet, oily mouth-feel, and vanilla and corn featuring on the well-balanced palate.

HENRY MCKENNA

Heaven Hill Distillery, 1701 West
Breckinridge Street, Louisville, Kentucky
www.heavenhill.com

Irish-born Henry McKenna emigrated to Fairfield, Kentucky, where, in 1855, he began to distil a whiskey that soon became very popular. McKenna died in 1893, and, later, Prohibition saw the closure of his distillery. However, McKenna's family re-opened the plant after Prohibition was repealed in 1933, and later sold it to Seagram's. The brand was eventually discontinued, and the name was purchased by Heaven Hill.

HENRY MCKENNA SINGLE BARREL 10-YEAR-OLD
BOURBON 50% ABV
Boasts an interesting blend of citrus fruits, charcoal, vanilla, and caramel on the nose. Contrasts continue to the palate, where spices and charred oak vie pleasingly with mint and honey.

WHISKY STYLES
CORN WHISKEY

Corn whiskey is distilled from a fermented mash of not less than 80 per cent corn at less than 80 per cent ABV. It is the one American whiskey that does not have to be aged in new, charred-oak barrels, and no minimum maturation period is specified. It is often sold new and clear and, when maturation does take place, it tends to be for a period of months rather than years.

Corn whiskey was a favourite illicitly distilled, "moonshine" product. The story is told of a well-known early 20th-century North Carolina moonshiner by the name of Quill Rose who, when asked by a judge whether ageing would not be beneficial to the liquor, is supposed to have replied, "Your honour has been misinformed. I have kept some for a week one time and I couldn't tell it was a bit better than when it was new and fresh." The growth in production of corn whiskey dates back to the years following the imposition of the first tax on spirits in North America during 1791, and the subsequent Whiskey Rebellion of 1794 by distillers and their supporters, who refused to pay the tax, assaulted excise officers, and marched on Pittsburgh in protest. The rebellion came to an end after 13,000 troops were assembled and marched down the Monongahela River, under the command of General George Washington.

After the rebellion had been suppressed, many disgruntled distillers of mainly rye whiskey subsequently moved south and west from Maryland, Pennsylvania, and Virginia into Indiana, Illinois, Kentucky, and Tennessee. As these were great corn-producing states, it was inevitable that this migration led to a growth in whiskeys made from corn rather than rye.

Today, the best-known commercial brands of corn whiskey include Georgia Moon *(see p.231)* and Mellow Corn from Heaven Hill *(p.246)*, while a number of micro-distillers also produce corn whiskeys.

Woodford Reserve *(see p.264)* may have the smallest distillery in Kentucky, but its triple-distilled bourbons are held in high regard. The distillery is operated by the Brown-Forman Corporation.

HUDSON MANHATTAN RYE

HUDSON NEW YORK CORN

HIGH WEST

27649 Old Lincoln Highway,
Wanship, Utah
www.highwest.com

High West was established by
David Perkins during 2007 in Park
City, Utah. However, since 2015,
distillation has taken place in a
6,000-litre (1,600-US-gallon) pot
still at Blue Sky Ranch, Wanship,
a facility described by its owners
as "...the world's only distillery-
dude-ranch...!" High West makes
a variety of whiskeys, including
Valley Tan Utah oat whiskey and the
Bourbon and rye "blend" Bourye.
The distillery is best known for its
ryes, especially those released
under the Rendezvous label.

HIGH WEST RENDEZVOUS RYE

RYE WHISKEY 46% ABV

*Rendezvous Rye is a blend of 16- and
6-year-old rye. The nose offers pepper
and spice, vanilla, and toffee, with an
intense, sweet, fruity, smoky palate and
a long, spicy, caramel-coated finish.*

HIRSCH RESERVE

Distributor: Preiss Imports

Hirsch Reserve is a drop of US
whiskey history. The spirit itself
was distilled in 1974 at Michter's
Distillery, the last surviving one
in Pennsylvania. Michter's closed in
1988, but one Adolf H. Hirsch had
acquired a considerable stock of
the spirit some years previously
and, after it had been matured for
16 years, it was put into stainless
steel tanks to prevent further
ageing. This whiskey is now
available from Preiss Imports but,
once gone, is gone forever.

HIRSCH RESERVE

BOURBON 45.8% ABV

*Caramel, honey, and rye dominate the
complex nose, with a whiff of smoke
also coming through. Oily corn, honey,
and oak on the rich palate, with rye and
more oak in the drying finish.*

HUDSON

Tuthilltown Distillery, 14 Gristmill Lane,
Gardiner, New York
www.tuthilltown.com

In 1825, New York State had
over 1,000 working distilleries
and produced a major share of
the nation's whiskey. These days,
Tuthilltown is New York's only
remaining distillery. Based in a
converted granary, the distillery
adjoins a gristmill, which dates
back to 1788 and is listed on
the National Register of
Historic Places.

Tuthilltown Distillery was
founded in 2001 by Brian Lee
and Ralph Erenzo, and is now
equipped with a 400-litre
(106-US-gallon) pot still that was
installed in 2005. Tuthill Spirits
produces a quartet of "Hudson"
bottlings, including a rich and
full-flavoured four-grain whiskey
and a rich, caramel single malt,
which is intended to be an
American "re-interpretation"

of traditional Scottish whiskies.
The distillery also produces Old
Gristmill Authentic American
Corn Whiskey. In 2010, William
Grant & Sons Ltd acquired
the Hudson Whiskey brand,
while Tuthilltown distillery
remains independent.

HUDSON MANHATTAN RYE

RYE WHISKEY 46% ABV

*The first whiskey to be distilled in New
York State for more than 80 years. Floral
notes and a smooth finish on the palate,
with a recognizable rye edge.*

HUDSON NEW YORK CORN

BOURBON 46% ABV

*Made with 100 per cent New York
State corn, this is the first bourbon ever
to be made in New York, and the first
pot-distilled whiskey to be produced
legally in New York since Prohibition.
It is a mildly sweet, smooth spirit with
subtle hints of vanilla and caramel.*

THE SECRETS OF...
JACK DANIEL'S

The story of Jack Daniel's, America's best-selling whiskey, begins with the birth of Jasper "Jack" Newton Daniel in Lincoln County, Tennessee, in 1846.

Legend has it that Jack did not get on with his stepmother and, at the age of just six, left home to live first with an elderly neighbour and his family, and then with local farmer and Lutheran lay preacher Dan Call, of Louse Creek, who also ran a whiskey still. It was one of Call's slaves, Nearest Green, who taught Jack the art of distilling.

Pressure from his congregation eventually forced Call to choose religion over whiskey-making, so young Jack took over the business and, by 1860, the precocious teenager owned the still.

Jack Daniel's Tennessee whiskey has come a long way from those modest beginnings, and enjoys an iconic status as one of the world's highest-profile drink brands. It is distilled in Lynchburg, to which, every year, hundreds of thousands of visitors flock in pilgrimage. However, while they can purchase any number of souvenirs bearing the Jack Daniel's name, they cannot buy the whiskey itself. Lynchburg is situated in Moore County, which is officially "dry".

Despite an image in which the figure of its founder plays a major part, since 1956, Jack Daniel's has belonged to Brown-Forman *(see p.220)*, which also owns Kentucky distilleries producing Old Forester *(p.248)*, Early Times *(p.224)*, and Woodford Reserve *(p.264)*.

▲ THE REAL JACK DANIEL
"Mr Jack" is a flamboyant figure in the history of American whiskey. He was reputedly quite a ladies' man, although he never married, and the brand name Old No. 7 is sometimes said to have referred to the number of his girlfriends.

▲ A TENNESSEE INSTITUTION
Licensed in 1886, the Jack Daniel Distillery is the oldest registered distillery in the US. Lem Motlow was Jack's nephew, who joined him in 1887 and inherited the business. The sign remains unchanged.

▼ TESTING THE SPIRIT

There is no set schedule to determine when the whiskey is ready, as maturation can vary from barrel to barrel, and by the relative positions of barrels in the warehouses. A panel of experts regularly noses the maturing spirit to decide when it's ready for bottling.

▲ NEW HAND-MADE CASKS

Jack Daniel is the only distillery to craft its own barrels by hand using new white oak. The interiors are then charred to caramelize the wood's natural sugars. As a result, the whiskey matured in these casks is deeply mellow, amber-hued, and aromatic.

◄ THE CHARCOAL ELEMENT

Jack Daniel creates its own charcoal by burning sugar maple wood in the rickyard, to be used in Tennessee whiskey's signature Lincoln County Process. This is a method of mellowing, in which the spirit is filtered slowly through 3 m (10 ft) of charcoal before being matured, resulting in a very smooth whiskey.

▲ MR JACK'S GRAVE

Jack Daniel died in 1911, having been unfortunate enough to contract blood poisoning after kicking his safe door in frustration when he forgot the combination. He is buried in Lynchburg's cemetery, close to his beloved distillery. The chairs are said to have been placed there for grieving Lynchburg ladies.

JACK DANIEL'S SINGLE BARREL

GENTLEMAN JACK

JACK DANIEL'S OLD NO. 7

MADE IN TENNESSEE

BOTTLED AT THE DISTILLERY

JACK DANIEL'S

280 Lynchburg Road,
Lynchburg, Tennessee
www.jackdaniels.com

Jack Daniel's has become an iconic brand worldwide, and is America's best-selling whiskey. Its founder, Jasper Newton "Jack" Daniel reputedly started to make whiskey as a child, and by 1860, was running his own distilling business at the tender age of 14.

Today, the Jack Daniel Distillery at Lynchburg, Tennessee, is owned by the Brown-Forman Corporation (*see p.220*) and is a major visitor attraction. Along with its fellow Tennessee distiller George Dickel (*p.230*), Jack Daniel's uses a version of the Lincoln County Process of charcoal mellowing prior to the spirit being put into barrels.

JACK DANIEL'S OLD NO. 7

TENNESSEE WHISKEY 40% ABV
Jack Daniel's presents a powerful nose of vanilla, smoke, and liquorice. On the palate it offers oily cough-mixture and
treacle, *with a final kick of maple syrup and burnt wood lingering in the surprisingly long finish. Not particularly complex, but decidedly muscular and certainly distinctive.*

JACK DANIEL'S SINGLE BARREL

TENNESSEE WHISKEY 47% ABV
Introduced in 1997, Single Barrel is charming and smooth on the nose, with notes of peach, vanilla, nuts, and oak. The comparatively dry palate offers depth, richness, and elegance, with oily corn, liquorice, malt, and oak. Malt and oak are also highlighted in the lengthy finish, along with a touch of rye spice.

GENTLEMAN JACK

TENNESSEE WHISKEY 40% ABV
After ageing for about four years, this is charcoal-mellowed once before barrelling. The result is a nose that is considerably more mellow, muted, and fruity than that of Old No. 7. The palate also yields more fruit, as well as notes of caramel, liquorice, and vanilla, and a whiff of smoke.

Jim Beam *(see overleaf)* is a global company with industrial-scale distilleries, but its American Outpost at Clermont, Kentucky, evokes the older traditions of whiskey.

JIM BEAM

Jim Beam Distillery, 149 Happy Hollow Road, Clermont, Kentucky
www.jimbeam.com

Jim Beam is the best-selling bourbon brand in the world, and its origins date back to the 18th century, when German-born farmer and miller Jacob Boehm travelled west into Bourbon County, Kentucky, from Virginia, carrying with him his copper pot still. He is reputed to have sold his first barrel of whiskey for cash in 1795, and subsequently moved his distilling operation into Washington County when he inherited land there from his father-in-law.

Jacob had two sons, John and David, and during David Beam's time at the helm, the distillery adopted the name Old Tub. In 1854, his son, also David, moved the venture to Nelson County, where the Clear Springs Distillery was established close to a railroad.

Jim (James Beauregard) Beam himself was Jacob Boehm's great-grandson. He joined the family business at the age of 16, in 1880, and trade prospered in the years before Prohibition forced the closure of Clear Springs.

Jim Beam founded the present Clermont Distillery close to Clear Springs soon after the repeal of Prohibition in 1933, despite being 70 years old at the time. He died in 1947, five years after ''Jim Beam'' first appeared on the bottle label, and two years after the firm had been sold to Harry Blum of Chicago, previously a partner in the company for several years.

The Beam family connection, however, carries on to this day through Fred Noe, great-grandson of Jim and a seventh generation Beam family member. Fred's father was Booker Noe, acknowledged as one of the true greats of bourbon distilling, and the man principally responsible for developing "small batch bourbon". Clermont, near the bourbon capital of Bardstown, remains the principal Jim Beam distillery, but its output is boosted by that of the nearby Boston distillery, which dates from 1953.

In addition to Jim Beam brands, a range of specialist whiskeys is also produced, including Baker's Kentucky (*see p.218*), Booker's Kentucky (*p.220*), Basil Hayden's (*p.219*), Knob Creek (*p.243*), Old Crow (*p.247*), Old Grand-Dad (*p.248*), and Old Taylor (*p.249*). Additionally, Beam Suntory Inc. operates the Maker's Mark Distillery (*p.244*) at Loretto.

JIM BEAM WHITE LABEL 4-YEAR-OLD

TENNESSEE WHISKEY 40% ABV

Vanilla and delicate floral notes on the nose. Initially sweet, with restrained vanilla, then drier, oaky notes develop, fading into furniture polish and soft malt in the finish. Once described, with some justification, as "a mellow baritone of a spirit".

JIM BEAM RYE

RYE WHISKEY 40% ABV

Light, perfumed, and aromatic on the nose, with lemon and mint, Jim Beam Rye is oily in the mouth, with soft fruits, honey, and rye on the palate, drying and spicy in the finish.

JIM BEAM BLACK LABEL 6-YEAR-OLD

BOURBON 43% ABV

The nose offers caramel, vanilla, and ripe oranges, while the palate is smooth, with honey, fudge, and citrus fruits.

JIM BEAM DEVIL'S CUT

BOURBON 45% ABV

Freshly planed wood and spicy vanilla on the nose, with vanilla and oak majoring on the palate, plus more vanilla and spice.

JIM BEAM BLACK LABEL 6-YEAR-OLD

JIM BEAM DEVIL'S CUT

JEFFERSON'S

McLain & Kyne Ltd (Castle Brands),
Louisville, Kentucky
www.jeffersonsbourbon.com

The Louisville company of McLain
& Kyne Ltd was formed by Trey
Zoeller to carry on the distilling
traditions of his ancestors. McLain
& Kyne specializes in premium,
very small batch bourbons, most
notably Jefferson's and Sam
Houston (see p.254).

JEFFERSON'S SMALL BATCH
8-YEAR-OLD

BOURBON (VARIABLE ABV)

*This bourbon has been aged in the heart
of metal-clad warehouses to accentuate
the extreme temperatures of Kentucky,
forcing the bourbon to expand deep
into the barrel and extract desirable
flavours from the wood. The nose is
fresh, with vanilla and ripe peach notes,
while the smooth, sweet palate boasts
more vanilla, caramel, and berries.
The finish is quite delicate, with toasted
vanilla and cream.*

JOHNNY DRUM

Kentucky Bourbon Distillers, 1869
Loretto Road, Bardstown, Kentucky
www.kentuckybourbonwhiskey.com

Johnny Drum is said to have
been a Confederate drummer boy
during the American Civil War,
and later a pioneer farmer and
distiller in Kentucky.

Johnny Drum bourbon was
formerly produced in the Willett
Distillery near Bardstown, but this
closed in the early 1980s when the
last of the Willett family members
retired. The plant was acquired by
Kentucky Bourbon Distillers Ltd,
for whom a range of whiskeys is
distilled under contract.

JOHNNY DRUM

BOURBON (VARIABLE ABV)

*Smooth and elegant on the nose, with
vanilla, gentle spices, and smoke. This
is a full-bodied bourbon, well-balanced
and smooth in the mouth, with vanilla and
a hint of smoke. The finish is lingering
and sophisticated.*

KENTUCKY
GENTLEMAN

Barton Distillery, 300 Barton Road,
Bardstown, Kentucky
www.sazerac.com

Kentucky Gentleman is offered
both as a blended whiskey and
as a straight bourbon.

According to its producers,
the blended version is created
from a blend of Kentucky straight
bourbon whiskey and spirits from
the finest grains.

The popular straight expression
enjoys a notably loyal following
in the southern states, particularly
Florida, Alabama, and Virginia.

KENTUCKY GENTLEMAN

BOURBON 40% ABV

*Made with a higher percentage of rye
than most Barton whiskeys, this offers
caramel and sweet oak aromas, and is
oily, full-bodied, spicy, and fruity in the
mouth. Rye, fruits, vanilla, and cocoa
figure in the lingering, flavourful, and
comparatively assertive finish.*

KENTUCKY TAVERN

Barton Distillery, 300 Barton Road,
Bardstown, Kentucky
www.sazerac.com

The Kentucky Tavern brand has
been established for over a century,
and was the leading whiskey
produced by the Louisville-based
Glenmore Distilleries Company.
It was named after a bar and
restaurant situated on the east
side of Louisville.

In 1992, Glenmore was acquired
by United Distillers, which has
since been amalgamated with
Diageo, and the Kentucky Tavern
brand was subsequently sold to
Sazerac Company Inc.

KENTUCKY TAVERN

BOURBON 40% ABV

*Assertive and oaky on the nose,
with apples and honey. Spices,
oak, more apples, and a note of
rye contribute to the palate, while
the medium-length finish is peppery
and oaky.*

GEORGIA PEACH

NEW YORK APPLE

KESSLER

Jim Beam Distillery, 149 Happy Hollow
Road, Clermont, Kentucky
www.jimbeam.com

One of the best-known and most
highly regarded blended American
whiskeys, Kessler traces its origins
back to 1888, when it was first
blended by one Julius Kessler, who
travelled from saloon to saloon
across the West, selling his whiskey
as he went. Kessler Whiskey was
acquired by The Seagram Company
during the mid-1930s, eventually
passing to Beam Inc., which was
then purchased by Suntory Holdings
in 2014. Kessler is now produced
by Beam Suntory, and is the
second-best-selling American
blended whiskey.

KESSLER

BLEND 40% ABV
*Lives up to its "Smooth as silk" slogan.
Light, fruity nose and sweet palate with
enough complexity of liquorice and leather
achieved by the blend's four-year ageing.*

KNOB CREEK

Jim Beam Distillery, 149 Happy Hollow
Road, Clermont, Kentucky
www.knobcreek.com

Knob Creek is the Kentucky town
where Abraham Lincoln's father,
Thomas, owned a farm and worked
at the local distillery. This bourbon
is one of three introduced in 1992,
when Jim Beam launched its Small
Batch Bourbon Collection. It is
made to the same high-rye formula
as the Jim Beam-distilled Basil
Hayden's *(see p.219)* and Old
Grand-Dad *(p.248)* brands.

Several new bottles have been
added to the Knob Creek range
since its launch, including, in 2012,
Knob Creek Straight Rye Whiskey
– the brand's first expression not to
carry an age statement.

KNOB CREEK 9-YEAR-OLD

BOURBON 50% ABV
*Nutty nose of sweet, tangy fruit and rye.
Malt, spice, and nuts on the fruity palate,
drying finish with notes of vanilla.*

LEOPOLD BROTHERS

5258 Joliet Street, Denver, Colorado
www.leopoldbros.com

Leopold Bros. is a family owned
and operated small batch distillery
based in Denver, Colorado, the home
state of brothers Scott and Todd
Leopold. Scott takes care of the
business side of the company, while
Master Distiller Todd Leopold
makes liqueurs, vodka, gin, rum,
absinthe, and flavoured whiskeys in
the distillery's 180-litre (48-US-
gallon) copper pot still. The
distillery specializes in small batch
blends, so all blends are made using
artisan processes and the bottles
are subsequently hand-numbered.

Unusual blends include a whiskey
made from the juice of Rocky
Mountain peaches and another
flavoured whiskey made in a similar
fashion from blackberries. These
fruit whiskies are matured in used,
charred bourbon barrels, so that the
sweetness of the fruit is balanced by
the smoothness of a bourbon finish.

Leopold Bros. now also produces
a "Small Batch Whiskey", made
from rye and American corn.

GEORGIA PEACH

FLAVOURED WHISKEY 30% ABV
*Peach juice is blended with small batch
whiskey, and matured in bourbon barrels.
The result is a peachy-sweet spirit with
oak, vanilla, and raisins.*

NEW YORK APPLE

FLAVOURED WHISKEY 40% ABV
*Blended with apples grown in New York
State, this whiskey is racked into used
bourbon barrels for additional ageing.
According to its producers, the barrels
add the oak, raisin, and vanilla finish,
while the mix of the sweet and tart
apples balances perfectly with the
charred oak finish.*

THE SECRETS OF...
MAKER'S MARK

The Maker's Mark Distillery stands on the banks of Hardin's Creek, near Loretto in Marion County, Kentucky. Established in 1805, its modern history dates from 1953.

That was the year Taylor William Samuels Sr bought the dilapidated distillery known as Happy Hollow. His great-great-great-grandfather had been a Kentucky whiskey-maker in the 1780s, and Taylor was in possession of the secret family recipe for bourbon. However, one of his first acts on taking over at Happy Hollow was symbolically to burn the recipe, declaring: 'Nothing that we need! To craft a truly new and soft-spoken bourbon, we will have to start from scratch."

By this, Samuels meant a more mellow whiskey than was the norm at the time. He achieved this using maize and malted barley, coupled with red winter wheat, rather than the usual rye. He used the spelling "whisky" from the outset, in honour of his Scottish ancestry.

Long acknowledged as one of Kentucky's great bourbons, in 1981, Maker's Mark passed out of family ownership. It is now part of Beam Suntory Inc., which also owns Jim Beam (see p.240).

▲ MASHBILL
The grain recipe, or mashbill, for Maker's Mark comprises 70 per cent corn, 16 per cent red winter wheat, and 14 per cent malted barley, producing a comparatively soft, gentle spirit – the "soft-spoken bourbon" that T.W. Samuels had envisioned from the beginning.

▼ COPPER POT STILLS
The "distiller's beer" is initially distilled in a five-storey column still, after which it undergoes a secondary distillation in copper pot stills in order to remove any remaining impurities, leaving a clear 65% ABV spirit.

▲ DISTILLER'S BEER
Yeast is added to the cooked mash in the traditional fermentation tanks or "washbacks" made of rare cypress wood. In these, the action of the yeast on the mash produces what is known as "distiller's beer"

◀ **CHARRING THE CASKS**
Barrels undergo a "charring" stage, in which their interiors are seared with fire. By law, bourbon must be matured in new, charred white-oak barrels. The layer of char on the wood facilitates the maturation process.

▼ **RICK HOUSES**
At Maker's Mark, barrels of spirit are stored in three-storey warehouses or "rick houses", and are periodically moved around within each warehouse to ensure consistency of maturation.

▲ **MONITORING THE CASKS**
The new make is put into oak barrels for maturation. A watchful eye is kept on the spirit while it's maturing to ensure that it is bottled at the peak of perfection. As part of this process, each barrel is sampled five times during the maturation period.

◀ **DIPPING IN WAX**
After being machine-filled, each bottle of Maker's Mark is labelled by hand and then its neck is dipped into hot wax for a few seconds to create the brand's characteristic red wax seal.

CREATING THE SEAL ▶
This was the brainchild of Marge Samuels, wife of T.W. "Bill" Samuels. She collected antique cognac bottles, many of which were sealed with wax. She also designed the "Maker's Mark" symbol itself.

MAKER'S MARK

Maker's Mark Distillery, 3350 Burks
Springs Road, Loretto, Kentucky
www.makersmark.com

Maker's Mark Distillery is located
on the banks of Hardin's Creek,
near Loretto. Established in 1805,
it is the US's oldest working
distillery remaining on its original
site. The Maker's Mark brand was
developed during the 1950s by Bill
Samuels Jr, and today is owned by
Fortune Brands Inc. The use of
the Scots spelling of "whisky",
rare among US brands, is a nod to
the Samuels' Scottish ancestry.

MAKER'S MARK

BOURBON 45% ABV

*A subtle, complex, clean nose, with
vanilla and spice, a delicate floral note
of roses, plus lime and cocoa beans.
Medium in body, it offers a palate of
fresh fruit, spices, eucalyptus, and ginger
cake. The finish features more spices,
fresh oak with a hint of smoke, and
a final flash of peach cheesecake.*

MCCARTHY'S

Clear Creek Distillery, 2389 NW Wilson
Street, Portland, Oregon
www.clearcreekdistillery.com

Steve McCarthy established
Clear Creek Distillery in 1986,
and has been distilling whiskey
for over two decades. He is of
the opinion that, since it is made
from peat-malted barley brought
in from Scotland, "our whiskey
would be a single malt Scotch if
Oregon were Scotland".

MCCARTHY'S OREGON

SINGLE MALT 40% ABV

*McCarthy's is initially matured in former
sherry casks for two or three years, then
for six to twelve months in barrels made
from air-dried Oregon oak. Kippery and
spicy on the nose, with a hint of sulphur,
peat, and vanilla, it is big-bodied and
oily, smoky-sweet on the meaty palate,
and with dry oak, malt, spice, and salt
in the long finish.*

MELLOW CORN

Heaven Hill Distillery, 1701 West
Breckinridge Street, Louisville, Kentucky

According to Heaven Hill, "The
forerunner and kissing cousin to
Bourbon, American straight corn
whiskey is defined by the US
Government as having a recipe
or mashbill with a minimum of
81 per cent corn, the rest being
malted barley and rye."

Today, Heaven Hill is the sole
remaining national producer of
this classic whiskey style, bottling
Georgia Moon (*see p.231*) in
addition to Mellow Corn.

MELLOW CORN

CORN WHISKEY 50% ABV

*Wood varnish and vanilla, with floral
and herbal notes on the nose. The palate
is big and oily, and fruity, with toffee
apples. More fruit, cinder toffee, and
understated vanilla complete the finish.
Young and boisterous.*

MICHTER'S

Michter's Distillery, 2351 New
Millennium Drive, Louisville, Kentucky
www.michters.com

Michter's whiskey was distilled
in Pennsylvania until 1989, when
its owners were declared bankrupt
and the distillery closed down. The
brand name was resurrected by
businessmen Joseph J. Magliocco
and Dick Newman a few years
later, and production now takes
place in the Michter's Distillery
in the Shively section of Louisville,
Kentucky. A number of ryes and
bourbons are marketed under the
Michter's label, along with an
unblended American whiskey and
a sour mash whiskey.

MICHTER'S US NO.1 BOURBON

BOURBON 45.7% ABV

*Very spicy on the nose, with caramel,
apricots, and cinnamon. Sweet palate
delivery, with more apricots, cloves,
black pepper, and a smoky note.
Spicy oak in the finish.*

NOAH'S MILL

Kentucky Bourbon Distillers Ltd,
Nelson County, Kentucky
www.kentuckybourbonwhiskey.com

Like Johnny Drum *(see p.242)*,
Noah's Mill was once distilled in
the now silent Willett Distillery,
which operated in Bardstown
from 1935 until the early 1980s.
In 1984, the site was bought by
Thompson Willett's Norwegian-
born son-in-law Even Kulsveen,
who runs Kentucky Bourbon
Distillers Ltd and plans to restore
the old distillery to production.
Noah's Mill is a hand-bottled,
small batch bourbon, currently
produced under contract.

NOAH'S MILL 15-YEAR-OLD

BOURBON 57.15% ABV
*Elegant and well-balanced on the nose,
with caramel, nuts, coffee, dark fruits, and
oak. Noah's Mill has a rich texture and is
notably dry on the palate, with background
notes of soft fruit and spice. The finish
is long and oaky.*

THE NOTCH

Triple Eight Distillery, 5&7 Bartlett
Farm Road, Nantucket, Massachusetts
www.ciscobrewers.com

Dean and Melissa Long started up
their Nantucket Winery in 1981,
and added the Cisco Brewery in
1995. Two years later, they founded
the region's first micro-distillery,
Triple Eight.

The first single malt whiskey
was distilled in 2000 and is called
The Notch Whiskey, because it is
"not Scotch", though it is produced
in the Scottish style. It is matured in
former bourbon barrels before
being finished in French oak
Merlot barrels.

THE NOTCH

SINGLE MALT 44.4% ABV
*Sweet aromas of almonds and fruit
on the nose, backed by vanilla and
toasted oak. Mellow honey and pear
notes are present on the palate, which
also contains a suggestion of Merlot.
The finish is lengthy and herbal.*

OLD CHARTER

Buffalo Trace Distillery, 1001 Wilkinson
Boulevard, Frankfort, Kentucky

The Old Charter brand dates
back to 1874, and the name is
a direct reference to the Charter
Oak tree, where Connecticut's
colonial charter was hidden from
the British in 1687. The Buffalo
Trace Distillery itself dates back
to the early 1900s and is listed
on the National Register of
Historic Places.

OLD CHARTER 8-YEAR-OLD

BOURBON 40% ABV
*Initially dry and peppery on the nose,
with sweet and buttery aromas following
through. Mouth-coating, with fruit, vanilla,
old leather, and cloves on the palate.
The finish is long and sophisticated.*

OLD CROW

Jim Beam Distillery, 149 Happy Hollow
Road, Clermont, Kentucky
www.jimbeam.com

Old Crow takes its name from
the 19th-century Scottish-born
chemist and Kentucky distiller
James Christopher Crow. Along
with Old Grand-Dad *(see p.248)*
and Old Taylor *(p.249)*, this brand
was acquired by Jim Beam *(p.240)*
from National Distillers in 1987,
and the three distilleries associated
with these bourbons were closed.
All production now takes place at
Jim Beam's distilleries in Boston
and Clermont.

OLD CROW

BOURBON 40% ABV
*Complex on the nose, with malt, rye, and
sharp fruit notes combining with gentle
spice. The palate follows through with spicy,
malty, and citric elements, with citrus and
spice notes to the fore.*

OLD FORESTER

OLD FORESTER BIRTHDAY BOURBON

OLD FITZGERALD

Heaven Hill Distillery,
1701 West Breckinridge Street,
Louisville, Kentucky
www.heavenhill.com

Old Fitzgerald was named by
John E. Fitzgerald, who founded
a distillery at Frankfort in 1870.
The brand moved to its present
home of Louisville when the
Stitzel brothers, Frederick and
Philip, merged their company
with that of William LaRue Weller
& Sons, and subsequently opened
the new Stitzel-Weller distillery
at Louisville in 1935.

VERY SPECIAL OLD FITZGERALD
12-YEAR-OLD

BOURBON 45% ABV
*A complex and well-balanced bourbon,
made with some wheat in the mashbill,
rather than rye. The nose is rich, fruity,
and leathery, while the palate exhibits
sweet and fruity notes balanced by
spices and oak. The finish is long and
drying, with vanilla fading to oak.*

OLD FORESTER

Brown-Forman Distillery,
850 Dixie Highway,
Louisville, Kentucky
www.oldforester.com

The origins of the Old Forester
brand date back to 1870, when
George Garvin Brown established
a distillery in Louisville, Kentucky
(*see Brown Forman, p.220*).
The whiskey initially used the
spelling "Forrester", and there
are several theories as to the
choice of name. Some say it was
selected to honour Confederate
army officer General Nathan
Bedford Forrest, and others that
it was inspired by George Garvin
Brown's physician Dr Forrester.
It has also been suggested that the
name was chosen to appeal to the
many timber workers in the area.

OLD FORESTER

BOURBON 43% ABV
*Complex, with pronounced floral notes,
vanilla, spice, pepper, fruit, chocolate,*

*and menthol on the nose. Full and fruity
in the mouth, where rye and peaches vie
with fudge, nutmeg, and oak. The finish
offers more rye, toffee, liquorice, and
drying oak.*

OLD FORESTER
BIRTHDAY BOURBON

BOURBON 47% ABV
*Since September 2002 there has
been an annual release of vintage Old
Forester to commemorate the birthday
of George Garvin Brown. The 2007
expression was distilled in the spring
of 1994, and consists of fewer than
8,500 bottles. According to Brown-
Forman, this vintage strikes a balance
between the previous two: 2005 was
heavy in cinnamon spice while 2006
had a pronounced mint note.*

*The 2007 release is sweet on the
nose, with cinnamon, caramel, and
vanilla, plus a contrasting whiff of
mint. The palate is full and complex,
with caramel, apples, and vanilla oak,
and a lengthy, warm, clean finish.*

OLD GRAND-DAD

Jim Beam Distillery,
149 Happy Hollow Road,
Clermont, Kentucky
www.theoldswhiskeys.com

Old Grand-Dad was established
in 1882 by a grandson of distiller
Basil Hayden (*see p.219*). The
brand and its distillery eventually
passed into the hands of American
Brands (Now Fortune Brands
Inc.) which subsequently closed
the distillery. Production of
Old Grand-Dad now takes place
in the Jim Beam distilleries in
Clermont and Boston.

OLD GRAND-DAD

BOURBON 43–57% ABV
*Made with a comparatively high
percentage of rye, the nose of Old
Grand-Dad reveals oranges and peppery
spices. Quite heavy-bodied, the taste is
full, yet surprisingly smooth, considering
the strength. Fruit, nuts, and caramel
are foremost on the palate, while the
finish is long and oily.*

OLD POTRERO

Anchor Distilling Company,
1705 Mariposa Street,
San Francisco, California
www.anchorbrewing.com

Fritz Maytag is one of the pioneers
of the American "micro-drinks"
movement, and has been running
San Francisco's historic Anchor
Steam Brewery since 1965. In
1994, he added a small distillery
to his brewery on San Francisco's
Potrero Hill. Here, Maytag aims to
"re-create the original whiskey of
America", making small batches
of spirit in traditional, open pot
stills, using 100 per cent rye malt.

OLD POTRERO 18TH CENTURY
STYLE WHISKEY

SINGLE MALT RYE 62.55% ABV

*An award-winning, "18th century style"
whiskey distilled in a small pot still, then
aged for a year in new, lightly toasted oak
barrels. Floral, nutty nose, with vanilla and
spice. Smooth on the palate, with mint,
honey, and pepper in the lengthy finish.*

OLD TAYLOR

Jim Beam Distillery,
149 Happy Hollow Road,
Clermont, Kentucky
www.jimbeam.com

Old Taylor was introduced by
Edmund Haynes Taylor Jr, who was
associated at various times with
three distilleries in the Frankfort
area of Kentucky, including what
is now Buffalo Trace *(see p.223)*.
He was the man responsible for
the Bottled-in-Bond Act of 1897,
which guaranteed a whiskey's
quality – any bottle bearing an
official government seal had to be
100 proof (50% ABV) and at least
four years old. Old Taylor was
bought by Fortune Brands in 1987.

OLD TAYLOR

BOURBON 40% ABV

*Light and orangey on the nose, with
a hint of marzipan; sweet, honeyed,
and slightly oaky on the palate.*

PARKER'S

Heaven Hill Distillery, 1701 West
Breckinridge Street, Louisville, Kentucky
www.heavenhill.com

Parker's Heritage Collection is
a limited annual series of rare
whiskeys that pays tribute to
Heaven Hill's sixth-generation
Master Distiller Parker Beam.

The first edition is a cask
strength 1996 bourbon that was
bottled at barrel-proof, the first
such barrel-proof bourbon release
by the distillers in the US. The
barrels were selected by Parker
Beam for their fine nose, robust
flavour, and long, smooth finish.

PARKER'S HERITAGE
COLLECTION (FIRST EDITION)

BOURBON 61.3% ABV

*Honey, vanilla, almonds, leather, and
cherries on the nose, while the palate
displays more vanilla, spicy fruit, and
caramel, with leather, pipe-tobacco,
and oak. The finish is long and fruity,
with spice and oak.*

PEREGRINE ROCK

Saint James Spirits, 5220 Fourth Street,
Irwindale, California
www.saintjamesspirits.com

Saint James Spirits was founded
in 1995 by teacher Jim Busuttil,
who learnt the craft of distilling
in Germany and Switzerland.
He has been making single malt
whisky (note the Scottish spelling)
since 1997, and Peregrine Rock
is produced from peated Scottish
barley in a 150-litre (40-US-gallon)
alambic copper pot still and
put into bourbon barrels for a
minimum period of three years,
thus mimicking the Scottish
method of production.

PEREGRINE ROCK
CALIFORNIA PURE

SINGLE MALT 40% ABV

*Floral on the nose, with fresh fruits and
a hint of smoke. The palate is delicate
and fruity, with a citric twist to it, while
sweeter, malty, and new-mown-grass
notes develop in the slightly smoky finish.*

Fermenting liquid in one of the washbacks at the Jack Daniel Distillery in Tennessee – at this stage of the process, the yeast is interacting with the sugars from the wort to create alcohol at a strength of about 8% ABV.

PIKESVILLE

Heaven Hill Distillery, 1701 West
Breckinridge Street, Louisville, Kentucky
www.pikesvillerye.com

Rye whiskeys fall into two
stylistic types, namely the
spicy, tangy Pennsylvania style,
as exemplified by Rittenhouse,
and the Maryland style, which
is softer in character. Pikesville
is arguably the only example
of Maryland rye still being
produced today. This whiskey
takes its name from Pikesville
in Maryland, where it was first
distilled during the 1890s, and
last produced in 1972. A decade
later the brand was acquired by
Heaven Hill.

PIKESVILLE SUPREME

RYE WHISKEY 40% ABV

*The crisp nose presents bubble gum, fruit,
and wood varnish, while on the palate
there is more bubble gum, spice, oak,
and overt vanilla. The finish comprises
lingering vanilla and oranges.*

RAGTIME

New York Distilling Company,
Richardson Street, Brooklyn, New York
www.nydistilling.com

Although the first distilleries
in Brooklyn, New York, were
established in the 18th century,
there was no legal whiskey
distillation in the "Big Apple" after
Prohibition. That was until 2009
when Tom Potter, co-founder of
Brooklyn Brewery, and Allen Katz,
former chairman of Slow Food USA,
established the New York Distilling
Co. In 2015, it started retailing its
Ragtime Rye alongside its range of
gins. This straight rye has a mashbill
of 72 per cent rye, 16 per cent corn,
and 12 per cent barley, and has been
aged for three years and six months.

RAGTIME RYE

RYE WHISKEY 45.2% ABV

*Rye spice, oak, and red berries on the
nose. The palate is full, with peppery rye,
cinnamon, nutmeg, and caramel. Finally
drying, with liquorice, spice, and oak.*

REBEL YELL

Heaven Hill Distillery, 1701 West
Breckinridge Street, Louisville, Kentucky
www.rebelyellbourbon.com

Made at the Bernheim Distillery
in Louisville, Rebel Yell is distilled
with a percentage of wheat in its
mashbill, instead of rye. Whiskey
was first made to the Rebel Yell
recipe in 1849 and, after enjoying
popularity in the southern states
for many years, the brand was
finally released on an international
basis during the 1980s. In addition
to the standard bottling, the Rebel
Yell range now includes American
Whiskey and Small Batch, as well
as a Small Batch Reserve.

REBEL YELL

BOURBON 40% ABV

*A nose of honey, raisins, and butter
leads into a big-bodied bourbon, which
again features honey and a buttery
quality, along with plums and soft
leather. The finish is long and spicier
than might be expected from the palate.*

RIDGEMONT

Barton Distillery, 300 Barton Road,
Bardstown, Kentucky
www.1792bourbon.com

The "1792" element of the name
pays homage to the year in which
Kentucky became a state, the 15th
state to become part of the US.
When this bourbon was introduced
to the market in 2004, it was
initially called Ridgewood Reserve
but, after litigation between
distillers Barton Brands and
Woodford Reserve's owners Brown-
Forman, the name was changed.

1792 RIDGEMONT RESERVE

BOURBON 46.85% ABV

*This comparatively delicate and complex
8-year-old, small batch bourbon boasts
a soft nose with vanilla, caramel, leather,
rye, corn, and spice notes. Oily and
initially sweet on the palate, caramel
and spicy rye develop along with
a suggestion of oak. The finish is oaky,
spicy, and quite long, with a hint of
lingering caramel.*

RITTENHOUSE RYE

Heaven Hill Distillery, 1701 West
Breckinridge Street, Louisville, Kentucky
www.heavenhill.com

Once associated with the rye
whiskey-making heartland of
Pennsylvania, Rittenhouse Rye
now survives in Kentucky, and
its mashbill comprises 51 per
cent rye, 37 per cent corn, and
12 per cent barley.

Rittenhouse was launched
by the Continental Distilling
Company of Philadelphia soon
after Prohibition was repealed in
1933, and was later acquired by
Heaven Hill, which continued to
produce the brand through the
lean years when rye whiskey as
a style was largely forgotten.

RITTENHOUSE STRAIGHT RYE

RYE WHISKEY 40% ABV
*Immediate aromas of rye, with black
pepper, spice, and cedar. Oily on the
palate, with more spicy rye, ginger, and
vanilla, leading to cinnamon notes.*

ROCK HILL FARMS

Buffalo Trace Distillery, 1001 Wilkinson
Boulevard, Frankfort, Kentucky
www.buffalotrace.com

This single cask brand was first
introduced to the Buffalo Trace
(see p.223) line-up in 1990, and is
named after the home farm of the
Blanton family. It was Colonel
Benjamin Blanton who first made
whiskey on the site of what is now
Buffalo Trace Distillery, just after
the American Civil War. The Rock
Hill mansion itself survives within
the Buffalo Trace complex.

ROCK HILL FARMS

BOURBON 50% ABV
*Oak, raisins, and fruity rye on the
nose, with a hint of mint. Medium- to
full-bodied, bitter-sweet on the palate,
with rye fruitiness, fudge, oak, and a
long, sweet, rye finish with a suggestion
of liquorice.*

ROCK TOWN

1216 E 6th Street,
Little Rock, Arkansas
www.rocktowndistillery.com

Founded in 2010 by Phil
Brandon, Rock Town is the
first legal distillery in the state
of Arkansas since Prohibition. All
corn, wheat, and rye used in the
distilling process is grown within
a maximum of 200 km (125 miles)
of the distillery. Rye and Hickory-
smoked whiskeys are made here,
along with Arkansas' first ever
bourbon, which is matured in
small, newly charred oak barrels
that were coopered in Arkansas
at Gibbs Brothers Cooperage. All
bottling takes place at the distillery.

ROCK TOWN ARKANSAS BOURBON

BOURBON 46% ABV
*The nose is smoky and sweet, with
roasted corn aromas, while the palate
is smooth and sweet, with almonds
and digestive biscuits.*

ROGUE SPIRITS

Rogue Brewery, 1339 NW Flanders,
Portland, Oregon
www.rogue.com

Dead Guy Ale was created in the
early 1990s to celebrate the Mayan
Day of the Dead (1 November, or
All Souls' Day) and, in 2008, the
Oregon-based producers launched
their Dead Guy Whiskey. It is
distilled using the same four malts
used in the creation of Dead Guy
Ale, and fermented wort from the
brewery is taken to the nearby
Rogue House of Spirits, where it
is double-distilled in a 570-litre
(150-US-gallon) copper pot still. A
brief maturation period follows, in
charred American white-oak casks.

DEAD GUY

BLENDED MALT 40% ABV
*Youthful on the nose, with notes of
corn, wheat, and fresh, juicy orange.
The palate is medium-dry, fruity, and
lively. Pepper and cinnamon feature
in the finish.*

RUSSELL'S RESERVE RYE

RUSSELL'S RESERVE 10-YEAR-OLD

RUSSELL'S RESERVE

Boulevard Distillery,
Lawrenceburg, Kentucky

Austin Nicholls' Master Distiller
Jimmy Russell and his son Eddie,
of Wild Turkey *(see p.262)* fame,
developed this small batch rye
whiskey, launched in 2007.

Jimmy is one of the great
characters of the bourbon world,
and is now a leading international
ambassador for the bourbon
industry. James C. Russell, to
give him his full name, has been
distilling whiskey since the
1950s and both his father and
grandfather were also distillers.
So, it was no great surprise when
his son Eddie joined the company
in 1980.

According to Jimmy Russell,
"rye whiskey is its own animal
and rye fans are a special breed".
His son, Eddie Russell, adds
that "we knew the whiskey
we wanted, but had never tasted
it before. This one really makes

the grade – deep character and
taste and, at six years, aged
to perfection."

RUSSELL'S RESERVE RYE

RYE WHISKEY 45% ABV
*Fruity, with fresh oak and almonds on the
nose. Full-bodied and robust, yet smooth.
Almonds, pepper, and rye dominate the
palate, while the finish is long, dry, and
characteristically bitter.*

RUSSELL'S RESERVE
10-YEAR-OLD

BOURBON 45% ABV
*The stable-mate to Russell's Reserve
Rye, this bourbon boasts a nose of pine,
vanilla, soft leather, and caramel. The
palate features more vanilla, along with
toffee, almond, honey, coconut, and the
appearance of a slightly unusual note
of chilli that continues through the
lengthy, spicy finish.*

SAM HOUSTON

McLain & Kyne Ltd (Castle Brands),
Louisville, Kentucky
www.samhoustonwhiskey.com

McLain & Kyne Ltd is best known
for what it terms "very small batch
bourbons", and the firm blends
whiskey from as few as eight to
12 barrels of varying ages for their
Jefferson's *(see p.242)* and Sam
Houston bourbon brands.

Sam Houston was introduced
in 1999 and is named after the
colourful 19th-century soldier,
statesman, and politician Samuel
Houston, who became the first
president of the Republic of Texas.

SAM HOUSTON AMERICAN
STRAIGHT WHISKEY

AMERICAN WHISKEY 43% ABV
*Apples and a hint of caramel on the
relatively light nose, while the palate
is very sweet, with more caramel and
emerging black pepper.*

SAZERAC RYE

Buffalo Trace Distillery, 1001 Wilkinson
Boulevard, Frankfort, Kentucky
www.buffalotrace.com

Sazerac Rye is part of the
annually updated Buffalo
Trace Antique Collection
(see p.223) and, having been
aged for 18 years, is the oldest
rye whiskey currently available.

Buffalo Trace says that the
18-year-old 2008 release is
comprised of whiskey that has
been ageing in its warehouse
on the first floor – this location
enables the barrels to age slowly
and gracefully.

SAZERAC RYE 18-YEAR-OLD

RYE WHISKEY 45% ABV
*Rich on the nose, with maple syrup
and a hint of menthol, this expression
is oily on the palate, fresh, and lively,
with fruit, pepper, and pleasing oak
notes. The finish boasts lingering
pepper, with returning fruit and a
final flavour of molasses.*

SEAGRAM'S 7 CROWN

Angostura Distillery,
Lawrenceburg, Indiana

One of the best known and most
characterful blended American
whiskeys, Seagram's 7 Crown
has survived the break-up of the
Seagram distilling empire and
is now produced by Caribbean-
based Angostura (of Angostura
Bitters fame).

This relative newcomer to the
US distilling arena has acquired
the former Seagram distillery at
Lawrenceburg, where 7 Crown
is made, along with the long-
shuttered Charles Medley
Distillery in Owensboro Kentucky.
The Lawrenceburg distillery is the
largest spirits facility in the US in
terms of production capacity.

SEAGRAM'S 7 CROWN

BLEND 40% ABV
*This possesses a delicate nose with
a hint of spicy rye, and is clean and
well structured on the spicy palate.*

ST. GEORGE

St. George Spirits, 2601 Monarch
Street, Almeda, California
www.stgeorgespirits.com

St. George Spirits was established
by Jörg Rupf in 1982, and the
distillery operates two Holstein
copper pot stills. A percentage
of heavily roasted barley is used,
some of which is smoked over alder
and beech wood. Most of the single
malt whiskey is put into former
bourbon barrels and matured for
between three and five years, with
a proportion matured in French
oak and former port casks.

ST GEORGE SINGLE MALT WHISKY (LOT 14)

SINGLE MALT 43% ABV
*The nose features apples, sweet
berry fruits, malt, and cocoa. Milk
chocolate, vanilla, dried fruit, and
spicy oak on the palate.*

STRANAHAN'S

Stranahan's Colorado Whiskey, 2405
Blake Street, Denver, Colorado
www.stranahans.com

Jess Graber and George Stranahan
established the Denver distillery
in March 2004, the first licensed
distillery in Colorado. Whiskey
is produced using a four-barley
fermented wash produced by the
neighbouring Flying Dog Brewery.
The distillation takes place in a
Vendome still and the spirit is put
into new, charred American oak
barrels. It is aged for a minimum of
two years, and each batch bottled
comprises the contents of between
two and six barrels.

STRANAHAN'S COLORADO WHISKEY

COLORADO WHISKEY 47% ABV
*The nose is quite bourbon-like, with
notes of caramel, liquorice, spice, and
oak. The palate is slightly oily, big,
and sweet, with honey and spices.
The fairly short finish is quite oaky.*

TEMPLETON RYE

East 3rd Street, Templeton, Iowa
www.templetonrye.com

Scott Bush's Templeton Rye
whiskey came onto the market
in 2006. It is distilled in a
1,150-litre (300-US-gallon)
copper pot still in Indiana before
being aged in new, charred-oak
barrels. Bush boasts that his
rye is flavoured to a Prohibition-
era recipe.

During the years of the Great
Depression, a group of farmers in
the Templeton area started to distil
a rye whiskey illicitly in order to
boost their faltering agricultural
incomes. Soon, "Templeton Rye"
achieved a widespread reputation
as a high-quality spirit.

TEMPLETON RYE SMALL BATCH

RYE WHISKEY 40% ABV
*Bright, crisp, and mildly sweet on
the palate. The finish is smooth,
long, and warming.*

TEN HIGH

Barton Distillery, 300 Barton Road,
Bardstown, Kentucky
www.sazerac.com

Ten High, a long-established name,
was first created in 1879 and is
now a Barton-owned brand. It
is a sour mash, which means that
it is made with a small quantity
of an old batch of mash containing
a certain strain of live yeast, which
ensures a consistent taste – similar
to the process of making sourdough
bread. The whiskey is matured in
white-oak barrels. The name Ten
High comes from a term used in
playing poker.

TEN HIGH KENTUCKY

BOURBON 40% ABV
*Grainy and slightly oaky on the nose,
Ten High is notably malty on the palate,
almost like a young malt Scotch, and
has notes of vanilla and caramel. The
finish is quite short and drying.*

THOMAS H. HANDY

Buffalo Trace Distillery, 1001 Wilkinson
Boulevard, Frankfort, Kentucky
www.buffalotrace.com

Thomas H. Handy Sazerac is
the newest addition to the Buffalo
Trace Antique Collection. It is
an uncut and unfiltered straight
rye whiskey, named after the
New Orleans bartender who first
used rye whiskey to make the
Sazerac Cocktail.

According to the distillers,
the barrels are aged six years
and five months on the fifth
floor of Warehouse M – "it's
very flavourful and will remind
drinkers of Christmas cake".

THOMAS H. HANDY SAZERAC
2008 EDITION

RYE WHISKEY 63.8% ABV
*Summer fruits and pepper notes on
the nose. The palate is a lovely blend
of soft vanilla and peppery rye, while
the finish is long and comforting, with
oily, spicy oak.*

TINCUP

Tincup Whiskey, Denver, Colorado
www.tincupwhiskey.com

Tincup is the latest whiskey venture
of Colorado-based Jess Graber, co-
founder of Stranahan's Whiskey
Distillery. Although Graber has
been distilling whiskey since 1972,
the ex-construction company boss,
firefighter, and rodeo rider more
recently, decided he wanted to offer
the market a Bourbon-style whiskey
with a more powerful, spicy flavour.
The result was Tincup, which has a
high rye content in its mashbill, and
is sourced from the MGP Distillery
at Lawrenceburg, Indiana. The
name recalls the days when gold
prospectors drank whiskey from
tin cups.

TINCUP AMERICAN WHISKEY

AMERICAN WHISKEY 40% ABV
*Lots of spice on the nose, with warm
apple pie, honey, and ginger. Cinnamon,
toffee, and more apple on the palate, with
caramel and lively spice in the finish.*

TOM MOORE

Barton Distillery, 300 Barton Road,
Bardstown, Kentucky
www.sazerac.com

This Barton Kentucky straight
bourbon brand takes its name
from the Tom Moore Distillery,
which was established in 1889
by Tom Moore and Ben Mattingly,
just a stone's throw from the
present Barton Distillery.

The plant was closed during
Prohibition but re-opened in 1934
and, a decade later, was acquired
by the Oscar Getz family, who
subsequently established the Barton
Distilling Company. The company
was bought by Sazerac in 2009.

TOM MOORE

BOURBON 50% ABV
*Distinct notes of rye and herbs on
the nose, along with vanilla, oak, and
cooked berries. Medium-bodied, the
palate is a blend of sugary sweetness
and spicy rye bitterness. Toffee and
ginger dominate the finish.*

WHISKY STYLES
US MICRO-DISTILLING

The US is currently undergoing a boom in small-scale or "micro" distilling, mirroring the country's earlier rapid growth of micro-brewing operations. Whiskey micro-distilling is a notably vibrant area of the market, where experimentation and innovation with different grains and production techniques are the norm. Distillers often operate outside the legally defined boundaries of bourbon, rye, or corn whiskies.

A micro-distillery is defined as one manufacturing fewer than 500 barrels of spirit per year. One of the early pioneers of the movement was San Francisco craft brewer Fritz Maytag, who set up the Anchor Distilling Company *(see Old Potrero, p.249)* in 1994. Since then, micro-distilleries have multiplied at a remarkable rate, being established in many states where there has been no distilling since the onset of Prohibition in 1920. Distilling now takes place in no fewer than 47 states, whereas 20 years ago, it was confined to no more than a handful. In the whiskey heartland of Kentucky, there are now ten operational micro-distilleries, while neighbouring Tennessee boasts nine.

In Virginia, Mount Vernon Distillery *(www.mountvernon.org)* is a working recreation of the whiskey-making facility established by President George Washington in 1797. Its 18th-century-style stills were installed in reconstructed buildings in 2006. Some of the more recently established US micro-distilleries which are majoring in whiskey include Black Bear *(www.blackbeardistillery.com)* in Colorado, which is ultra-traditional in style and plans to produce an Irish-style whiskey. Bent Brewstillery *(www.bentbrewstillery.com)* in Minnesota is, as the name suggests, a combined brewery and distillery, and some of its single malt whiskey has been aged in a combination of charred oak and charred applewood. California-based Venus Spirits *(www.venusspirits.com)* uses a hand-beaten Spanish alembic still to produce single malt, rye, and bourbon, while Alabama's John Emerald Distilling Company *(www.johnemeralddistilling.com)* makes a single malt using barley flavoured with peach wood and southern pecan during malting. Clearly, the spirit of innovation and experimentation in US micro-distilling is more alive than ever.

VAN WINKLE

2843 Brownsboro Road
Louisville, Kentucky
www.oldripvanwinke.com

Buffalo Trace *(see p.223)* has been in partnership with Julian Van Winkle since 2002, making and distributing his whiskeys. The current expressions were produced at a number of distilleries, and matured at the Van Winkle's now silent Old Hoffman Distillery.

Julian is a grandson of legendary Julian P. "Pappy" Van Winkle Sr, who started working as a salesman for W.L. Weller & Sons in Louisville in 1893 at the age of 18 and went on to become famous for his Old Fitzgerald bourbon.

Van Winkle specializes in small-batch, aged whiskeys. The bourbons are made with wheat, rather than cheaper rye. This is said to give the whiskeys a smoother, sweeter flavour during the long maturation period favoured by Van Winkle. All whiskeys are matured for at least 10 years in lightly charred mountain oak barrels. The range includes the rare 23-year-old and the 107 proof 10-year-old.

OLD RIP VAN WINKLE 10-YEAR-OLD

BOURBON 45% ABV
Caramel and molasses on the big nose, then honey and rich, spicy fruit on the profound, mellow palate. The finish is long, with coffee and liquorice notes.

PAPPY VAN WINKLE'S FAMILY RESERVE 20-YEAR-OLD

BOURBON 45.2% ABV
Old for a bourbon, this has stood the test of time. Sweet vanilla and caramel nose, plus raisins, apples, and oak. Rich and buttery in the mouth, with molasses and a hint of char. The finish is long and complex, with a touch of oak charring.

OLD RIP VAN WINKLE 10-YEAR-OLD

PAPPY VAN WINKLE'S FAMILY RESERVE 20-YEAR-OLD

PAPPY VAN WINKLE'S FAMILY RESERVE 15-YEAR-OLD

BOURBON 53.5% ABV

A sweet caramel and vanilla nose, with charcoal and oak. Full-bodied, round and smooth in the mouth, with a long and complex finish of spicy orange, toffee, vanilla, and oak.

VAN WINKLE FAMILY RESERVE RYE 13-YEAR-OLD

RYE WHISKEY 47.8% ABV

An almost uniquely aged rye. Powerful nose of fruit and spice. Vanilla, spice, pepper, and cocoa in the mouth. A long finish pairs caramel with black coffee.

WHISKY STYLES
AMERICAN RYE

The heritage of rye whiskey in North America probably dates back to the 1600s. Its development owes much to Irish and Scottish settlers, who found rye less difficult than barley to grow there. The Irish were already familiar with the use of rye in whiskey-making.

Rye whiskey was particularly associated with the states of Pennsylvania and Maryland, with each making a distinctive style of the spirit; however, most rye is now distilled in Kentucky. At one time much more widely consumed in the US than bourbon, rye whiskey never fully recovered from Prohibition. Its distinctive, peppery, slightly bitter character probably worked against it as drinkers developed a taste for blander spirits. However, there has been a slow revival in rye's fortunes, with a number of US micro-distilleries *(see p.257)* producing small quantities of rye for appreciative connoisseurs. For example, in 1996, the pioneering Fritz Maytag of San Francisco's Anchor Brewery began distilling Old Potrero *(see p.249)* from 100 per cent malted rye. Moreover, the recreated Mount Vernon Distillery in Virginia *(see p.257)* now distils rye whiskey to a recipe developed by Scottish-born farm manager, James Anderson.

By law, rye whiskey has to be made from a mash of not less than 51 per cent rye, with the other ingredients usually being corn and malted barley. It has to be distilled to no more than 80% ABV and casked at 62.5% ABV or less. As with bourbon, virgin charred-oak barrels are used for maturation and the minimum maturation period is two years. Leading brands of rye whiskey include Pikesville *(see p.252)*, Rittenhouse *(p.253)*, and Sazerac *(p.254)*. Jim Beam *(p.240)* and Wild Turkey *(p.263)* also produce expressions of rye.

VIRGINIA GENTLEMAN

A. Smith Bowman Distillery, Bowman Drive, Fredericksburg, Virginia
www.asmithbowman.com

The only full-scale distillery in a state that once made more whiskey than Kentucky, and founded by Abram Smith Bowman in 1935, it was acquired in 2003 by Sazerac, which also owns Buffalo Trace *(see p.223)*. Virginia Gentleman's first run is fermented and distilled at Buffalo Trace before a second, slow run through a copper pot doubler still on the Smith Bowman site, where it is also matured in charred white-oak barrels. A higher corn percentage than many bourbons gives it a greater sweetness.

VIRGINIA GENTLEMAN

BOURBON 45% ABV
A light, sweet, toasted nut aroma, and spicy rye, sweet corn, honey, caramel, and cocoa on the palate. A complex finish, with rye, malt, and vanilla.

VIRGINIA LIGHTNING

Belmost Farm of Virginia, 13490 Cedar Run Road, Culpeper, Virginia
www.belmontfarmdistillery.com

For Virginia Lightning, distiller Chuck Miller uses an original, secret family recipe, a blend of corn, wheat, and barley that is mashed and fermented in copper fermentation tanks. Distillation takes place in a 1930s, 7,600-litre (2,000-US-gallon) copper still. Finally, it is passed through a doubler still to increase strength and remove impurities. It is then bottled unaged. Its assertive sister spirit, Kopper Kettle, is charcoal-filtered; oak and apple-wood chips are used to boost maturation before it is barrel-aged for two years.

VIRGINIA LIGHTNING

CORN WHISKEY 50% ABV
Corn and alcohol on the nose, smooth and sugary on the palate, with oily corn, plus a powerful kick in the finish.

WASMUND'S

Copper Fox Distillery, 9 River Lane, Sperryville, Virginia
www.copperfox.biz

In spring 2003, Rick Wasmund purchased an existing Virginia distillery from which to launch Copper Fox Whisky, and in 2005, the operation moved to its present, newly built site at Sperryville.

One of the few US distilleries to do all its own malting, Wasmund malts barley in the traditional Scottish manner and then dries it using apple, cherry, and oak wood. It is distilled in a double pot still in single barrel batches and matured using an original "chip and barrel" ageing process, which dramatically speeds up maturation.

WASMUND'S

SINGLE MALT WHISKY 48% ABV
Honey, vanilla, watermelon, and leather on the nose, and a well-balanced blend of sweet and dry flavours on the palate, with nuts, smoke, spices, and vanilla.

W.L. WELLER

Buffalo Trace Distillery, 1001 Wilkinson Boulevard, Frankfort, Kentucky
www.buffalotrace.com

Distilled by Buffalo Trace, W.L. Weller is made with wheat as the secondary grain, for an extra smooth taste.

William LaRue Weller was a prominent 19th-century Kentucky distiller, whose company ultimately merged in 1935 with that of the Stitzel brothers. A new Stitzel-Weller Distillery was subsequently constructed in Louisville.

W.L. WELLER SPECIAL RESERVE

BOURBON 45% ABV
Fresh fruit, honey, vanilla, and toffee characterize the nose, while the palate has lots of flavour, featuring ripe corn and spicy oak. The medium-length finish displays sweet, cereal notes and pleasing oak.

WILD TURKEY KENTUCKY SPIRIT

WILD TURKEY

Boulevard Distillery, US Highway
62 East, Lawrenceburg, Kentucky
www.wildturkeybourbon.com

Wild Turkey's Boulevard Distillery is situated on Wild Turkey Hill, above the Kentucky River, near Lawrenceburg, in Anderson County. Wild Turkey has been owned by the Pernod Ricard Group since 1980, when the French drinks giant took over the New-York-based Austin Nichols Distilling Co. The distillery was first established in 1905 by the three Ripy brothers, whose family had been making whiskey in the nearby distilling centre of Tyrone since the year 1869.

The Wild Turkey brand itself was conceived in 1940, when Austin Nichols' president, Thomas McCarthy, chose a quantity of 101 proof straight bourbon from his company stocks to take along on a wild turkey shoot. Today, Wild Turkey is distilled under the watchful eyes of legendary Master Distiller Jimmy Russell, the world's longest-tenured active Master Distiller, and his son Eddie, who is the fourth generation Russell to work at the distillery. In 2015, Eddie was named Master Distiller in his own right after 35 years of working with the Wild Turkey brand. The Russells have also created some other highly regarded brands, including Russell's Reserve (see p.254) and American Spirit (see p.218).

Wild Turkey is matured in American oak barrels which are subjected to the deepest No.4 "Alligator" char, and they are filled with spirit at a lower proof than that of some competitors. This means less water has to be added before bottling, allowing more flavours imparted from the barrel to be retained.

WILD TURKEY 101 PROOF

WILD TURKEY RARE BREED

WILD TURKEY KENTUCKY STRAIGHT RYE

WILD TURKEY 81 PROOF

BOURBON 40.5% ABV

Spicy corn, vanilla, oak, and coffee on the nose. The palate yields big caramel and honey notes, plus cinnamon and allspice.

WILD TURKEY KENTUCKY SPIRIT

BOURBON 50.5% ABV

A single barrel whiskey, each one being personally selected by Jimmy Russell to be fuller-bodied than normal. A fresh, attractive nose, with oranges and notes of rye. Complex palate with almonds, honey, more oranges, and a hint of leather. Long and sweet finish, darkening and becoming more treacly.

WILD TURKEY 101 PROOF

BOURBON 50.5% ABV

Jimmy Russell maintains that 50.5% (101 proof) is the optimum bottling strength for Wild Turkey. This has a remarkably soft yet rich aroma for such a high proof whiskey, due in part to its eight years of maturation. Caramel,

vanilla, soft fruits, and a touch of spice on the nose, full-bodied, rich, and robust in the mouth, with more vanilla, fresh fruit, and spice, plus brown sugar and honey. Notes of oak develop in the long, powerful, yet smooth finish.

WILD TURKEY RARE BREED

BOURBON (VARIABLE ABV)

Launched in 1991, this brand comprises 6- to 12-year-old whiskeys. Aroma and flavour are notably smooth for a bourbon with such a high alcohol content. Complex, initially assertive nose, with nuts, oranges, spices, and floral notes. Honey, oranges, vanilla, tobacco, mint, and molasses make for an equally complex palate. Long, nutty, finish, with spicy, peppery rye.

WILD TURKEY KENTUCKY STRAIGHT RYE

RYE WHISKEY 50.5% ABV

This straight rye has a pleasingly firm nose, crammed with fruit. The body is full and rich, and the well-balanced palate offers intense spices and ripe fruit. A profoundly spicy, nutty finish.

WOODFORD RESERVE

7855 McCracken Pike,
Versailles, Kentucky
www.woodfordreserve.com

Woodford Reserve is unique among bourbon distilleries in that it uses a triple distillation method and three copper pot stills for a portion of its production – the distillate comes from a column still at a separate facility also owned by Woodford Reserve.

Woodford Reserve is operated by the Louisville-based Brown-Forman Distiller Corporation, which also owns Jack Daniel's *(see p.236)*, but the distillery's origins can be traced back as far as 1797. Brown-Forman only began to distil there in 1996, when it was known as the Labrot & Graham Distillery. The company subsequently spent $10.5 million restoring the plant, and in 2003, the present Woodford Reserve name was adopted for both the distillery and its whiskey.

WOODFORD RESERVE DOUBLE OAKED

WOODFORD RESERVE STRAIGHT RYE

In 2005, the first bottling in the Master's Collection range was released under the Four Grain Bourbon name, and two years later, a Sonoma-Cutrer Finish was added to the line-up. The Master's Collection 1838 Sweet Mash was released in 2008 to commemorate the year in which the present Woodford Reserve Distillery was constructed, and also to celebrate the historic "sweet mash" method of bourbon production.

WOODFORD RESERVE MASTER'S COLLECTION 1838-STYLE WHITE CORN

BOURBON 45.2% ABV

Malt, apple, mixed nuts, and popcorn on the soft nose, while the palate yields new leather, more popcorn, spicy lemon, and pepper.

WOODFORD RESERVE DISTILLER'S SELECT

BOURBON 45.2% ABV

Distiller's Select is elegant yet robust on the nose, perfumed, with milk chocolate raisins, dried fruit, burnt sugar, ginger, and a touch of saddle soap. Equally complex on the palate, Distiller's Select is fragrant and fruity, with raspberries, camomile, and ginger. The finish displays lingering vanilla notes as well as peppery oak.

WOODFORD RESERVE DOUBLE OAKED

BOURBON 45.2% ABV

Oak, caramel, dark berry fruits on the nose, with orange and fudge in the background. Black pepper, vanilla, caramel, and honey on the lingering palate.

WOODFORD RESERVE STRAIGHT RYE

RYE WHISKEY 45.2% ABV

Light on the nose, with rye, black pepper, pears, and fresh oak. Rye, malt, and honey on the peppery palate, with a hint of mint.

NORTHWEST
TERRITORIES

BRITISH
COLUMBIA

ALBERTA

SASKATCHEWAN

MANITOBA

HUDSON
BAY

ONTARIO

EDMONTON

Alberta

CALGARY

Highwood

VANCOUVER   Black Velvet   REGINA

Crown Royal

WINNIPEG

USA

Canadian Mist   OTTAWA

TORONTO   Kittling
Ridge

Hiram Walker
(Canadian Club)

miles
0   300
0   300
kilometres

N
W   E
S

FORTY CREEK

GLEN BRETON

CROWN ROYAL

QUÉBEC

NEWFOUNDLAND
AND LABRADOR

QUÉBEC · NEW · Glenora
NTRÉAL · BRUNSWICK · (Glen Breton)
NOVA
SCOTIA

The golden age of Canadian whisky was from late 19th to mid-20th centuries, with whisky makers such as Hiram Walker, creator of Canadian Club, and Sam Bronfman at Seagram forming vast commercial empires. These two dominated much of the world market. From this high point, however, Canadian whisky experienced a marked decline in the second half of the 20th century, and it now operates on a far more modest scale. Where once 200 distilleries produced rivers of whisky to serve a seemingly insatiable American market, now Canada has fewer than a dozen distilleries, most of which are owned by US bourbon companies or international spirits producers. Seagram's — a name so closely associated with Canada — is still the brand name for a handful of whiskies, but the Seagram's empire itself is gone. It remains to be seen if the remaining producers can take their nation's whisky industry back to being a major player on the world stage.

CANADA

ALBERTA

WISER'S

SEAGRAM'S V.O.

CANADIAN CLUB

CANADIAN MIST

WHISKY STYLES
CANADIAN WHISKY

All Canadian whisky is blended, apart from Glen Breton, a single malt *(see p.275)*. Production is in column stills, but each distillery produces a range of styles, and each blend will use between 15 and 50 different whiskies. As in Scotland, the spirit must be matured for at least three years, although much is aged six to eight years. The base spirit is light and relatively neutral in character, distilled from rye, barley, wheat, or corn. Unlike in the US, there is no constraint upon the mashbill. A proportion of rye or malted rye spirit, which adds spice to the blend and body, is added to the mix, and this provides Canadian whisky with its chief characteristics. It is often described as rye whisky, but is of a different style to American rye whiskey.

Early immigrants to Canada found a country blessed with the necessities for making whisky. By 1840, there were about 200 distillers in the country. Commercial distilleries usually began as offshoots of grain mills – among them were Hiram Walker, Joseph Seagram, J.P. Wiser, and Gooderham & Worts. Their business was not easy because of a Puritan ethic that constrained the sale of alcohol. Today, liquor stores are run by the state, except in Alberta. Ironically, it was the imposition of Prohibition in the US, between 1920 and 1933, that provided Canadian whisky with the impetus it needed. The major players – Seagram, Schenley, and Hiram Walker – realized that they could build an export market for the future. Today, the US consumes more Canadian whisky than any other spirit, including American whiskey. Indeed, a great deal of Canadian whisky is blended specifically for the US market, having a light and smooth style, the former coming from a very pure base spirit, and the latter from other elements in the blend.

ALBERTA SPRINGS 10-YEAR-OLD

ALBERTA PREMIUM

ALBERTA

1521 34th Avenue Southeast,
Calgary, Alberta
www.albertarye.com

Alberta Distillery was founded in
Calgary in 1946 to take advantage
of the immense prairies of the
Canadian west and the fine water
cascading down from the Rocky
Mountains. It has capacity to
produce 20 million litres (over
5 million gallons) per annum in its
beer, column, and pot stills, and,
since 1987, has been owned by
Jim Beam. As well as the Alberta
labels, other brands from this
distillery include Tangle Ridge
and Windsor Canadian (see p.277).

Rye is at the heart of many
Canadian whiskies, and is
predominant in all the whiskies
that come from Alberta. The bulk
of the distillery's blends are made
up of a base spirit made with rye
rather than corn. This is first
distilled in a beer still, then in a
continuous rectifier. A separate

rye spirit is also made up. This is
distilled once only, leaving oils and
congeners in the spirit to make it
heavy, oily, and rich in flavour.
The two spirits are then blended
together. Maturation takes place
in first-fill bourbon casks, or even
in new white-oak casks.

ALBERTA SPRINGS
10-YEAR-OLD

CANADIAN RYE 40% ABV
*A sweet aroma, with rye bread and
black pepper. The taste is very sweet,
even somewhat cloying, becoming
charred and caramelized.*

ALBERTA PREMIUM

CANADIAN RYE 40% ABV
*Described as "Special Mild Canadian
Rye Whisky". The aroma presents
vanilla toffee, a hint of spice, light
citric notes, and fruitiness. The taste
is sweet above all, with stewed apples,
plums, and marzipan.*

BLACK VELVET

2925 9th Avenue North,
Lethbridge, Alberta
www.blackvelvetwhisky.com

Black Velvet is the third best-selling
Canadian whisky in the US. It
was created by Gilbey Canada
in the 1950s as Black Label, and
made at the Old Palliser Distillery
in Toronto. It was so successful
that, in 1973, the Black Velvet
Distillery was established at
Lethbridge, in the shadow of the
Rockies, only a couple of hours
drive from the US border. In 1999,
both Black Velvet and Palliser were
sold to Barton Brands, now a
division of Constellation Brands.

BLACK VELVET 8-YEAR-OLD

BLEND 40% ABV
*The nose is light, with citrus fruit, while
the soft palate yields orchard fruits,
pepper, oak, and grain.*

CANADIAN MIST

202 MacDonald Road,
Collingwood, Ontario
www.canadianmist.com

Launched in 1965, this whisky
now sells 3 million cases a year
in the US. Its distillery is odd in
several ways: the equipment is
all stainless steel; it is the only
Canadian distillery to use a mashbill of corn and malted barley; and
it imports its rye spirit from sister
distillery Early Times (see p.224)
in Kentucky. Almost all the spirit is
tankered to Kentucky for blending.
In addition to the popular Canadian
Mist brand, the 1185 Special
Reserve is also available.

CANADIAN MIST

BLEND 40% ABV
*Lightly fruity on the nose, with vanilla
and caramel notes. Mild, sweet flavour
with traces of vanilla toffee.*

CANADIAN CLUB 1858

CANADIAN CLUB SMALL BATCH SHERRY CASK

CANADIAN CLUB

Hiram Walker Distillery, Riverside Drive
East, Walkerville, Ontario
www.canadianclub.com

Canadian Club is the oldest and
most influential whisky brand in
Canada. Created by businessman
Hiram Walker in 1884, it was
named simply "Club" and aimed at
discerning members of gentlemen's
clubs. Unusually, in an era when
most whiskies were sold in bulk,
it was supplied in bottles, and thus
could not be adulterated by the
retailer, a practice soon adopted
by other Canadian and American
distillers. The company has had
numerous Royal Warrants, from
Queen Victoria to Elizabeth II.

A less lofty customer, Al Capone,
smuggled thousands of cases across
the border during Prohibition.

In 1927, Hiram Walker & Sons
was bought by Harry Hatch, who
owned the Gooderham & Worts
Distillery in Toronto. The merged
company was the largest distiller
in the world. Entrepreneur Hatch
made a fortune during Prohibition. In
1935, he took a controlling interest
in H. Corby (*see Wiser's, p.277*).
Then, in 1937, he bought Ballantine's
(*p.35*) and a clutch of malt whisky
distillers, and built the Strathclyde
grain distillery. Allied Distillers
acquired the company in 1987.

The Canadian Club brands were
sold to Fortune Brands, the owner
of Jim Beam (*see p.240*), in 2005.

Canadian Club is always "blended at birth" — that is, the component whiskies are mixed prior to a maturation of at least five years.

CANADIAN CLUB 1858

BLEND 40% ABV

Floral notes on the nose, with dried fruits and rye. The palate is oily, sweet, fruity, and mildly herbal, with white pepper.

CANADIAN CLUB SMALL BATCH SHERRY CASK

BLEND 41.3% ABV

Rye, pine, freshly sawn timber, ginger, and discreet sweet sherry on the nose, while the palate yields vanilla, caramel, black pepper, and light fruit notes.

CANADIAN CLUB SMALL BATCH CLASSIC 12

BLEND 40% ABV

Caramel, orange, and hand rolling tobacco on the nose, with cereal, honey, and spice. More caramel and oranges on the gently spiced palate, with almonds and dates.

CANADIAN CLUB RESERVE 9-YEAR-OLD

BLEND 40% ABV

Vanilla, maple syrup, rye, and fresh oak on the nose, while the palate offers spicy rye, butterscotch, and milk chocolate, underpinned by corn notes.

Canada's huge grain silos, standing
starkly against the sky, are an icon of the
country's landscape and agricultural heritage,
including its whisky distilling industry.

CROWN ROYAL BLACK

CROWN ROYAL RYE

CROWN ROYAL DELUXE

CROWN ROYAL

Distillery Road, Gimli, Manitoba
www.crownroyal.com

Crown Royal was created by Sam Bronfman, President of Seagram (*see p.276*), to mark the state visit to Canada of King George VI and Queen Elizabeth in 1939, with its "crown-shaped" bottle and purple velvet bag. Although it was only available in Canada until 1964, it is now one of the best-selling Canadian whiskies in the US.

Although it has been produced at Gimli Distillery on Lake Winnipeg since 1992, Crown Royal was originally made at Waterloo Distillery, founded in 1857, and sold to the Distillers Corporation in 1928. The driving force behind this company was Sam Bronfman, or "Mr. Sam", a man of energy, daring, ruthlessness, and passion. With the help of his brothers, he built Seagram into the largest liquor company in the world. Prohibition was their big break,

though Sam tended to draw a veil over this period in later life. "We shipped a lot of goods. Of course, we knew where it went, but we had no legal proof. I never went to the other side of the border to count the empty Seagram bottles." In 2001, the company shed its alcohol interests – Gimli Distillery and Crown Royal went to Diageo.

CROWN ROYAL DELUXE

BLEND 43% ABV

Nose of toffee, vanilla, and cereal. Smooth palate of caramel, peaches, and oak.

CROWN ROYAL BLACK

BLEND 45% ABV

Rum and raisin ice cream sprinkled with black pepper on the nose, while vanilla, caramel, and oak dominate the fruity palate.

CROWN ROYAL NORTHERN HARVEST RYE

BLEND 45% ABV

Rye, cinnamon, and caramel on the nose. Spicy rye, ginger, and black pepper on the sweet palate.

FORTY CREEK

Kittling Ridge Distillery,
Grimsby, Ontario
www.fortycreekwhisky.com

Kittling Ridge was named 2008
Canadian Distillery of the Year by
Whisky Magazine. Unusually, it
uses pot stills as well as column
stills, and a mashbill mix of rye,
barley, and corn. Built in 1970, it
is part of a well-respected winery
and was originally designed to make
eau de vie. John Hall, its owner
since 1992, brings the skills of a
winemaker to distilling: "I am not
so bound by tradition as inspired by
it". Whisky critic Michael Jackson
called Forty Creek "the most
revolutionary whisky in Canada".

BARREL SELECT

BLEND 40% ABV

*A complex, fragrant nose, with soft
fruit, honeysuckle, vanilla, and some
spice. A similar palate, with traces of
nuts and leather, and a smooth finish
with lingering fruit and vanilla.*

GLEN BRETON

Glenora Distillery, Route 19,
Glenville, Cape Breton, Nova Scotia
www.glenoradistillery.com

This is North America's only malt
whisky distillery. Cape Breton
Island has a strong Scottish
heritage, but the Scotch Whisky
Association has criticized the name
for sounding too much like a Scotch.

Production began in June 1990,
halting within weeks due to lack
of funds. The distillery was later
bought by Lauchie MacLean, who
has re-distilled earlier, inconsistent
spirit, and bottles at 8 or 9 years.

Glenora has its own maltings and
uses Scottish barley that is given a
light peating. The two stills it uses
are made by Forsyths of Rothes.

GLEN BRETON RARE

SINGLE MALT 43% ABV

*Butterscotch, heather, ground ginger, and
honey nose. Light to medium body, with
a creamy mouthfeel and notes of wood,
almonds, caramel, and peat.*

HIGHWOOD

114 10th Avenue Southeast,
High River, Alberta
www.highwood-distillers.com

Unusually for Canada, Highwood,
founded in 1974, is independently
owned. It makes a range of spirits
and is the only distillery in Canada
using just wheat in its column stills
as the base spirit for its blends. In
2005, it bought the Potter's and
Cascadia distilleries. Potter's is a
separate brand from Highwood.
It is mixed with sherry, and this
flavour adds another dimension.

HIGHWOOD

CANADIAN RYE 40% ABV

*A blend of wheat and rye spirits. The
oaky, vanilla-scented nose has traces of
rye spice, orange blossom, and honey.
The palate balances sweetness with oak
tannins and nuts.*

HIRSCH

Distribution: Preiss Imports Inc,
San Diego, California

This whisky is no longer being
made, but is still available via a
US distributor. Although Canadian
whisky is often referred to as
"rye", only a few brands contain
more than 50 per cent rye spirit,
which is what makes it a true
rye whisky. Hirsch is one, and
connoisseurs claim it rivals the
best Kentucky ryes.

The whiskies are bottled in
small batches, made in column
stills, aged in ex-bourbon barrels,
selected by Preiss Imports, and
bottled by Glenora Distillers,
Nova Scotia (*see Glen Breton*).

HIRSCH SELECTION 8-YEAR-OLD

CANADIAN RYE 43% ABV

*Solvent and pine essence, then sweet
maple sap on the nose. The taste is
sweet, with caramel, dry coconut, and
oakwood; full-bodied. A bitter-sweet
finish with a few earthy notes.*

SEAGRAM'S V.O.

SEAGRAM'S 83

SEAGRAM'S FIVE STAR

SEAGRAM'S

Diageo Canada, West Mall,
Etobicoke, Ontario
www.diageo.com

Joseph Emm Seagram's family
emigrated to Canada from Wiltshire,
England, in 1837. In 1864, he was
appointed manager of a flour mill
at Waterloo, Ontario, where he
became interested in distilling as
a way of using surplus grains. By
1869, he was a partner in the
company, and, in 1883, by which
time distilling was the core business,
he was the sole owner. The brand
83 commemorates this. The V.O.
brand stands for 'Very Own'' and
was once the bestselling Canadian
whisky in the world. It was
also Sam Bronfman's favourite
tipple (*see p.274*).

Joseph Seagram's sons sold the
company to Bronfman's Distillers
Corporation Ltd, which used
Seagram's stocks of old whisky
to good advantage once Prohibition
was repealed in 1933. After

further changes of ownership,
the Seagram's portfolio, which
includes other spirits and wines,
was bought out in 2001 by a
partnership between Diageo and
Pernod Ricard. Diageo now controls
the Canadian Seagram's labels,
as well as Seagram's 7 Crown
(*see p.255*), which is marketed
as an American whiskey.

SEAGRAM'S V.O.

BLEND 40% ABV

*The nose presents pear drops, caramel,
and some rye spice, along with butter.
Light-bodied, sweet, and lightly spicy,
with a slightly acerbic mouthfeel.*

SEAGRAM'S 83

BLEND 40% ABV

*At one time, this was even more
popular than V.O. Now it is a standard
Canadian: smooth and easy to drink.*

SEAGRAM'S FIVE STAR

CANADIAN RYE 40% ABV

*A perfectly acceptable budget whisky
of good mixing quality.*

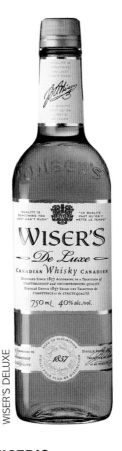

WISER'S DELUXE

WISER'S SMALL BATCH

TANGLE RIDGE

Alberta Distillery, 1521 34th Avenue
Southeast, Calgary, Alberta

This whisky from the Alberta
Distillery *(see p.269)* is sweeter
than its stablemates, although,
like the other Alberta whiskies,
it is made exclusively from rye.
Introduced in 1996, it is one of the
new school of premium Canadian
whiskies: aged 10 years in oak, it is
then "dumped" and small amounts
of vanilla and sherry are added.
The spirit is then re-casked for a
time to allow the flavours to marry.

Its name comes from a limestone
wall in the Canadian Rockies that
was discovered by distinguished
explorer, artist, and writer Mary
Schaffer (1861–1939).

TANGLE RIDGE DOUBLE CASK

CANADIAN RYE 40% ABV
*Butterscotch and burnt caramel on the
nose, velvet-smooth mouthfeel, and a
very sweet taste, with a hint of sherry.
Lacks complexity, however.*

WINDSOR CANADIAN

Alberta Distillery, 1521 34th Avenue
Southeast, Calgary, Alberta

One might think that this comes
from the Hiram Walker Distillery
at Windsor, Ontario; actually, it
is made at the Alberta Distillery
(see .p269). The name is no doubt
meant to recall the British Royal
Family, but it should not be confused
with the Scotch Windsor *(see
p.178)*. Like other whiskies made
at Alberta, Windsor Canadian is
exclusively rye-based.

WINDSOR CANADIAN

BLENDED CANADIAN RYE 40% ABV
*Honey, peaches, pine nuts, and cloves
on the nose. A medium body and
a sweet taste, with cereal and wood
notes. An unassuming whisky; great
value for money.*

WISER'S

Hiram Walker Distillery, Riverside Drive
East, Walkerville, Ontario
www.wisers.ca

John Philip Wiser may well have
been the first distiller to use the
term "Canadian Whisky" on his
label, at the Chicago World's Fair
in 1893. He was the son of Dutch
immigrants and, in 1864, he took
over a distillery on the banks of
the St Lawrence River at Prescott,
Ontario, from a business partner.
By the early 1900s, it was the third
largest distillery in Canada, and its
whiskies were being exported to
China and the Philippines, as well
as the US.

Not long after the death of
J.P. Wiser in 1917, the company
decided to form a merger with
the H. Corby Distillery Company,
which was founded by Henry
Corby in 1859 at Corbyville in
Ontario. Production of Wiser's
brands was moved to here in 1932.
Three years later, Hiram Walker,

Gooderham & Worts acquired 51
per cent of the company. In 1969,
Hiram Walker was bought by Allied
Lyons. Corby Distillery was closed in
1989, and production of the Corby/
Wiser whiskies moved to the Hiram
Walker Distillery at Walkerville,
which is now owned by Pernod
Ricard, as are the brands. Today,
Wiser's are the fifth best-selling
Canadian whiskies in Canada.

WISER'S DELUXE

BLEND 40% ABV
*A fruity and spicy nose, with cereal
and linseed oil, vanilla, and toffee.*

WISER'S SMALL BATCH

BLEND 43.4% ABV
*A recent addition to Wiser's range, Small
Batch is a full-flavoured Canadian whisky,
with vanilla, oak, and butterscotch on
the nose and in the taste. The slightly
higher strength makes for more flavour
and texture.*

SUNTORY YAMAZAKI

KIRIN KARUIZAWA

NIKKA PURE MALT

HOKKAIDO

Nikka
Yoichi

SAPPORO

AOMORI

Nikka Miyagikyo

SENDAI

HONSHU

Chichibu

Suntory Hakushu

TOKYO

Kirin Gotemba

KYOTO

OSAKA

Suntory Yamazaki

HIROSHIMA

SHIKOKU

FUKUOKA

KYUSHU

NAGASAKI

miles
0   100

0   100
kilometres

NIKKA YOICHI

HANYU

Suntory is Japan's biggest whisky producer and has two large whisky distilleries at Yamazaki and Hakushu. Its main competitor, Nikka, has two distilleries at Yoichi and Miyagikyo. The drinks company Kirin has whisky facilities at Gotemba, while other working distilleries making whisky are Miyashita Shuzo, Shinshu, White Oak, and Chichibu. The rest of Japan's distilleries abandoned whisky-making after the Asian financial crisis of 1997, either closing down or shifting their focus to making *shochu*, the traditional Japanese potato spirit. Nikka's Yoichi Distillery is situated on Hokkaido, Japan's northernmost island, where the climate is similar to that in Scotland. The others are located on Honshu island in central Japan. Unlike distilleries in Scotland and other parts of the whisky-making world, Japanese distillers do not trade whiskies with each other for making blends. Instead, they each produce a range of whiskies to make up their own blends.

SUNTORY HIBIKI

SUNTORY HAKUSHU

NIKKA TAKETSURU

NIKKA MIYAGIKYO

KIRIN FUJI-GOTEMBA

ICHIRO'S MALT – ACE OF DIAMONDS, DISTILLED 1986, BOTTLED 2008

CHICHIBU

Venture Whisky, Saitama Prefecture
www.one-drinks.com

The newest Japanese distillery was founded in 2007 by Ichiro Akuto, previously of Hanyu (see Hanyu). A small plant, it features what might be the only Japanese oak washbacks in the world. Ageing takes place in a mix of more than 20 cask types, including ex-bourbon, ex-sherry, ex-Madeira, and ex-cognac casks. Some 10 per cent of the barley used is malted on site, and batches of peated spirit are distilled annually. Chichibu releases are highly prized and difficult to obtain, even in Japan.

ICHIRO'S MALT CHICHIBU THE PEATED 2015

SINGLE MALT 62.5% ABV
Warm asphalt, earthy peat, lemon, new oak, and sea spray on the nose. The palate is smooth, with sweet peat, new leather, liquorice, citrus fruit, and plain chocolate.

GOLDEN HORSE

Toa Shuzo, Chichibu
www.toashuzo.com

The Golden Horse brand is still owned by Toa Shuzo, the firm which used to own the Hanyu distillery (see Hanyu), and the whiskies are drawn from its last remaining stocks. There are bottlings at 8, 10, and 12 years. They are rarely seen on the export markets, and, at the time of writing, it is unclear what will happen to the Golden Horse brand once the Toa Shuzo stocks have disappeared.

GOLDEN HORSE 8-YEAR-OLD

SINGLE MALT 40% ABV
A quite vibrant nose with light malt extract notes and some oak. There's a basic sweetness to this lightly perfumed malt, which has just a wisp of smoke on the finish, but a nagging acidic touch in some bottlings.

HANYU

Toa Shuzo, Saitama Prefecture
www.one-drinks.com

The Hanyu distillery was built by the Akuto family in the 1940s for producing *shochu*. Full production of whisky began in 1980, and Hanyu enjoyed success until the financial crisis of 1996 triggered the end of the whisky boom in Japan. The distillery had to close in 2000. When the firm was bought out in 2003, Ichiro Akuto (see *Ichiro's Malt*) was given a few months to buy back as much stock as he could before the distillery was demolished.

HANYU 1988 CASK 9501

SINGLE MALT 55.6% ABV
Vibrant and intense, with vanilla, some citrus, and a delicate cocoa-butter character. The Japanese oak adds a bitter-sweet edge. On the palate there's a rich depth. The finish shows smoke.

ICHIRO'S MALT

Hanyu Distillery, Saitama Prefecture
www.one-drinks.com

Ichiro's Malt is a range of bottlings from Ichiro Akuto, who was the former president of Hanyu (see *Hanyu*), and the grandson of Hanyu's founder, Isouji Akuto. The whiskies are drawn from the 400 casks of Hanyu single malt that Akuto managed to obtain after the Hanyu distillery was closed down.

As a young man, Ichiro Akuto had worked as a brand manager at Suntory and developed a strong feel for marketing. The bulk of Hanyu's remaining stock is being released by Akuto in a series of 53 whiskies named after playing cards. This Card Series, as it is known, is memorable not only for its distinctive branding but also for the high quality of many of its expressions.

Distillation dates for the Card Series range from 1985 to 2000,

ICHIRO'S MALT – ACE OF SPADES, DISTILLED 1985, BOTTLED 2006

ICHIRO'S MALT DOUBLE DISTILLERIES

ICHIRO'S MALT & GRAIN

with some of the expressions being given secondary maturation in other types of barrel – Japanese oak, cognac, and sherry among them. Other old Hanyu casks were re-racked into either new wood or American oak. Some are still untouched. All of the Card Series bottlings are now extremely rare and highly collectable.

ICHIRO'S MALT – ACE OF DIAMONDS, DISTILLED 1986, BOTTLED 2008

SINGLE MALT 56.4% ABV

Mature nose, with Seville orange, furniture polish, rose, pipe tobacco, and when diluted, sloe and Moscatel. Spicy and chocolatey on the tongue.

ICHIRO'S MALT – ACE OF SPADES, DISTILLED 1985, BOTTLED 2006

SINGLE MALT 55% ABV

The Ace of Spades – sometimes called the Motorhead malt, after the band best known for singing "Ace of Spades" – is one of the oldest in the

Card Series. Bold, rich, and fat with masses of raisin, some tarry notes, and treacle. The palate is chewy and toffee-like, with some prune and a savoury finish.

ICHIRO'S MALT DOUBLE DISTILLERIES

BLENDED MALT 46% ABV

The nose is sweet and oaky, with sawdust and hints of sandalwood. Malt and spice on the palate, with developing oak and liquorice.

ICHIRO'S MALT & GRAIN

BLEND 46% ABV

Honey, vanilla, malt, and apricots on the nose. The palate offers more honey, plus citrus fruit, ginger, pepper, and sweet hay. Tropical fruits in the peppery finish.

GOTEMBA FUJISANROKU 18-YEAR-OLD

GOTEMBA FUJISANROKU 50°

KIRIN GOTEMBA

Shibanta 970, Gotembashi, Shizuoka

Spectacularly situated in the cool foothills of Mount Fuji, 620 m (2,000ft) above sea level, Kirin's Gotemba distillery was built in 1973 as part of a joint venture with the former Canadian giant Seagram *(see p.276)*. It contains both a grain-whisky distillery and a malt plant.

The distillery's output is much in line with the light flavours typical of Seagram's house style. In the 1970s, this was also the style preferred by the Japanese consumer and was intended to partner Japanese cuisine. That said, the distillery had to supply all the needs of Kirin's blends, so it made three different grain whiskies and three styles of malt, including peated.

Gotemba Distillery is open to the public, but is currently not in production. Its whiskies are available through specialist retailers in Japan and some overseas outlets.

GOTEMBA FUJISANROKU 18-YEAR-OLD

SINGLE MALT 40% ABV

Gotemba's new 18-year-old bottling, Fujisanroku is more floral and restrained than the "old" Fuji Gotemba 18-year-old, with less of the oakiness. Some peach, lily, and a zesty grapefruit note. The honey found in the grain reappears here.

FUJISANROKU TARUJUKU 50°

BLEND 50% ABV

Vanilla and light oak on the slightly spirit-y nose, while the palate is oaky, with malt and allspice, leading to a short finish.

WHISKY STYLES
JAPANESE WHISKY

The Japanese whisky industry was founded in the 1920s with a partnership between Shinjiro Torii, the owner of a firm importing Scotch, and Masataka Taketsuru, a distiller who had studied whisky-making in Scotland. Torii built Yamazaki *(see p.298)*, Japan's first malt distillery, and employed Taketsuru as his distiller. Torii's company grew to become the drinks giant Suntory. In 1934, Taketsuru founded his own distillery at Yoichi; his company became Suntory's great rival, Nikka.

While Taketsuru preferred a heavier, more Scottish, peaty style that he could develop on Japan's northern island, Hokkaido, Torii continued to develop a light style of whisky in the mild climate of central Japan. These rivals were joined by a handful of other distilleries starting in the 1950s. Like Scotch, the initial success of the Japanese industry was built on blended varieties. By the 1980s, the biggest-selling single whisky brand in the world was Suntory Royal, which was selling more than 15 million cases in its home market. Also like Scotch, the Japanese whisky industry's recent surge has come through the burgeoning interest in single malt and a discovery by whisky lovers around the world of the Japanese purity of flavour.

The Japanese art of distilling is based on an in-depth, quality-driven, scientific knowledge of production. The minutiae of whisky-making – water, barley, yeast types, mashing, fermentation, distillation, and maturation in different oaks – has been investigated by the Japanese in depth. This allows firms to produce a wide range of different flavours of single malt from a single distillery, which, in turn, takes Japanese single malt away from the Scotch model. Most Japanese single malts today are blends of different flavoured malts from the same distillery.

Like other whisky bars in Japan, The Crane in Tokyo has a distinctly Scottish feel, though a Japanese barman is more likely to wear a bow tie and hand cut ice than his Scottish counterpart. Japanese whiskies are also based on Scotch models, but have their own character.

KARUIZAWA 1986

KARUIZAWA1995: NOH SERIES

KARUIZAWA 1971

KIRIN KARUIZAWA

Maseguchi 1795–2, Oaza,
Miyotamachi, Kitasakugun, Nagano
www.kirin.co.jp

Originally a winery, Kirin's second distillery was converted to whisky production in the 1950s. Unusually for most Japanese distilleries, it made only one style of whisky. Whereas the majority of Japan's malts tend to be light and delicate, Karuizawa always specialized in a robust, big-hitting, and smoky style. To achieve this, it retained techniques that are rare now even in Scotland: the heaviness of the Golden Promise strain of barley used is accentuated by the small stills, while maturation in ex-sherry casks adds a dried-fruit character.

The distillery is no longer in production, but, in recent years, single cask bottlings of Karuizawa have become extremely collectable, being sold at very high prices.

KARUIZAWA 1986: CASK NO. 7387, BOTTLED 2008

SINGLE MALT 60.7% ABV

Incense on the nose along with wax, crystallized fruits, dried fig, cep, cassia, tamarind paste, smoke, and spice. The palate needs water to bring forth dried fruits, rosewood, and coffee.

KARUIZAWA 1995: NOH SERIES, BOTTLED 2008

SINGLE MALT 63% ABV

The nose is hugely resinous, mixing tiger balm, geranium, boot polish, prune, and heavily oiled woods. There's also mint chocolate with water. The palate is lightly astringent and needs a drop of water to release the tannic grip. An exotic and floral whisky.

KARUIZAWA 1971: CASK NO. 6878, BOTTLED 2008

SINGLE MALT 64.1% ABV

Beeswax and sandalwood becoming fragrant with tea, molasses, and smoke. The palate is resinous with walnut, long pepper, and Bolivar cigar.

NIKKA COFFEY MALT WHISKY

NIKKA WHISKY FROM THE BARREL

NIKKA PURE MALT RED

NIKKA – GRAIN & BLENDS

Nikka 1, Aobaku, Sendaishi, Miyagiken; Kurokawacho 7–6, Yoichimachi, Yoichigun, Hokkaido
www.nikka.com

Japan's second-largest distillery company was founded in 1933 by Masataka Taketsuru. This charismatic distiller had learned the art of whisky-making in Scotland – at Longmorn in Speyside and Hazelburn in Campbeltown. Back in Japan, he initially worked with Shinjiro Torii, helping to establish Yamazaki distillery (*see p.298*), which is now owned by Suntory. He then went to Hokkaido island in Japan, where conditions were closer to those in Scotland, and founded Yoichi distillery.

Taketsuru's company, Nikka, now part of Asahi Breweries, operates two malt distilleries at Yoichi and Miyagikyo. It also has grain plants and an ever-growing portfolio of styles, including blends and single malts. Like its domestic rivals, it produces all the whiskies for its in-house blends.

In recent years, Nikka has been focusing on the export market. Although its blends are available overseas, the thrust of its commercial push has been through its single-malt range branded as Nikka Miyagikyo (*see p.290*) and Nikka Yoichi (*p.294*). Its blends include the Pure Malt Series (opposite) and Nikka Taketsuru Pure Malt range (*p.291*).

NIKKA COFFEY MALT WHISKY
MALT WHISKY 45% ABV
Lemon sprinkled with black pepper and background vanilla on the feisty nose. The palate continues those themes, with the addition of milky coffee and prune juice.

NIKKA WHISKY FROM THE BARREL
BLEND 51.4% ABV
Nikka's award-winning blend of malts and grain is given further ageing in first-fill bourbon casks. The nose is

NIKKA PURE MALT WHITE

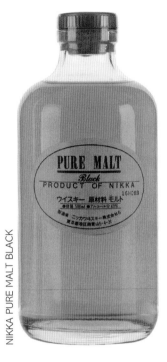

NIKKA PURE MALT BLACK

upfront, and slightly floral, with good intensity, peachiness, and a lift akin to rosemary oil and pine sap. The palate is lightly sweet, with some vanilla, a hint of cherry, and plenty of spiciness on the finish. This is a top blend.

NIKKA PURE MALT SERIES

This trio of "pure" (blended) malts are drawn from the wide range of different styles made at Nikka's two malt distilleries, Yoichi and Miyagikyo.

NIKKA PURE MALT RED

BLENDED MALT 43% ABV

Red is light and fragrant, with faint hints of pineapple, fresh apple, pear, and a gentle almond-like oakiness. This delicacy continues on the palate, along with a light citric finish.

NIKKA PURE MALT WHITE

BLENDED MALT 43% ABV

The smokiest member of the trio, with plenty of salt spray, fragrant dried lavender, and soot on the nose, and the same herbal, oily note as From The Barrel. The palate is rich and soapy.

NIKKA PURE MALT BLACK

BLENDED MALT 43% ABV

Rich and sweet, with lots of black fruits, dark chocolate, and a little polished oak. More substantial than the Red, with an extra layer of smokiness and greater depth and power on the palate. Peppery on the finish.

NIKKA COFFEY GRAIN WHISKY

SINGLE GRAIN 45% ABV

Sweet spicy aromas, with vanilla, cereal, and coconut. Tropical fruit, digestive biscuits, toffee on the palate, with developing sweet oak.

NIKKA COFFEY GRAIN WHISKY

WHISKY TOUR: JAPAN

Tokyo is a good starting point for the whisky lover. The city has myriad whisky bars and excellent train connections to the distilleries at Chichibu, Hakushu, and Gotemba. Further afield, Suntory's flagship distillery, Yamazaki, is also accessible by train, and can be easily combined with a visit to Kyoto or Osaka.

JAPAN

TOUR STATISTICS

DAYS: 6	**LENGTH:** 530miles (850 km)	**DISTILLERIES:** 4
TRAVEL: Shinkansen (bullet trains), local trains		**REGION:** Central Honshu, Japan

THE STILLS AT CHICHIBU

DAY 1: CHICHIBU DISTILLERY

1 **Chichibu**, Japan's newest distillery, started by Ichiro Akuto, has no visitor facilities yet, but whisky enthusiasts can arrange a personal tour by contacting the distillery in advance. Chichibu city is 90 minutes by train from Tokyo's Ikebukuro station. A taxi can be taken from the station to the distillery, which is outside the city. *(+81 (0)494 62 4601)*

Shinjiro Torii is revered in Japan as the founder of Suntory, which operates the Yamazaki and Hakushu distilleries on this tour.

MATSUE

Chugoku Expy YAMAZAKI KYOTO

KOBE OSAKA

4

Chugoku Expy **FINISH**

OKAYAMA

Sanyo Expy

HIROSHIMA

FUKUOKA

START

SENDAI

FUKUSHIMA

NIIGATA

Banetsu Expy

Hokuriku Expy

Tohoku Expy

Kanetsu Expy

NAGANO

CHICHIBU

1

TOKYO

HAKUSHU **2**

HONSHU

JR Chuo Line

JR Asigiri Line

GOTEMBA **3**

Tokaido Shinkansen Line

AGOYA

miles
0   50

0   50
kilometres

DAY 2: SUNTORY'S HAKUSHU DISTILLERY

2 Situated in the southern Japanese Alps, the Suntory Distillery at **Hakushu** is surrounded by a lovely nature reserve. The nearest station is Kobuchizawa, which is 2 hours 30 minutes by express train (JR Chou Line) from Tokyo's Shinjuku Station. After exploring the distillery and museum you can try some of the hiking trails that run through the forest. It is then best to return to Tokyo to get a fast train connection to Gotemba. *(+81 (0) 551 35 2211)*

HAKUSHU DISTILLERY

DAYS 3–4: KIRIN'S GOTEMBA DISTILLERY

3 The town of **Gotemba** is the start of one of the main routes up Mount Fuji. It is also home to Kirin's Gotemba Distillery. Many visitors come to visit both. They start climbing Fuji in the afternoon to reach the 8th or 9th stage by nightfall, where there are huts for pilgrims. The summit of Fuji is reached at dawn. After descending, it is possible to get a bus back to Gotemba to visit the distillery. Although not the

MOUNT FUJI AND TRAIN

prettiest of distilleries, this has good facilities for visitors and a spectacular view of Fuji from its rooftop terrace. The train from Tokyo's Shinjuku Station takes about 1 hour 40 minutes. *(+81 (0) 550 89 4909)*

DAYS 5–6: SUNTORY'S YAMAZAKI DISTILLERY

YAMAZAKI DISTILLERY

4 It is best to take the bullet train to either Kyoto or Osaka to make a base for visiting the Suntory Distillery at **Yamazaki**, the company's original and flagship whisky-making plant. Local trains from either city stop at Yamazaki station. The distillery is a 10-minute walk from the station. There are extensive visitor facilities, including an impressive tasting bar with exclusive bottlings. The distillery offers well-heeled clients a chance to buy a cask through its Owner's Cask scheme. There is also a traditional Shinto shrine to visit. *(+81 (0) 75 961 1234; www.theyamazaki.jp/en/distillery)*

NIKKA MIYAGIKYO 12-YEAR-OLD

NIKKA MIYAGIKYO 15-YEAR-OLD

NIKKA MIYAGIKYO 10-YEAR-OLD

NIKKA MIYAGIKYO

Nikka 1, Aobaku, Sendaishi, Miyagiken
www.nikka.com

Also known as Sendai after its
nearest main town, Nikka's
Miyagikyo was the second
distillery built by Nikka founder,
Masataka Taketsuru. Today, it
has a malt distillery with eight
stills, a grain plant with two
different set-ups, and extensive
warehousing. Like most Japanese
distilleries, it makes a wide range
of spirit styles. The predominant
one – which is most common in the
single-malt bottlings – is lightly
fragrant and softly fruity. That
said, there are some peaty
examples, too. The distillery is
open to the public, and is home
to Nikka's Coffey Grain Whisky.

A new release is a Miyagikyo
without an age statement, which
is made to be drunk *mizuwari*-style
(with water). The nose is floral
and light, and the palate shows
a touch of sultanas.

NIKKA MIYAGIKYO 10-YEAR-OLD

SINGLE MALT 45% ABV

*Typical of the main distillery character,
this has an attractive floral lift: lilies, hot
gorse, lilac, with a touch of anise in the
background. The palate shows balanced,
crisp oak, some butterscotch notes, and
a pine-like finish.*

NIKKA MIYAGIKYO 12-YEAR-OLD

SINGLE MALT 45% ABV

*The extra two years fill out the nose with
flowers, giving way to soft tropical fruits,
such as mango and persimmon, as well
as richer vanilla pod character. Good
structure with a wisp of smoke.*

NIKKA MIYAGIKYO 15-YEAR-OLD

SINGLE MALT 45% ABV

*Bigger, with raisiny ex-sherry cask notes
alongside the toffee and super-fruits.
The gentle distillery character is in
evidence, along with hint of the fresh
floral nature of youth. The richest of
the expressions.*

NIKKA MIYAGIKYO 10-YEAR-OLD

NIKKA TAKETSURU 17-YEAR-OLD

NIKKA TAKETSURU 21-YEAR-OLD

NIKKA TAKETSURU PURE MALT

NIKKA TAKETSURU

Nikka 1, Aobaku,
Sendaishi, Miyagiken;
Kurokawacho 7–6, Yoichimachi,
Yoichigun, Hokkaido
www.nikka.com

This small range of blended
(vatted) malts is named after
the founder of Nikka, Masataka
Taketsuru. Like the Pure Malt
range, it is made up of component
whiskies from the firm's two sites
although, given the range of malts
produced at each of them, it would
be difficult to guess which element
came from which distillery.

NIKKA TAKETSURU PURE MALT

BLENDED MALT 43% ABV

*Sweet, sherried, and spicy on the nose,
with vanilla, honey, and red berries. Rich,
fruity notes in the mouth, with a hint of
smokiness and a relatively short finish.*

NIKKA TAKETSURU 17-YEAR-OLD

BLENDED MALT 43% ABV

*The biggest-selling expression in
the range, the 17-year-old has all*
the complexity you would expect from
mature stock. There's more obvious
smoke at work than in the 12-year-old:
some cigar-box aromas, varnish, and
light leather. When diluted, a fresh
tropical-fruit character comes out. This
is what leads on the palate, before the
peat smoke begins to assert itself.
A clean, precise, and complex whisky.

NIKKA TAKETSURU 21-YEAR-OLD

BLENDED MALT 43% ABV

*With this multi-award winner, the smoke
is immediate while the spirit behind is
thicker, richer, and darker: ripe berries,
cake mix, oak, and a touch of mushroom
or truffle indicative of age. Fruit syrups,
figs, prune, smoke, and multi-layered,
complex whisky.*

Nikka's Miyagikyo Distillery is set among the mountains and cherry orchards of Miyagi Prefecture to the northeast of Tokyo. Company legend has it that master distiller Masataka Taketsuru came here in the 1960s, tasted the water, and pronounced it good.

NIKKA YOICHI 10-YEAR-OLD

NIKKA YOICHI 12-YEAR-OLD

NIKKA YOICHI 20-YEAR-OLD

NIKKA YOICHI

Kurokawacho 7–6, Yoichimachi,
Yoichigun, Hokkaido
www.nikka.com

Although Yoichi's malts are most definitely Japanese, they do have close resemblances to their cousins in Scotland – the whiskies of Islay and Campbeltown in particular. A wide range of styles is made, but Yoichi is famous for its complex, robust, oily, and smoky malts.

The most youthful Yoichi, without an age statement, is intended as an introduction to the distillery and should be drunk *mizuwari-style* (with water) or *sodawari* (with soda). It is crisp and clean with light smoke, a hay-like note, and a sweet spot in the middle of the palate.

NIKKA YOICHI 10-YEAR-OLD

SINGLE MALT 45% ABV
There's a hint of maltiness in here, unusual for a Japanese single malt. Salt spray and light smoke on the nose initially,
with some caramelized fruit notes. Yoichi's oiliness coats the tongue while the smoke changes from fragrant to sooty with dried flowers towards the finish.

NIKKA YOICHI 12-YEAR-OLD

SINGLE MALT 45% ABV
The understated qualities have been banished here. This is classic Yoichi – big, deep, robust, and complex. The peatiness adds an earthy character to the coal-like sootiness. Poached pear and baked peach give a balancing sweetness, offset by smoke, liquorice, and heather.

NIKKA YOICHI 20-YEAR-OLD

SINGLE MALT 52% ABV
A huge, uncompromising nose, where the oiliness apparent in all the expressions is now to the fore. Deck oil or gun oil, seashores, kippers, and the funky notes of great maturity – leather, cedar, yew, and leaf-mould. Clean turmeric and coriander spiciness. The palate is massive, with decent mouthwatering acidity balancing the dry oak and smoke. Still fresh on the finish.

SUNTORY HAKUSHU

Torihara 2913–1, Hakushucho,
Komagun, Yamanashi
www.suntory.co.jp

Located in a forest high in the
Japanese Alps, Hakushu was once
the largest malt distillery in the
world, with two huge stillhouses
producing a vast array of different
makes for the Suntory blenders.
These days, only one of the
stillhouses is operational, but the
ethos of variety is still adhered to.
Nowhere else offers such an array
of shapes and sizes of pot stills.
The Suntory bottlings of Hakushu
as a single malt seem to echo the
location, being light, gentle, and
fresh, though there are also smoky
and heavy versions.

SUNTORY HAKUSHU
12-YEAR-OLD

SINGLE MALT 43.5% ABV
*The best-selling Hakushu, the 12-year-old has a very cool nose, with cut grass
and a growing mintiness. There's a hint*
*of linseed oil, suggestive of youth.
The palate is sweet but quite slow, with
that minty, grassy character being given
a little depth by apricot fruitiness and
extra fragrance by a camomile note.*

SUNTORY HAKUSHU
18-YEAR-OLD

SINGLE MALT 43% ABV
*Balanced and slightly restrained. Once
again a vegetal note, this time more
like a tropical rainforest. There's also
plum, mango, hay, and fresh ginger.
Good acidity and toasty oaky finish.
There's a general fresh acidity, cut
with a generous delicate sweetness.
The palate is direct and shows more
toasty oak.*

SUNTORY HAKUSHU
DISTILLER'S RESERVE

SINGLE MALT 43% ABV
*The nose is herbal, with wet grass,
pine cones, and cucumber, and the
palate carries on those notes, along
with a waft of smoke and mint.*

SUNTORY HIBIKI 17-YEAR-OLD

SUNTORY HIBIKI 21-YEAR-OLD

SUNTORY HIBIKI 30-YEAR-OLD

SUNTORY HIBIKI

Torihara 2913–1, Hakushucho,
Komagun, Yamanashi
www.suntory.co.jp

Japan's most powerful distiller
was founded in 1923 by Shinjiro
Torii. Its fortunes were built on
blended whiskies based on malts
from its two distilleries: Yamazaki
and Hakushu. Although there
is a move towards single malts
globally, Suntory's blends, such
as the Hibiki range, are still
regarded as very important.

The Hibiki 12-year-old is the
most recent member of the stable.
It has a nose akin to Victoria plum,
pineapple, lemon, then fudge and
fresh, sappy oak. It is sweet
and thick on the tongue with
a menthol-like finish.

SUNTORY HIBIKI
17-YEAR-OLD

BLENDED MALT 43% ABV
*This, the original Hibiki, has a soft,
generous nose featuring super-ripe fruits,*
light peatiness, a hint of heavy florals
(jasmine), and citrus. On the palate,
there's caramel toffee, black cherry,
vanilla, rosehip, and light oak structure.

SUNTORY HIBIKI 21-YEAR-OLD

BLENDED MALT 43% ABV
*Deep and sensual, with the density
and musty nature of great aged
whisky. Black butter, sandalwood,
and an intriguing green herbal thread.
Perfumed and hinting at light smoke.
The palate is thick and ripe with
plenty of flowers and dried fruits.
Sweet and long on the tongue.*

SUNTORY HIBIKI 30-YEAR-OLD

BLENDED MALT 43% ABV
*This multi-award winner (it won Best
Blend in the World two years in a row
at the World Whiskies Awards) is huge
in flavour, with a compote of different
fruits: Seville orange, quince paste,
quite assertive wood, and walnuts,
followed by aniseed and fennel, and a
deep spiciness. The palate is sweet and
velvety, with Old English Marmalade to
the fore, along with sweet, dusty spices.*

THE YAMAZAKI 12-YEAR-OLD

THE YAMAZAKI DISTILLER'S RESERVE

THE YAMAZAKI 25-YEAR-OLD

THE YAMAZAKI 18-YEAR-OLD

SUNTORY YAMAZAKI

Yamazaki 5–2–2, Honcho,
Mishimagun, Osaka
www.suntory.co.jp

Yamazaki claims to be the first
malt distillery built in Japan,
and was home to the fathers of
the nation's whisky industry,
Shinjiro Torii and Masataka
Taketsuru. Like Hakushu, it
produces a huge range of styles.
The official single-malt bottlings
concentrate on the sweet fruity
expression. Single-cask bottlings
have also been released. Most of
the older expressions have been
aged in ex-sherry casks, but there
is the occasional Japanese-oak
release for Japanese malt converts.

THE YAMAZAKI 12-YEAR-OLD

SINGLE MALT ABV 43%

*The mainstay of the range, the 12-year-
old is crisp, with a fresh nose of pineapple,
citrus, flowers, dried herbs, and a little
oak. The palate is sweet and filled with
ripe soft fruits and a hint of smoke.*

THE YAMAZAKI
DISTILLER'S RESERVE

SINGLE MALT 43% ABV

*Fragrant and delicately fruity, with
sandalwood on the nose. Summer fruits,
vanilla, and subtle spice on the palate,
with nutmeg and cinnamon at the close.*

THE YAMAZAKI 25-YEAR-OLD

SINGLE MALT 43% ABV

*A huge, concentrated, almost balsamic
sherried nose, with sweet raisin,
pomegranate, molasses, fig jam, prune,
rose petal, musk, leather, and burning
leaves. The palate is bitter and quite
tannic. It's very dry.*

THE YAMAZAKI 18-YEAR-OLD

SINGLE MALT 43% ABV

*With age, Yamazaki acquires more
influence from oak. The estery notes
of younger variants are replaced by
ripe apple, violet, and a deep, sweet
oakiness. This impression continues
on the palate with a mossy, pine-like
character and the classic Yamazaki
richness in the middle of the mouth.
This is an extremely classy whisky.*

THE SECRETS OF ...
YAMAZAKI

When Shinjiro Torii bought land near a small village on the old road between Kyoto and Osaka in 1921, he had a grand vision. There was no reason, he believed, that Japan couldn't make its own whisky. And he would create it here, at Yamazaki.

The only thing missing in his great scheme was someone with whisky-making knowledge. He found this in Masataka Taketsuru, a young scientist who had gone to Scotland to study chemistry, returning home with a Scots wife and a passion for whisky making. Yamazaki began distilling in 1924, and five years later, Japan's first whisky, Shirofuda (White Label), was launched.

Yamazaki is one of the world's most remarkable distilleries, and experimentation has never ceased. This is in part due to the Japanese distillers' idiosyncrasy in using only their own whiskies for their blends. Thus, the more complex the blend,

the more whiskies are required, so constant innovation is essential. Yamazaki is also at the forefront of the new, export-driven Japanese whisky industry. The domestic boom is long over, but distillers are courting a new generation. Though weaned on *shochu* (a traditional spirit), young Japanese, like their international contemporaries, are interested in single malt, individuality, and premium.

Who knows if Torii's vision ran to selling his whiskies in direct competition with Scotch, or if he dreamed that they would one day be seen as the equals of Scottish single malts. The fact is that they are.

▲ PLACE OF POWER
Yamazaki is the place where, in the 16th century, Sen no Rikyu, the creator of *cha-noyu* (tea ceremony), built his first tea house. The waters of three rivers merge here. Torii needed water and wanted humidity to help with maturation; this wooded site also simply felt right to him.

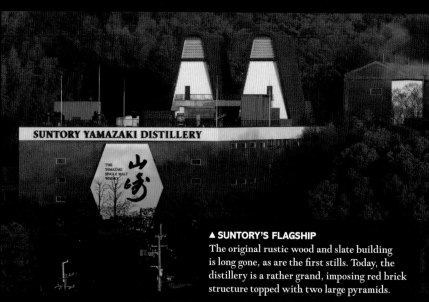

SUNTORY YAMAZAKI DISTILLERY

▲ SUNTORY'S FLAGSHIP
The original rustic wood and slate building is long gone, as are the first stills. Today, the distillery is a rather grand, imposing red brick structure topped with two large pyramids.

WASHBACKS

Yamazaki processes unpeated, lightly peated, and heavily peated malt. The two mash tuns produce different types of wort, and various yeast strains are used. Wort and yeast come together in the washbacks, and fermentation begins, although the length varies.

TASTING NEW MAKE

Suntory's most recent preference for direct firing and smaller stills adds weight to the new make spirit. This new make is a medium-bodied, fruity malt with a subtle depth in the middle of the palate. Future bottlings are likely to contain a whiff of smoke.

STILLS

The stillhouse at Yamazaki contains a remarkable collection of stills, which are mostly run in tandem. They include steam-fired stills of differing shapes and sizes. This distillery is renowned for its willingness to experiment; the smaller, direct-fired stills were added in 2005.

MATURATION

A broad range of woods is used for maturation including new oak, ex-bourbon, and ex-sherry casks. There is even a whisky that has been matured in casks formerly used to age plum liqueur. The official number of Yamazaki

RIEDEL TENNESSEE YEAST DRA
MATURATION BOURBON GRAIN PIN
OLD FASHIONED MALTING SCOTCH D
COPITA SWING MASH TUN POT S
PATENT ISLAY SINGLE MALT
BLENDS PEAT FERMENTATION BLEN
AND HOGSHEADS STARCH COFFEY
YEAST DRAM RYE QUAICH CEREALS
PINCH GLENMORANGIE WHEAT HI
DISTIL PETARD RIEDEL TENNESSEE
STILL MATURATION BOURBON GRA
OLD FASHIONED MALTING SCOTCH D
COPITA SWING MASH TUN POT S
WOOD PATENT ISLAY SINGLE MALT
BLENDS PEAT FERMENTATION BLEN
AND HOGSHEADS STARCH COFFEY
YEAST DRAM RYE QUAICH CEREALS
PINCH GLENMORANGIE WHEAT HI
DISTIL PETARD RIEDEL TENNESSEE
STILL MATURATION BOURBON GRA
OLD FASHIONED ISLAY SINGLE MALT

WHISKIES WORTH THE WAIT

REST OF THE WORLD

EUROPE • ASIA
AUSTRALASIA • AFRICA

WHISKY STYLES
EUROPEAN WHISKY

Outside the key whisky nations of Scotland and Ireland, there is a smattering of whisky distilleries across Western Europe. Northern countries such as Germany and Sweden have been distilling "aqua vitae" from grains for centuries, mainly in the form of vodka, gin, akvavit, korn, and schnapps. Southern countries such as France have long traditions of distilling fruits into eaux-de-vie.

In recent years, with global interest in whisky increasing, some of these mostly small-scale, family-owned European distilleries have expanded into whisky-making. In the north, such operations are often an extension of existing beer breweries, whereas in the south, the stills used for brandy may also be used for whisky. For that reason, southern-European whiskies often turn out fruitier than their northern counterparts. The use of a range of former wine casks for maturation also adds significantly to the sweet flavours of southern European whiskies.

The output of most European distilleries is small, but with a dedicated local following, so whisky releases can sell out within a few days. Apart from the Swedish Mackmyra, few are available outside their own countries. Other tiny whisky operations include Weutz (Austria), Fisselier (France), Brasch, Gruel, Höhler, Zaiser, and Rabel (Germany), Maison Les Vignettes and Bauernhof (Switzerland).

Further east, Turkey's state-owned brand Tekel cannot technically be called "whisky" because it is made from a mash of malted barley and rice. Kizlyar distillery in Dagestan, Russia, was founded in 2003 and produces single malt, grain, and blended whiskies.

PENDERYN LEGEND

SINGLE MALT 41% ABV

Light on the nose, with tropical fruit, vanilla, and honey, while the palate yields more vanilla, honey, and fruit, notably ripe bananas, leading into a relatively short peppery finish.

PENDERYN LEGEND

PENDERYN PEATED

PENDERYN MYTH

PENDERYN
WALES

Penderyn, near Aberdare
www.welsh-whisky.co.uk

Currently the only whisky distillery in Wales, Penderyn was named "Microdistillery Whisky of the Year" in 2008 by leading American whisky magazine *Malt Advocate*. It is indeed micro, producing only one cask a day. After a slow start, the distillery is now acknowledged worldwide as making exquisite whiskies. In his *Whisky Bible 2009*, Jim Murray describes Penderyn as "a prince of a Welsh whisky truly fit for the Prince of Wales". It was HRH Prince Charles himself who opened the distillery to the public in June 2008, eight years after the first distillate ran off the single still. Capacity was greatly increased with the introduction of a second still in 2013 and a pair of traditional pot stills the following year.

Whisky-making in Wales started long before that: according to Penderyn, the Welsh may have been making whisky ("*gwirod*") in the 4th century. It is also said that the American whiskey pioneers Evan Williams and Jack Daniel were from Welsh stock.

The core Penderyn range includes Legend, Peated, and Myth, with the latter undergoing its entire maturation in ex-Bourbon casks.

PENDERYN PEATED

SINGLE MALT 46% ABV

Sweet, aromatic smoke followed by vanilla, green apples, and refreshing citrus notes.

PENDERYN MYTH

SINGLE MALT 41% ABV

Vanilla, apple juice, and coconut milk on the light nose, with a thin palate offering citrus fruits, chocolate-flavoured ice cream, and spicy notes in the medium to long finish.

THE ENGLISH WHISKY CO.
ENGLAND

St George's Distillery, Harling Road,
Roudham, Norfolk
www.englishwhisky.co.uk

According to Alfred Barnard, in his
1887 tome Distilleries of the United
Kingdom and Ireland, England had
at least four distilleries in the 1800s.
These had all gone by the turn of the
20th century and it was not until
2006 that pot stills produced malt
spirit in England again, thanks to
The English Whisky Co. Whisky
has been released in sequential
chapters, in both unpeated and
peated formats, while more
mainstream Classic and Peated
expressions are also available.

THE ENGLISH WHISKY CO. CHAPTER 14
SINGLE MALT 46% ABV

*The nose is floral and fruity, with honey,
vanilla, and orange. Oily on the palate,
very fruity, vanilla custard, and ultimately
a lengthy, drying finish.*

THE ENGLISH WHISKY CO. CHAPTER 15
SINGLE MALT 46% ABV

*This heavily peated, five-year-old
expression features bonfire and citrus
notes on the nose, with more citrus fruit
on the palate, along with vanilla and
chilli, leading into a dry, oaky finish.*

ADNAMS
ENGLAND

Copper House Distillery, Adnams PLC, Sole Bay Brewery, Southwold, Suffolk, www.adnams.co.uk

Adnams Brewery has been a feature of the Suffolk town of Southwold since 1872; in 2010, a licence was granted to distil on the site, and distilling equipment was subsequently installed in a redundant brew-house building.

Adnams released its first two whiskies in 2013: Triple Grain No.2 and Single Malt No.1. Both are produced from local, East Anglian grains, with the former matured in American oak barrels and the latter in French oak casks. Adnams also distil gin, vodka, and absinthe.

ADNAMS COPPER HOUSE SINGLE MALT NO.1

SINGLE MALT 43% ABV
New oak opens the nose, soon followed by vanilla, honey, and spices. Caramel, apples, and black pepper on the palate.

HICKS & HEALEY
ENGLAND

Healey's Cornish Cyder Farm, Penhallow, Truro, Cornwall www.thecornishcyderfarm.co.uk

St Austell Brewery produces the mash for Healey's whiskey – which employs the Irish and US spelling – and this is then double distilled in a small pair of Scottish-made copper pot stills at the Cornish Cyder Farm, located near Newquay. The stills were installed in 2000, and in 2011, a single cask was bottled, with its 7-year-old single malt whiskey subsequently hitting the shelves. This was the oldest English whisk(e)y available, and batches are bottled each year, with a 2004 distillation being released aged eight.

HICKS & HEALEY SINGLE MALT CORNISH WHISKEY 8-YEAR-OLD

SINGLE MALT 60.2% ABV
Sweet fruits on the early nose, then malt, ginger, and vanilla. Baked apple, cinnamon, and caramel on the spicy palate.

FRYSK HYNDER
THE NETHERLANDS

Us Heit Distillery, Snekerstraat 43, 8701 XC Bolsward, Friesland www.usheitdistillery.nl

Us Heit (Frisian for "Our Father") was founded as a brewery in 1970. In 2002, owner Aart van der Linde, an avid whisky enthusiast, decided to start distilling whisky with barley from a local mill. It is the same barley from which Us Heit beer is made and it is malted at the distillery. A 3-year-old single malt whisky, Frysk Hynder, has been released in limited quantities every year since 2005. Us Heit uses different types of cask for maturing its whisky, from ex-bourbon barrels to wine casks and sherry butts.

FRYSK HYNDER 3-YEAR-OLD SHERRY MATURED

SINGLE MALT 43% ABV
Sweet nose, with sherry, soft spice, oak, and figs. Smooth, sherried palate with developing dark chocolate and spicy oak.

MILLSTONE
THE NETHERLANDS

Zuidam, Weverstraat 6, 5111 PW, Baarle Nassau www.zuidam.eu

What started as a gin distillery some 50 years ago is now a company with a second generation of the Zuidam family at the helm. It produces beautifully crafted single malts, alongside excellent young and old *jenevers*, as the Dutch call their gin. The Millstone 5-year-old single malt whisky was introduced in 2007, to be followed by an 8-year-old sibling. Zuidam uses ex-bourbon as well as ex-sherry casks to mature its whisky. A 10-year-old expression is in the making.

MILLSTONE 5-YEAR-OLD

SINGLE MALT 40% ABV
Delicate tones of fruit and honey combined with vanilla, wood, and a hint of coconut. Rich honey sweetness, delicate spicy notes, and a long vanilla oak finish.

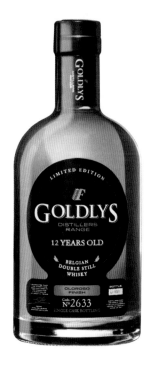

THE BELGIAN OWL
BELGIUM

The Owl Distillery, Rue Sainte
Anne 94, B4460 Grâce-Hollogne
www.belgianwhisky.com

Master Distiller Etienne
Bouillon founded this distillery
in the French-speaking part
of Belgium in 2004. He uses
home-grown barley and first-
fill bourbon casks to produce
a 3-year-old single malt whisky.
The first batch was bottled in
the autumn of 2007. The Belgian
Owl Distillery was formerly
known under the names
Lambicool and PUR-E.

BELGIAN SINGLE MALT
SINGLE MALT 46% ABV
*This non-chill filtered malt offers vanilla,
coconut, banana, and ice cream, topped
with fig, followed by a crescendo of
other flavours such as lemon, apples,
and ginger. A long finish, with ripe
fruits and vanilla.*

GOLDLYS
BELGIUM

Graanstokerij Filliers,
Leernsesteenweg 5, 9800 Deinze
www.filliers.be

Flemish distiller Filliers has been
making grain spirits since 1880. In
2008, it surprised the whisky world
by launching two whiskies it had
been maturing for years. Their name
comes from the River Lys, which
is nicknamed the "Golden River"
because of the flax retted (soaked)
in it. Goldlys uses malt, rye, and
corn, and is distilled twice, first
in a column still, then in a pot still
– a similar process to making
bourbon. The spirit is then matured
in ex-bourbon casks, and a number
of "finishes" are available.

GOLDLYS 12-YEAR-OLD
OLOROSO CASK FINISH
DOUBLE STILL WHISKY 43% ABV
*Vanilla, honey, and citrus on the nose.
Oily palate of sherry and raisin leads
to a lengthy finish.*

GOUDEN CAROLUS
BELGIUM

Brouwerij Het Anker, Guido Gezellelaan
49, B-2800 Mechelen
www.hetanker.be

The Belgian beer brewery Het
Anker – makers of the famous
Gouden Carolus Tripel beer – first
ventured into whisky-making in
2003. The current owner, Charles
Leclef, is the fifth generation of
the de Van Breedam family to
own the company. In 2008, 2,500
bottles of Gouden Carolus Single
Malt were bottled and distributed.

GOUDEN CAROLUS
SINGLE MALT 40% ABV
*Nicely balanced for a young whisky,
with fruity, woody notes.*

ARMORIK
FRANCE

Distillerie Warenghem, Route de
Guingamp, 22300 Lannion, Bretagne
www.distillerie-warenghem.com

The Warenghem Distillery
was founded in 1900 to produce
apple cider and fruit spirits.
It was not until 99 years later
that the owners decided to start
making other types of spirits,
including malted beers and
whisky. There are now two
types of whisky made here:
Armorik, a single malt, and
WB (Whisky Breton), a blend.
The type of casks used for
maturation is not specified.

AMORIK WHISKY
BRETON CLASSIC
SINGLE MALT 46% ABV
*Citrus fruits, spicy malt, hazelnuts,
and vanilla on the nose, while the full,
oily palate yields malt, honey, vanilla,
and dried fruits, before a spicy and
slightly salty finish.*

EDDU GOLD

EDDU GREY ROCK

EDDU SILVER

EDDU
FRANCE

Des Menhirs, Pont Menhir, 29700
Plomelin, Bretagne
www.distillerie.bzh

This is from the land of *menhirs*
(standing stones) and Calvados
distilled from apples. The Des
Menhirs Distillery started life as
a manufacturer of apple cider in
1986, but in 1998, branched out
into whisky. Most fruit distillers
that venture into whisky-making
use their existing equipment to
distil whisky on the side. Not so
this company: Des Menhirs built
a separate still for the exclusive
production of whisky, which it
distils not from barley but from
buckwheat (*eddu* in Breton). The
distillery currently carries three
different expressions of its Eddu
whisky – Silver, Gold, and Grey
Rock. The types of cask used are
not specified. In 2006, the distillery
was extended and now houses
a shop as well.

EDDU SILVER

BUCKWHEAT WHISKY 40% ABV
*Aromatic rose and heather on the
nose. Fruity, with a touch of honey,
marmalade, and some nutmeg.
Velvety body, with vanilla and
oak in the finish.*

EDDU GOLD

BUCKWHEAT WHISKY 43% ABV
*Almost identical to its Silver sibling –
with the same flowers and spices –
but higher in alcohol.*

EDDU GREY ROCK

BLEND 40% ABV
*A blended variety containing 30 per
cent buckwheat. Orange and apricot
flavours combine with broom flower.
A faint sea breeze is framed by a
hint of cinnamon. Balanced flavours
and a long, long finish.*

GLANN AR MOR
FRANCE

Crec'h ar Fur, 22610 Pleubian, Bretagne
www.glannarmor.com

Glann ar Mor means "by the sea" in Breton. The distillery opened in 2005 after eight years of planning. On 17th November 2008, the contents of one cask were emptied and bottled, rendering 305 bottles. The Glann ar Mor distillery now produces an unpeated single malt named Glann ar Mor and a peated single malt named Kornog (meaning "The West Wind" in Breton). Maturation takes place in first-fill Sauternes wine barriques and first-fill bourbon barrels. The company is building a new Scotch distillery at Gartbreck on Islay.

GLANN AR MOR
SINGLE MALT 46% ABV
Fairly complex, with ginger, vanilla, and a whiff of the sea, then grassy and leafy. Big fruit, including ripe apples and pears, framed in fine oak.

GUILLION
FRANCE

Hameau de Vertuelle,
51150 Louvois, Champagne
www.distillerie-guillon.com

The Guillon Distillery is located in the Champagne region of France, and was purpose-built in 1997 to produce whisky. It started distilling in 1999, distinguishing itself by the use of a variety of ex-wine casks for maturation. For the first maturation period, ex-Burgundy casks are used. After that, the whisky is finished for six months in casks that used to contain sweet wines like Banyuls, Loupiac, and Sauternes. Guillon bottles a premium blend at 40% ABV. The various single malts are bottled at 42, 43, and 46% ABV.

GUILLON CUVEE 42
SINGLE MALT 42% ABV
Barley, berry fruits, and a slight hint of smoke on the nose, with more barley plus apples, before a slightly ashy, fiery finish.

P&M
FRANCE

Domaine Mavela, Brasserie Pietra,
Route de La Marana,
20600 Furiani, Corsica
www.corsican-whisky.com

P&M is a fruitful cooperation between two companies on the Mediterranean island of Corsica. Founded as a brewery in 1996, Pietra produces the mash that is distilled at Mavela. The single malt whisky is aged in casks made from oak from the local forest. As well as single malts, P&M also produces a blended variant.

P&M PURE MALT
MALT 42% ABV
This complex, aromatic whisky has a subtle aroma of honey, apricot, and citrus fruit, and a rich flavour.

UBERACH
FRANCE

Bertrand Distillery, 3 rue du Maréchal
Leclerc, BP 21, 67350 Uberach, Alsace
www.distillerie-bertrand.com

The Bertrand brandy and liqueur distillery in Alsace dates from 1874 and has been run by the same family ever since. The Alsace region is blessed with particularly fertile, alluvial soil and the area around the distillery produces a range of fruits that are used in some of Bertrand's spirits. The company also produces beer and two non-filtered whiskies, Uberach Single Malt and Uberach Single Cask.

UBERACH SINGLE MALT
SINGLE MALT 42.2% ABV
Floral, fruity, and spicy, with black tea and hints of plums, as well as wax, and tobacco notes. Aromatic with good balance and an oaky, fruity finish.

WAMBRECHIES
FRANCE

1 Rue de la Distillerie, 59118
Wambrechies, Nord-Pas-de-Calais
www.wambrechies.com

Wambrechies was founded in
1817 as a *jenever* (gin) distillery
and is one of only three stills
left in the region. It continues
to produce an impressive range
of *jenevers*, as well as one malt
whisky and a *jenever* beer.
Wambrechie whiskies are bottled
at three and eight years old, with
the younger whisky consisting
of a lighter, floral blend and the
older having a deeper, spicy
character. They have also released
two 12-year-old expressions.

WAMBRECHIES 8-YEAR-OLD

SINGLE MALT 40% ABV
*Delicate nose, with aniseed, fresh paint,
vanilla, and cereal notes. Smooth on
the palate, with a fine malty profile.
Spicy finish, with powdered ginger
and milk chocolate.*

HOLLE
SWITZERLAND

Hollen 52, 4426 Lauwil, Basel
www.single-malt.ch

Until 1st July 1999, it was strictly
forbidden in Switzerland to distil
spirit from grain, which was
considered a food staple. After
a change in the law, the Bader
family, who had been making fruit
spirits for a long time, started to
distil from grains, and became the
country's first whisky producer.

HOLLE

SINGLE MALT 42% ABV
*Delicate aromas of malt, wood,
and vanilla, with a flavour of wine.
There are two varieties: one is matured
in a white-wine cask, the other in a
red-wine cask. A cask strength version
is bottled at 51.1% ABV.*

SINGLE LAKELAND
SWITZERLAND

Zürcher Nägeligässli 7,
2562 Port

The Zürcher Distillery was set up
in 1968 by Heinz Zürcher, although
he had been distilling and selling
spirits since 1959. Whisky was
first distilled at Zürcher in 2003.
The spirit matures in Oloroso
sherry casks for three years.
The first bottling was released
in 2007. Due to its popularity
and low production rates, the
single malt sells out very quickly.

SINGLE LAKELAND

SINGLE MALT 42% ABV
DISTILLED 2005 BOTTLED 2008
*Perfectly balanced. Flavours of
tannin and smoke. Smooth vanilla
and cinnamon aromas.*

WHISKY CASTLE
SWITZERLAND

Schlossstrasse 17, 5077 Elfingen
www.whisky-castle.com

Käsers Schloss (the Swiss name of
the distillery) is owned by Ruedi
and Franziska Käser. The couple
started producing whisky in 2000
and expanded the business in 2006
to include themed events such as
whisky dinners and whisky
conferences at their premises.
The brand name of their whisky
in English is Whisky Castle, and
there are a number of expressions,
including Double Wood, Terroir,
Smoke Barley (aged in new French
oak casks), Smoke Rye, Full Moon,
and Château (matured in Château
d'Yquem wine casks).

WHISKY CASTLE FULL MOON

SINGLE MALT 43% ABV
*This is made from smoked, malted
barley during a full moon, hence the
name. It is a young whisky with a
sweetish aroma and taste.*

NOCK-LAND
AUSTRIA

Wolfram Ortner, Untertscherner Weg 3,
9546 Bad Kleinkirchheim
www.wob.at

Ortner specializes in luxury
products, especially cigars, glasses,
and fruit liqueurs. The company
started producing Nock-Land
whisky in 1996, named after the
Nockberg Mountains nearby. Since
2014, two principal expressions have
been available, namely Nock-Land
Single Malt XV Double Matured
(15-year-old) and the 6-year-old
Double Matured, which has been
finished in charred Limousin oak.

NOCK-LAND WHISKY

MALT 48% ABV
*Sweet and malty with heavy notes of
spice and tobacco. Rounded off with
a faint whiff of honeycomb.*

REISETBAUER
7-YEAR-OLD

SINGLE MALT 43% ABV
*Delicate and multi-layered
on the nose, with slightly
roasted aromas reminiscent
of hazelnuts and dried
herbs. Pleasant notes of
bread and cereals on the
palate. Slightly smoky,
with fine spice.*

REISETBAUER 12-YEAR-OLD

REISETBAUER
AUSTRIA

Axberg 15, 4062 Kirchberg-Thening
www.reisetbauer.at

Han Reisetbauer made his name
as a quality distiller of fruit. He
started distilling whisky in 1995,
claiming to be the first Austrian
to do so. Waldviertler Roggenhof
Distillery *(see next entry)* makes
the same claim.

Reisetbauer grows his own
barley, and does his own malting
and fermentation. The wash
is double distilled, and he uses
Trockenbeeremauslee and
Chardonnay casks, allowing
the spirit to absorb traces of
fruit left in the wood, enhancing
its flavour. His first bottling
was released in 2002.

REISETBAUER 12-YEAR-OLD

MALT 48% ABV
*Similar to the 7-year-old, with greater
emphasis on fruit notes from the wine
barrels used for maturation.*

WALDVIERTLER J.H. SPECIAL PURE RYE MALT "NOUGAT"

WALDVIERTLER J.H. SPECIAL SINGLE MALT "KARAMELL"

WALDVIERTLER J.H. ORIGINAL RYE WHISKY

RYE WHISKY 41% ABV
Extremely sweet and dense on the nose, with honey, ripe peaches, and spicy rye. The palate is equally full and sweet, with honey, caramel, and a hint of lemon. An after-dinner dram.

WALDVIERTLER
AUSTRIA

Whiskydestillerie J. Haider OG,
3664 Roggenreith 3
www.whiskyerlebniswelt.at

The Waldviertler Roggenhof Distillery was founded in 1995 and, like Reisetbauer *(see previous entry)*, claims to be the first whisky distillery in Austria. It produces five different whiskies. Two are single malts – J.H. Single Malt and J.H. Special Single Malt "Karamell". The other three are rye whiskies – J.H. Original Rye, J.H. Pure Rye Malt, and J.H. Special Pure Rye Malt "Nougat".

The company uses casks made from Manharstberger oak trees that grow in the local region. The whiskies are matured for between three and twelve years and offered as single-cask bottlings. Alcohol percentages vary from 41–54% ABV, and the flavours range from light vanilla to caramel, chocolate, and nougat.

Johann Haider, the master distiller and joint owner of Waldviertler Roggenhof, has also created the "Whisky Experience" on the premises, consisting of an audio-visual tour and a café in which to sample various whiskies in coffee. Seminars are given on Haider's book *Fascination Whisky*. Other spirits made here include vodka, gin, and brandy, but – unusually for a Continental European distillery – whisky is the main focus.

WALDVIERTLER J.H. SPECIAL PURE RYE MALT "NOUGAT"

RYE WHISKY 41% ABV
A gentle, sweet taste of honey, harmonizing perfectly with the light vanilla taste.

WALDVIERTLER J.H. SPECIAL SINGLE MALT "KARAMELL"

SINGLE MALT 41% ABV
Smoky and dry, with an intense caramel flavour.

HAMMERHEAD
CZECH REPUBLIC

www.stockspirits.com

Hammerhead whisky was distilled during 1989 at the Pradlo Distillery near Plzen, in western Czechoslovakia. The distillery had been making pot-still spirits for many years before experimenting with single malt whisky. This experiment is believed to be the only Bohemian single malt in the world.

Stock Spirits purchased the distillery without knowing of the whisky's existence. It was first bottled in 2011, and further releases have ensued since.

HAMMERHEAD 25-YEAR-OLD
SINGLE MALT 40.7% ABV
A very drinkable whisky made from Czech barley and finished in casks made of Czech oak. It has a nutty, floral nose, spiced palate of dried fruit, and an oaky, liquorice finish.

GOLD COCK
CZECH REPUBLIC

Jelinek Distillery,
Razov 472, 76312 Vizovice
www.rjelinek.cz

Jelinek Distillery was founded at the end of the 19th century, and acquired the Gold Cock brand from Tesetice, a Czech distillery that no longer exists. For its two expressions – Red Feathers and a 12-year-old – Jelinek uses Moravian barley and water is sourced from an underground well that is rich in minerals. The type of cask used is not specified.

GOLD COCK RED FEATHERS
BLEND 40% ABV
Light and grainy, slightly metallic, and sweetish.

AMMERTAL
GERMANY

Hotel Gasthof Lamm, Jesinger
Hauptstrasse 55/57, 72070 Tübingen
www.lamm-tuebingen.de

Volker Theurer, the owner of Hotel Gasthof Lamm, is also a distiller and makes a whisky known as Black Horse Original Ammertal for a local market. The mash consists of 70 per cent malted barley and 30 per cent rye and wheat. It is aged in German oak ex-bourbon barrels and ex-sherry casks and is matured for a minimum of seven years.

ORIGINAL AMMERTAL
BLEND 40% ABV
Slightly nutty with some coffee notes and sweet grains.

BLAUE MAUS
GERMANY

Fleischmann, Bamberger Strasse 2,
91330 Eggolsheim-Neuses
www.fleischmann-whisky.de

The Fleischmann brandy distillery was founded in 1980 on the premises of the original family company – a grocery and tobacco shop. In 1996, after nearly 14 years of experimentation with whisky distillation, the company launched their first whisky expression. There are now eight different single cask malt whiskies available, including Blaue Maus, Grüner Hund, and Old Fahr, along with a single cask grain whisky – Austrasier.

BLAUE MAUS OLD FAHR
SINGLE MALT 40% ABV
The nose offers plain chocolate, ginger, and a slight oiliness. The oiliness continues onto the soft palate, which features contrasting vanilla and drying oak notes, with plain chocolate returning in the finish.

FRÄNKISCHER
GERMANY

Reiner Mösslein, Untere Dorfstrasse 8, 97509 Zeilitzheim
www.weingeister.de

Reiner Mösslein Distillery produces just one malt whisky – Fränkischer – and a variety of schnapps. The whisky is distilled from a blend of home-grown barley and grain. The spirit then matures in charred-oak casks for five years, lending it a smoky aroma.

FRÄNKISCHER 5-YEAR-OLD
GRAIN WHISKY 40% ABV
Chocolate and smoke on the nose, leading on to earthy flavours with oaky notes.

GLEN ELS
GERMANY

Hammerschmiede Spirituosen, Elsbach 11A, 37449 Zorge
www.hammerschmiede-spirituosen.de

The Hammerschmiede company was founded in 1984, and its first distillation of single malt whisky took place in autumn 2002. The spirit is stored in a smithy dating from 1250, and matures in Bordeaux and German oak casks that previously contained Amontillado, Fino, Manzanilla, Oloroso, and cream sherries, plus port, Marsala, or Madeira. Glen Els is only available as a single cask expression bottled at cask strength. The distillery operates with relatively small copper pot stills.

GLEN ELS THE JOURNEY
SINGLE MALT 43% ABV
A whiff of smoke on the nose, along with vanilla, toffee, and citrus fruits. The palate is sweet, with more vanilla and fudge, before a gentle smoky note develops.

SLYRS
GERMANY

Bayrischzellerstrasse 13 , 83727 Schliersee, Ortsteil Neuhaus
www.slyrs.de

Slyrs was founded in 1999 and makes a well-regarded whisky, which is distributed by Lantenhammer, a schnapps distillery located in the same Bavarian village. Slyrs is bottled after maturing for an unspecified time in new American white-oak barrels. Sherry cask matured and cask strength expressions have also been released.

SLYRS
SINGLE MALT 43% ABV
Some flowery aromas and spicy notes deliver a nice and easy dram. The taste varies according to the vintage.

BRAUNSTEIN
DENMARK

Braunstein, Carlsensvej 5, 4600 Koge
www.braunstein.dk

A microbrewery located in an old warehouse in Koge harbour, Braunstein was established in 2005 and uses a small still to make spirit from malted barley. The resulting spirit is clean, fresh, and fruity. Maturation takes place in ex-Oloroso sherry casks. A new edition of the whisky is added each year. The distillery also manufactures aquavit, herbal spirits, schnapps, and a beer called BB Amber Lager. Tastings are held each month, and there is a notably active Braunstein Whisky Club.

BRAUNSTEIN
SINGLE MALT (VARIABLE ABV)
Fruits, raisins, and chocolate come to the fore in this single malt that varies in strength from batch to batch.

BOX EXPLORER

TEERENPELI
FINLAND

Teerenpeli, Hämeenkatu 19, Lahti
www.teerenpeli.com

The first Teerenpeli Brewery was founded in May 1995 in Restaurant Teerenpeli, and the beer won several medals. In 2002, the new brewery and distillery were opened in Restaurant Taivaanranta. The brew house is situated in the dining room, while the fermentation and distilling equipment are in the cellar, along with a visitor centre. Casks of Teerenpeli new malt whisky are available for sale to private individuals or corporate groups.

TEERENPELI 3-YEAR-OLD NO. 001

SINGLE MALT 43% ABV

A lot of grain (barley), vanilla, and oak wood with a slightly thick body.

BOX
SWEDEN

Sörviken 140, 872 96 Bjärtrå
www.boxwhisky.se

The Box Distillery came on stream in 2010, situated at the old Box Power Station, constructed in 1912 in the heart of the Ädalen region of Sweden. The distillery has two conventional, Scottish-built pot stills, and produces two styles of spirit – one unpeated, the other peated with imported Islay peat.

Box has issued a number of limited edition bottlings to date, and they have been met with great enthusiasm from Swedish whisky fans. The Pioneer, released in 2014, sold out its 5,000-bottle run in only seven hours.

BOX EXPLORER

SINGLE MALT 48.3% ABV

Light on the nose, with tropical fruit, honey, oak, and sweet peat smoke. Palate has lots of black pepper and peat smoke, with a gingery oak finish.

SPIRIT OF HVEN TYCHO'S START SINGLE MALT

SPIRIT OF HVEN SEVEN STARS NO.3 PHECDA'S SINGLE MALT

GOTLAND
SWEDEN

Gotland Whisky AB,
Sockerbruket, Romakloster
www.gotlandwhisky.se

Many decades ago, Sweden had
a thriving whisky industry, and
recent years have seen the number
of operational distilleries in the
country rise to eight. Gotland was
created in a former sugar factory,
not far from the historic city of
Visby, and the first spirit flowed
from the Scottish-built pot stills in
2012. Local barley is used in whisky
production, with on-site maltings
in operation, and both peated
and unpeated whiskies are being
produced. It is called "Isle of Lime"
because of the large quantity of
limestone found on Gotland island.

GOTLAND ISLE OF LIME
SINGLE MALT 40% ABV
*Light and fruity on the nose, with
vanilla, straw, and a hint of coconut
on the medium-bodied palate.*

HVEN
SWEDEN

Backafallsbyn AB,
Isle of Hven, S:t Ibb
www.hven.com

Spirit of Hven micro-distillery
is located on the island of Hven,
found in the Oresund Strait
between Sweden and Denmark.

Opened in 2008, the Hven
Distillery has only the third
pot still built in Sweden, older
Swedish distilleries often
importing second-hand stills
from Scottish distilleries.

Today, some malting is practised
on site, with Swedish peat (and
even seaweed) used in the drying
process. As well as whisky, the
distillery also produces rum, gin,
Calvados, and aquavit.

Among the whiskies currently
available are Urania (made using
barley from Scotland, Belgium,
and Hven, and matured in
casks from America, France,
and Spain), Seven Stars No.2

Merak Single Malt Whisky, and
Sankt Claus (matured in French
oak casks that previously held
Merlot wine).

SPIRIT OF HVEN TYCHO'S
STAR SINGLE MALT
SINGLE MALT 41.8% ABV
*New leather and orchard fruits, peat
smoke, and a slight sea salt on the
nose. More peat on the palate, with
freshly cut hay, orange, and pepper.*

SPIRIT OF HVEN SEVEN STARS
NO.3 PHECDA'S SINGLE MALT
SINGLE MALT 45% ABV
*Barbecue smokiness, brine, and ginger
on the nose, with developing honey and
pepper. The palate is quite oily, with
cinnamon, honey, more smoke, and
increasingly spicy and dry nutty
and oak notes.*

SMÖGEN
SWEDEN

Smögen Whisky AB, Ståleröd Heather
Liden 1 Hunnebostrand,
www.smogenwhisky.se

Smögen, a farm-based distillery
on the west coast of Sweden,
started producing whisky in 2010.
Designed by its owner, lawyer and
whisky aficionado, Pär Caldenby,
it has a 900-litre (200-gallon) wash
still and a 600-litre (130-gallon)
spirit still, with an annual capacity
of some 35,000 litres (7,700
gallons). Caldenby imports heavily
peated malt from Scotland.

Smögen's first release, Smögen
Primör, came in 2013. It is a
3-year-old cask strength matured
in European oak and ex-Bordeaux
wine casks.

SMÖGEN PRIMÖR
SINGLE MALT 63.7% ABV
*Earthy nose of sweet smoke, salt,
leather, and cocoa. Sweet peat on
the palate, with berries and spices.*

MACKMYRA
SWEDEN

Mackmyra, Kolonnvägen 2, Gävle
www.mackmyra.se

Mackmyra was founded in 1999 by the Swedish engineer Magnus Dardanell and a group of friends. In 2012, a remarkable new 37-metre-tall (120-ft), gravity-fed distillery opened a few miles from the Valbo original, and all commercial distilling now takes place on that site. The first Mackmyra distillery has been retained, however, and is still used for occasional special runs and to host marketing activities.

Having first released a series of six "Preludium" expressions during 2006 and 2007, many other bottlings have followed, and the core range now consists of Brukswhisky, Svensk Ek (matured in Swedish oak barrels), and the smoky Svensk Rök.

Mackmyra matures its spirit in several locations, including in a series of underground warehouses in the old Bodås mine, on Fjäderholmarna (an island near Stockholm), at Häckeberga Castle, and on the historic Gut Basthorst estate in Germany.

MACKMYRA SVENSK EK
SINGLE MALT 46.1% ABV
Toasted oak notes on the nose, with honey and citrus fruits. More honey and citrus notes on the palate, with malt, ginger, pepper, and spicy oak.

MACKMYRA BRUKSWHISKY
SINGLE MALT 41.4% ABV
The nose is light, with pine, cereal, citrus, and spicy toffee. The palate is also light and approachable, with cinnamon, vanilla, raspberries in cream, lively spices, and mild oak.

MACKMYRA SVENSK RÖK
SINGLE MALT 46.1% ABV
Peat smoke, citrus fruit, and vanilla on the nose, with a palate displaying sooty peat, more citrus fruit, and a hint of honey, with lingering spiciness.

DYC FINE BLEND

DYC PURE MALT

DYC 8-YEAR-OLD

DYC
SPAIN

Beam Global España SA,
Pasaje Molino del Arco, 40194
Palazuelos de Eresma, Segovia
www.dyc.es

The first whisky distillery in
Spain was founded in 1959 close
to Segovia and started producing
whisky in 1963. It stands next to
the River Eresma, famous for the
excellent quality of its water.
The distillery is now owned by
Beam Suntory. DYC (which stands
for Destilerías y Crianza del
Whisky) comes in four versions.
There is an unaged expression,
called Fine Blend, and an
8-year-old; these are both blends
of various grains. The pure malt,
which has no age statement, is a
blended malt, and, since 2009,
there has also been a 10-year-old
single malt.

The spirits mature in American
oak barrels and are primarily sold on
the home market. The Spanish tend

to drink it in a mix with cola and
ask at the bar for a "whisky-dyc",
pronouncing it "whisky-dick".

DYC 8-YEAR-OLD

BLEND 40% ABV

*Floral, spicy, smoky, grassy, with
a hint of honey and heather. Smooth,
creamy mouthfeel; malty with hints
of vanilla, marzipan, apple, and citrus.
A bitter-sweet, long, smooth finish.*

DYC PURE MALT

BLENDED MALT 40% ABV

*Sophisticated, fragrant bouquet with
vanilla. Full-bodied, rich malt flavour.
The finish is long, sophisticated, and
subtle, with hints of heather, honey,
and fruit.*

DYC FINE BLEND

BLEND 40% ABV

*Clean, with a hint of fruit, spice, and
toasted wood. Malty, spicy, smooth,
and creamy mouthfeel. The finish is
smoky and spicy.*

WHISKY STYLES
ASIAN WHISKY

India is the largest consumer of whisky in the world. Along with other parts of Asia, its spirits industry was founded by European expatriates in the 18th century. Western spirits such as gin and whisky were known throughout these countries as "locally made foreign liquor" (LMFL). In India, the British Raj named it "Indian-made foreign liquor" (IMFL).

To this day, the raw materials and processes for LMFL/IMFL are not defined by law. However, a brand of "Indian whisky" made from molasses alcohol and whisky essence is not allowed to bear the name "whisky" within the EC and many other export markets. The Thai Mekhong brand used to be described as "whisky", but is now marketed as "rum". Most LMFL and IMFL spirits are made in industrial ethanol plants. However, there are a few grain and pot still malt distilleries in India, Pakistan, Taiwan, and Israel.

Categories of Asian whisky:

Extra Neutral Alcohol (ENA) Made by fermentation and distillation in continuous stills, typically of molasses, rice, millet, buckwheat, or barley. Basic Asian whiskies are made from ENA mixed with whisky essence and other artificial flavourings.

Blended Whisky A mix of ENA whisky and locally produced malt whisky and/or bulk imported whisky. Where an age statement is given, this is the age of the imported whisky. The product does not pass the EC definition as "whisky".

Malt Whisky Blends of 100 per cent malt whiskies, domestic or foreign, qualify as "whisky" in the EC if matured for at least three years.

Single Malt Whisky Made from malted barley in a single distillery. So long as this is matured for at least three years, it meets EC regulations.

MURREE'S CLASSIC 8-YEAR-OLD

MURREE'S RAREST 21-YEAR-OLD

8PM CLASSIC

8PM ROYALE

MURREE
PAKISTAN

Murree Distillery, National
Park Road, Rawalpindi
www.murreebrewery.com

Murree began life in 1860 as a
brewery serving the needs of British
troops stationed in the Punjab, and
today, it still makes the leading
brand of beer in Pakistan. It was
built in Ghora Gali, 1,830m
(6,000ft) above sea level in the
foothills of the Western Himalayas,
and took its name from a nearby hill
station. In 1889, the company built
another brewery in Rawalpindi,
and it was here, 10 years later,
that the distillery was installed.

By this time, Rawalpindi was
part of Pakistan, but a dispensation
was granted to the non-Muslim
owners to distil alcoholic drinks
"for visitors and non-Muslims".
This makes it the only distillery
of alcoholic beverages in a
Muslim country; the oldest
continuing industrial enterprise

in Pakistan; and one of the
oldest public companies on
the sub-continent.

The barley comes from the
UK and is malted in floor maltings
and Saladin boxes. The four large
open-air wash stills have stainless-
steel pots and copper heads and
condensers. Two spirit stills are
under cover. Some of the spirit
is filled into cask, most into large
vats (some made from Australian
oak), and matured in cellars
equipped with a cooling system.

MURREE'S CLASSIC 8-YEAR-OLD
SINGLE MALT 43% ABV
*A flowery, buttery nose and finish,
somewhat green, with a boiled-sweets
taste. Unlikely to be pure malt whisky.*

MURREE'S RAREST
21-YEAR-OLD
SINGLE MALT 43% ABV
*This is the oldest whisky to have been
produced in Asia and has developed and
deepened the Murree key notes with
a big dose of wood-extractive flavours.*

8PM
INDIA

Owner: Radico Khaitan
www.radicokhaitan.com

Launched as recently as 1999,
8PM had the singular distinction
of selling a million cases in its first
year. The brand owner is Radico
Khaitan, which describes itself as
"one of India's oldest and largest
liquor manufacturers". It is owned
and managed by veteran distiller
Dr Lalit Khaitan and his son
Abhishek. The company owns
other whisky brands, including
Whytehall (see p.324), and it
has recently formed a partnership
with Diageo, the world's largest
drinks conglomerate, to produce
Masterstroke (see p.322).

The company's headquarters
are at Rampur Distillery, Uttar
Pradesh. Established in 1943,
it is now a gigantic unit with
a capacity of over 90 million litres
(20 million gallons) of alcohol
a year in three distinct operations:

a small malt distillery, a recently
opened grain distillery, and a
molasses distillery making ENA
(see p.318), rectified spirit, and
anhydrous alcohol, ethanol,
and gasohol (which is mixed with
petrol and used as fuel). As well as
whisky, Radico Khaitan produces
rum, brandy, gin, and vodka.

8PM CLASSIC
BLEND
*Made from "a mix of quality grains",
this has a core that promises "thaath"
(boldness, opulence) and "the reach
of a man to the dream world".*

8PM ROYALE
BLEND
*A blend of Indian spirits and mature
Scotch malt whiskies.*

AMRUT PEATED INDIAN SINGLE MALT

AMRUT SINGLE MALT

AMRUT INDIAN SINGLE MALT CASK STRENGTH

AMRUT
INDIA

www.amrutwhisky.co.uk

The family-owned company of Amrut Distilleries was founded in 1948 by Shri J.N. Radhakrishna Jagdale to supply bottled liquor to the Ministry of Defence. He was succeeded in 1976 by his son, Shri Neelakanta Rao Jagdale, the current chairman, who has focused on innovation, product quality, and transparency in the IMFL industry.

In 2002, Amrut trialled the sale of miniatures in Indian restaurants in the UK. It was very successful in Glasgow, and the brand now features at European whisky fairs.

In Hindu mythology, the *amrut* was a golden pot containing the elixir of life. The whisky of the same name is made from barley grown in the Punjabi foothills of the Himalayas. This is malted in Jaipur and distilled in small batches 900 m (3,000 ft) above sea level in Bangalore, where it is also matured in ex-bourbon and new oak casks and bottled without chill-filtration.

AMRUT INDIAN SINGLE MALT CASK STRENGTH

SINGLE MALT 61.9% ABV

Lightly fruity and cereal-like, with the bourbon cask introducing toffee. More woody, spicy, and malty with water. Similar in profile to a young Speyside malt.

AMRUT PEATED INDIAN SINGLE MALT

SINGLE MALT 62.78% ABV

Cereal and kippery smoke on the nose; oily, with salt and pepper. The taste is sweet and malty, with a whiff of smoke in the finish.

AMRUT SINGLE MALT

SINGLE MALT 40% ABV

A fresh, grassy, and fruity nose, with a trace of spice, ginger, and aniseed. The taste is smooth and sweet, with cereal and toffee apples. The finish is short.

ANTIQUITY
INDIA
Owner: United Spirits
www.unitedspirits.in

Antiquity is owned by the long-established Indian trading firm Shaw Wallace, now part of United Spirits. It is India's most expensive whisky, and won a gold award at the World Beverage Competition in 2007 in the "Scotch Whisky" category. It is, in fact, a blend of Scotch whisky, Indian malt whisky, and ENA.

United Spirits is the largest spirits company in India, and among the top three in the world. It is also the spirits division of the massive United Breweries Group.

ANTIQUITY
BLEND 42.8% ABV
A mild, biscuity nose, with some well-integrated fruit and floral notes. The taste is sweet overall, with some sulphur traces in the medium-length finish.

ARISTOCRAT
INDIA
Jagatjit Industries,
91 Nehru Place, New Delhi
www.jagatjit.com

Aristocrat comes from Jagatjit Industries – the third largest spirits producer in India, and a leading producer of IMFL from grains rather than molasses. The company was founded in 1944 by L.P. Jaiswal, under the patronage of the Maharaja of Kapurthala, Jagatjit Singh, with the guiding philosophy "Spirit of Excellence". Aristocrat is widely referred to as "AC" ("A" for "Aristo", "C" for "Crat") and a brand with this abbreviated name recently joined the portfolio.

ARISTOCRAT PREMIUM
BLEND 42.8% ABV
This is certainly not a pure malt whisky. Indeed, some commentators reckon it might be an IMFL with a dash of malt extract.

BAGPIPER
INDIA
Owner: United Spirits
www.unitedspirits.in

Formerly "The world's No.1 non-Scotch whisky", Bagpiper occupied fourth place with sales of 11.6 million cases in 2013. An IMFL, probably made from molasses alcohol and concentrates, it was launched by the United Spirits subsidiary Herbertson's in 1987 and, in its first year, sold 100,000 cases. The brand has always been closely associated with Bollywood, India's huge film-production industry, and has successfully won accreditation from many film stars. The company also broadcasts a weekly Bagpiper show on TV, and sponsors talent-spotting programmes.

BAGPIPER GOLD
BLEND 42.8% ABV
Gold is the premium expression of Bagpiper, but it still has a somewhat artificial taste and is best drunk with a mixer like cola.

BLENDERS PRIDE
INDIA
Owner: Pernod Ricard
www.pernod-ricard.com

Since it fell under the ownership of Pernod Ricard, the brand has been neck and neck with Royal Challenge (see p.324) as the bestseller in its sector. It is a premium IMFL (made from Scotch malts and Indian grains), whose name comes from a story about the master blenders who exposed a cask of whisky to the warmth of the sun at regular intervals. The delicate sweetness and aromatic flavour of the blend are testimony to the success of their experiment.

BLENDERS PRIDE
BLEND 42.8% ABV
A smooth and rich mouthfeel, with a sweet taste that gives way to a disappointingly dull finish.

IMPERIAL BLUE
INDIA

Owner: Pernod Ricard
www.pernod-ricard.com

Imperial Blue is Pernod Ricard's
second-best-selling brand in
India, selling around 11 million
cases in 2013. Launched in 1997,
it was previously a Seagram's
brand, benefiting hugely from
Pernod Ricard's acquisition of
Seagram in 2001, jumping from
producing under half a million
cases to over a million by 2002.
Imperial Blue hit the headlines
in 2008 when some bottles in
Andhra Pradesh were found to
be under-strength. It later
transpired that they had been
sabotaged by disgruntled workers.

IMPERIAL BLUE
BLEND 42.8% ABV
*In spite of the "grain" in its name,
Imperial Blue is a blend of imported
Scotch malt and locally made neutral
spirit. It is light, sweet, and smooth.*

MASTERSTROKE
INDIA

Owner: Diageo Radico
www.radicokhaitan.com
www.diageo.com

Masterstroke De Luxe Whisky,
an IMFL priced for the "prestige"
category, was launched by Diageo
Radico in February 2007. The
company is a joint 50:50 venture
between Radico Khaitan Ltd *(see
8PM, p.319)*, "India's fastest-
growing liquor manufacturer",
and the world's largest drinks
company, Diageo. It is their
first joint venture.

Within three months, the brand
was being endorsed by Bollywood
superstar Shah Rukh Khan.

MASTERSTROKE
BLEND 42.8% ABV
*A rich nose and mouthfeel, lent by
a liberal amount of Blair Athol single
malt. Well-balanced, with the light
finish characteristic of Indian-made
foreign liquors.*

MCDOWELL'S
INDIA

Owner: United Spirits
www.unitedspirits.in

Scotsman Angus McDowell founded
McDowell & Co. in Madras in 1826
as a trading company specializing
in liquor and cigars. In 1951, it was
acquired by Vittal Mallya, owner
of United Breweries. McDowell's
No.1 was launched in 1968, and
currently sells over 23 million cases
a year, making it the second-best-
selling Indian-produced whisky
in India.

A malt whisky distillery was
commissioned by McDowell & Co.
at Ponda, Goa, in 1971. It employs
the distilling regime used for
Scotch malt, with maturation in
ex-bourbon casks for around three
years. It is claimed that the heat
and humidity of Goa leads to a
more rapid maturation.

The product is described as "the
first-ever indigenously developed
single malt whisky in Asia". Three

main expressions are available: two
blends, called No. 1 Reserve and
Signature Rare, and a single malt.
McDowell also produces "the
world's first diet whisky", as it
calls it. This is a blend of "reserve"
whisky and garcenia, an Indian
herb reputed to control cholesterol
levels and burn off fat.

MCDOWELL'S NO.1 RESERVE
BLEND 42.8% ABV
*"Blended with Scotch and Select Indian
Malts", this has a nose of dried figs
and sweet tobacco and, later, prunes and
dates. A sweet taste initially, then burnt
sugar and a short finish.*

MCDOWELL'S SINGLE MALT
SINGLE MALT 42.8% ABV
*A true single malt, with a fresh cereal
and fruity nose and a sweet, pleasantly
citric taste, not unlike a young Speyside.*

PAUL JOHN BOLD

PAUL JOHN BRILLIANCE

PAUL JOHN EDITED

OFFICER'S CHOICE
INDIA

Owner: Allied Blenders and Distillers
www.abdindia.com/officers_choice

Available in some 18 countries, Officer's Choice has become one of the largest whisky brands in the world since its 1988 launch. Sales have risen at 14 per cent per annum over the past five years, with sales of 23 million cases between 2014 and 2015. It enjoys a 37 per cent share in the Indian whisky market, jostling for a top spot with McDowell's No.1 Reserve. Two "semi-premium" variants of Officer's Choice are also available: Blue, which appeared in 2012, and Black, released two years later. All expressions comprise Indian grain whisky and Scottish blended malts.

OFFICER'S CHOICE

BLEND 42.8% ABV
The nose is spirit-y, with a hint of rum, while the palate yields caramel and cinnamon before a short finish.

PAUL JOHN
INDIA

John Distilleries Pvt. Ltd.,
110, Pantharapalya, Mysore Road,
Bangalore 560 039
www.pauljohnwhisky.com

Paul John single malts are produced on the tropical coast of Goa, using six-row barley grown on the foothills of the Himalayas. Distillation takes place in traditional copper pot stills, which can yield up to 3,000 litres (660 gallons) of spirit per day. Casks are stored in a temperature-controlled cellar, but the climate of Goa means that whiskies mature relatively quickly. The first single malt was distilled in 2007 and the initial release took place in autumn 2012.

Paul John established John Distilleries Ltd (JDL) in 1992, and, as well as whisky, the company also produces brandy and wine. Its "flagship" brand Original Choice Whisky sells over 10 million cases a year. In recent times, however, there has been a conscious effort to focus on single malts, and a range of peated and unpeated expressions is now available, featuring both single malts and single cask single malts.

PAUL JOHN BOLD

SINGLE MALT 46% ABV
Vanilla, honey, lively spices, and peat on the nose. Honey, oak, spice, and smoke on the full palate.

PAUL JOHN BRILLIANCE

SINGLE MALT 46% ABV
Honey, cinnamon, and spice on the fragrant nose. Sweet, spicy, and smooth on the palate, with a suggestion of milk chocolate.

PAUL JOHN EDITED

SINGLE MALT 46% ABV
The nose is fruity, with honey, coffee, and gentle smoke. Grassy and peaty on the palate, with more coffee coming through.

ROYAL CHALLENGE
INDIA
Owner: United Spirits
www.unitedspirits.in

This "blend of rare Scotch and matured Indian malt whiskies" is owned by Shaw Wallace, a part of United Spirits since 2005. It is described as "the iconic" premium Indian whisky and, until 2008, it was also the best-selling premium Indian whisky, but is now severely challenged by Blenders Pride.

ROYAL CHALLENGE
BLEND 42.8% ABV
A soft, rounded nose, with traces of malt, nuts, caramel, and a light rubber note. These aromas translate well in the taste at full strength. With water, it remains dense and full-bodied but the taste, diluted, is not as heavy. Very sweet, slightly nutty, and mouth-drying, but with a longish finish.

ROYAL STAG
INDIA
Owner: Pernod Ricard
www.pernod-ricard.com

Seagram's Royal Stag broke the million-cases-a-year barrier in 2000. Early the following year, it was acquired by Pernod Ricard, when the Seagram empire was carved up between the French company and Diageo. The new owner continued the Seagram name, adopting the brand as its leader in the "prestige" sector of the vigorous Indian market. It also improved the blend, which is a combination of blended Scotch malts and Indian grain whiskies. Sales in 2013 amounted to 14.7 million cases, making it the third-best-selling Indian whisky.

ROYAL STAG
BLEND 42.8% ABV
For a standard blend, this shapes up well: fresh and sweet to start, with spice and cereal notes, and a firm finish.

SIGNATURE
INDIA
Owner: United Spirits
www.unitedspirits.in

The recently introduced Signature Rare Aged Whisky comes from the McDowell's stable, owned by United Spirits, and has the slogan "Success is Good Fun". It is a blend of Scotch and Indian malt whiskies and is the fastest-growing brand in the company's portfolio, selling over 600,000 cases in 2006–07. It has also won a clutch of international awards, including a gold in the Monde Selection 2006.

SIGNATURE
BLEND 42.8% ABV
A rich nose, with a distinct medicinal note. Straight, the taste is surprisingly sweet, with smoky and medicinal undertones, becoming less sweet with water. Relatively light in body, with a distinct peaty, smoky edge.

WHYTEHALL
INDIA
Owner: Radico Khaitan
www.radicokhaitan.com

Another Radico Khaitan brand (*see 8PM, p.319*), Whytehall became a part of the portfolio after Radico bought out the stake of its former joint venture partner, Bacardi, in Whytehall India Limited in July 2005.

Whytehall is made in the company's distillery at Hyderabad, and now sells half a million cases per annum. The brand won a silver medal at the International Wine and Spirit Competition 2007 and a gold medal at the Monde Selection in Belgium in 2008.

WHYTEHALL
BLEND 42.8% ABV
A superior IMFL blend of aged Scotch malts and Indian spirits.

KAVALAN PODIUM SINGLE MALT

KAVALAN KING CAR CONDUCTOR SINGLE MALT

KAVALAN CLASSIC SINGLE MALT

KAVALAN CONCERTMASTER PORT CASK FINISH SINGLE MALT

KAVALAN
TAIWAN

Kavalan Distillery, No. 326, Sec. 2,
Yuanshan Road, Yuanshan, Yilan
www.kavalanwhisky.com

The distillery is located in north-eastern Taiwan and was created by the King Car Food Industrial Company, with Scottish whisky consultant Dr Jim Swan playing a significant role in its design. The distillery, completed in March 2006, was equipped with two pairs of copper pot stills, giving an annual capacity of 1.5 million litres (330,000 gallons).

The year 2015 saw capacity dramatically increase to around 4.5 million litres (990,000 gallons) with addition of six more stills. The intention is for production to increase to 9 million litres (7.8 million gallons) per annum.

This expansion is due to the overwhelmingly positive response the whiskies have received since first released in 2008. The distillery visitor centre now welcomes more than one million people per year.

Although the Classic Single Malt is the best-selling Kavalan, there is a wide range of other expressions available. Most are around three years of age as Taiwan's sub-tropical climate enhances early maturation and leads to significant spirit losses due to evaporation.

KAVALAN PODIUM SINGLE MALT

SINGLE MALT 46% ABV

The nose is light and fresh, with honey, coconut, and vanilla. Ripe bananas, honey, and ginger on the palate, with spicy oak.

KAVALAN KING CAR CONDUCTOR SINGLE MALT

SINGLE MALT 46% ABV

A fresh nose of banana, apple, and floral notes. More banana on the voluptuous palate, with coconut milk, and vanilla.

KAVALAN CLASSIC SINGLE MALT

SINGLE MALT 40% ABV

Vanilla and fruit cocktail on the nose, tropical fruits, spice, vanilla, and soft oak on the palate.

KAVALAN CONCERTMASTER PORT CASK FINISH SINGLE MALT

SINGLE MALT 40% ABV

Port, berry fruits, honey, and milk chocolate on the nose, while tropical fruits and sweet oak develop on the palate.

WHISKY STYLES
AUSTRALASIAN WHISKY

Australia and New Zealand have a significant number of whisky distilleries producing malt. Some of these malts have been favourably compared with the best from Scotland. Tasmania, in particular, has ideal conditions for whisky production. However, Australasian whiskies can be hard to track down outside the continent, as the markets are mainly domestic.

Until 1938, Australasia was the largest export market for Scotch whisky, and it is hardly surprising that enterprising settlers of Scots descent established distilleries in Australia and New Zealand during the 19th century. Most were illicit farm stills, but there were a couple of short-lived industrial ventures, like the New Zealand Distillery, Dunedin (1867–73), and the Crown Distillery, Auckland, New Zealand (1865–79), which both opened in response to the halving of duties on locally made spirits. They soon closed when duties rose again, following pressure on the government by Scottish banks, which were payrolling the construction of the country's railways.

The first attempt to revive the distilling tradition in New Zealand was Wilson's Willowbank Distillery at Dunedin (1964–95), whose Lammerlaw brand became reasonably well known in Europe and East Asia, as well as in its home market. During the 1990s, however, the focus for revival was in Australia, particularly in Tasmania, where five distilleries opened, and that number has now grown to nine. The reasons for this are a combination of climate – Tasmania has the purest air in the world, and copious clean water dumped on the island by the Roaring Forties – and plenty of fertile country for growing barley. Away from Tasmania, Australia now boasts a further nine distilleries, located in Victoria, Albany, New South Wales, Queensland, and South Australia. These concerns are all "boutique" operations – small by choice and design – but they are now producing malt whiskies with a uniquely Australasian character.

BAKERY HILL PEATED MALT

BAKERY HILL CASK STRENGTH PEATED MALT

BAKERY HILL DOUBLE WOOD

BAKERY HILL
AUSTRALIA

28 Ventnor Street,
North Balwyn, Victoria
www.bakeryhilldistillery.com.au

"Single malt whisky is more than a craft, it's our passion." So says David Baker, chemist and founder (together with his wife, Lynn) of Bakery Hill Distillery near Melbourne, Victoria. Their first spirit flowed in 2000.

The barley strains Australian Franklin and Australian Schooner are sourced locally and sometimes malted over locally cut peat. The wash is brewed in 1,000-litre (264-gallon) batches and distilled twice in a single copper pot still. Maturation is on-site in barrels from Jack Daniel Distillery (see p.236). The ambient temperature at Bakery Hill is 10–30°C (50–86°F), so maturation is quicker than in Scotland.

Baker was determined to prove that top-quality malt whisky could be made in Australia, and he has succeeded: his single cask, non-chill filtered malts are already winning awards. Bakery Hill whiskies are now available well beyond their Victoria homeland.

BAKERY HILL PEATED MALT

SINGLE MALT 46% ABV

A sweet and oaky balance of peat and malt on the nose. These aromas carry through in the taste.

BAKERY HILL CASK STRENGTH PEATED MALT

SINGLE MALT 59.88% ABV

Intense peatiness on the nose, with dark cherry. The taste is sweet (toffee, honeycomb), with some salt and smoke. It has a good texture.

BAKERY HILL DOUBLE WOOD

SINGLE MALT 46% ABV

Finished in French oak ex-wine casks after ex-bourbon-cask maturation. Apricot, coconut, and plum, then syrup, fruitcake, and cloves. Sweet taste, with orange marmalade and oak.

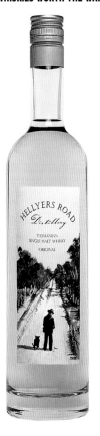

LARK'S SINGLE MALT

LARK'S PM

HELLYERS ROAD
AUSTRALIA

153 Old Surrey Road, Burnie, Tasmania
www.hellyersroaddistillery.com.au

Hellyers Road, opened in 1999, and owned by the Betta Milk Cooperative, now has about 3,000 ex-bourbon casks under maturation; it also produces a Tasmanian barley-based, pot-still vodka. The experience gained in running a milk processing plant has provided owner Laurie House with all the knowledge he needs to run this modern and highly automated plant.

The distillery is named after Henry Hellyer who, in the 1820s, created the first road into the interior of Tasmania, the same road that now leads to the distillery.

HELLYERS ROAD ORIGINAL

SINGLE MALT 46.2% ABV
A light-bodied, pale-coloured malt, un-tinted and non-chill filtered. The nose is fresh and citric, with vanilla notes.

LARK
AUSTRALIA

14 Davey Street, Hobart, Tasmania
www.larkdistillery.com

The modern revival of whisky-making in Australia began in Tasmania, with the opening of this small distillery in Hobart in 1992. It was the brainchild of Bill Lark, who, the story goes, was inspired by a bottle of single malt Scotch consumed during a fishing trip with his father-in-law, which prompted the question "why is nobody making malt whisky in Tasmania today?" Lark realized that the island has all the right ingredients: plenty of rich barley fields, abundant pure soft water, peat bogs, and a perfect climate for maturation.

Lark located his distillery on the harbourfront at Hobart, and is now assisted by his wife Lyn and daughter Kristy. They use locally grown Franklin barley, 50 per cent of it re-dried over peat.

The Distilling Act 1901 required a minimum still capacity of 2,700 litres (600 gallons) – Lark's first task was to have this law amended so that they could use smaller stills. The distillery produces 10 to 12 100-litre (22-gallon) barrels of whisky a month, as well as a range of other spirits, including liqueurs using the indigenous pepperberry spice. The malt is bottled from single casks at three to five years. Unusually, all Lark's products are Kosher Certified.

LARK'S SINGLE MALT

SINGLE MALT 58% ABV
Malty and lightly peated, with peppery notes. A smooth mouthfeel, with rich malt, apples, and oak-wood, and some spice in the finish.

LARK'S PM

BLENDED MALT 45% ABV
Sweet and smoky on the nose and in the mouth; clean and lightly spicy. This can be regarded as a well-made "barley schnapps".

LIMEBURNERS
AUSTRALIA

Great Southern Distilling Company, 252 Frenchman Bay Road, Albany, Western Australia
www.distillery.com.au

The Great Southern Distillery was built in 2007, the brainchild of lawyer and accountant Cameron Syme. Its location was chosen for Albany's cool, wet winters and enough breeze to provide 75 per cent of its energy needs by wind power. It is close to the Margaret River wineries, which supply the ingredients for schnapps and liqueur-making. Limeburners whisky is offered in single barrel bottlings: the first, M2, launched in April 2008, won an award.

LIMEBURNERS BARREL M11

SINGLE MALT 43% ABV
The fourth bottling (M11), nicknamed "The Dark One", is from a French oak ex-brandy cask, re-racked into a second-fill ex-bourbon barrel.

OVEREEM PORT MATURED – CASK STRENGTH

OVEREEM SHERRY CASK MATURED

OVEREEM BOURBON CASK MATURED – CASK STRENGTH

OVEREEM
AUSTRALIA

Old Hobart Distillery, Blackman's Bay,
Tasmania, Australia
www.overeem.co.uk

Overeem single malt whiskies
were first produced in Tasmania
by businessman and whisky
aficionado Casey Overeem, who
built the bespoke Old Hobart
Distillery, complete with copper
pot still, within walking distance
of his family home. He was granted
a licence to distil in 2005, and
started production two years
later. Overeem visited no fewer
than 15 Scotch whisky distilleries
in one trip to the UK to expand
his knowledge of the whisky
distillation process.

Distillation takes place in a pair
of copper pot stills, using a wash
with a lightly peated element
that is produced to Overeem's
specifications at the nearby Lark
Distillery. Maturation takes place
in ex-bourbon, port, or sherry
casks. Since 2014, Lark Distillery
Pty Ltd has owned old Hobart
Distillery and the Overeem brand.

OVEREEM PORT MATURED –
CASK STRENGTH
SINGLE MALT 60% ABV
*Summer fruits and vanilla on the
softly spicy nose, while the palate
offers more vanilla and spice, with
liquorice and oak.*

OVEREEM SHERRY
CASK MATURED
SINGLE MALT 43% ABV
*The nose yields vanilla, milk chocolate,
and spicy raisins, while the palate
delivers orange, sweet sherry, caramel,
dark chocolate, and cloves.*

OVEREEM BOURBON CASK
MATURED – CASK STRENGTH
SINGLE MALT 60% ABV
*Fresh and green on the early nose, with
nutty vanilla and caramel. Big flavours
of ripe apple, vanilla, and coconut.*

SULLIVANS COVE AMERICAN OAK CASK

SULLIVANS COVE DOUBLE CASK

NANT
AUSTRALIA

The Nant Estate, Bothwell, Tasmania
www.nant.com.au

The Nant estate in Tasmania, founded in 1821, was bought by Keith and Margaret Batt in 2004 with a view to building a distillery on the historic working farm. With the expert guidance of Bill Lark *(see Lark, p.328)*, the distillery went into production in April 2008. The plan is to produce a limited number of casks each year. The barley and water for the distillery come from the estate, while a restored mill provides the grist. There is also an elegant new visitor centre.

NANT DOUBLE MALT
BLENDED MALT 43% ABV
This is a vatting of two casks selected from other Tasmanian distilleries, and gives an idea of what Nant's own whisky will taste like in the future. Sweet and fruity, with plums and cream soda, it is medium-bodied and smooth.

SMITH'S
AUSTRALIA

Yalumba, Angaston, South Australia
www.yalumba.com

Samuel Smith arrived in Angaston in 1847, one of the first settlers. He was a brewer by trade and, within two years, had set up the Yalumba Winery, having made a small fortune in the goldfields of Victoria. In the early 1930s, the company that bears his name installed a pot still at the winery to make brandy. This was used three times to distil a mash of locally grown barley malt (in 1997, 1998, and 2000). It was matured in a mix of sherry, French wine, bourbon, and new American oak casks. After a period of silence, the still is active once more, and a 12-year-old single malt is now available.

SMITH'S ANGASTON
BLENDED MALT 40% ABV
Hay, vanilla, and toffee on the nose; sweet, light, and delicate, with vanilla and nuts to taste; clean and sweet in the finish.

SULLIVANS COVE
AUSTRALIA

Tasmania Distillery, Lamb Place, Cambridge, Tasmania
www.sullivanscovewhisky.com

Sullivans Cove was the original British settlement at Hobart, on the island of Tasmania. There was a great deal of distilling taking place on the island – legal and illegal – until a total prohibition on distillation was introduced in 1838. The ban lasted until the early 1990s, when it was overturned.

In 1994, a small distillery was established in what is now Hobart, but the malt whisky produced was named after the area's original name: Sullivan's Cove. The distillery changed hands in 2003, when the equipment was moved to Cambridge, on the outskirts of the city of Hobart.

The whisky is now winning awards (a gold and silver in blind tastings by the Whisky Society of

Australia in 2007). The spirit is brewed at Cascade Brewery, distilled in a Charentais-style pot still, and bottled from single casks by hand. Like most other Australian distilleries, Tasmania also makes gin, vodka, and liqueurs.

SULLIVANS COVE
AMERICAN OAK CASK
SINGLE MALT 47.5% ABV
The initially sweet nose develops pepper and oaky notes. The palate has malt and vanilla.

SULLIVANS COVE
DOUBLE CASK
SINGLE MALT 40% ABV
Vanilla, orange, lemon, honey, figs, and allspice on the nose. The mildly herbal palate delivers honey, ginger, dried fruits, then white pepper in the finish.

Barley is grown in the foothills of the Stirling Ranges and in other pockets of Australia and New Zealand. Some distilleries, such as Lark, have experimented with new strains of barley that tolerate local conditions better than the strains grown in Europe.

LAMMERLAW
NEW ZEALAND

Bottled by Cadenhead
www.wmcadenhead.com

In 1974, the Wilson Brewery and
Malt Extract Company produced
New Zealand's first legal whisky
for 100 years. Unfortunately, its
pot stills were made from stainless
steel, and the spirit was horrible.
In 1981, the distillery was acquired
by Seagram, who vastly improved
quality and produced a 10-year-old
single malt – Lammerlaw – named
after the nearby mountain range.
The distillery was dismantled
in 2002, and the casks passed to
Milford's owners *(see Milford)*.
Cadenhead has bottled Lammerlaw
in its World Whiskies series.

CADENHEAD'S LAMMERLAW
10-YEAR-OLD

SINGLE MALT 47.3% ABV
*Light-bodied and somewhat "green"
and cereal-like, but pleasant to taste.*

MACKENZIE
NEW ZEALAND

Southern Distilleries,
Stafford Street, Timaru
www.hokonuiwhiskey.com

The eponymous Mackenzie was
a shepherd and sheep-rustler
during the 1850s, and gave his
name to that part of the Southern
Alps between Canterbury and
Otago where he operated. He
and his dog are commemorated
by monuments in the district.
Scotch was his drink, and this
re-creation of his favourite tipple
is a blend of Scotch and New
Zealand malts from Southern
Distilleries, which also makes
Old Hokonui *(see entry)*. The
process and reduction water
used in Mackenzie's creation
flows from the Mackenzie Basin.

THE MACKENZIE

BLENDED MALT 40% ABV
*A light and refreshing dram, with
plain caramel and oak notes.*

MILFORD
NEW ZEALAND

The New Zealand Malt Whisky
Company & Preston Associates,
14–16 Harbour St, Oamaru
www.thenzwhisky.com

Milford whisky was originally
made at Willowbank Distillery
in Dunedin, South Island, which
was owned by the Wilson Brewery
(see Lammerlaw). The New
Zealand Malt Whisky Company
now owns the Milford label (and
also the less prestigious Prestons
label). It has also opened a retail
warehouse named Cellar Door
at Oamaru, where a wide range
of expressions of New Zealand
whisky are available.

MILFORD 10-YEAR-OLD

SINGLE MALT 43% ABV
*Often compared to a Scottish Lowland
malt, Milford's 10-year-old has a light,
dry, and fragrant nose; the taste is
sweet, then dry, with a slightly
woody, short finish.*

OLD HOKONUI
NEW ZEALAND

Southern Distilleries,
Stafford Street, Timaru
www.hokonuiwhiskey.com

Southern Distilleries has two
small pot stills producing Old
Hokonui Moonshine, single malt,
and blended malts, using – as
the distillers put it – "Murdoch
McRae's original 1892 recipe".

McRae was the leading illicit
distiller in the district, having
learned the craft from his mother,
with whom he had arrived from
Kintail, Scotland, in 1872. Many
of his descendants also became
distillers and their story is told
with memorabilia in the Hokonui
Museum at Gore.

OLD HOKONUI

BLEND 40% ABV
*Pale in colour, and light-bodied, with
a smooth mouthfeel, and an oaky
taste with distinct smoky notes.*

THREE SHIPS
SOUTH AFRICA

James Sedgwick Distillery, Wellington
East, Drakenstein 7655, South Africa
www.threeshipswhisky.co.za

The James Sedgwick Distillery
was founded around 1886 and
is named after the Yorkshire-
born Western Cape-based
businessman Captain James
Sedgwick. Despite the age of
the distillery, whisky has only
been produced there since 1990.
Today, the distillery is owned
by the Distell Group Ltd.

The distillery's Three Ships
brand was originally a blend
of imported Scotch and native
South African whisky and this
tradition has continued in the
Select and Premium Select
expressions, the latter aged
for five years. These blends
have now been joined by two
newer expressions. First was
the limited edition 10-year-old
Single Malt – South Africa's first

single malt whisky – of which
there have been three subsequent
releases since its initial launch in
2003. Second was the Special
Release, the first blend made
entirely of South African whisky
that is matured for three years
before being finished in bourbon
casks for six months.

THREE SHIPS 10-YEAR-OLD

SINGLE MALT 43% ABV
The nose is floral, with just a hint of
brine, plus barley and fresh pears.
The palate is rounded and malty, with
ripe peaches, honey, and soft spices.

Your Tasting Notes...

You can use these pages to make your own notes about the appearance, aroma, taste, and finish of different whiskies that you have the opportunity to sample.

WHISKY			
TYPE			
BOTTLER			
AGE			
APPEARANCE			
AROMA			
TASTE			
WITH WATER			
FINISH			
VERDICT	AGAIN & AGAIN SAME AGAIN NEVER AGAIN	AGAIN & AGAIN SAME AGAIN NEVER AGAIN	AGAIN & AGAIN SAME AGAIN NEVER AGAIN

WHISKY			
TYPE			
BOTTLER			
AGE			
APPEARANCE			
AROMA			
TASTE			
WITH WATER			
FINISH			
VERDICT	AGAIN & AGAIN SAME AGAIN NEVER AGAIN	AGAIN & AGAIN SAME AGAIN NEVER AGAIN	AGAIN & AGAIN SAME AGAIN NEVER AGAIN

Your Tasting Notes...

You can use these pages to make your own notes about the appearance, aroma, taste, and finish of different whiskies that you have the opportunity to sample.

WHISKY			
TYPE			
BOTTLER			
AGE			
APPEARANCE			
AROMA			
TASTE			
WITH WATER			
FINISH			
VERDICT	AGAIN & AGAIN SAME AGAIN NEVER AGAIN	AGAIN & AGAIN SAME AGAIN NEVER AGAIN	AGAIN & AGAIN SAME AGAIN NEVER AGAIN

WHISKY			
TYPE			
BOTTLER			
AGE			
APPEARANCE			
AROMA			
TASTE			
WITH WATER			
FINISH			
VERDICT	AGAIN & AGAIN SAME AGAIN NEVER AGAIN	AGAIN & AGAIN SAME AGAIN NEVER AGAIN	AGAIN & AGAIN SAME AGAIN NEVER AGAIN

Your Tasting Notes...

You can use these pages to make your own notes about the appearance, aroma, taste, and finish of different whiskies that you have the opportunity to sample.

WHISKY			
TYPE			
BOTTLER			
AGE			
APPEARANCE			
AROMA			
TASTE			
WITH WATER			
FINISH			
VERDICT	AGAIN & AGAIN SAME AGAIN NEVER AGAIN	AGAIN & AGAIN SAME AGAIN NEVER AGAIN	AGAIN & AGAIN SAME AGAIN NEVER AGAIN

WHISKY			
TYPE			
BOTTLER			
AGE			
APPEARANCE			
AROMA			
TASTE			
WITH WATER			
FINISH			
VERDICT	AGAIN & AGAIN SAME AGAIN NEVER AGAIN	AGAIN & AGAIN SAME AGAIN NEVER AGAIN	AGAIN & AGAIN SAME AGAIN NEVER AGAIN

GLOSSARY

ABV (alcohol by volume) This is the proportion of alcohol in a drink, expressed as a percentage. Whisky is most commonly at 40% or 43% ABV.

Analyser still *see* continuous distillation

Angels' share The expression given for the amount of liquid that evaporates from the cask during the period of *maturation*.

Batch distillation Distillation carried out in batches, as opposed to *continuous distillation*. Each batch may be marginally different, which gives the method an artisanal quality.

Barrel *see* cask

Blended malt A mix of single malt whiskies from more than one distillery.

Blended whisky A mix of malt whiskies and grain whiskies.

Cask The oak container in which whisky is matured. There are many different styles and sizes of cask as well as a principle distinction between the type of wood used: American or European oak. In the US, whisky is most commonly matured in barrels (180–200 litres/40–45 gallons). American barrels are re-used elsewhere; in Scotland they are often broken down and re-assembled as hogsheads (250 litres/55 gallons). Butts and puncheons (both 500 litres/110 gallons) are the largest casks used for maturing whisky, having first been seasoned with, or used to age, sherry.

Cask finishing The practice of using a different cask (such as port, Madeira, French wine, or rum casks) for the final period of the whisky's maturation.

Cask strength Whisky that is bottled straight from the cask rather than first being diluted. It is typically around 57–63% ABV.

Column still Also known as a Coffey, Patent, or continuous still, this is the type of still used for *continuous distillation*.

Condenser The vaporized spirit driven off the stills is turned into liquid in a condenser. The traditional type of condenser is a "worm tub" – a tapering coil of copper pipe set in a vat of cold water outside the still house. Worm tubs have largely been superseded by shell-and-tube condensers, usually situated inside the still house.

Continuous distillation The creation of spirit as an ongoing process, as opposed to *batch distillation*. Continuous distillation uses a column still (also known as a Patent or Coffey still) rather than a *pot still*. It has two connected columns: the Rectifier and the Analyser. The cool wash travels down the Rectifier in a sealed coil, where it becomes heated. It then passes to the head of the Analyser, down which it trickles over a series of perforated copper plates. Steam enters the foot of the Analyser and bubbles through the wash, driving off alcoholic vapour, which rises up the Analyser then passes to the foot of the Rectifier. Here it again ascends, to be condensed by the cool wash (which is thus heated) as it rises in a zig-zag manner through another series of perforated copper plates. As the vapour rises, it becomes purer and of higher strength, until it is drawn off at the "striking plate" at 94% ABV.

Cut points In the process of pot still distillation, the operator divides the run into three "cuts" to separate the useable spirit from rejected spirit, which must be re-distilled. The first cut contains the foreshots; the middle cut is the section of useable spirit; the end cut contains the feints or aftershots.

Draff The Scottish name for the remains of the grain after mashing. It is a nutritious cattle fodder, used either wet or dried and pelletized.

Drum maltings Large cylinders in which grain is germinated during the industrial *malting* of barley. The drums are ventilated with temperature-controlled air and rotate so the grains do not stick together.

Dumping Emptying the contents of a cask into a vat, either prior to bottling or before putting into a different kind of cask.

Eau de vie Literally, "water of life", and usually used in reference to grape-based spirits. Compare with *uisge beatha*.

Expression The term given to a particular whisky in relation to the overall output of a distillery or spirits company. It may refer to the age, as in 12-year-old expression, or to a particular characteristic, such as a cask strength expression.

Feints The final fraction of the spirit produced during a distillation run in batch distilling. Feints (also called tails or aftershots) are aromatically unpleasant, and are sent to a feints and foreshots receiver to be mixed with *low wines* and re-distilled with the next run.

Fermenter Another name for *mash tun*.

First fill The first time a cask has been used to hold whisky other than bourbon, it is referred to as first-fill cask. A first-fill sherry cask will have held only sherry prior to its use for maturing whisky; a first-fill bourbon cask will have been used once only to hold bourbon prior to its use in maturing whisky.

Foreshots The first fraction of the distillation run in pot-still distillation. Foreshots (also known as heads) are not pure enough to be used and are returned to a feints and foreshots receiver to be re-distilled in the next run.

Grist Ground, malted grain. Water is added to grist to form the *mash*.

Heads *see* foreshots

High wines (US) A mix of spirit that has had its first distillation and the foreshots and feints from the second distillation. With a strength of around 28% ABV, high wines undergo a second distillation to create *new make*.

Independent bottler/bottling A company that releases bottles of whisky independently of the official distillery bottlings. They buy small quantities of casks and bottle the whisky as and when they choose.

Kilning In the process of *malting*, kilning involves gently heating the "green malt" to halt its germination and thereby retain its starch content for turning into sugars (in the mashing stage). Ultimately these sugars will be turned into alcohol. Peat may be added to the kiln to produce a smoky-flavoured malt.

Lomond still This pot still was designed so that a distillery could vary the character of spirit being produced. The level of *reflux* could be altered by way of an additional condenser on the still, so that a heavy or light style of spirit could be made, as required.

Low wines The spirit produced by the first distillation. It has a strength of about 21% ABV. Compare with *high wines*.

Lyne arm (or "lye pipe") The pipe running from the top of the still to the condenser. Its angle, height, and thickness all have a bearing on the characteristics of the spirit.

Malting The process of deliberately starting and stopping germination in grain to maximize its starch content. As the grain begins to germinate (through the influence of heat and moisture), it becomes "green malt" (grain that has just begun to sprout). The green malt undergoes kilning to produce malt.

Marrying The mixing of whiskies prior to bottling. It most often applies to blends, where whiskies of different types and from several distilleries are combined for a period in vats or casks to blend more fully before the whisky is bottled.

Mash The mix of grist and water.

Mashbill The mix of grains used in the making of a particular whisky. In the US, there are specific requirements about the percentage of certain grains for making bourbon, Tennessee whiskey, and rye, for example.

Mash tun The vessel in which the grist is mixed with hot water to convert starch in the grain into sugars, ready for fermentation. The fermentable liquid that results is known as wort; the solid residue (husks and spent grain) is *draff*.

Maturation For *new make* to become whisky, it must go through a period of maturation in oak casks. The length of time varies: in Scotland and Ireland, the minimum period is three years; in the US, the minimum maturation is two years.

Middle cut *see* cut points

New make The clear, useable spirit that comes from the spirit still. It has a strength of about 70% ABV and is diluted to around 63–64% before being put into

casks for maturation. In the US, new make is called white dog.

Peating Adding peat to the kiln ovens when *malting* barley to impart a smoky, phenolic aroma and taste to the whisky. Barley that has undergone this process is known as peated malt.

Phenols A group of aromatic chemical compounds. In whisky-making, the term is used to refer to the chemicals that impart smoky and medicinal flavours to malt and the whisky made from it, which may be described as phenolic. Phenols are measured in parts per million (ppm). Highly phenolic whiskies, such as Laphroaig and Ardbeg, will use malt peated to a level of between 35 and 50ppm.

Poteen *see* uisce poitín

Pot still The large onion-shaped vessels, nearly always made of copper, used for batch distillation. Pot stills vary in size and shape, and these variations affect the style of spirit produced.

ppm *see* phenols

Proof The old term for the alcoholic proportion of a spirit, now superseded by ABV. The American proof figure, which is different to Imperial proof, is twice that of the ABV percentage.

Rectifier *see* continuous distillation

Reflux The process by which heavier alcoholic vapours fall back into the still rather than passing along the lyne arm to the condenser. By falling back, these vapours are re-distilled, becoming purer and lighter. The size, height, and shape of the still, and how it is operated, contribute to the degree of reflux, and therefore to the lightness and character of the spirit. Long-necked stills have

a greater degree of reflux and produce a more delicate style of spirit than squatter stills, which tend to make heavier, "oilier" whiskies.

Run In batch distillation – as carried out using pot stills – the extent of distillation is referred to as a run. The spirit produced during the run is variable in quality, and is divided by *cut points*.

Saladin box Used in the industrial *malting* of barley, these are large rectangular troughs in which the grains are germinated. Air is blown through the barley in the trough and the grain turned by mechanical screws to prevent the grains from sticking together.

Silent distillery A distillery in which whisky production has stopped – possibly only temporarily.

Single cask A bottling that comes from just one cask (often bottled at *cask strength*).

Single malt A malt whisky that is the product of just one distillery.

Spirit safe A glass-fronted cabinet through which the distilled spirit passes and which is used to monitor the purity of the spirit. The stillman operates the spirit safe during a run to assess its quality and make *cut points*.

Spirit still In *batch distillation*, the spirit still is used for the second distillation, in which the spirit from the wash still is distilled again to produce *new make*.

Still The vessel in which distillation takes place. There are two basic types: a *pot still* for *batch distillation* and a *column still* for *continuous distillation*.

Triple distillation Most batch distillation involves two distillations: in a *wash still* and

in a *spirits still*. Triple distillation – the traditional method in Ireland – involves a third distillation, which is said to produce a smoother and purer spirit.

Uisge beatha / uisce beatha The Scottish Gaelic and Irish Gaelic terms, respectively, from which the word whisky derives. The term means "water of life", and so is synonymous with *eau de vie* and *aqua vita*.

Uisce poitín Historically, the Irish Gaelic term for non-licensed whiskey, usually known as poteen.

Vatting The mixing of whisky from several casks. This is usually done to achieve a consistency of flavour over time. (*see also* Marrying)

Viscimetric whorls The eddies and vortices observed when water is added to whisky. The capacity of an individual whisky to sustain viscimation is termed its viscimetric potential.

Wash The resultant liquid when yeast is added to the *wort*, fermenting into a kind of ale. Wash has an alcoholic strength of about 7% ABV. It passes into a *wash still* for the first distillation.

Wash still In *batch distillation*, the wash still is used for the first distillation, in which the wash is distilled.

Washbacks The fermenting vessels in which yeast is added to the *wort* to make *wash*. Called "fermenters" in the US.

Wood finish *see* cask finish

Worm / worm tubs *see* condensers

Wort The sweet liquid produced as a result of mixing hot water with grist in a *mash tun*.

REFERENCE

WHISKY OWNERSHIP

It can, at times, be difficult to work out exactly which company owns a specific whisky brand or distillery. As firms have merged or been bought out by larger business groups, the trail is sometimes rather elusive and confusing. Here is a brief summary of the major conglomerations, which elucidates how they have emerged and transformed over time into the key big players in the world of whisky today: Diageo, Chivas Brothers/Pernod Ricard, United Spirits (the UB group), and Beam Global (itself part of Fortune Brands).

THE RISE OF DIAGEO

The Distillers Company Limited (**DCL**) was founded in 1877 as an amalgamation of six leading grain whisky distilleries. In 1894, it opened its first malt whisky distillery (Knockdhu), and, in the early 20th century, began to acquire blending companies and their brands. Following "The Big Amalgamation" in 1925, when the big blending firms Walkers, Dewars, and Buchanans joined DCL, it became the largest distiller in the world at the time.

In 1987, DCL was acquired by Guinness, and the whisky side of the business was re-named United Distillers. Then, in 1998, Guinness merged with Grand Metropolitan, who had a drinks subsidiary called Independent Distillers & Vintners. The combined operating name for this subsidiary and United Distillers became United Distillers & Vintners (**UDV**).

In the same year (1998) that Guinness merged with Grand Metropolitan, **Diageo** was formed as the holding company. Two years later, the corporate structure was simplified and UDV was replaced as the trading entity by Diageo.

Diageo owns a plethora of whisky brands, including verable old blends such as Buchanan's, Haig, and Johnnie Walker. It also owns many Scotch whisky distilleries – its flagships are the 12 that produce the Classic Malts range: Caol Ila, Cardhu, Clynelish, Cragganmore, Dalwhinnie, Glen Elgin, Glenkinchie, Knockando, Lagavulin, Oban, Talisker, and Royal Lochnagar.

CHIVAS & PERNOD RICARD

Founded in Aberdeen in 1801, **Chivas Brothers** was a wine & spirits merchant. It was acquired by the Canadian distiller Seagram in 1949. Seagram went on to acquire or build nine distilleries and a number of leading blends.

In 2001, Seagram decided to divest itself of its alcoholic beverages divisions, which was divided between Diageo and Pernod Ricard. Chivas remains the whisky arm of Pernod Ricard.

The French distiller **Pernod Ricard** entered the Scotch whisky industry with the purchase of Aberlour Distillery in 1974, but moved into the "First Division" when it acquired part of the Seagram's drinks empire in 2001. This included The Glenlivet Distillery, together with the Chivas Regal brand, and six of Allied-Domecq's distilleries in 2005, together with Ballantine's. Pernod Ricard owns brands such as Ballantine's, Chivas Regal, Jameson, Paddy, and Powers, and prestigious distilleries such as Glenlivet, Aberlour, Scapa, and Longmorn. In the States, it owns the Wild Turkey brand and, in Canada, Wiser's.

IRISH DISTILLERS

The story of Irish Distillers goes back to 1867, when five small distillers in County Cork amalgamated to form The Cork Distillers Company (**CDC**), which consolidated its production at Midleton Distillery.

That was the status quo until almost 100 years later, when, in 1966, The Irish Distillers Group (**IDG**) was formed by the merger of Powers, Jameson's, and CDC. Powers and Jameson's historic distilleries in Dublin were closed by the early 1970s, and a large new distillery was built at Midleton in 1975 to accommodate production of all the whiskeys in the IDG stable. IDG was taken over by Pernod Ricard in 1988.

UNITED SPIRITS

Part of the UB Group, **United Spirits** became the third-biggest spirits producer (after Diageo and Pernod Ricard) when it acquired **Whyte & Mackay** in 2007. With this purchase came several Scottish distilleries, including Dalmore and Jura. However, in 2014, Emperador Inc. bought the Whyte & Mackay business from United Spirits.

BEAM SUNTORY INC.

This subsidiary of Suntory Holdings Ltd owns the Jim Beam brand, as well as Maker's Mark and Canadian Club. Its Scotch whisky ownership includes Laphroaig and the Teacher's blend.

BACARDI

The famous rum maker **Bacardi** joined the Scotch whisky industry in 1992 with the acquisition of William Lawson Ltd, owner of Macduff Distillery (*see Glen Deveron*). In 1998, Bacardi acquired John Dewar & Sons, together with four distilleries from Diageo, making it a major player in Scotch whisky.

ALLIED-DOMECQ

Though now broken up, Allied-Domecq in its 1990s heyday was one of the world's biggest whisky companies. It began as **Allied Breweries**, which acquired Teacher's in 1976, and changed the name of its spirits division to **Allied Distillers** when it bought Hiram Walker, owner of Ballantine's brands and distilleries, in 1987. Three years later, the company acquired Whitbread's whisky interests and moved into the big league.

In 1993, with the acquisition of the Spanish distiller and sherry-maker Pedro Domecq, the name was changed to **Allied-Domecq**, which became the third-largest drinks company in the world. Allied-Domecq was broken up in 2005, with Teacher's going to Beam Global and Ballantine's to French drinks giant Pernod Ricard.

WHISKY RANGES

Throughout this book, and when studying or buying whisky, three key whisky ranges are regularly mentioned: Flora & Fauna, Classic Malts, and Rare Malts. Here is a little background information about each of them.

Classic Malts A range of six malts was introduced by United Distillers in 1987/88. The malts came from UD's Cragganmore, Dalwhinnie, Glenkinchie, Lagavulin, Oban, and Talisker distilleries. Under the ownership of Diageo, the range has been expanded to 12 of its flagship malts: the six original members of the range, plus Caol Ila, Cardhu, Clynelish, Glen Elgin, Knockando, and Royal Lochnagar.

Flora & Fauna In the early 1990s, UDV introduced the Flora & Fauna range of single malt bottlings from all of its distilleries. Diageo continued to produce the range but recently decided that it will be discontinued.

Rare Malts A selection of small batch bottlings from UDV at natural strength and colour, without chill-filtration. They were released between 1995 and 2006, and 36 distilleries were represented in the range.

WHISKY SHOPS

AUSTRALIA

**Scotch Malt Whisky
Society in Australia**
mail order to members only
www.smws.com.au

Single Malt Whisky Club
PTY LTD
Unit M3, 63 Mandoon Road
Girraween, 2145
+ 61 (4)58 109 110
www.singlemalt.com.au

AUSTRIA

Potstill
Laudongasse 18, 1080 Wien
+43 (0)664 118 85 41
www.potstill.org

BELGIUM

Whiskycorner
Kraaistraat 18, 3530 Houthalen
+32 (0)89 386233
www.whiskycorner.be

Jurgen's Whiskyhuis
Gaverland 70, 9620 Zottegem
+32 (0)9 336 51 06
www.whiskyhuis.be

FRANCE

La Maison du Whisky
20 rue d'Anjou, 75008 Paris
+33 (0)1 42 65 03 16
www.whisky.fr

also at 47 rue Jean Chatel
97400 Saint-Denis
+33 (0)2 62 21 31 19

GERMANY

Cadenhead's Whisky Market
Luxemburger Strasse 257
50939 Köln
+49 (0)221 283 1834
www.cadenhead.de

Celtic Whisk(e)y & Versand
Otto Steudel, Bulmannstrasse 26
90459 Nürnberg
+49 (0)911 45097430
celtic.whiskymania.de

Weinquelle Lühmann
Lubeckerstrasse 145
22087 Hamburg
+49 (0)40 256 391
www.weinquelle.com

Whisky & Cigars
Sophienstrasse 8-9
10178 Berlin-Mitte
+49 (0)30 282 03 76
www.whiskyandcigars.de

Whisky Corner
Reichertsfeld 2
92278 Illschwang
+49 (0)96 6695 1213
www.whisky-corner.de

IRELAND

Celtic Whisky Shop
27—28 Dawson Street
Dublin 2
+353 (0)1 675 9744

Mitchell & Son
The CHQ building
IFSC Docklands
Dublin 1
+353 (01)612 5540
www.mitchellandson.com

also at Glasthule
54 Glasthule Road
Sandycove
County Dublin
+353 (01)230 2301

JAPAN

Shinanoya
Kabukicho 1-12-9, Shinjuku
Kabukicho, Tokyo
+81 (0)3 3204 2365
(more branches throughout Tokyo)

Kawachiya
5-40-15 Nakakasai
Edogawa-ku
Tokyo, 134-0083
+81 (0)3 3680 4321
(more branches throughout Tokyo)

Tanakaya
3-4-14 Mejiro, Toshima-ku, Tokyo
+81 (0)3 3953 8888

NEW ZEALAND

The Whisky Shop
www.whiskyshop.co.nz

RUSSIA

Whisky World Shop
9 Tverskoy Boulevard
123104 Moscow
+7 495 787 9150
www.whiskyworld.ru

UNITED KINGDOM

Berry Brothers & Rudd
3 St James's Street
London SW1A 1EG
+44 (0)20 7022 8973
www.bbr.com

**Cadenheads Whisky Shop
and Tasting Room**
26 Chiltern Street
London W1U 7QF
+44 (0)20 7935 6999
www.whiskytastingroom.com

Gordon & MacPhail
58—60 South Street, Elgin
Moray IV30 1JY
+44 (0)1343 545110
www.gordonandmacphail.com

Loch Fyne Whiskies
Inverary, Argyll PA32 8UD
+44 (0)1499 302 219
www.lfw.co.uk

Milroy's of Soho
3 Greek Street
London W1D 4NX
+44 (0)20 7437 2385
shop.milroys.co.uk

Royal Mile Whiskies
379 High Street, Royal Mile
Edinburgh EH1 1PW
+44 (0)131 225 3383
www.royalmilewhiskies.com

also at 3 Bloomsbury Street
London WC1B 3QE

Scotch Malt Whisky Society
mail order to members only
www.smws.com

The Vintage House
42 Old Compton Street
London W1D 4LR
+44 (0)20 7437 2592
www.sohowhisky.com

Whisky Castle
6 Main Street, Tomintoul,
Ballindalloch, Moray, AB37 9EX

+44 (0)1807 580 213
www.whiskycastle.com

The Whisky Exchange
2 Bedford Street, Covent Garden
London WC2E 9HH
+44 (0)20 7100 0088
www.thewhiskyexchange.com

The Whisky Shop
12 branches in England and Scotland
+44 (0)14 1427 2977
www.whiskyshop.com

The Whisky Shop Dufftown
1 Fife Street, Dufftown, Keith,
Moray AB55 4AL
+44 (0)1340 821097
www.whiskyshopdufftown.co.uk

USA

D&M
2200 Fillmore Street
San Francisco, CA 94115
+001 (415) 346 1325
(800) 637 0292
www.dandm.com

Park Avenue Liquor Shop
270 Madison Avenue
New York, NY 10017
+001 (212)685 2442
www.parkaveliquor.com

Binny's Beverage Depot
1132 South Jefferson Street
Chicago, IL 60607
+001 (312)768 4440
www.binys.com

The Whisky Shop
360 Sutter Street
San Francisco, CA, 94108
+001 (415)989 1030
www.whiskyshopusa.com

WHISKY WEBSITES

www.maltmadness.com
www.maltmaniacs.net
www.nonjatta.com
www.whiskyadvocate.com
www.whiskycast.com
www.whiskyforum.se
www.whiskymag.com
www.whisky-pages.com
www.youtube.com/user/SingleMaltTv

INDEX

PICTURE CREDITS

Old Charter, Rock Hill Farms, Sazerac Rye, Thomas H. Handy, W.L. Weller; Bunnahabhain Distillery; Burn Stewart Distillers: Black Bottle, Deanston, Scottish Leader; The Old Bushmills Distillery Co: Bushmills, The Irishman, Knappogue Castle; Campari Drinks Group: Glen Grant, Old Smuggler, Wild Turkey 81 Proof; Cardhu Distillery; Castle Brands Inc.: Jefferson's; Chichibu Distillery: The Peated 2015; Chivas Brothers: 100 Pipers, Ballantine's, Chivas Regal, Clan Campbell, Long John, Passport, Queen Anne, Royal Salute, Something Special, Stewarts Cream of the Barley, Strathisla, Tormore; Clear Creek Distillery: McCarthy's; Clontarf Distillery; Clynelish Distillery; Compass Box Delicious Whisky; Constellation Spirits Inc.: Very Old Barton®, Kentucky Gentleman®, Kentucky Tavern®, Ridgemont®, Ten High®, Tom Moore®, Black Velvet®; Cooley Distillery: Connemara, Cooley, Inishowen, Kilbeggan, Locke's, Tyrconnell, Wild Geese; Copper Fox Distillery: Wasmund's; Corby Distilleries: Wiser's; Craigellachie Distillery; Cragganmore Distillery; Des Menhirs: Eddu; Deerstalker Whisky: Allt-a-Bhainne; Diageo plc: Bell's, Black & White, Buchanan's, Bulleit Bourbon, Bushmills, Cameron Brig, Caol Ila, Cardhu, Crown Royal, Dalwhinnie, Dimple, Glen Elgin, Glen Ord, Haig Club, J&B, Johnnie Walker, Lagavulin, Linkwood, Mortlach, Oban, Old Parr, Royal Lochnagar, Teaninich, VAT 69, White Horse, Windsor; Diageo Canada: Seagram's; Domaine Charbay: Charbay; Domaine Mavela: P&M; Echlinville Distillery: Dunville's; Edrington: Glenturret Peated, The English Whisky Co.; The Famous Grouse; The Fleischmann Distillery; Four Roses Distillery; The Gaelic Whisky Co.: Mac Na Mara, Poit Dhubh; Garrison Brothers Distillery: Texas Straight Bourbon; George A. Dickel & Co.: George Dickel; Georgetown Trading Co.: 1776; Girvan Distillery; Glan ar Mor; Glencadam Distillery; Glendalough Distillery; Glendronach Distillery; Glendullan Distillery; Glenfarclas Distillery; Glenfiddich Distillery; Glenglassaugh Distillery; Glengoyne Distillery; Glengyle Distillery: Kilkerran; Glenkinchie Distillery; Glenlivet Distillery; The Glenmorangie Company: Glenmorangie, James Martin's; Glen Moray Distillery; Glenora Distillery: Glen Breton; Glenrothes Distillery; Glenturret Distillery; Gotland Whisky AB; Graanstokerij Filliers: Goldlys; Great Southern

Distilling Company: Limeburners; Guillon Distillery; Healeys Cornish Cyder Farm: Hicks & Healey; Heaven Hill Distilleries, Inc.: Bernheim, Elijah Craig, Evan Williams, Heaven Hill, Georgia Moon, Mellow Corn, Old Fitzgerald, Parker's, Pikesville, Rittenhouse Rye; Highland Park Distillery; Highwood Distillers; Holle; Hotel Gasthof Lamm: Ammertal; Ian MacLeod: Glengoyne 18-year-old, Langs, Tamdhu; International Beverage Holdings: anCnoc 2000, anCnoc 18-year-old, Balblair, Hankey Bannister Original Blend; Inver House Distillers: Catto's, Hankey Bannister, Inver House, MacArthur's, Pinwinnie Royale, Speyburn; Isle of Arran: Robert Burns; Jagatjit Industries: Aristocrat; John Distilleries Pvt. Ltd: Paul John; Jura Distillery; Käsers Schloss: Whisky Castle; Kavalan Distillery; Kentucky Bourbon Distillers, Ltd.: Johnny Drum, Noah's Mill; Kilchoman Distillery; Kirin Holdings Company: Kirin Gotemba, Kirin Karuizawa; Kittling Ridge Distillery: Forty Creek; Knockdhu Distillery: anCnoc; Knockeen Hills; La Maison du Whisky: Nikka; La Marttiniquaise: Label 5; Lark Distillery: Lark Overeem Port Cask Matured; Last Drop Distillers; Leopold Bros; Loch Lomond Distillery Group: Glen Scotia; Luxco Spirited Brands: Rebel Yell; Macallan; Macduff International: Grand Macnish, Islay Mist, Lauder's; Mackmyra; McMenamin's Group: Edgefield; Midleton Distillery: Clontarf, Crested Ten, Dungourney, Green Spot, The Irishman, Jameson, Midleton, Paddy, Powers, Redbreast, Tullamore D.E.W.; Morrison Bowmore Distillers: Auchentoshan, Bowmore, Glen Garioch, McClelland's, Yamazaki; Murree Distillery; The Nant Estate; New York Distilling Company: Ragtime Rye ;The New Zealand Malt Whisky Company: Milford; The Nikka Whisky Distilling Co.; Chichibu, Number One Drinks Company: Hanyu, Ichiro's Malt; Old Pulteney Distillery; The Owl Distillery: The Belgian Owl; Pernod Ricard: Glen Keith, Glenlivet Founder's Reserve, Longmorn Cask Strength, Miltonduff, Scapa, Strathclyde; Pernod Ricard USA: American Spirit, Russell's Reserve, Wild Turkey; Piedmont Distillers: Catdaddy; Preiss Imports; Radico Khaitan: 8PM, Whytehall; Reiner Mösslein:Fränkischer; Reisetbauer; Richard Joynson: Loch Fyne; Rock Town Distillery: Rock Town Arkansas Bourbon; Rogue Spirits; Rosebank Distillery;

Saint James Spirits: Peregrine Rock; Scapa Distillery, Smögen Whisky AB; Southern Distilleries: MacKenzie, Old Hokonui; Spencerfield Spirits: Pig's Nose; Speyside Distillery: Spey; Springbank Distillers: Hazelburn, Longrow, Springbank; St George Spirits; Stock Spirits: Hammerhead; Stranahan's Colorado Whiskey; Suntory Group: Suntory Hakushu, Suntory Hibiki; Tasmania Distillery: Sullivan's Cove; Teeling Distillery; Teerenpeli; Templeton Rye; Talisker Distillery; Tobermory Distillery: Ledaig, Tobermory; Tomatin Distillery: The Antiquary, The Talisman, Tomatin; Tomintoul Distillery; Triple Eight Distillery: The Notch; Tullibardine Distillery; Tuthilltown Distillery: Hudson; United Spirits: Signature; Us Heit Distillery: Frysk Hynder; Waldviertler Whiskydestillerie; Walsh Whiskey: Writers Tears; Wambrechies Distillery; Welsh Whisky Company: Penderyn; Wemyss Malts: Invergordon, Longmorn Bitter Sweet Barley 1997; West Cork Distillers: The Pogues; Whyte & Mackay: The Claymore, Cluny, The Dalmore, Fettercairn, John Barr, Tamnavulin, Whyte & Mackay; William Grant & Sons: Balvenie Portwood 21-year-old, Balvenie Caribbean Cask 14-year-old, Balvenie Single Barrel 12-year-old, Blavenie 30-year-old, Clan MacGregor, Glenfiddich, Grant's, Monkey Shoulder; Wolfram Ortner: Nock-Land; Woodford Reserve Distillery: Woodford Reserve Double Oaked, Woodford Reserve Straight Rye, Woodford Reserve Master's Collection 1838 White Corn; Yalumba: Smith's; Zuidam Distillery: Millstone; Zürcher Brewery: Single Lakeland

ACKNOWLEDGMENTS

FIRST EDITION

Thameside Media would like to thank the following people and companies for their help and kind permission to photograph at their premises:

Jane Grimley at Aberfeldy Distillery, Ann Miller at Aberlour Distillery, Michael Heads at Ardbeg Distillery, Rob, Robbie, and Brian at Balvenie and Glenfiddich Distilleries, Adam Holden at Berry Brothers & Rudd, Dave and Heather at Bowmore Distillery, Mark and Duncan at Bruichladdich Distillery, John MacLellan at Bunnhabhain Distillery, Ewan Mackintosh at Caol Ila Distillery, the staff and owners of The Canny Man's in Edinburgh, Stephanie Macleod at Dewar's, Ian and Claire at Gordon & MacPhail, Cathy and Ruth at Kilchoman Distillery, Ruth and Ian (Pinky) at Lagavulin Distillery, Vicky Stevens, Graham Holyoake, and David McLean at Laphroaig Distillery, Margaret and Morag at Macallan Distillery, staff at The Mash Tun in Aberlour, Philip Shorten at Milroy's of Soho, Graham Logie at Port Ellen Maltings, Gary at Speyside Cooperage, The Whisky Shop Dufftown.

Thameside Media would also like to thank the following individuals for their kind assistance with the project: Sukhinder Singh and staff at The Whisky Exchange, London *(www.thewhiskyexchange.com)*, Marisa Renzullo, Casper Morris, Becky Offringa of The Whisky Couple, Aparna Sharma at DK India office.

First edition produced for Dorling Kindersley by **THAMESIDE MEDIA** www.thamesidemedia.com

DIRECTORS Michael Ellis, Rosalyn Ellis

EDITORS Fay Franklin, Michael Fullalove, Caroline Blake, Zoe Ross

DESIGNERS Nora Zimerman, Kate Leonard, Ian Midson

RETOUCHER Steve Crozier

For **DK**

PROJECT EDITOR Danielle Di Michiel

PROJECT DESIGNER Will Hicks

EDITORIAL ASSISTANCE Andrew Roff

SENIOR JACKET CREATIVE Nicola Powling

MANAGING EDITOR Dawn Henderson

MANAGING ART EDITOR Christine Keilty

PRODUCTION EDITOR Ben Marcus

CREATIVE TECHNICAL SUPPORT Sonia Charbonnier

And a big thank you to Stuart Bale and Luca Saladini at The Albannach bar in London for guidance with, and mixing of, the cocktails featured on pp.110–111.

SECOND EDITION

DK would like to thank Jane Simmonds for proofreading, Marie Lorimer for compiling the index, and Karen Constanti, Bhavika Mathur, Juhi Sheth, Suzena Sengupta, and Vikas Sachdeva for design assistance.

WRITERS

FIRST EDITION

DAVE BROOM

Dave is editor of *Whisky Magazine Japan*, contributing editor to *Whisky Magazine*, a regular columnist on many periodicals, has written a dozen books, and won three Glenfiddich Awards for his writing. He is a respected taster, and in demand as a teacher and lecturer. For the first edition, Dave wrote the section on Japanese whisky.

TOM BRUCE-GARDYNE

Tom is an expert on Scotch malt and has written several books on the subject, including *The Scotch Whisky Book* and *Scotch Whisky Treasures*. He is a regular contributor to *Unfiltered* and *scotchwhisky.com* and wrote a weekly drinks column for *The Herald*. Tom wrote the entries on Scotland's malt whiskies for the first edition.

IAN BUXTON

Elected Keeper of the Quaich (1991) – the Scotch Whisky industry's highest accolade – and a Liveryman of the Worshipful Company of Distillers, Ian is a member of *Whisky Magazine's* "World Whiskies Awards" tasting panel and also Director of the World Whiskies Conference. He writes for *Whisky Magazine*, *Scottish Field*, and *The Times*, among other titles. He recently edited and contributed to the Gedenkschrift for Michael Jackson *Beer Hunter*, *Whisky Chaser*, and is currently working on a history of Glenglassaugh Distillery. Ian wrote the entries on Scotland's blended whiskies for the first edition.

CHARLES MACLEAN

Charlie has been writing about whisky since 1981, and has published 15 books on the subject – *The Times* describes him as "Scotland's leading whisky expert". In 2009, he was elected Master of the Quaich (the whisky industry's highest accolade) and, in 2012, won the 'Outstanding Achievement Award' at the International Wines & Spirits Competition. Visit his website at *whiskymax.co.uk*. Charles is Editor-in-Chief of this book, and also wrote the sections on Canadian, Asian, and Australasian whiskies for the first edition.

PETER MULRYAN

Peter is the author of four books on spirits: *The Whiskeys of Ireland*, *Poteen – Irish Moonshine*, *Bushmills – 400 years*, and *Irish Whiskey Guide*. He has contributed to numerous publications, including *Whisky Magazine*, and, as a television producer, specializes in food and drink programmes. Peter wrote the section on Irish whiskey for the first edition.

HANS OFFRINGA

An eclectic bilingual author and photographer, among other works, Hans has written and translated more than 20 books on whisky, and numerous articles for various publications across the globe. He is one of very few writers to have been named Kentucky Colonel as well as Keeper of the Quaich. For more information about Hans's work, see *www.thewhiskycouple.com*. Hans wrote the section on European whisky for the first edition.

GAVIN D. SMITH

Gavin is the author of some 25 published books, more than a dozen of which are whisky-related, such as *The A–Z of Whisky* and *Whisky Opus* (with Dominic Roskrow). He regularly contributes to various whisky magazines and websites, including *Whisky Magazine* and *scotchwhisky.com*, as well as hosting whisky events. Gavin is a Keeper of the Quaich. He wrote the USA chapter for the first edition.

SECOND EDITION

All revisions for the second edition were carried out by Gavin D. Smith.

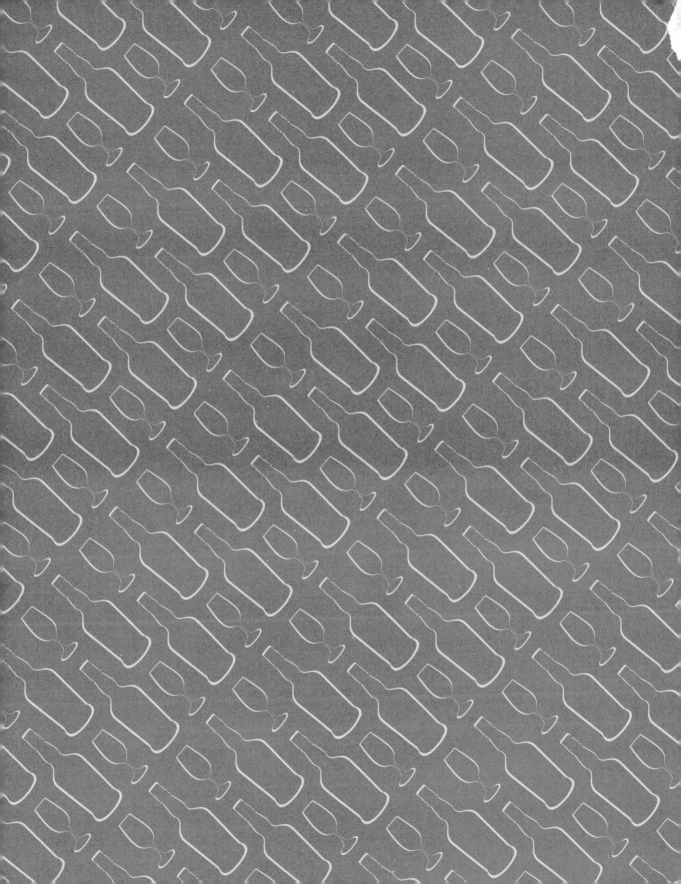